Political Discourse in the Media

Pragmatics & Beyond New Series (P&BNS)

Pragmatics & Beyond New Series is a continuation of Pragmatics & Beyond and its Companion Series. The New Series offers a selection of high quality work covering the full richness of Pragmatics as an interdisciplinary field, within language sciences.

Volume 160

Political Discourse in the Media. Cross-cultural perspectives
Edited by Anita Fetzer and Gerda Eva Lauerbach

Political Discourse in the Media

Cross-cultural perspectives

Edited by

Anita Fetzer
Universität Lüneburg

Gerda Eva Lauerbach
Johann Wolfgang Goethe-Universität Frankfurt am Main

John Benjamins Publishing Company

Amsterdam / Philadelphia

^{TM} The paper used in this publication meets the minimum requirements of American National Standard for Information Sciences – Permanence of Paper for Printed Library Materials, ANSI z39.48-1984.

Library of Congress Cataloging-in-Publication Data

Political discourse in the media : cross-cultural perspectives / edited by Anita Fetzer and
    Gerda Eva Lauerbach.
    p. cm. -- (Pragmatics & Beyond New Series, ISSN 0922-842X ; v. 160)
    Includes bibliographical references and index.
    1. Mass media--Political aspects. 2. Mass media and language. 3. Discourse analysis--
    Political aspects. I. Fetzer, Anita, 1958- II. Lauerbach, Gerda.
    P95.8.P6435   2007
    323.44--dc22   2007009990
    ISBN 978 90 272 5403 0 (Hb; alk. paper)

John Benjamins Publishing Co. · P.O. Box 36224 · 1020 ME Amsterdam · The Netherlands
John Benjamins North America · P.O. Box 27519 · Philadelphia PA 19118-0519 · USA

Table of contents

Acknowledgements

This edited volume developed from an international panel organized by the editors within the IADA conference in Salzburg 2003. We are deeply grateful to the participants of the panel and to the audience for their critical and stimulating comments. Our appreciation also goes to Pragmatics & Beyond New Series Editor, Andreas Jucker, and the anonymous reviewers of the manuscript, as well as to Isja Conen.

PART I

Introduction

Political discourse in the media

Cross-cultural perspectives

Gerda Eva Lauerbach and Anita Fetzer
University of Frankfurt, Germany / University of Lüneburg, Germany

1. Introductory remarks

The goal of this volume is to examine the phenomenon of media communication from a cross-cultural perspective. The focus in the contributions is on the analysis of political discourse in the media which, in mediatized mass democracies, is for most people the only way in which they ever encounter politics. The cross-cultural perspective adopted in this collection of papers involves two basic approaches: on the one hand, culture-specific discourse practices of journalists and politicians are described and compared. The (mainly) implicit assumption is that the recipients for whom these interactants design their discourse are counterfactually conceived of as a culturally homogeneous audience. This is different for international media outlets, and special attention is given, on the other hand, to international broadcasting and its ways of addressing the communicative needs of a culturally heterogeneous audience.

Within this comparative approach, the contributions to the volume focus on television, especially on the genres of political interview, debate, public address and a generically complex media event. Some contributions start from a formal linguistic device and explore its discursive functions, while others use a function to form approach, departing from discursive goals, strategies and tactics, and exploring their realizations in context. The data are taken from discourses in a range of national and international media which are conducted in Arabic, British and American English, Finnish, Flemish, French, German, Hebrew and Swedish. Thus a comparative perspective on the discursive practices and strategies with which participants construct culturally specific as well as international media discourses can enrich "[a] phenomenology of media language [that] would have as its task the job of investigating the connections between media, language and the world" (Scannell 1998:263).

2. Politics, the media and the public sphere

The analysis of political discourse on television should, ideally, be an interdisciplinary enterprise: political communication, media studies, and cultural studies are only some of the disciplines that could provide valuable contextualization for the discourse analytic study of verbal data taken from the mass media. Although the contributors to this volume all work within a framework of discourse analysis, in some papers a response to the pressure to cross disciplinary boundaries into the domain of the visual code of television can be observed (e.g. Lauerbach, Sauer, Scheithauer, Schieß). Also, all authors are aware of the importance of the social, cultural and situational context of their data by providing background for their analyses. But since the scope of an empirical paper rarely leaves room for the discussion of the wider issues of the exercise one is involved in, there are two interrelated points that shall be briefly addressed in this section. The first is what the theory and method of a constructivist approach to the analysis of political discourse involves, and the second is the relation between politics, the media, and the public sphere.

As to the first point, constructivism is the dominant view in media studies, cultural studies and discourse studies alike: the phenomena under scrutiny are not conceived of (merely) as static domains whose structural characteristics are the object of inquiry, but as being achieved or produced through the dynamic interaction of the members of the social domain under review. This is the classical view of ethnomethodology, and it marks the turn from the analysis of social structures to the analysis of social processes, that is, to the *methods* the members of a social group themselves use in collaboratively producing those structures. This view also involved a turn away from the analysis of the macro-level of social institutions to the analysis of the micro-level of conversational interaction, and earned ethnomethodology the label of "micro-sociology" (see e.g. Heritage 1984; Levinson 1983). The problem ever since has been how to account for the relations between the micro and macro-levels, a problem that also besets the analysis of political discourse in the media. A *moderate constructivist* approach involves the assumption that the micro-structural interactions of social members *only partly* construct, maintain and change the macro-structures of a society, i.e. its institutions, just as they are in turn partly constructed, maintained and changed by them – complex systems of further factors and processes on various levels are involved in the relations of the micro and macro levels of social organization (cf.

for instance Fairclough's 1995, 1998 models for how this may work for the micro-level of text and the orders of discourse that construct what elsewhere would be called the macro-level institutions of say, education, law, religion, economics or politics).

Turning to the second point, politics, the media and the public sphere have traditionally been conceived of as macro-structural phenomena and much theorizing on the part of sociology, media studies and political communication has gone into elucidating the relations between them. The political discourse disseminated in the mass media, for instance, has been conceptualized as "symbolic politics". The term is based on a distinction by Edelman (1976) between an instrumental and an expressive dimension of politics, which Sarcinelli (1987) calls the production and the presentation of politics. The production of politics for the greatest part takes place behind the scenes, and the public very rarely has access to it (if it does – as is the case e.g. in the case of parliamentary commissions publicly probing into political scandal – this happens only in retrospect and within strict limits). The presentation of politics by contrast takes place on the public stage that the media provide (televised parliamentary debates would seem to be a complex boundary case). The term "symbolic politics" may create confusion however, since any type of politics is done through language and, thus, symbolically constituted (Fairclough 1998; Chilton & Schäffner 2002). Yet due to the access problem mentioned, most of the data that discourse analysis deals with belong to mediatized politics, that is to say not to the production but to the presentation variety. And this latter variety, due to the staging constraints and commercial interests of the mass media, has become ritualized, formatted and schematized to such an extent that it is justified to speak of a "semblance" of political reality (Sarcinelli 1994; Bentele 1992, translation G.L.). It is this negative interpretation that has become the dominant meaning of "symbolic politics" in political communication studies (Tenscher 1998). This reading should also not be confused with the "symbolic politics" of celebrating national holidays, for instance (cf. Sauer, this volume).

The relations between politics and the media have also been described as an "existential exchange system" (Sarcinelli 1987:218, translation G.L.) or a "happy symbiosis" (Boorstin 1987), in which information (on the part of the politicians) is exchanged for publicitiy (on the part of the media) – a bond that keeps growing tighter as the media become more and more subject to the commercial imperative (Tenscher 1998). Such a "happy symbiosis" between politics and the media runs counter to the media's role as a neutral mediator and critical monitor of politics, and it is not democratically legitimated. It is therefore unlikely to show itself on the surface of "symbolic politics". Rather, it is to be expected to manifest itself in other phenomena, such as e.g. the staged antagonism observable in political interviews. Such covert practices are hard to capture with the methods of media studies, but they fall squarely into the field of discourse analysis with its focus on the micro-level phenomena of not just explicit, but also implicit communication.

Regarding the present state of the relations between politics, the media and the public, the relevant discourses in communication studies, political communication, and discourse analysis are very sceptical. There is criticism that it falls short of the democratic ideal according to which free, objective and scrupulous media inform the public on political decisions and issues, at the same time controlling the actors in the political sphere by insisting on the transparency of the political process and on the justification of its decisions to the public. Instead, the media are accused that, due to time constraints and other production pressures, they have fallen into rigid routine, which in turn leads to the simplification of complex states of affairs. Also, due to the commercial pressure exerted through audience ratings or number of copies sold, the media are said to be giving in to a tendency to make political discourse more entertaining by trivializing, personalizing, dramatizing, conversationalizing, in short by "boulevardizing" a social domain which depends on an informed public, respectively electorate for democracy to work (Swanson 1992; Blumler & Gurevitch 1995; Curran 1991; Curran & Gurevitch 1991; Negrine 1996). The politicians for their part are criticised for using the mass media to influence public opinion instead of providing factual information, by employing professional public relations strategies and "spinning" what information they do provide (Cook 1998).

The relations between politics, the media and the public have been captured in the model of a system of political communication created by Blumler and Gurevitch (1995). The model comprises four interrelated subsystems: the system of political institutions with respect to their communication aspects, the system of the media with respect to their political aspects, the system of the public's expectations and orientations regarding political communication, and communication-relevant aspects of political culture. Depending on the aims of inquiry, one can focus on one subsystem at a time, while keeping in mind its relations to the others. Possible complementary participant roles for the agents in the subsystems are hypothetically proposed as follows (1995:15):

Audience	*Media personnel*	*Politicians*
Partisan	Editorial Guide	Gladiator
Liberal citizen	Moderator	Rational persuader
Monitor	Watchdog	Information provider
Spectator	Entertainer	Actor/performer

Different configurations of participant roles across the subsystems will yield different types of political communication in a society, a culture, or a media corporation. The table shows how difficult a comprehensive analyis of all three components would be. Blumler and Gurevitch's model has informed their own cross-culturally comparative research on the agenda-setting role of British (BBC) and US-American (NBC) television in reporting on election campaigns (1995). It also provides a useful frame of reference for empirical research beyond communication studies. In discourse analysis, for instance, the focus of inquiry in media discourse has so far mainly been on the study of journalistic practices in certain genres, or on the discourse practices of politicians, less frequently on how they interact, and discourse analytic audience reception research is so far still a fairly neglected field (but see Holly 1996; Holly, Püschel & Bergmann 2001).

The goal of discourse analysis is to describe the coding and interpretation conventions of a culture in certain discursive domains, as well as the culture's underlying common ground assumptions. In cross-cultural analysis, it then goes on to confront its results with comparable phenomena of another culture. Such comparative research, according to Gurevitch and Blumer (1990: 308f.), possesses significant advantages over a mono-cultural approach: Due to its wide and varied data base, and the constant comparison between culturally specific ways of doing things, comparative research counteracts any culture-centric bias that may remain unreflected in mono-cultural analysis. Further, the process of comparison renders visible the unchallenged assumptions in the analyst's own culture. And lastly, the confrontation with different ways of doing the "same" thing, which is advocated by critical discourse analysis in order to de-naturalize the dominant readings of a culture (see Section 3 below), is built into the very heart of the comparative method.

3. Culture and cross-cultural discourse analysis

Culture is a concept whose definition is often presupposed in the domains of linguistics, pragmatics and discourse analysis. In other disciplines, it has been defined for instance as the world view reflected in the classification systems of languages, as systems of beliefs, values and attitudes shared by the members of a community, as shared ways of doing things or as the sum of the artefacts produced by the members of a culture over time. Some views involve a static perspective on culture, focusing on a culture's products and ideas, some a dynamic one, focusing on the interactive processes employed by members in collaboratively creating them. Some views favour a cognitive perspective, focusing on the knowledge shared by a culture's members about the physical, the social and the subjective world. Most traditional views conveive of culture as an autonomous, homogeneous, territorially confined unity that is "contained" within the boundaries of a nation state and that contains, in turn, all the properties that define it and make it different from other cultures.

What is of relevance for this volume on political media discourse across cultures is the premise that members of a speech community know about their community's appropriate ways of producing and interpreting explicit and implicit meaning, about its discourse practices and genres and about the socio-cultural contexts of their use, and that they are not necessarily familiar with the ways of other communities (Hanks 1996; Ochs 1996). We shall therefore approach the problem of defining culture by asking what constitutive conditions need to be satisfied for members of a culture to successfully interact with each other (cf. Lauerbach 2002). Very briefly, the position taken here is that three dimensions are necessarily involved when we talk about what is necessary for members of a culture to be able to communicate: they have to share knowledge regarding symbolic sign systems, above all language; they have to share knowledge about systems of pragmatic principles and social practices, above all those of verbal interaction; and they have to share systems of knowledge about the physical, the social and the subjective world (which worlds also include the artefacts of a culture). They also have to share knowledge about how these systems interact. In addition, there are stores of knowledge involving normative conditions on appriopriate interaction in all three dimensions. These relate e.g. to standards of social tact and politeness, and of rational argumentation, and to how these are expressed in speech acts and genres in culturally situated discourses. There are many open questions here regarding the dimensions of this interactionally relevant knowledge, for instance of how explicit these types of knowledge have to be, and how consistent and free of contradictions within and between the systems, about meta-levels of knowledge, about how the systems interact, how they are accessed and continuously monitored in interaction, about how this complex of knowledge is socially distributed, etc. All of these questions are well beyond the scope of this introduction, except the last.

The store of interactionally relevant knowledge is a potential, a resource from which members of a culture can choose for the realisation and interpretation of contributions to discursive events. If there are, between members, grave asymmetries between the stores of interactionally relevant knowledge, miscommunication will occur. This is aggravated if members of different cultures are involved (see Günthner & Luckmann 2001). In the context of inter-cultural communication, marked deviations from expected interactional norms become a rich source of cultural stereotyping. However, interpersonal communication between different cultures *is* possible, and this points to the fact that there has to be a core of interactionally relevant knowledge that is universally shared.

Cross-cultural discourse analysis is about both: about a core which can be presupposed as shared, and about the rest, where languages and other semiotic systems, social and discursive practices, and conceptualisations of reality are culturally specific to a degree that may be communicatively disruptive (or interesting for e.g. social, political or philosophical reasons). For the dimension of language, the project of cross-cultural analysis includes all levels of the linguistic system, from prosody to textual organisation. For the dimension of interaction it addresses the ways in which the social and discursive practices of a culture work. But the focus is also on what happens if interactants are unaware of this and are led to to misguided evaluations regarding e.g. the group membership of their interlocutors, their social status, personality features, or even their intelligence (see Gumperz 1982). In the domain of world knowledge, cross-cultural analysis is about how the dominant discourses of different cultures shape their members' perspective on the world.

Depending on the dimension of knowledge and the type of product looked at (sentence or discourse), scholars attempt to reconstruct the grammar of a language and speakers' knowledge of linguistic principles, categories and relations, or they try to reconstruct the "grammar" of interaction and speakers' knowledge about pragmatic principles, categories and relations. Earlier Chomskian grammars, with their reconstruction of linguistic competence, are examples of the first approach. The ethnography of communication (Hymes 1974; Saville-Troike 1989), with its reconstruction of communicative competence in contexts of culture, is a case of the second. Interactional meaning, according to Hymes (1974), can be captured through a number of contextual factors which constrain appropriate linguistic behaviour. He has assembled them in his well-known s-p-e-a-k-i-n-g acronym, anchoring a speech community's knowledge about linguistic code and social practice to the components of situation, that is the physical setting and the psychological scene, participants, viz. speaker, hearer and audience and their statuses, ends, namely the goal and the purpose of the speech event from a socio-cultural viewpoint, act sequence, that is *how* something is said as regards message form and sequence, and *what* is said as regards message content, key, e.g. mock or serious, instrumentalities, e.g. channels (spoken, written, visual, etc.) and forms (vernacular, dialect or standard) of speech, norms of interaction and interpretation, and genres.

Yet a focus on interaction does not necessarily imply one on cultural context as well, as the enthnomethodological paradigm shows. According to the ethnomethodological enterprise of reconstructing participants' orientation to principles of conversational organisation, cultural context does not pre-exist the interaction. Rather, it is interactionally constituted and collaboratively constructed by its members in and through the process of communication (Prevignano & Thibault

2003). Consequently, the research paradigm of ethnomethodological conversation analysis focusses on the methods of interaction with which participants produce the structural components of discourse, while ignoring the cultural and social contexts in which the interaction takes place. The extreme position that social context is constructed solely through the interaction of the participants, rather than facilitating and constraining it, has not gone without criticism. The argument of the critics is that the approach precludes the possibility of contextual factors informing a critical analysis (see the debate between Billig and Schegloff in *Discourse and Society*: Billig 1999; Schegloff 1997, 1999). A cross-cultural discourse analysis will need to complement such approaches by theories that allow for the fact that in communication, interactants collaboratively construct their relevant context(s) for producing and interpretating utterances, without the implication that context arises wholly and solely as a product of interactive construction. Such theories have to account for the fact that, to use John Gumperz' felicitous phrase, context is both brought along and brought about.

In the tradition of Foucault and Bourdieu, Fairclough (1995) has formulated such a theory, with a focus on media discourse. The goal of the theory is to account, in a multilevel model, for the relations between the linguistic/semiotic micro-structure of the text and the context of the sociocultural macro-structure. Fairclough understands the macro-structural *Order of Discourse* as a configuration of *Types of Discourse* of social domains or institutions (e.g. the family, education, politics, the mass media). Types of Discourse, in their turn, are constituted by *Genres* and *Discourses*. The latter are a society's representations of a social domain under a particular perspective (e.g. politics from a liberal, socialist, or marxist perspective). *Texts* are produced and consumed according to *discursive practices*, and these, in turn, are embedded in *sociocultural practices*. Text analysis has a double focus – on the structure of the text and on the discursive practices with which it was produced within the wider context of the type of discourse it is a part of. The key categories for the mediation between the Order of Discourse and the Text are those of *Genre* and of *Discourse*, and the key processes are those of the *discursive practices of production and consumption* (which, in Fairclough's framework, are more than just coding and interpretation but include the conditions of the production and reception situation of, e.g. media products). Let us focus here on the category of genre.

The category of *Genre* is central to discourse analysis and can be taken to be its basic unit of analysis. Communicative genres (rather than literary ones) or *activity types* (Levinson 1979) are conventionalised patterns for the communicative solution of social "problems". These problems give rise to a genre's external (social, institutional) structure, while the communicative practices of working through those problems yield its characteristic internal (discursive, textual) structure

(Luckmann 1986, 1988; Kress 1993). Genres can vary across cultures, historical eras, social classes and sub-cultures (Luckmann 1986, 1988; Günthner & Luckmann 2001), and they are indicators of social change (Bakhtin 1987; Fairclough 1995; 2003). The internal-external-structure constitution of communicative genres points to their function as points of articulation between the socio-cultural and the textual, or between culture and language. Levinson (1979: 368), drawing attention to the category's indeterminate boundaries, defines *activity type* (which corresponds to genre) as

> a fuzzy category whose focal members are goal-defined, socially constituted, bounded events with *constraints* on participants, setting and so on, but above all on the allowable contributions.

Genres provide a context for understanding "over and beyond whatever meaning the words or sentences may have *in vacuo*" (Levinson 1979: 367), and a cognitive frame of reference, which is strongly influenced by sociocultural constraints, for the interpretation of implicit meaning:

> ...there is another important and related fact, in many ways the mirror image of the constraints on contributions, namely the fact that for each and every clearly demarcated activity there is a set of *inferential schemata*. These schemata are tied to (derived from, if one likes) the structural properties of the activity in question. (Levinson 1979: 370)

To sum up, communicative genres are socio-culturally conventionalised, sometimes even ritualised patterns for dealing with recurring social problems, they provide standardised frames of interpretation and genre-specific ways of inferring implicit meaning. Actual texts, on the other hand, always offer a range of potential reading positions but suggest preferred interpretations by privileging one of those positions over the others. The privileged reading positions reaffirm shared cultural coding conventions, interpretation rules, norms and values. They may therefore appear to be the only ones, to be "natural". From the point of view of cultural studies and of critical discourse analysis, these preferred interpretations are nothing but the naturalization of the hegemonial view, achieved due to the relations of power in a society and by the privileged access of the powerful to the public sphere (cf. Bell & Garrett 1998; Fowler 1987, 1991; Fowler & Kress 1979; Fairclough 1989, 1992, 1995; Hall 1973, 1980). Genres, due to their conventionality, must be considered a powerful factor in promoting such preferred interpretations. This can be taken to hold in particular for the standardised genres of the mass media.

The view that cultures are well-bounded, homogeneous unities based on systems of naturalised meanings, as well as the role of the mass media in the processes of naturalisation, has provoked critical inquiry from various quarters. In critical discourse analysis, for instance, with its goal of addressing relations of discursive power within a society, the method is to lay open a society's underlying naturalized assumptions, coding conventions and preferred reading positions by close linguistic analysis. These are then confronted with alternative ones that are also possible, but not commonly realized in a culture (cf. Wodak & Meyer 2001). In cultural studies, Hall (1980) introduced the idea that recipients actually do use more ways of reading a text than the ones priviledged by the culture. Over and above the dominant reading, by which recipients accept the interpretation preferred by the text, he distinguishes two further types: negotiated and oppositional readings. In both, recipients do not follow the preferred interpretation offered by the text. In the negotiated reading, recipients modify the offered interpretation to some extent without totally rejecting it, in the oppositional reading, they reject this interpretation altogether and substitute it with their own. Deviant readings point to sub-cultural differences of dealing with discursive meaning and thus challenge the presumption of the homogeneity of cultures. But if cultures are internally differentiated according to sub-cultural milieus, lifestyles and communication practices, then this presents a complication for cross-cultural discourse analysis.

Another complication comes from outside the individual culture. The acceleration of the globalisation process has led to world-wide economical, political, social and cultural connections which render it problematic to continue speaking of separate, autonomous, territorially defined cultures (Welsch 1999). Traditional cultures have been modified by forms of life and cultural styles which are not contained within their boundaries. Rather, they traverse them. These lifestyles cannot be captured within the old concept of culture, which is why Welsch proposes the term of *transculture* (cf. also Hepp 2006:63). In a similar vein, Hall (1997), in a paper on "The centrality of culture", argues that, due to advanced communication technologies and world-wide media networks, a cultural revolution has taken place which has made cultural products a major factor in the global economy. The media, above all the internet but also television, have become a major force in the globalisation process, and the motor of world-wide social and cultural change. We may add that world-wide media networks, globally operating media corporations and international television channels, like CNN International, BBC World, Al Dschazira or the newcomer Al Dschazira English, create new cultural spaces whose extension coincides with the reaches of their airwaves. These new territories are inhabited by a global audience which, due to the international distribution of information and advertising in a few world languages, is in the process of becoming a global information elite. For these audiences, global media events, especially in times of crisis, are not only "sites of maximum visibility and turbulence" in the flow of global discourses (Fiske 1996:7), but also arenas for the construction of transcultural identities.

What is the influence of global cultural products on local contexts? Is it a unidirectional process, from Western-dominated media to the rest of world? Naturally, there is a way in which global culture leaves traces in local contexts, but global products are also selected and imported according to local preferences, and these preferences, in turn, have an effect on production. The production and global marketing of television soap operas or the advertising campaigns of globally operating corporations are examples of such strategies of "glocalisation". Due to the fact that cultural products and signifying practices have become available transculturally, there is indeed an effect on local cultures, in that cultural differences are beginning to show structural similarities (Hannerz 1992:53). We can hypothesise that such changes will show up in the communicative genres of a culture, presumably as a tendency towards hybridisation.

To sum up, there are two factors that cast into doubt a homogenous, autonomous, teritorially bounded concept of culture: the sub-cultural differentiations from within a culture, and the transculturalisation processes that affect it from outside. What are the consequences of this for the methods of culturally comparative research? Cross-cultural analysis is, after all, based on the premise of independent systems with definite boundaries as objects of its analyses (cf. Pfetsch & Esser 2003:28). Does not the existence of internal differentiation and of transcultural processes undermine the comparative enterprise by depriving it of its objects of inquiry?

The answer to this is twofold, concerning the underlying concept of culture on the one hand, and the units and methods of inquiry on the other. As to the first, the concept of culture as formulated above is based on the constitutive and normative conditions of verbal and nonverbal interaction of the members of a speech community. As such, it is not bound to territory, nor does it presuppose the homogeneity of the speech community. But what kinds of cultural manifestations, in terms of texts and genres, can be the objects of transcultural discourse analysis? Is there a way in which cross-cultural differences as well as transcultural communalities can be captured? For the study of transcultural communication, Hepp (2006:78ff.) proposes what he terms an *international comparative semantics*. This includes a comparative analysis of the media system of culture one and culture two, *complemented* by an analysis of areas of intensified cultural contact, involvement, exchange on the level of global media capitalism. Such areas could be from sub-cultural domains such as popular culture, religious and social movements, diaspora groups, or politics. In this manner, transcultural phenomena could be put into relation to mono- and cross-cultural ones. The approach seems to be still very much in the programmatic stage, but it is certainly worth thinking about how this could work in other fields of inquiry.

Let us therefore narrow the focus by looking at discourse analysis, of media discourse, on the domain of politics, as in the contributions to this volume. By analysing and comparing genres, and within them certain discursive practices or linguistic devices, one can focus on a specific, narrowly circumscribed domain of a culture's media, and not on whole media systems. The focus is then on a phenomenon of a sub-culture, as it were. But this is the accepted method of linguistic and discourse analytic contrastive research already. One the other hand, one can ask if there are certain genres of political discourse in the media which are likely to be more resistent to transcultural influences, in contrast to others which are more likely to embrace them, and test this hypothesis by studying the differences between them. Parliamentary debates broadcast on the radio or on television, as well as Christmas addresses by heads of state may be cases of the first type. Political interviews, on the other hand, might be a genre that is more open to transcultural standardisation. One could also do a comparative analysis of one genre, say political interviews, in the media of "old" and "new" democracies. This approach should yield interesting results, if indeed the genres should prove to be comparable across the two domains. Lastly, one can transfer the Heppian paradigm to media discourse analysis and look at particular genres in national and international media. This will presumably yield differences between the two types – but can we draw conclusions from this to transcultural traces in the national media genres? What kind of comparative design might give us an answer to this question? Presumably it would be interesting to do longitudinal studies and to look at the changes within a genre in national and international media over time. Generally, ethnographic descriptions of the cultural and transcultural context should be part of any analysis, and an essential element of this should be the description of the discourse type to which the genres analysed belong. It is to this we turn now for the project pursued in this volume.

4.   Political discourse in the media

Political discourse in the media is a complex phenomenon: it is institutional discourse, media discourse, and mediated political discourse. As institutional discourse, it differs from everyday conversation in being subject to institutional goals and procedures. As media discourse it is different from other types of institutional discourses by being, above all, public discourse addressed to a mass media audience. This sets it apart from the discourse of other institutions, such as medicine, the law, or education. As mediated political discourse, it is the outcome of the encounter of two different institutional discourses – those of politics and of the media. Just what constitutes the goals and purposes, subtypes, genres and discursive practices of this hybrid discourse, is the question pursued in political discourse analysis.

"Political discourse in the media" as a term is ambiguous in its referential domain: it can refer to the discourse *of* political agents in the media, or the discourse of journalists *with* politicians in the media, or to the discourse of journalists *about* politics and political agents in the media. Discourse *of* politicians or other political agents like spokespersons are for instance speeches on important issues and occasions, e.g. in parliamentary debates, at party conferences, summit meetings, etc., also statements, press conferences and the like. These events are embedded in journalistic news discourse and, in the case of the broadcasting media, may be carried live, to be repeated as soundbites in later programming. Discourse *with* politicians and other political personnel are dialogic speech events in which political representatives interact with journalists in interviews. Focusing again on the broadcasting media, such interviews can take place in radio and television news, in news magazines or in talk shows, or they can be an event in their own right. They can be conducted on a one-on-one or a panel/debate basis (Clayman & Heritage 2002). Discourse *about* politics and politicians is journalistic discourse in the genres of report, analysis, commentary, etc. by the speakers of news programmes, the anchors of news magazines, by studio experts and correspondents on location. This discourse *about* politics can, and usually does, embed other voices: In quoting the voices of politicians and spokespersons of different parties on an issue, journalists can create a debate that may not actually have taken place in this way. In interviewing the politicians themselves, they can monitor and critically observe the political process on behalf of the audience. In interviewing or quoting outside experts on the issue they provide explanations of what it means in the wider context of society. In asking ordinary people about their opinions, they demonstrate how it may concern the man or woman in the street. Vox pops can also be heard in audience participation programmes, through the voices of members of a studio audience, or by members of the home audience calling in, or sending faxes or e-mails.

Discourse *about* politics is thus the overarching category in which the others can be embedded. Various journalistic genres are involved; they can be monological, in which case the audience is addressed directly, or dialogical, in which case the participants address the audience via their interaction with their interlocutors. In the sense of Goffman (1974: 539ff., 1981: 137ff.), media discourse belongs to what he calls *podium events*. These are defined as social events which are either addressed to or performed for a live or mass media audience (e.g. lectures, sermons, staged plays; radio and television news, interviews, talk shows).The participation framework of political discourse in the media consists of journalists, as representatives of a media institution, of political actors as representatives of the institution of politics, of actors from other social institutions, of lay people as representatives of the world of everyday life, and the audience, as representatives of the public. Focusing on television, members of all of these groups can be heard and seen, but their importance and status are very different. Although political actors are the newsmakers of political discourse, so that the discourse is always *about* them, they do not necessarily have to be present. This is different for the journalists and the audience – both of them are constitutive for media discourse about any discursive domain. However, for the dialogical genre of political interview, political actors are, of course, necessary participants. Actors from other institutions can participate for analysis and commentary, but this could also be done by experts from within the media. The evaluations and other reactions from lay persons, the studio and/or mass audience likewise are not necessary but optional constituents of media discourse. There is a further distinction between the participants as to whether they are "on the podium", or in the audience. The first group can be called first-frame participants, the second, second frame participants. The conditions of participation are different for the diverse partipant groups, and they are subject to the specific discursive practices within the institution of media discourse.

In comparison with everyday discourse, institutional discourse is therefore often looked upon as something artificial which adheres to its own regularities and discourse practices. From an analytic viewpoint, however, institutional discourse and everyday communication share all of the fundamental pragmatic premises for felicitous communication, but differ with respect to their instantiations in context. This holds for the conversation-analytic concepts of sequentiality and turn-taking (Fetzer & Meierkord 2002; Sacks, Schegloff & Jefferson 1974; Sacks 1992), for the interpersonal-communication concepts of face and footing (Brown & Levinson 1987; Goffman 1981), for speech-act theory's felicity conditions and the overarching pragmatic premise of intentionality of communicative action, with its subsequent differentiation between what is said and what is meant (Grice 1975; Searle 1975, 1995). The meaning of an interlocutor's contribution may thus go beyond the level of what is said in both types of discourse. In both types of discourse, participants may flout conversational maxims in order to trigger conversational implicatures and to express conversationally implicated meaning (Grice 1975), and in both the communicative meaning of what speakers intend to communicate needs to be worked out by the addressees. Yet in institutional contexts, this meaning may not be freely negotiable due to constraints on possible participant roles and on the number of participants, as well as on the kinds of contributions, the turn-length and the kinds of sequencing expected or allowed.

Furthermore, the strategies of coding and interpretation are not just dependent on the type of institution, but also on the type of genre or activity type engaged in. This raises a problem for all general pragmatic principles, including Grice's (1975) system of conversational logic, for which Levinson (1979: 376) offers two basic solutions for discussion:

> There are two ways in which the conflict between Grice's general principles of conversation and the particular expectations of specific activities can be reconciled. The first is to seek for a more sophisticated statement of Grice's principles that will allow differing degrees of application of each maxim and the corresponding adjustment of implicatures. The second is to accept Grice's maxims as specifications of some *unmarked* communication context, deviations from which however common are seen as special or *marked*.

If one opts for the second way of dealing with the problem, then the effort of institutional discourse analyis has to go into accounting for the parameters of markedness that distinguish types of discourses and their genres from the unmarked type of everyday conversation and its genres.

The most consequential feature of media discourse is that it is addressed to an absent mass audience and not to a group of co-present participants. The fact that media discourse is produced for such an audience influences both its content and its form. In the case of dialogic interaction being broadcast, the audience may be directly addressed by the journalists and, in rare cases, also by their studio guests. As a rule, however, it will be in the position of a ratified overhearer (Goffman 1981), as for instance when journalists and politicians talk to each other in order to display their discourse to the audience. This has consequences for the way in which such discourse is constructed, as has been demonstrated for the news interview by analysts working within the framework of conversation analysis. In refraining from giving feedback to their interviewees, interviewers indicate that the interviewees' answers are not addressed to them but to the audience (Clayman & Hertitage 2002: 120ff.).

Another consequence of media discourse being addressed to an absent mass audience concerns the construction of meaning by the first-frame participants. Both in ordinary and in mediated face-to-face dialogues, participants may initiate repair sequences. In contrast to everyday discourse, however, there are constraints on the negotiation of meaning in mediated discourse. First, the length of a repair sequence is constrained by the programme's strict time schedule, and second, the audience cannot directly intervene in this process between the first-frame participants by asking clarification questions. It may, however, participate in a mediated manner if there is audience participation, or through other types of mediated discourse, for instance letters to the editor, phone-ins, email, chat, or through meta-discourse with other members of the audience. However, such attempts at the negotiation of meaning are always delayed or after the event.

The consequences for the first-frame participants are that they have to take particular care in recipient-designing their discourse for an audience that cannot intervene with comprehension questions. This holds equally for monologue addressed to the audience. The orientation to a heterogeneous mass audience whose members may have different stores of background knowledge leads to formal features of the discourse like the explanation of possibly unfamiliar referential terms, or the explication of inferences and jokes.

There is a connection between the features of recipient design of media discourse, its public character, and the rights and obligations of its participants:

> ...the design features ... indicate that it is meant for reception by absent audiences. And this, in turn, establishes the intrinsically public nature of broadcast talk. Talk-in-public, especially political talk, is 'on the record' and this has consequences on what can and cannot be said and for ways of saying and not saying. (Scannell 1998: 260)

So, in being produced for a mass audience, mediated discourse is necessarily public discourse. The public and mediated status of its participants and of the activity engaged in is one of the decisive factors which differentiate their rights and obligations from those of the participants of communicative events in other social domains. Thus interviewees are in a different position from, for instance, suspects being questioned by the police:

> American citizens have a constitutionally protected right to remain silent in the face of police questioning, so that silence cannot be treated as incriminating in courts of law. But public figures have no such protection in the court of public opinion constituted by the news interview. (Clayman & Heritage 2002: 241)

This is why, if e.g. interviewees do not wish to answer a question, they are faced with a dilemma. Answering the question will lead to undesirable consequences. Yet there are strong pressures – from interviewers, the audience, and subsequent media exposure – to "just answer the question". In the political arena, politicians may chose, under specific circumstances, to explicitly opt out of the event (Lauerbach 2003b), but they do not have the right to remain silent and, should they decide to do so, this is generally used against them by portraying them as uncooperative, if not insincere (Fetzer 2002). Moreover, the silence is loaded with additional generalised and particularised inferential meaning: politicians are considered to not fulfill their obligation of informing the public and the electorate in an appropriate manner and, more specifically, to have a problem with the question asked.

Since media discourse is public discourse by definition, it is accessible to a general public, including other media, who have the right to comment on it and to recontextualize it, thus constructing intertextuality (Fetzer & Weizman 2006; Scannell 1998). And it is those intertextual references to "on-the-record" utterances and the subsequent construction of intertextuality which are at the heart of media discourse. This is reflected, for instance, in the genre of political interview in which politicians are challenged with prior statements and claims, and in the discursive practices of journalists in news programmes in which politicians' talk is explicitly taken up through direct and indirect quotes.

The absent mass audience that journalists, politicians and other participant groups of first-frame participants orient to is counterfactually conceptualized as an over-arching category for a more or less culturally homogeneous entity. But there is a tension here between the media publicly broadcasting to a mass of addressees who receive this discourse as individuals or small groups mainly in their private environment. Practices of audience address and occasional informal style show the media's orientation to this fact. Also, audiences are differentiated as to sub-cultural milieus, and first-frame participants may intend to address specific segments of the audience in particular, such as members of a political party in the context of a political interview or speech, the electorate in the context of a political interview or debate, and sometimes a nation, or a nation and its allies, in the context of a president's speech.

In international broadcasting, the multi-layered participant structure of media communication becomes even more complex. This is because the mass audience addressed in the second frame no longer represents a more or less culturally homogeneous group, and neither the first- nor the second-frame participants may orient to culturally shared background knowledge, value systems and discursive practices. In international broadcasting, the situation is also more complex linguistically. The broadcasters may e.g. use standard or regional varieties of English (or Spanish, or Arabic), interact with interviewees and other guests who speak the language used as a lingua franca, and the audiences addressed are at least bilingual and belong to different cultures.

Before being overly impressed by the challenge to international media that lies in recipient-designing their programme for such heterogeneous audiences, we should consider that the global media are no doubt also a factor in shaping their audiences' orientation to international media culture and in homogenizing their patterns of reception. Cameron (2003) has shown for a particular aspect of global business communication how such homogenization is achieved by strictly prescribing certain modes of interaction. In her study of global call-centre communication, she discusses prescribed scripted salutations, simulated friendliness and a relentless positive politeness. Similar manuals exist for the broadcasting personnel of international television companies to ensure consistent patterns of discursive behaviour which become, in turn, partially constitutive both of a channel's culture and of the reception habits of transcultural audiences. Such handbooks regulate the language varieties and formality levels to be used, the relation of image, text, and on-screen characters, the forms of audience address and of the address and referential terms for journalists and guest, etc.

Turning at last to political discourse in the media, we have seen that it is institutional, mediated discourse collaboratively produced for the major part by the interaction of the representatives of two macro-institutions of modern societies, of the institution of politics and of the institution of the media. It is the presentation of politics, not its production (see Section 2).

Politics has its events and genres within and through which it conducts its business, and the media have their events and genres within and through which they conduct theirs. Some political events occur independently of the media, such as party conferences, parliamentary debates, the reports of parliamentary commissions and election campaigns; some are events staged by the media or by the representatives of the political system, or both. They are staged to be carried live or to be reported on, such as national and other addresses, press conferences, or press releases on the part of politics, and interviews, talk shows, new reports, current affairs debates or news magazine portraits on the part of the media. However, the fact that political events may occur independently from media instigation does not mean that they are not shaped by the media. A good example are election campaigns or national holiday addresses (cf. Blumer & Gurevitch 1990, 1995; ben-Aaron 2005; Sauer, this volume).

The goals of the institutions of politics and the media as well as their symbiotic relationship have already been remarked on in section two, as have as their respective and reciprocally influential practices of "boulevardization" on the part of the media, and of spinning and soundbite design on the part of politics. The fact that politics is interest-driven negotiation over limited resources within a society and across nations has consequences for the readings offered to a mass audience when its representatives talk to or talk with the media. One of the constitutive conditions of mediated political texts is that they are addressed to audiences whom their authors know to be divided as regards their interests and political affiliations, on most issues, and whom they will consequently try to persuade to stay within or to come into their camp. Thus political discourse in the media is persuasive discourse.

From a pragmatic angle, political discourse in the media can be conceived as communicative action (Fetzer & Weizman 2006). As in all types of persuasive discourse, and thus for the analysis of how politicians interact with the media, the contrast between perlocutionary act (Austin 1962) and perlocutionary effect (Searle 1969) deserves particular attention. The distinction is one of (1) intended versus achieved effects, and (2) between the audience as a whole, and subsets of hearers and audiences as its parts. The relevance of the intention/effect duality is explicitly highlighted by Chilton and Schäffner (2002: 11), who draw the connection between a pragmatic approach to political discourse and media studies by pointing out that the concept of perlocutionary effect "is (...) of crucial importance in political discourse analysis in particular, because it points to the potential discrepancy between intended effect (that is, effect that some hearers may infer to be intended) and the actual effect on the hearer."

Here lies a particular challenge for political discourse analysis in that the heterogeneous audiences in mass-media discourse may comprise not only different national and international targets, but also different ideologically defined groups. This requires research on both the sides of the communicative process – of the practices of both production and reception. On the reception side, this means discourse analytic audience reception research, which is still in its infancy. What we can look for on the production side is the discursive traces of politicians' and journalists' orientation to multiple addressees with different, if not conflicting, interests and affiliations on the one hand, and with different (sub-)cultural backgrounds, on the other.

Just as other discourses of a society, the discourse of politics, and its ways of interacting with the discourse of the mass media, is subject to constant change (see Section 2). Such changes manifest themselves through the hybridization of its communicative genres – by incorporating features of one genre into another, and/or by a blending of generic styles, or by drawing on other or more discourses than before, e.g. by incorporating elements of economical, ecological and scientific discourse into political discourse (Fairclough 1995). The contemporary political interview in the Anglo-Saxon media is a particularly clear case of this happening. A particular kind of change has been triggered by a change in the participant structure of the political interview, or rather, in the status of the participating politicians. The arrival of grass-roots political movements and the appearance of their representatives in the public sphere have introduced a new type of politician to public interaction whose expertise may lie more in the fields of science and eco-technology than in politics. In dealing with professional politicians who have all present-day commodities and any possible personal and technical support at their disposal, and with professional interviewers who have the media know-how at their fingertips, they may be assigned therefore the status of partial experts, if not lay persons, and be treated accordingly. Present-day political discourse in the media thus has become hybrid in that it articulates together the orders of discourse of the political system (conventional, official politics), of the media, of science and technology, of grassroots sociopolitical movements, of ordinary private life, and so forth – but in an unstable and shifting configuration. (Fairclough 1998: 146f.)

Another change that can be observed is the incorporation of the familiar, "soft and feel-good" style of everyday conversation with its norms of politeness into the serious political interview:

Political interviews typically mix their genres and their discourses. In complex ways, politicians characteristically shift into conversational genre, and draw upon lifeworld discourses, in finding ways to address mass audiences who are listening or watching in mainly domestic environments. (Fairclough 1998: 151)

The tendency towards everyday discourse holds for interviewers as well, but as yet seems to show itself more in the private than in the public media, at least in Britain (Lauerbach 2004). If hybrid genres can be considered indicators of social change in general, a particular composition of hybrid elements can indicate a particular state of social development:

A particular articulation of genres and discourses within a generic complex is a particular effect of power corresponding to a particular state of hegemonic relations. It is also a potential focus for resistance and struggle. To take an example, not all professional politicians are willing to go along with more aggressive and contestatory styles of political interview which fit in with the media priorities to make programmes more entertaining by subordinating political discussion to gladiatorial contest. (Fairclough 1998: 151)

However, the manner in which journalists define their roles and professional identities can vary across channels within one culture (for instance for professional interviewers in the British television channels BBC and ITV, cf. Lauerbach 2004). Variation across cultures, which is the focus of the papers in this volume, is of course to be expected all the more. For instance, in the participant structure of news programmes, in some cultures one prominent anchor who is in sole control may be preferred, in others two or more anchors conversationally interacting as a team. Since cultures can differ in their preferred discourse styles for certain social domains, the conversationalization of institutional discourse and especially of media discourse, which has been found to hold for the Anglo-American context (Fairclough 1995), may not necessarily be found in other cultural contexts, such as the German, Flemish, Finnish or Swedish ones, or in those of the "new" democracies. And since discourse styles may also be evaluated differently across cultures, the Anglo-American phenomenon of conversationalization may, for instance, be interpreted as an appropriate style for political discourse in some cultures while it will be looked upon as a non-serious mode of communication in another one, where it may be appropriate for talk shows but not for news interviews. In a similar vein, what may be conceived of as a public domain in one culture, for instance a politician's family and their intimate interpersonal relationships, may be conceived of as a private domain in another culture. The interesting point in comparative analysis comes when such features can be shown to cluster in a meaningful way, so that they support generalising interpretations.

Based on interviews with journalists in a media studies context, Köcher (1986) studied the self-images of British and German media professionals. Her results yielded roughly two groups: "bloodhounds" for the British media, and "missionaries" for the German ones. Twenty years later, and with the more fine-grained methods of micro-level discourse analysis, such clear-cut categories are presumably not to be achieved, but the papers collected in this volume should nevertheless contribute to our understanding of how political discourse in the media can vary cross-culturally.

The contributions

The contributions in this volume fall in three parts. The papers in the first part start off from the textual micro-phenomenon of linguistic form and examine its functions in discourse, those in the second part employ a textual meso-perspective and investigate genre-specific discourse practices, and those in the third part are based on a textual macro-outlook and analyse political media events – national addresses, and the multi-generic macro-texts of election nights.

Part I, *From linguistic device to discourse practice*, comprises two contributions. Anne-Marie Simon-Vandenbergen, Peter R. R. White and Karin Aijmer's *Presupposition and 'taking-for-granted' in mass communicated political argument. An illustration from British, Flemish and Swedish political colloquy* examines to what extent taken-for-grantedness is used as a strategy in political media language as a genre across cultures, and whether it is characterised by similar choices at the interpersonal level. The data are taken from British, Flemish and Swedish radio and television interviews and debates. Rut Scheithauer's *Metaphors in election night television coverage in Britain, the United States and Germany* is based on Lakoff and Johnson's (1980) cognitive-constructivist theory of metaphor. It presents a quantitative and qualitative analysis of the use of metaphors by nine television stations covering the British general election of 1997, the German parliamentary election of 1998 and the US presidential election of 2000.

Part II, *Discursive practice in political interviews*, contains four contributions. Annette Becker's *"Are you saying ...?" A cross-cultural analysis of interviewing prac-*

tices in TV election night coverages employs an integrated framework informed by pragmatics, conversation analysis, and appraisal theory. It examines the form and function of question-answer-routines in political and expert interviews on the basis of data recorded during international and national coverages of the UK and German General Elections (1997/1998), and during the US Presidential Elections in 2000. Marjut Johansson's *Represented discourse in answers. A cross-cultural perspective on French and British political interviews* examines the communicative function of represented discourse from a cross-cultural perspective in a dialogic framework by focussing on the different functions and contexts of use in French and English political TV-interviews. It compares and contrasts its descriptive and argumentative uses in the two sociocultural contexts. Anita Fetzer's *Challenges in political interviews: an intercultural analysis* is set in a sociopragmatic frame of reference. It examines language- and culture-specific preferences for communicating, interpreting and contextualizing challenges. The study is based on a corpus of British and German political interviews from the general elections in Britain (1997) and Germany (1998). Elda Weizman, Irit Levi and Isaac Schneebaum's *Variation in interviewing styles: challenge and support in Al-Jazeera and on Israeli television* explores patterns of interviewers' challenge and support in TV news interviews conducted by two interviewers – Faysal al-Qasem in Arabic (on Al-Jazeera) and Ben Kaspit in Hebrew (Israel Television, Channel 1), focusing on topic introduction in the openings, explicit comments and elaborative reformulations in triadic interviews with two interviewees. It compares and contrasts symmetric and asymmetric configurations in the two sociocultural settings and interprets the differences in terms of challenge and support.

Part III, *Media events: from public address to election nights*, comprises three contributions. Christoph Sauer's *Christmas Messages by heads of state: multimodality and media adaptations* employs a frame of reference informed by functional pragmatics and critical discourse analysis. It investigates the multimodal quality of Christmas Messages by European heads of state on TV giving particular attention to the 'multimedia show' by the British Queen in 2003 and the 'sermon' by the Finnish President in 2004, thus accommodating the complex relationship between what TV viewers see and what they hear. Raimund Schieß's *Information meets entertainment: a visual analysis of election night TV programs across cultures* analyses the semiotic work, techniques and conventions used by TV stations to articulate the transitions between inside and outside and to produce a spatially fragmented yet coherent televisual text in the context of the broadcast studio. It compares and contrasts the techniques used by the stations BBC, BBC World, ITV, CNN International, CNN, NBC, ARD and RTL, and analyses their strategies. Gerda Eva Lauerbach's *Presenting television election nights in Britain, the United States and Germany. Cross-cultural analyses* examines the discursive practices with which presenters interact with various types of participants inside the studio and on outside locations. It focusses on the ways in which they construct from this a comprehensible and coherent text for the television audience. The data are national and international broadcasts covering the British and German parliamentary elections of 1997 and 1998, respectively, and the US presidential elections of 2000.

References

Austin, J. L. 1962. *How to do Things with Words*. Cambridge: Cambridge University Press.

Bakhtin, M. 1987. *The Dialogic Imagination: 4 Essays*. Austin: University of Texas Press.

Bell, A. and Garret, P. (eds) 1998. *Approaches to Media Discourse*. Oxford: Blackwell.

ben-Aaron, D. 2005. *Given and News. Media Discourse and the Construction of Community on National Days*. University of Helsinki: Pragmatics, Ideology and Contacts Monographs 4.

Bentele, G. 1992. "Symbolische Politik im Fernsehen." In *Kulturkonflikt – Medienkonflikt – Konflikt in den Medien*, E. Hess-Lüttich (ed), 215–232. Opladen: Westdeutscher Verlag.

Billig, M. 1999. "Whose terms? Whose ordinariness? Rhetoric and ideology in conversation analysis." *Discourse and Society* 10(4): 534–582.

Blumler, J. and Gurevitch, M. 1995. *The Crisis of Public Communication*. London: Routledge.

Boorstin, D. 1987. *Das Image – Der Amerikanische Traum*. Reinbek: Rowohlt.

Brown, P. and Levinson, S. 1987. *Politeness: Some Universals in Language Usage*. Cambridge: Cambridge University Press.

Cameron, D. 2003. "Globalizing 'communication.'" In *New Media Language*, J. Aitchison and D.M. Lewis (eds), 27–35. London: Routledge.

Chilton, P. and Schäffner, C. 2002. "Introduction: themes and principles in the analysis of political discourse". In *Politics as Text and Talk: Analytical Approaches to Political Discourse*, P. Chilton and C. Schäffner (eds), 1–41. Amsterdam: Benjamins.

Clayman, S. and Heritage, J. 2002. *The News Interview. Journalists and Public Figures on the Air*. Cambridge: Cambridge University Press.

Cook, T. 1998. *Governing with the News: The News Media as a Political Institution*. Chicago: The University of Chicago Press.

Curran, J. 1991. "Mass Media and Democracy: A Reappraisal." In *Mass Media and Society*, J. Curran and M. Gurevitch (eds), 82–117. London: Edward Arnold.

Curran, J. and Gurevitch, M. (eds.). 1991. *Mass Media and Society*. London: Edward Arnold.

Edelman, M. 1976. *Politik als Ritual*. Frankfurt: Campus.

Fairclough, N. 1989. *Language and Power*. London, New York: Longman.

Fairclough, N. 1992. *Discourse and Social Change*. Cambridge: Polity Press.

Fairclough, N.1995. *Media Discourse*. London: Edward Arnold.

Fairclough, N. 1998. "Political discourse in the media: an analytical framework." In *Approaches to Media Discourse*, A. Bell and P. Garret (eds), 142–162. Oxford: Blackwell.

Fairclough, N. 2003. *Analysing Discourse. Textual Analysis for Social Research*. London: Routledge.

Fetzer, A. 2002. "'Put bluntly, you have something of a credibility problem'. Sincerity and cred-ibility in political interviews". In *Politics as Text and Talk: Analytical Approaches to Political Discourse*, P. Chilton and C. Schäffner (eds), 173–201. Benjamins: Amsterdam.

Fetzer, A. and Meierkord, C. (eds) 2002. *Rethinking Sequentiality: Linguistics meets Conversational Interaction*. Amsterdam: Benjamins.

Fetzer, A. and Weizman, E. 2006. "Political discourse as mediated and public discourse". *Journal of Pragmatics* 38(2):143–153.

Fiske, J. 1996. *Media Matters. Race and Gender in U.S. Politics.* Minneapolis: University of Minnesota Press.

Fowler, R. 1987. "Notes on Critical Linguistics." In *Language Topics: Essays in Honour of Michael Halliday*, T. Threadgold and R. Steele (eds), 481–492. Amsterdam: Benjamins.

Fowler, R. 1991. *Language in the News: Discourse and Ideology in the Press.* London: Routledge.

Fowler, R. and Kress, G. 1979. "Critical Linguistics." In *Language and Control*, Fowler, B. Hodge, G. Kress and T. Trew (eds), 185–213. London, Boston, Henley: Routledge and Kegan Paul.

Goffman, E. 1974. *Frame Analysis. An Essay on the Organization of Experience.* New York: Harper & Row.

Goffman, E. 1981. *Forms of Talk.* Oxford: Basil Blackwell.

Grice, H.P. 1975. "Logic and conversation". In *Speech Acts. (=Syntax and Semantics. Vol. III)*, M. Cole and J. Morgan (eds), 41–58. New York: Academic Press.

Günthner, S. and Luckmann, T. 2001. "Asymmetries of Knowledge in Intercultural Communication. The relevance of cultural repertoires of communicative genres." In Di Luzio, A., Günthner, S. and Orletti, F. (eds), *Culture in Communication. Analyses of Intercultural Situations*. Pragmatics and Beyond 81. Amsterdam/Philadelphia: John Benjamins, 3–85.

Gumperz, J. 1977. "Sociocultural knowledge in conversational inference". In *Linguistics and Anthropology*, M. Saville-Troike (ed), 191–211. Washington: Georgetown University Press.

Gumperz, J. 1982. *Discourse Strategies.* Cambridge: Cambridge University Press.

Gumperz, J. 1992. "Contextualization and understanding". In *Rethinking Context: Language as an Interactive Phenomenon*, A. Duranti and C. Goodwin (eds), 229–252. Cambridge: Cambridge University Press.

Gurevitch, M. and Blumler, J.G. 1990. "Comparative research: the extending frontier". In *New Directions in Political Communication*, D. Swanson and D. Nimmo (eds), 305–325. London: Sage.

Hall, S. 1973. "A World at One with Itself." In *The Manufacture of News*, St. Cohen and J. Young (eds), 85–94. London: Constable.

Hall, S. 1980. "Encoding/decoding." In *Culture, Media, Language. Working Papers in Cultural Studies, 1972–79.* St. Hall et al. (eds), 128–138. London: Hutchinson.

Hall, S. 1997. "The Centrality of Culture: Notes on the Cultural Revolutions of our Time." In Thompson, K. (ed), *Media and Cultural Regulation.* London: Sage, 207–238.

Hall, S. 2000. *Cultural Studies. Ein politisches Theorieprojekt.* Ausgewählte Schriften 3. Hamburg: Argument.

Hanks, W.F. 1996. "Language form and communicative practice". In *Rethinking Linguistic Relativity*, J. Gumperz and S. Levinson (eds), 232–270. Cambridge: Cambridge University Press.

Hannerz, U. 1992. *Cultural Complexity: Studies in the Social Organization of Meaning.* New York: Columbia University Press.

Hepp, A. 2006. *Transkulturelle Kommunikation*. Konstanz: UVK Verlagsgesellschaft.

Heritage, J. 1984. *Garfinkel and Ethnomethodology*. Cambridge: Polity Press.

Holly, W. 1996. "Hier spricht der Zuschauer – ein neuer methodischer Ansatz in der sprach-wissenschaftlichen Erforschung politischer Fernsehkommunikation." In *Sprach-strategien und Dialogblockaden*, H. Diekmannshenke and J. Klein (eds), 101–121. Berlin, New York: de Gruyter.

Holly, W., Püschel, U. and Bergmann, J. (eds). 2001. *Der sprechende Zuschauer. Wie wir uns Fernsehen kommunikativ aneignen*. Wiesbaden: VS Verlag für Sozialwissenschaften.

Hymes, D. 1974. *Foundations in Sociolinguistics: An Ethnographic Approach*. Philadelphia: University of Philadelphia Press.

Köcher, R. 1986. "Missionaries and Bloodhounds: Role Definitions of British and German Journalists." *European Journal of Communication* 1 (1): 43–64.

Kress, G. 1993. "Genre as Social Process." In *The Powers of Literacy – A Genre Approach to Teaching Writing*, B. Cope and M. Kalantzis (eds), 22–37. London: Falmer.

Lakoff, G. 1987. *Women, Fire, and Dangerous Things: What Categories Reveal about the Mind*. Chicago: Chicago University Press.

Lakoff, G. and Johnson, M. 1980. *Metaphors we Live by*. Chicago: University of Chicago Press.

Lauerbach, G. 2003a. "Context, Contextualization, and Re-contextualization." In Mengel, E., H.-J. Schmid and M. Steppat (eds), *Anglistentag 2002 Bayreuth. Proceedings*. Trier: Wissenschaftlicher Verlag, 411–422.

Lauerbach, G. 2003b. "Opting out of the Media-Politics Contract – Discourse Strategies in Confrontational Political Interviews." In Bondi, M. and Stati, S. (eds), *Selected Papers from the 10th IADA Anniversary Conference, Bologna 2000*. Tübingen: Niemeyer, 283–294.

Lauerbach, G. 2004 . "Political Interviews as a Hybrid Genre." *TEXT* 24 (3): 353–397.

Lauerbach, G. this volume. "Presenting televison election nights in Britain, the United States and Germany. Cross-cultural analyses".

Levinson, S. 1979. "Activity types and language". *Linguistics* 17: 365–399.

Levinson, S. 1983. *Pragmatics*. Cambridge: Cambridge University Press.

Levinson, S. 1988. "Putting linguistics on a proper footing: explorations in Goffman's concepts of participation". In *Erving Goffman. Exploring the Interaction Order*, P. Drew and A. Wootton (eds), 161–227. Cambridge University Press: Cambridge.

Luckmann, T. 1986. "Grundformen der gesellschaftlichen Vermittlung des Wissens: Kommunikative Gattungen." *Kölner Zeitschrift für Soziologie und Sozialpsychologie. Sonderheft 27 (Kultur und Gesellschaft)*: 191–211.

Luckmann, T. 1988. "Kommunikative Gattungen im Haushalt einer Gesellschaft." In *Der Ursprung der Literatur*, G. Schmolka-Koerdt et al. (eds), 279–288. München: Fink.

Negrine, R. 1996. *The Communication of Politics*. London: Sage.

Ochs, E. 1996. "Linguistic resources for socializing humanity". In *Rethinking Linguistic Relativity*, J. Gumperz and S. Levinson (eds), 407–437. Cambridge: Cambridge University Press.

Pfetsch, B. and Esser, F. 2003. "Politische Kommunikation im internationalen Vergleich: Neuorientierung in einer veränderten Welt." In Esser, F. and Pfetsch, B. (eds), *Politische Kommunikation im internationalen Vergleich*. Wiesbaden: Westdeutscher Verlag, 9–31.

Prevignano, C. and Thibault, P. (eds) 2003. *Discussing Conversation Analysis*. Amsterdam: Benjamins.

Sacks, H. 1992. *Lectures on Conversation*. [Ed. by Gail Jefferson]. Oxford: Blackwell.

Sacks, H., Schegloff, E. and Jefferson, G. 1974. "A simplest systematics for the organization of turn-taking for conversation". *Language* 50 (4): 696–735.

Sarcinelli, U. 1987. *Symbolische Politik*. Opladen: Westdeutscher Verlag.

Sarcinelli, U. 1994. "Fernsehdemonkratie." In *Öffentlichkeit und Kommunikationskultur*. Vol. 2, W. Wunden (ed), 21–41. Hamburg, Stuttgart.

Sauer, C. this volume. "Christmas messages by heads of state: multimodality and media adaptations".

Saville-Troike, M. 1989. *The Ethnography of Speaking*. Oxford: Blackwell.

Scannell, P. 1998. "Media-language-world". In *Approaches to Media Discourse*, A. Bell and Garrett. P. (eds), 252–267. Oxford: Blackwell.

Schegloff, E. 1997. "Whose text? Whose context?" *Discourse and Society* 9(2): 165–187.

Schegloff, E. 1999. "Schegloff's texts as Billig's data: A critical reply." *Discourse and society* 10(4): 558–572.

Scheithauer, R. this volume. "Metaphors in election night television coverage in Britain, the United States and Germany."

Schieß, R. this volume. "Information meets entertainment: a visual analysis of election night TV programs across cultures."

Searle, J.R. 1969. *Speech Acts*. Cambridge: Cambridge University Press.

Searle, J.R. 1975. "Indirect Speech Acts." In *Pragmatics (Syntax and Semantics 9)*, Cole, P. and J. Morgan (eds), 59–82. New York: Academic Press.

Searle, J.R. 1995. *The Construction of Social Reality*. New York: The Free Press.

Swanson, D. 1992. *The Political-Media Complex. Communication Monographs* 59: 397–400.

Tenscher, J. 1998. "Politik für das Fernsehen – Politik im Fernsehen – Theorien, Trends und Perspektiven." In *Politikvermittlung und Demokratie in der Mediengesellschaft*, U. Sarcinelli (ed.), 184–208. Bonn: Bundeszentrale für politische Bildung.

Welsch, W. 1999. "Transculturality – The Changing Forms of Cultures Today." In Bundesministerium für Wissenschaft und Verkehr/Internationales Forschungszentrum für Kulturwissenschaften ed., *The Contemporary Study of Culture*. Wien: Turia & Kant, 217–244.

Wodak, R. and Meyer, M. (eds) 2001. *Methods of Critical Discourse Analysis*. London: Sage.

PART II

From linguistic device to discourse practice

Presupposition and 'taking-for-granted' in mass communicated political argument

An illustration from British, Flemish and Swedish political colloquy

Anne-Marie Simon-Vandenbergen, Peter R. R. White
and Karin Aijmer
Ghent University, Belgium / University of Adelaide, Australia /
Göteborg University, Sweden

The aim of this paper is to examine to what extent taken-for-grantedness is used as a strategy in political media language as a genre across cultures, and whether it is characterised by similar choices at the interpersonal level. The data are taken from British, Flemish and Swedish radio and television interviews and debates.

Starting from a close analysis of the use of the marker of expectation *of course* and its equivalents, the study shows that this adverb is part of a much wider range of frequently used explicit and implicit markers of presupposed common knowledge. Second, we show that various markers of presupposition are typically used in the three cultures examined for the same purposes. This indicates that the genre of political media debate is to a large extent conventionalised at the interpersonal level and that the conventionalisation operates in similar ways in the three cultures.

1. Introduction

Recent linguistic research on media political language, whether the concern is with the written or the spoken media, can roughly be divided into three groups of studies. In one type of studies the focus is on ways in which language reflects explicit or implicit ideologies. Typically these studies have aimed at laying bare the means by which speakers/writers convey political opinions regarding crucial societal issues such as class, gender or race relations. The linguistic framework within which most of these studies are carried out is critical discourse analysis in the broadest sense. The ultimate goal of this type of research is to raise awareness of language as an instrument of power and thereby to attempt to have an impact on power relations, to contribute to lifting inequality. These studies hence have a clear ideological starting-point and purpose. Examples are van Dijk (1998a, 1998b), Fairclough (1995, 2001), Wodak et al. (2000), Blommaert and Bulcaen (1997), and many articles in the journal *Discourse and Society*.

The second group of studies on media political language focus on the mechanisms of interaction and ways in which participants engage in talk. These studies are not so much interested in the ideologies of the speakers as in the way media interaction develops in different genres such as radio or television interviews and debates. The linguistic framework within which these studies are to be situated is typically conversation analysis in some variant. Examples of such work are Greatbatch (1992) and Clayman and Heritage (2002).

The third group comprises studies which take a functional approach to discourse in a broad sense and concentrate on the linguistic means, lexical and grammatical, of persuasion. The focus is on participants' rhetorical strategies by means of which they attempt to get their points across and reach their goals as political speakers. This type of research shares with the first group of studies its interest in the power of linguistic choices and with the second group its interest in the way speakers deal with the demands made by the various genres in which they are involved – for example how is it that speaker answer face-threatening questions, deny accusations or strengthen their own arguments. This type of research tends to go into detailed analyses of linguistic choices as rhetorical devices employed by political speakers to reach certain goals which are crucial in the presentation of themselves in the media. Examples are Harris's study (1991) on answering questions, Simon-Vandenbergen (1996, 1997) on image building, Lauerbach (2004) on political interviews as a hybrid genre.

The present article is to be situated within the third group. Its aim is to study strategic uses of lexicogrammatical means in an attempt to persuade. More specifically the focus is on the use of a set of resources which we see as construing 'taken-for-grantedness' – certain formulations by which propositions are treated as generally known or agreed upon, and hence as uncontentious and not at stake argumentatively. Our specific focus will be upon two modes of taken-for-grantedness – that associated with what the literature terms presupposition (see e.g. Bertuccelli Papi 1997; Caffi 1998; Lambrecht 1994) and that associated with metadiscursive locutions such as *of course* and its Dutch and Swedish equivalents *natuurlijk* and *ju* respectively. The research elaborates on previous work on the use of modality and evidentiality in British political discourse (especially Simon-Vandenbergen 1992) and on cross-linguistic research in this area (especially Simon-Vandenbergen and Aijmer 2005; Lewis 2004). Our goal is threefold.

The first aim is to look at taken-for-grantedness as a persuasive strategy in political TV debates. This paper builds on Sbisà (1999) and takes the argumentation further in the direction of finding an answer to the question why speakers find it useful to treat certain propositions as generally known or agreed upon or otherwise not at issue. It is often assumed that such formulations are used with the aim of making propositions unarguable, or at least with the aim of making them less accessible to argumentation. For instance, Caffi (1998) writes:

> Obviously, it is more difficult to question something that is communicated only implicitly rather than something which is communicated openly, if only because what is implicit must be recognized before being attacked. This is proved by the highly polemical and aggressive value underlying any attack to presuppositions; such an attack is seriously face-threatening. (1998:753)

However, in the type of media data examined in this paper the taken-for-granted material does, at least with some regularity, get challenged. This finding forces us to look beyond some simple notion of unarguability in seeking to identify the rhetorical purposes which may be served by these formulations in the mass communicated political arguments which constitute our current data set.

The second aim of this paper is of a more general linguistic nature. Starting from the system of engagement as developed by Martin (1997, 2000) and elaborated by White (1998, 2000, 2002, 2003) we want to argue that presupposition deserves a place in that framework as one of the options. While a consideration of presupposition is absent in the model presented in White (2003), both White (2006) and Martin and White (2005) do discuss what is termed 'taken-for-grantedness' and in this context consider the potential intersubjective and rhetorical effects associated with the use of presupposing formulations. The account in this paper is generally supportive of the approach taken by White and by Martin and White but seeks to consider the rhetorical function of taken-for-grantedness in greater depth, and in the context of cross-linguistic comparisons.

Thirdly, the data are taken from political debates in three closely related cultural contexts, the British, Flemish and Swedish ones. We believe that by studying closely linguistic choices in similar data in different languages and cultures the resources which are exploited surface more visibly. Furthermore, if it appears that the choices are similar we can hypothesise that political discourse in these cultures relies on the same tactics. However, in order to reach this third goal of studying strategies from an intercultural point of view much more research is called for, on a larger amount of data from more widely different cultures. We therefore see this third goal as mainly exploratory in nature.

First we briefly introduce the framework we are using and its relevance for the data under consideration (Section 1). Section 2 discusses the data. We then outline our view of the rhetorical effect of 'taken-for-grantedness' as it operates in connection with the discourse marker *of course* and its Flemish and Swedish equivalents (Section 3). The use of presupposing constructions across the British, Flemish and Swedish data is dealt with in Section 4. Section 5 gives the discussion of and conclusions from the findings.

2.   The system of engagement (White 2003; Martin & White 2005)

Various authors working within a functional approach to language have argued for a view of modality which goes beyond the formal categories of modal auxiliaries and epistemic adverbs to include a wide range of lexical and grammatical expressions of speakers' attitudes towards the truth value of their propositions (especially Stubbs 1986). In such encompassing definitions of modality various systems which are kept apart in more formal approaches are brought together in that they serve similar aims in positioning the speaker vis-à-vis their utterances. These systems form a heterogeneous group including evidentials, hedges, concession, negation and others. From a rhetorical perspective it makes indeed good sense to treat choices from these different systems as working together to create semantic prosodies such as confidence and authority (Simon-Vandenbergen 1992, 1996, 1997). White (2003) and Martin and White (2005), elaborating the system of engagement as introduced by Martin (1997), accommodate these different types of expressions in an encompassing system of choices which all express the ways in which "the textual voice engages with alternative voices and positions" (White 2003: 261). White's and Martin and White's contribution to the research on the functionality of modal and evidential expressions has been to draw attention to the fact that a primary functionality of these resources is to enable the speaker/writer to expand or contract the dialogic space available to alternative positions. In developing this argument, they have demonstrated that commitment to the truth-value of the propositions is to be seen as one factor but not the only one and often not even the most important one.

Within the model (White 1998; White 2003; Martin & White 2005) the main choice is between monoglossic and heteroglossic utterances, the former being bare statements whereby propositions are declared absolutely. For example,

(1)   Two years on, the British government has betrayed the most fundamental responsibility that any government assumes – the duty to protect the rule of law. It is a collusion in an international experiment in inhumanity, which is being repeated and expanded around the world.
       [*The Guardian*, January 10, 2004, leader pages – 24]

Such utterances are seen as undialogic in that they ignore the backdrop of alternative viewpoints and other voices against which such utterances always operate, offering no recognition of these alternative points of view. In this they contrast with formulations which do recognize the communicative context as heteroglossic in that the speaker/writer is presented as responding to prior utterances, as positioning him-or herself with respect to other viewpoints, or as anticipating the responses of those to whom the utterance is addressed. This is achieved through modalisation, attribution and a range of additional metadiscursive qualifiers including negation, concession and the *of course* locutions which are our current concern. White claims that the contexts in which the barely asserted 'monoglossic' option is typically found are either those in which knowledge is established and therefore need not be argued for, or contexts in which the textual voice "constructs itself as being in solidarity with a readership which holds the same (...) views" (2003:264). In Martin and White (2005), the model is further developed to allow for a difference between bare assertions such as those just listed and those which involve presupposition, as the term has been defined in the literature. Presuppositions, of course, are those formulations in which the proposition survives even under negation. For example, the proposition that the Canadian government has betrayed its promises is presupposed in the following.

(2)   After nine years of **the government's betrayal of the promised progressive agenda**, Canadians have a gut feeling that their country is slipping away from them.
[Canadian Hansard, www.parl.gc.ca/37/2/parlbus/chambus/house/debates/002_2002-10-01/han002_1215-E.htm]

Martin and White contend that un-presupposing bare assertions of the type listed earlier present the proposition as still in play argumentatively in some way, while the presupposing formulation presents it as a 'given' which puts nothing at stake argumentatively. (See Martin & White 2005: Chapter 3.) It is precisely this latter rhetorical effect that we are interested in in this article and we shall come back to this monoglossic option in Section 3.

In contrast with the monoglossic utterance, the heteroglossic one is dialogistic in the sense that, as just indicated, it engages with alternative positions (White 2003:265). It can do so in two main ways, i.e. by expanding or contracting the space for other voices and alternative positions. The expansive options actively recognize alternative positions or allow for their possibility and hence lower the interpersonal cost for any who might advance such a viewpoint. For example, in the following two extracts, *it's possible, would, I believe* and *will* are dialogistically expansive in actively allowing for alternative dialogic possibilities.

(3)   **it's possible that** a severe shake-up **would** bring your husband to realize how much you really mean.
The sad aspect of all this is that by giving support to this invasion Blair will be destroying the UN and **I believe will** have betrayed the British people.

In contrast, the contractive options operate to challenge, head off, deny or exclude dialogic alternatives, even while in some way allowing for, or engaging with these alternatives Thus negation is the archetypal dialogically contractive option in that, in denying some proposition, it necessarily invokes and hence allows for that contrary position, even while asserting that the denied proposition is unsustainable. The locution which is our current concern, *of course,* is included among these dialogically contractive options in that it (a) presents the speaker/writer as dialogically engaged with the putative addressee in anticipating that the proposition is something which will already be known or agreed upon, and (b) construes any contrary proposition as going against common sense or common knowledge. Under White's engagement framework, it is classified as an instance of 'concurrence' in that it presents the addressee as inevitably sharing this piece of information or this viewpoint with the speaker/writer.

It is our proposal in this paper that even while presupposition is 'monoglossic' in Martin and White's terms and locutions such as *of course* are 'heteroglossic', they nonetheless do share one important aspect of their rhetorical functionality. Both formulations, in their different ways, present the proposition as a 'given', as informational or evaluative content which the speaker/writer is presented as taking for granted. In this we are extending Martin and White's notion of taken-for-grantedness, which for them is limited to 'monoglossic' presupposition, to include the heteroglossic concurring option of *of course* (and related formulations.)

In Sections 3 and 4 we look at taken-for-grantedness as construed via formulations such as *of course* and at taken-for-grantedness as construed via presupposition respectively.

3.   The data

The British data used for this study are taken from the programme *Question Time* (BBC1 8 January 2004) and from a corpus comprised of some fifty episodes of the BBC radio programme, *Any Questions* (June 2003 – December 2004), the Flemish data[1] are from the programmes *Ter zake Zaterdag* (Canvas, 7 February 2003)

---

1.   The word *Flemish* is used here to indicate that the programmes were broadcast in Flanders (i.e. on Flemish television) and that they were debates between Flemish politicians. When refer-

and *De Zevende Dag* (Canvas, 8 February 2003). The data cover 6 debates. The Swedish data are from a debate on nuclear energy broadcast on 21 March 1980.[2] These programmes share a number of features, including that the protagonists are politicians, that the topics are political issues, and hence that these are interactions which all fall under the heading of 'political discourse'. Further, in all cases the interaction is managed by an interviewer or moderator. Thirdly, in all cases these are broadcast programmes, whether on the radio or on television. For the purposes of this study the difference between radio and television programmes is less important. The crucial factor is that the discourse is political, the issues controversial, and the interaction takes place for an audience of viewers or listeners. On the other hand there are some differences between the genres which these data represent that may have an impact on the discursive choices, and thus potentially on the use of presupposition as a tactic. We shall briefly comment on these genres.

The English and the Flemish programmes belong to the genre which Greatbatch (1992) and, following him, Clayman and Heritage (2002) call 'the panel interview'. According to Greatbatch, the advantage of panel interviews over one-to-one interviews is that the former solve the journalist's problem of having to reconcile combative questioning with the preservation of neutrality. By asking questions of two or more interviewees, typically representing different parties and viewpoints, the interviewer can provoke lively debate while maintaining neutrality. The liveliness results from disagreement among the interviewees. The disagreement can be voiced at different places in the turn-taking and can be addressed to the interviewer or to another interviewee. Greatbatch (1992) points out that the strength of disagreement in this genre increases with the abandonment of the expected question-answer format and with the identity of the addressee. The extracts given in the discussion will show that both the English and the Flemish data display the features of this genre. Not infrequently do interviewees address each other and in some cases they even deviate from the topic to become personal

---

ence is to the linguistic features we prefer to use the term *Dutch*, a variant of which is spoken in Flanders.

2.   The Flemish programmes are weekly debates in which a number of politicians take place and in which various topics are discussed. This explains why the examples from the Flemish data are 'heterogeneous' as far as speakers and topics are concerned. In contrast, all Swedish examples are from one debate, on the topic of nuclear energy. The reason why it is used for illustration, even though it is quite old (1980) is that it was a heated as well as much discussed debate at the time. We do not think that the time gap is relevant to the points we want to illustrate.

in an escalation of heated and unmitigated disagreement (see Clayman & Heritage 2002: 313ff. on the escalation from disagreement to confrontation).

The Swedish data are well described in Hirsch (1989). The genre is a formal television debate in which the turn-taking can be characterized as "mechanistic or almost completely predetermined" (1989: 118). The debate in question took place in the last days before the referendum on nuclear energy in Sweden held on 23 March 1980. In this debate, the representatives of the three lines met. Line 1 is in favour of nuclear energy, while line 3 wants to abolish it. Line 2 is a compromise, neither radically for nor against it. The three lines were represented by four speakers, and a well-known news broadcaster acted as moderator or "master of ceremonies". The primary goal of the activity was to influence the voting behaviour of the home audience. From the interaction point-of-view it is important to mention that the turns were very strictly timed, that claims made by one speaker are answered by another speaker only indirectly, and hence that there is no overlapping talk, no interruptions, no abandonment of "institutionalised footing" (Greatbatch 1992: 287), no escalation of disagreement towards confrontation.

The passages given in the following sections as illustrations follow normal orthographic and punctuation conventions for readability's sake. We have opted against a detailed CA transcript for the sake of uniformity: while the Flemish data were recorded and transcribed by us, the Swedish data have been transcribed at the Department of Linguistics, Göteborg University and this transcription has been used here (although some conventions have been changed for the sake of consistency with the other data). The *Question Time* data were transcribed by us, while the data from *Any Questions* were collected from the BBC website at www. bbc.co.uk/radio4/anyquestions.shtml.

4.   *Of course* and its equivalents in the Flemish and Swedish data

It has appeared from previous research that the adverb *of course* is extremely frequent in British political discourse. Both Simon-Vandenbergen (1992) and Lewis (2004) demonstrate that it fulfils some very useful rhetorical functions in this type of context. It is over-archingly a mechanism by which the speaker/writer announces that the current proposition is so generally known or so generally agreed upon as to be self-evident. It is thus a dialogistically anticipatory gesture in that either a state of knowledge or a value position is projected onto the audience. In English, *of course* shares this functionality of announcing self-evidence with a few other locutions, for example, *naturally, it goes without saying, needless to say, as you know* and *obviously*. For the purposes of this paper we have chosen to confine ourselves to *of course* (and its Dutch and Swedish counterparts) because it is overwhelmingly the most frequently used of these locutions in our data. For example, in our database of transcripts of the *Any Questions* programmes, *of course* occurs in all 55 transcripts at an average of 7 instances per transcript (373 instances in 55 transcripts) while *obviously* occurs 137 times in 48 transcripts and *naturally* only 7 times in 7 transcripts (and only half of those instances construe 'concurrence'). In the Dutch and Swedish data we have looked at *natuurlijk* and *ju* respectively because (a) they too are announcements of self-evidence and (b) as announcers of self-evidence they are the closest to *of course,* and (c) because, like *of course,* they are the most frequently occurring announcers of self-evidence. In the Dutch data *natuurlijk* occurs 24 times in 6 transcripts, i.e. with an average of 4 per transcript. In the Swedish data *ju* occurs 169 times in the 90-minute debate, while *naturligtvis* occurred only twice and the synonymous *förstås* and *givetvis* were not found at all. In a study of the translation equivalents of *of course,* Simon-Vandenbergen and Aijmer (2003–4) have found that the word *natuurlijk* was the prototypical equivalent of *of course* in all its functions. In Swedish, it is striking that the most frequent translations of *of course, naturligtvis* and *förstås* (as found in Simon-Vandenbergen and Aijmer 2003–4) were (almost) absent from the debate, which indicates that they do not have the rhetorical function of *of course.* The frequency of *ju* is accounted for further in this section.

The rhetorical functions served by *of course* can be grouped together under two broad headings. In the first instance it can be seen as having a 'politeness' function. For example,

(4)   DIMBLEBY (moderator)
Welcome to Petersfield in Hampshire which is decked out for Christmas and where we're in St. Peter's Church, which is renowned architecturally for its fine Norman tower and socially for its concerts, plays, exhibitions and civic events, as well as being **of course** a place of Christian worship.

In such instances the announcement of self-evidence acts as a form of dialogic apology cum explanation which can be accounted for by reference to the Gricean maxim of 'quantity' (Grice 1975). Since the informational content of the framed proposition is presented as being so widely known as to be self-evident, such formulations involve the speaker saying 'more' than is necessary. They are thus an apparent breach of 'quantity'. The speaker indicates an awareness of the apparent breach, while at the same time signalling that there is some other good reason why he/she needs to announce information which the addressee already knows – for example, in order to foreground a particular piece of information, in order to put together all the steps in a chronology, to ensure that the addressee knows where the speaker is coming from argumentatively, and so on. When used in this way, then, *of course* can be seen as a signal of discursively necessary redundancy. In such cases, *of course* has *as you know* as its near synonym – i.e.

> ...we're in St. Peter's Church, which is renowned architecturally for its fine Norman tower and socially for its concerts, plays, exhibitions and civic events, as well as being, **as you know,** a place of Christian worship.

In the above instance, the proposition at issue involved entirely uncontentious and uncontested informational content – that St Peter's Church was a place of Christian worship. Such uses are rare in our data and are not of major interest in the context of this paper's central concern with political argument and conflict. However, we also find this politeness-oriented, apparent redundancy signalling function in connection with evaluative or speculative, and hence potentially more contentious, propositions. Consider by way of example the following two extracts,

(5) a.   If there is to be a war on terror, and perhaps there must be, because **of course** September 11th was an outrage

b.   I think the terrible thing is that you knew from the very first moment that it really didn't matter what anybody said or anybody did this unfortunate man was going to meet the most terrible death. A man obviously not involved in the day-to-day difficulties. And a man who had gone there to do a constructive job. So **of course** you think first of the family.

Here the signalled assumption is that all will share the speaker's view of the attack on the World Trade Centre in New York in 2001, and that all will respond in the same way to the news that Iraqi insurgents had executed the British man they had taken hostage during the US and British invasion of Iraq in 2004. Despite the material being evaluative rather than 'factual', the same apology cum explanation effect applies. Since these are value positions which are presented as self-evidently the case, their expression is, on the face of it, redundant. The speakers signal their awareness of this apparent breach of the maxim of quantity, alerting their listeners that there is, nevertheless, some good communicative reason why they are being told something they already know to be the case. Once again the *of course* functions as a signal of necessary redundancy. The ideological potential of such uses is obvious. Not only do they project particular value positions onto the putative addressee, but they also construe that value position as universally shared, thus positioning any who might dissent from the viewpoint as at odds with what is common knowledge or common sense. In such cases, *of course* has *needless to say/it goes without saying* as a near synonym. For example

> If there is to be a war on terror and perhaps there must be because, **it goes without saying,** September 11th was an outrage

In the second instance, in contrast with this solidarity and politeness function, *of course* serves an oppositional function. Here the announcement of self-evidence acts as a dialogic 'put-down' by which the speaker's immediate interlocutor is presented as having dealt inappropriately with informational or evaluative material. The interlocutors have either shown themselves to be ignorant of, to have overlooked, or to have omitted to mention a point of some significance, or, alternatively, they have made too much out of some point, for example presenting it as argumentatively significant or crucial when, from the current speaker's perspective, it is too well known to have any such rhetorical potential. Consider by way of example the following extract. The current speaker presents the previous speaker's arguments in favour of a ban on fox hunting (then being proposed by the British government) as flawed in that the previous speaker has failed to take into account evidence against the pro-ban position provided by recent experiences in Scotland.

(6)   JENKIN
      Well I myself would never break the law but you've got a problem where so
      many people feel that a law is unjust. We've had chief constables speaking
      publicly about the huge amount of resources that are going to be necessary to
      police a ban on foxhunting and **of course** they've already tried to ban foxhunt-
      ing in Scotland and the legislation is a complete nonsense because they carry
      on foxhunting and they just shoot the foxes at the end instead of catching
      them by hounds.

The 'put-down' effect applies here as this counter evidence is presented as universally known. In failing to take it into consideration, the prior speaker is construed either as grossly ill-informed (he is ignorant of what is commonly known) or as dissembling (he seeks to misrepresent the case at hand by suppressing common knowledge). There is also a further positioning effect by which the wider audience is presented as standing with the current speaker, and against the former speaker, in sharing this view of the significance of the Scottish experience. In such cases, *of course* has *as everyone knows* as its near synonym. For example,

      We've had chief constables speaking publicly about the huge amount of
      resources that are going to be necessary to police a ban on foxhunting and, **as
      everyone knows,** they've already tried to ban foxhunting in Scotland and the
      legislation is a complete nonsense because they carry on foxhunting and they
      just shoot the foxes at the end instead of catching them by hounds.

Alternatively, *of course* is employed as the current speaker presents some key point of the prior speaker's argument as self-evident and hence not relevant or at issue in the current debate. Consider by way of example the following, in which the speakers are Dimbleby (D) and Bryant (B):

(7)   D: What do you make then of the point that Peter Hitchens was making – making, to the effect that the marriage is fundamental to the belief of the church and fundamental to its identity, as he believes it also to be in a coherent civilised society?

      B: **Of course** marriage is absolutely essential to a coherent and a good society and for the vast majority of people it's the way they're going to live their lives but there are some people, like myself, who are gay or are lesbian who are never going to have the opportunity of marriage, who might want to live in long trusting loving relationships and I think the church should be helping people to do that rather than making it more difficult.

Here the current speaker (Bryant) doesn't simply concede the prior speaker's point about the social role of the family, but, via the use of *of course*, construes it as so evidently the case as to be irrelevant to the issues which are actually under consideration. With such uses of *of course*, it is usual for the locution to be followed by some adversative connective such as *but* or *yet*. Once again this is a use of *of course* by which the prior speaker is cast as either foolish (they have overestimated the significance of some argumentative point) or as rhetorically unscrupulous (they have sought to base an argument on a point they know to be irrelevant). And once again there is a positioning effect by which the current speaker is construed as aligned with the wider audience against the prior speaker. However, in this instance it is an assessment of the argumentative significance of some point which the current speaker supposedly shares with the wider audience. In such cases, *of course* has *it goes without saying/needless to say* as its near synonym. For example,

> **It goes without saying that** marriage is absolutely essential to a coherent and a good society....

In summary, then, of this section, we can say that in English all uses of *of course* are announcements by the speaker that they regard the current proposition to be so widely known or so widely agreed upon to be 'self evident'. Within this broader functionality, instances of *of course* may vary according to whether they are serving a solidary or an oppositional function. In the first instance they act as dialogic apologies cum explanations, as the speaker signals a discursively necessary redundancy. In the second instance they act as put-downs by which some prior speaker is indirectly accused of understatement (having ignored or failed to mention some relevant point) or, alternatively of overstatement (having made too much out of some essentially irrelevant point).

    In Flemish *natuurlijk* can serve they same functions as *of course* in English as they have been outlined above. That is to say, it is an announcer of self evidence which can be either solidary ('apologetic' signal of necessary redundancy) or oppositional (a 'put-down'), and within the oppositional, it either implies 'understatement' (failure by the dialogic opponent to note some very widely known significant point) or 'overstatement' (making too much argumentatively out of some universally known point).[3] Its use is illustrated in the following extract.[4] The politician is Rik Daems (RD).

(8)   I: Well, Mr Daems, what is Mr Van Rossem saying there? He says the executive board was perfectly aware of the plans of the Swiss and apparently the VLD party chairman Karel De Gucht knew about it, too. Do you know about that scenario?

RD: Not at all. I think that the inquiry committee has revealed a number of things which are important. I think that we regrettably find that we have landed in a party political situation where some people have at particular moments stooped to personal attacks but if you distance yourself from that for a moment then I think that you find in the report a number of aspects ...

I: Yes

RD: ...mainly to well financially it was an enterprise in which a number of very bad decisions were taken, mainly under the impulse of the Swiss and what struck me especially is that now a few days ago it appeared from the Ernst & Young report in Switzerland that well in fact there had been premeditated deception

I: Yes and according to Mr Van Rossem...

RD: [overlap] which of course doesn't mean...

I: ...according to Mr Van Rossem the executive board knew about this, some VLD people knew about it and nothing was done, he says.

---

3. Perhaps a note on the semantic relationship between the cognates Dutch *natuurlijk* and English *naturally* is in order here. We have checked the Dutch equivalents of *naturally* in a translation corpus (Triptic Namur Corpus: debates of the European Parliament and fiction, see Paulussen 1999 for a description). English *naturally* is translated by *natuurlijk* and by *vanzelfsprekend* ('it goes without saying'). It is striking that its frequency in English original data is much below its frequency in English translations from Dutch. As a translation, *naturally* is the equivalent of *natuurlijk* (most frequent), *uiteraard* and occasionally *het ligt voor de hand* ('it is evident'). So *natuurlijk* covers both *of course* and *naturally*.

4. For the sake of readability, all Dutch and Swedish extracts are given in English translation. The original extracts are added in the Appendix. In the transcripts abbreviations stand for the names of political speakers. The letter I stands for 'Interviewer'. In the Dutch transcripts [...] in turn final position indicates that the current speaker is interrupted and [...] in turn initial position indicates that the speaker continues his/her utterance after interruption or overlap. The symbol [.] indicates a slight pause.

RD: [overlap] Well, Karel De Gucht **of course** hadn't become party chairman by 1997 because that was the time of the purchase of those air buses...

I: Hmmm

RD: ...so I think that things are being mixed up and that Mr Van Rossem...

I: Is he mistaken and talking nonsense, Mr Van Rossem?

RD: Well I think Mr Van Rossem **of course** now that he wants to become a politician is perhaps a little bit influenced by that but the essence of the story, Mr Belet, is that you have to look at the conclusions of the report because what is important for me is that we have uncovered to some extent where the causes are of such a large company going bankrupt: bad management, wrong financial decisions.

In the above extract Rik Daems (RD), federal Minister of State Enterprises is being interviewed on the bankruptcy of Sabena, the national airline company. The interviewer refers to Mr Van Rossem, one of the senior dismissed Sabena pilots who became the spokesman for the Sabena pilots at the time and accused the government of not having disclosed knowledge of the Swiss plans to stop their financial input. Van Rossem claimed the government had known about it for a long time and should have reacted. RD uses the word *natuurlijk* (the Flemish equivalent of *of course*) twice in this extract. The first time it functions to convey that 'as everybody knows' Karel De Gucht could not have been responsible as he wasn't party chairman at the time, in contrast with what Van Rossem claims. The implication is that the accusation of Van Rossem is therefore clearly unjustified and it is plain for everyone to see that. This usage of *natuurlijk*, then, clearly parallels the use of *of course* as an oppositional 'put-down' in English which we exemplified above. More specifically, it is the first type of 'put-down' where the dialogic opponent is construed as guilty of 'understatement'. They are represented as either ignorant of, or as deceitfully failing to mention, some significant point which is known to the rest of us. As was the case with the equivalent *of course* in English, the adverb builds up a solidary relationship between the current speaker and the audience against the dialogic opponent.

The second occurrence of *of course* (source item *natuurlijk*) occurs in association with the dialogically expansive items *I think* and *perhaps*. The reason is that the interviewee is making a strong statement here about the dishonest intentions of the Sabena pilot but has no evidence for making claims about intentions. Therefore the accusation is hedged even though the word *of course* at the same time closes down the dialogue. Here we see the Flemish equivalent of English *of course* where the functionality is to signal necessary redundancy. That Van Rossem, as a would-be politician, might be expected to distort or misrepresent is construed as a proposition which is self-evident and which, accordingly, wider audience members will already know and take for granted. The speaker 'apologises' for proposing a point of which the audience is supposedly only too well aware, signalling that, despite this apparent redundancy, he still needs to make this point for the purposes of advancing his own argument. The effect, obviously, is highly ideological as the view that would-be politicians are by nature deceitful is projected onto the audience and construed as universally held. The speaker, in his capacity as an established politician, thus implicitly distinguishes between 'real' and 'would-be' politicians.

The above examples show *natuurlijk* as 'put-down' (understatement) and as 'apology' (signalling of necessary redundancy). In the following passage *natuurlijk* functions as 'put-down' (overstatement).

(9)   VR: Yes, **of course** the threat of war is something something terrible and we must do everything to forestall that. It goes without saying. The people want that. Of course we want that, too uhm but we must also have a consistent policy, I think. Uhm . Mr Michel was in New York at the end of January. He was impressed by what he heard there. He asked for an understanding of the American viewpoint. There was even mention of a U-turn. He has . he denied that. Uhm he comes back to Europe and then we adopt a viewpoint that is in fact completely in contradiction with the impression which he gave in New York.

The speaker, MP for the opposition, disagrees with the government's refusal to give defensive support to Turkey, as has been asked by the US. The government spokesperson in this interview argues that Belgium must do everything to avoid a war against Iraq. This is the point where the speaker in the above extract comes in with *of course*, which, while expressing agreement with the government's argument, presents it as an overstatement, which does not detract from the opposition's line of argumentation.

In Swedish political speech the word *ju* is extremely frequent (see Simon-Vandenbergen and Aijmer 2005). It clearly differs, however, from *of course* and *natuurlijk* in that it does not cover the same oppositional functions. Its function is mainly to mark self-evidence and to construe a relationship of solidarity. As shown in Simon-Vandenbergen and Aijmer (2003–4), it can be seen as a rhetorical equivalent of *of course* in that it also functions to announce self evidence and thereby to construe a relationship of solidarity between the speaker and their audience. In contrast with Dutch *natuurlijk*, however, it is not the most frequent translation equivalent of *of course*. However, just like *of course* and *natuurlijk* it represents the proposition as an undisputed truth and hence is used by political speakers as a ploy to create a power imbalance with the opponent. In contrast with English *of course* and Dutch *natuurlijk,* Swedish *ju* is a modal particle rather than an adverb. This means that it can for instance not be fronted or moved around and is much less salient. It can be said to have a 'sneaked in' character. The following extract illustrates this use of *ju* (translated as *of course*). The speaker is Rune Molin (RM):

(10)   RM: Why do we get such different contradictory messages? **Of course** it can't be demanding too much that the voters should get information about what is going to happen to the electricity supply, how you are going to ration, how you are going to raise the prices and so on, because that is **of course** what is going to be the consequence when one is going to lower the electricity supply in the eighties. Dahleus is **of course** going to leave the scene himself after the 23rd of March I have read in the papers, but could you not before that tell us who will carry out your political message?

In conclusion, it has appeared from recent research that at least in British, Flemish, Swedish and French (Lewis 2004) political discourse the rhetorical mode of 'concurrence' (White's term 2003) is favoured in contexts where speakers wish to contract the dialogue in the sense of making it difficult to challenge the proposition as it is presented as shared knowledge. The use of items indicating shared knowledge typically confirms solidarity in contexts where interactants already share a great deal of common ground and a common outlook (see Holmes 1988). Their use in contexts where very little is actually to be taken for granted, as differences in opinion are the very 'raison d'être' of the genre (political debate), is aimed at construing solidarity with those who need to be persuaded, i.e. the audience, against the opponent.

5.   The use of presupposition as another tactic

5.1 The monoglossic statement

It appears from the data in all three languages concerned that the concurrence strategy discussed in the previous section is just one of the more encompassing range of linguistic choices which in political discourse raise the interpersonal stakes for any who might want to question, challenge or reject a proposition being taken-for-granted by the speaker. In White's taxonomy (2003), the dialogic contraction devices, while being heteroglossic in recognising the theoretical possibility of alternative opinion, at the same time close down the dialogue by making challenges difficult. Such dialogic contraction is therefore closer to the monoglossic mode than the dialogic expansion devices. White points out that the monogloss option is also typically used where textual voice and audience either do share a common outlook or where the textual voice, for persuasive purposes, creates solidarity with a particular readership, who possibly hold an opinion distinct from other sections of the community. In White's taxonomy it is the bare assertion which realises the meaning of the monoglossic mode.

It appears indeed that in the data political speakers do present highly controversial judgements in a monoglossic way by expressing them as bare unmodalised statements. Here is an example from the Flemish data. The speaker is a member of the opposition and criticizing the safety policy of the government. The opposition's viewpoint is that even though a lot of money is being spent on police reform, the result is less safety than before:

(11)   VR: The central theme: safety. And they spend a lot more money to have fewer people who take care of safety. That's an incomprehensible story.

The strength of the argument lies in the juxtaposition of the different propositions. While the government cannot deny that money has been spent on police reform (objective fact), nor that the reforms involve a re-allocation of tasks so that there are fewer policemen on the streets (objective fact), the subjective elements in the utterance are the following: first, the vague quantifier *a lot more* is a subjective assessment; secondly, the presentation of having fewer people who take care of safety as the goal (in the form of a subordinated purpose clause) is the speaker's subjective assessment of the facts; thirdly, the nominal phrase *fewer people who take care of safety* to refer to policemen on the street is strategically chosen because it emphasizes the paradoxical situation. However, it expresses a contestable equation of the class of policemen on the street with the class of people taking care of safety. The evaluative comment *That's an incomprehensible story* merely sums up the argument: the government's policy has been presented by the speaker in a monoglossic way as indeed paradoxical.

However, there is another type of strategy which is at least as common as the bare statement to construe solidarity and to block dialogue. This is the presentation of material as presupposed. We want to argue that within the taxonomy of engagement modes it is the most dialogistically restrictive of all the engagement options, limiting the scope for dialogic alternatives even more thoroughly than bare assertions of the type just exemplified. Under this option, the speaker does not simply decline to offer any recognition that the proposition is in some way problematic or subject to contestation (as is the case with non-presupposing bare assertions). They go beyond this to present the proposition as simply not at issue, as a proposition which can be assumed and hence need not be asserted. While a non-presupposing monoglossic statement presents at least part of the information as new, presupposition structures present the information as known. While monoglossic utterances do not build in the possibility of dialogic alternatives, they are nevertheless dialogically 'upfront' in making a statement which can be affirmed or denied. Presupposed material, on the other hand, is 'sneaked in' as it were. Not only does it not open up a dialogue but it definitely shifts attention away from the thus backgrounded material.

Presupposition takes many forms and has been widely discussed in the linguistic literature. It is not our ambition here to give an exhaustive account of the different types as they occur in the data. What we want to do by giving some examples of different manifestations of presupposition is to show that it is an important means of persuasion in political discourse. In the next section we specify the way in which we are using the notion in this paper.

5.2 The term *presupposition*

The term *presupposition* covers many different things. One important distinction that has been made is between semantic and pragmatic presupposition. According to Caffi (1998: 752) "[t]he concept of semantic presupposition is quite clear". This is true to the extent that there are clear criteria which allow us to decide under what conditions we can claim that some material is semantically presupposed. Semantic presupposition is defined in terms of truth-conditions, as a subtype of entailment, in the sense that a proposition which is presupposed remains true under negation and questioning. The following example is from Bertuccelli Papi (1997). The sentence 'Sue is dancing a macarena' presupposes that there is a person named Sue and there is a dance which is the macarena. This type of existential presupposition survives even when the sentence is negated or turned into a question: 'Sue is not dancing a macarena' and 'Is Sue dancing a macarena?'. Semantic presupposition manifests itself in various lexical expressions and grammatical structures, and Bertuccelli Papi (1997) gives the following list: definite descriptions (including proper names), factive predicates including epistemic verbs (like *know, realize*) and emotive predicates (like *be surprised, regret, forget, deplore, resent*), implicative verbs (like *manage, remember*), change of state, inchoative and iterative verbs (like *stop, start*), verbs of judging (like *accuse, blame, criticize*), clefting and pseudo-clefting, prosodic emphasis, temporal clauses, non-restrictive relative clauses and counterfactuals. Semantic presupposition is conceptually different from pragmatic presupposition, which is defined in terms of common ground or background knowledge. Lambrecht (1994) gives the following definition of pragmatic presupposition:

> The set of propositions lexicogrammatically evoked in a sentence which the speaker assumes the hearer already knows or is ready to take for granted at the time the sentence is uttered. (1994: 52)

While this definition clearly distinguishes pragmatic from semantic presupposition, in practice it appears that the two concepts are hard to keep apart. The same types of lexicogrammatical structures are given for both types. In fact the distinction has, as Lambrecht points out (1994:61), "been all but abandoned in the literature", and Bertuccelli Papi remarks in the same vein that semantic presuppositions "have to be treated as pragmatic phenomena" (1997:11). The types of lexicogrammatical structures mentioned above are the ones we shall look for in the data at hand, even though what we are interested in are not the truth-conditions but the fact that these structures evoke situations, events which are presented by the speaker as background knowledge, propositions whose truth the speaker takes for granted. Thus when a speaker says *I regret that you told these lies* we have a case of semantic presupposition (the truth of the main proposition depends on the truth of the subordinated proposition, and the presupposition that 'you told these lies' survives under negation in *I don't regret that you told these lies*). However, what is more interesting from the point of view of interaction is that in uttering *I regret that you told these lies* the proposition 'you told these lies' is presented as common ground, while the assertion which is at stake is that 'I regret this'. Why is this the crucial point in interaction?

There are two reasons. One is that by encoding something as background, shared knowledge, the speaker at the same time presents a proposition as one whose truth is accepted by the hearer. In other words, pragmatically it is not the logical entailment which is of interest in the analysis of verbal interaction as much as the speaker's assumption of what can be taken for granted. Secondly, in terms of information structuring it is important that the presupposed material is backgrounded as old information, while the information in the assertion is foregrounded as new. Presuppositions in this way contribute to the structuring of the discourse, and "determine the point of view from which the text develops" (Bertuccelli Papi 1997:13). Both these factors play a role in the choices which speakers make with regard to what can be encoded as presupposed material.

The pragmatic view of presuppositions obviously entails that they are not static but are negotiated and interactively construed. But it also entails the possibility of exploitation. Bertuccelli Papi puts it as follows:

> It is therefore legitimate to wonder by whom pragmatic presuppositions should be taken for granted and by whom they are granted. The most plausible answer is that speakers treat presuppositions as noncontroversial, even though they may in fact be controversial and not taken for granted by the addressee. (1997:12–13)

Similarly, Lambrecht (1994:65) mentions the "conscious or unconscious exploitation of presuppositions for special communicative purposes". The reason why presuppositions are exploitable is that they are harder to challenge. As Lambrecht points out, the 'lie-test' shows that if the addressee wishes to challenge the 'old' information in the presupposition, he/she has to use other strategies than the straightforward 'That's not true'. For example, if the addressee replies *That's not true* to the utterance *I finally met the woman who moved in downstairs* she is challenging that the speaker met her, not that she moved in downstairs. If the addressee wishes to challenge the taken-for-granted nature of the presupposed proposition she would have to say something like *I didn't know that you had a new neighbour* or *What are you talking about?* (1994: 52). In such cases Lambrecht demonstrates that presuppositions are based on the assumption of shared knowledge which is not put up for discussion. There is, however, also the cognitive principle of 'pragmatic accommodation' (Lambrecht 1994: 66), which means that speakers frequently create a new presuppositional situation which can then be the starting-point for the further development of the conversational exchange. If someone says *My car broke down* this does not necessarily imply that the speaker thinks that the addressee knew that she has a car. Even if the addressee did not have this information she will accommodate to the new situation. Such cases of pragmatic accommodation are, however, to be distinguished from what Lambrecht refers to as "devious" cases of exploitation (1994: 70). The difference lies in the effects aimed at: devious cases are not aimed at conveying information indirectly but at creating "a fictitious presuppositional situation" for certain rhetorical purposes. In this paper we shall examine which types of presuppositions are used by political speakers and for what purposes.

It is important to emphasise that, whatever the pragmatic effect in specific contexts, certain lexicogrammatical expressions by themselves trigger presuppositions. It is these expressions that we will examine. We shall, on the other hand, not be concerned with pragmatic presupposition in the very broad sense in which it has been used by some, to include all knowledge that language users have and which is brought into the production and comprehension of utterances. Kempson (1975: 166ff.), for instance, refers to the 'Pragmatic Universe of Discourse', defined as the "body of facts which both speaker and hearer believe they agree on" in a conversation. Mey (1998: 186) claims that a "serious theory of pragmatic presuppositions (...) inquires *metapragmatically* into the ways in which an utterance is understood in the context of the language users' 'common ground'". And Mey further points out that it is then important not only to inquire how people say things but why they say them at all (1998: 187).

In this paper we are focusing on structures that are traditionally subsumed under semantic presupposition, while recognising that they need to be studied from a pragmatic point of view, both in their exploitation and their understanding. We are not concerned with pragmatic presupposition in the broadest sense, which includes various forms of implicitness such as conversational implicatures (whether particularized or generalized).

5.3 Previous research on presupposition for persuasive purposes: Sbisà (1999)

Sbisà (1999) discusses the use of presupposition for persuasive purposes in the Italian daily press. One interesting question she deals with is why presuppositions should ever be persuasive, why there is "a default tendency" in the addressee to take the presupposed information for granted (1999:501). The answer, according to Sbisà, lies in the normative nature of presuppositions: they are to be defined not as shared assumptions but as assumptions that ought to be shared. This entails that speakers violate norms of interaction if they take for granted that information is shared while it is not. If therefore presuppositions are not satisfied, addressees will consider speakers as uncooperative. Thus, ideally, speakers should strive towards producing utterances which trigger presuppositions only when the "objective context" indeed contains those presuppositions. The reason why presuppositions are useful for transmitting ideologies is then that they tend to be left unchallenged, since they are backgrounded. Explicitation and challenging of presuppositions are options available to the addressee but, as Sbisà points out, dispreferred ones (1999:506).

The data examined in this paper differ from those discussed in Sbisà (1999) in several ways. First, they are spoken instead of written, and there is an interlocutor who has the option of choosing the dispreferred reaction. Studying the reactions of hearers adds an important aspect to the discussion of the motives behind presupposition. Secondly, it will be shown that the dispreferred reaction is not infrequent in this genre. While we notice that in our data there are instances of presupposition where the proposition is not challenged, it is significant that, where the presupposition involves currently contentious material, it was not unusual for the presupposed material to be rejected or otherwise challenged in some way. Here is an example from the British data, an exchange between Dimbleby (D) and May (M):

(12) D: Theresa May, why dump on returning officers? [presupposes that 'dumping on returning offices' has taken place]
     M: Well I'm not dumping on returning officers.

5.4 Presupposition in the data

The following extract from the programme *Question Time* illustrates the type of structures and meanings that we are interested in. The issue of debate is the government's plans to introduce top-up fees for university students, for which they could get a loan. David Willits (W), Shadow Secretary, voices the Conservative party's opposition to this plan. David Dimbleby (D) asks the question:

(13)   D: David Willits, you were asked whether Tories will be voting in the lobbies for this because your position purports to be that you're against top-up fees.

W: We are against them, we are against them and we're against them because we don't think we want to see our students any other perhaps on the latest proposals 23,000£ of debt when they leave university. I don't think that's the right way to go. And as a Conservative I want to encourage people to save and I hear Ministers in the areas that I debate particularly, pensions, things like that, say they've got to encourage people to save. **I don't see how** getting saddling young people with 23,000 pounds' worth of debt is gonna help them start off in their lives and **we should remember how** we got into this. We got into this **because** the government set a target, an arbitrary target for the expansion of universities, that they should reach this target of 50%. Well, I completely agree with what PhylisJames said, I don't think it's in the best interests of the people in this country, you do need a better education to set such a target, they need [interruption by moderator]

The first instance of a construction which exploits presupposition is 'I don't see how...'. This expression is synonymous to other expressions such as 'I don't understand how'. The proposition in the subordinated interrogative clause, in this case a *how*-clause, is in such structures presented as known information, since the only unknown element, the missing bit is the element in the *wh*-word (i.e. *how*). In this concrete example, the speaker presents as presupposed that the government is going to 'saddle young people with 23,000£ worth of debt'. The term *saddle* is evaluative, which means that the negative judgement is simultaneously absorbed in the message as presupposed and non-negotiable. We have a similar example in the expression 'we should remember', a factive verb. In the above instance, what needs to be remembered is that the government took the wrong decision ('bad for them'), and again an evaluative term, *arbitrary*, is smuggled into the presupposed material.

The next example is from the Swedish nuclear debate. The speaker is Per Unckel (a member of the Conservative Party and in favour of nuclear energy, line 1). The addressee (Ulla Lindström) is a member of the Social Democratic party and is in favour of line 3 and abolishing nuclear energy.

(14)   if Ulla Lindström does not trust lines one and two I suppose Ulla Lindström anyhow trusts the developing countries themselves **when** they shake their heads and wonder how we in Sweden can think about doing away with nuclear energy/**when** this implies that the pressure on scanty oil resources/ which could be of use to the developing countries becomes still harder

The tactically relevant presupposed material in this passage is in the two *when*-clauses *when they shake their heads (...)* and *when this implies (...)*. The speaker first presents the disapproving attitude of the developing countries towards Sweden's plans to do away with nuclear energy as self evident by putting the proposition in a *when*-clause. Next, at a deeper level of subordination, the proposition that these plans would harm the developing countries by increasing the pressure on resources, is also presented as presupposed in a *when*-clause.

The following extract is also from the Swedish material. The speaker is Per Unckel (line 1):

(15)   the election is about whether **in addition to** the global energy crisis we have already to a large extent been affected by, we should place **additional** burdens which may be too heavy for us

What is presupposed in the above utterance is that there is 'a global energy crisis'. Further, the comparative referential term *additional* is relevant here in terms of presupposition, since it presupposes the current existence of a burden (in the form of the 'global energy crisis').

Here follow some more examples of presuppositional structures from the Flemish and Swedish data.

(i) Factive predicates

The presupposition trigger of factive predicates can be illustrated with the following example from the Flemish data, from an interview with Jean-Luc Dehaene (DH), former Prime Minister of Belgium:

(16)   DH: Well I call that continuing the debate after the elections and so I thought that this hype uh was unnecessary uh totally artificial uh and **some people apparently did not see** that they were thereby undermining the verve of the innovation...
       I: Hmm
       DH: ...and and and the campaign that should revolve around the innovation.

What is presented as new information is that some people apparently did not see something. That they were undermining the innovation is presented as to be taken for granted. The verb 'see' is indeed frequently used as an evidential and has a factive meaning: you can only see what is there. Another example from the same interview:

> (17)   DH: But **when I see** that this position uh damages my party, that through the way in which they handle this in my party they damage themselves, then I have to stop this.

The following is an example from the Swedish data, with Lennart Dahleus (LD) speaking:

> (18)   LD: Yes, **Per Unkel knows of course that** there are more possibilities for serious accidents than those we have discussed, steam explosions, **and that** nuclear power is a dangerous source of energy **and that** it contains enormous risks ranging from uranium mining to waste disposal that we probably agree on **and that** there are risks which have no equivalent in other sources of energy.

(ii) Relative clauses

Consider the following extract from the Flemish data:

> (19)   RD: This of course doesn't alter the fact that the government has approved an investment plan in the long term, a framework within which the NMBS [National Railways Company] must try to become healthy again, and one thing should certainly not be forgotten and that is a very important thing after all...
>
> I: [overlap] Yes
>
> RD: ...in a few months the liberalisation of this goods transport starts and therefore ...
>
> I: [overlap] Precisely. Uhm.
>
> RD: ...we must really urgently take a number of measures **which**...
>
> I: [overlap] Yes
>
> RD: ...**in so many years were not taken** because otherwise competition is going to hit very hard.
>
> I: [overlap] **Well, Mr Van Rompuy, it's the previous government's fault again.**
>
> VR: **Yes, well, we're getting used to that.**

On the face of it the relative clause gives information which is quite innocent: there would be no point in taking measures if they had indeed been taken before. The fact that the information is added at all raises the question of why it is added and why it is added in the form it is. The shared knowledge of the world which we need in order to explain the workings of this utterance is that 'in so many years' is a reference to the previous legislature, when the speaker's party was in the opposition and his opponent in the debate was in the government. This utterance is a way of reversing the tables in holding the opponent responsible for 'what is bad'.

The next extract is an example from the Swedish debate. The speaker is Rune Molin, who represents line 2 in the referendum which was neither clearly for nor against nuclear energy.

(20)   RM: It is self-evident that if we use our nuclear plants, the possibilities will increase considerably for cutting a dependence on oil **which is wrecking the economy of the whole of Swedish society.**

Below is another example from the Swedish debate. The speaker is Per Unckel (line 1):

(21)   PU: In this nuclear debate there has been one feature which I myself have appreciated much// and this is a feature characteristic of many of those who still support line three// **which implies a demand for a more tolerant society with room for more human concern and closeness/** if it was this that this referendum was actually about/ I think that no one would have any doubts about its outcome.

The relative clause carries the presupposition that people in line three want a more tolerant society with room for human concern and closeness, which is obviously positively evaluated. However, the speaker draws attention to this as already known or old information in order to then foreground that this is not what the referendum is about. His own viewpoint is that this desire for a better society is actually a reason to use nuclear energy not to abolish it. What we have here is a 'put down' of line three's position by presenting its argumentation as an overstatement, something everyone agrees on but which does not solve the problem.

Similarly in the next example from the Swedish data, the addressee is obviously assumed to share the presupposition conveyed in the *which*-clause. The speaker is Per Unckel (line 1) and the addressee Lennar Daleus (line 3):

(22)   PU: yes Lennart Daleus was surprised that I spoke about oil in a referendum about nuclear energy/the reason is of course that we have decided to use our nuclear reactors in order to open up the possibility of us being forced to reduce our dependence on oil, **which is well on the way to getting out of hand**

(iii)   Conditional clauses

(23)   VR: Do people feel safer?
       RD: [overlap] **Well of course if** in politics, colleague Van Rompuy, you get
             important people such as Mr Dehaene is an important man, **who want
             to create the impression** among the population that unsafety in-
             creases...
       VR: **Oh, it's Mr Dehaene?**
       RD: ...then I think that's bad. What m...
       VR: **Oh dear, Mr Dehaene creating unsafety.**
       RD: ...what matters is reality...
       VR: [overlap] **That is that is...**
       RD: ...and I'll give you another example.
       VR: [overlap] **very new to us, that is very new.**
       I: Yes, you must conclude, Mr Daems.
       VR: [overlap] **that is very new.**

By presenting the contestable information in the conditional clause of an *if...then*
structure which expresses a general truth that information is backgrounded as
given and the focus is on the result, namely the value judgement 'I think that's
bad'. It will be noted that the speaker makes use of several closing down strategies at the same time: *of course* (concurrence), subordination in an *if* clause in a
general truth statement (presupposition), subordination in a relative clause (presupposition).

The following example is from the Swedish data (the speaker is Per Unckel,
line 1):

(24)   But it is clear that /**if** one now decides to demolish nuclear reactors / **which
       correspond to all the energy that we get from water power**/then this cannot
       pass without a trace / and line three confirms I suppose also this by claiming
       that there is no other country which is so dependent on nuclear power as
       Sweden

In (24) the speaker uses the conditional clause structure, which includes the relative clause with presupposed material, to convey the following message: 'if one
decides to do away with nuclear energy, one does away with all the energy we get
from water power'.

(iv)   Existential structures

By 'existential structures' we refer in this context to structures with definite noun
phrases triggering the presupposition of the existence of their referents. A very

frequent type in political argumentation is an identifying clause with as subject 'the problem'. It is illustrated by the following example:

(25) RV: The problem of Mr Dewinter is that he only...
      DW: It is linked...
      I: [overlap] Yes
      DW.:   ...to it.
      RV: ...looks at the past. And we want to do something...
      I: [overlap] Okay
      RV: ...about the future and Mr Dewinter refuses to discuss that.
      I: No, he has a clear thesis. His future is: full is full.
      DW: [overlap] immigration stop.

The topic of discussion is immigration and Robert Voorhamme (RV, Socialist party) is attacking Filip Dewinter (DW, Flemish Bloc) for his thesis that the government policy does not work. He uses the expression 'The problem ... is that ...' In this type of structure two propositions are semantically presupposed, namely the identified and identifying elements. In this case these are firstly that there is a problem which the opponent has (the identified element), and secondly that he only looks at the past (the identifier element). What is new information is thus that the problem is now identified as such. How do we have to understand the workings of this type of utterance? First, 'problem' is a judgement term: whether something is a problem or not is a subjective assessment of a state-of-affairs. Second, 'he only looks at the past' is pragmatically to be understood as a judgement as well, since our knowledge of the world tells us that politicians need to look at the future. This is indeed explicit in the contrast with the speaker's own party ('And we want to do something about the future'). Through this structure a negative judgement (a criticism of the opponent as a politician) is made into presupposed material.

(v) Pseudo-cleft structures

(26) DW: [overlap] **What you are doing**...
      AD: [overlap] That's not possible, according to the law...
      DW: [overlap] ...by slowing down...
      VR: [overlap] Mr Dewinter
      DW: [overlap]...**by slowing down integration**...
      AD: [overlap] human rights...
      DW: [overlap]...**is**...
      AD: [overlap]... says very clearly...
      DW: [overlap] importing...
      I: [overlap] This is incomprehensible. Let's...

DW: [overlap] … **importing backwardness**. And that is the wrong position.

There is a lot here which is presupposed in Filip Dewinter's (DW) statement: that the government is slowing down integration and that there is backwardness associated with the Islam culture. What is presented as new information is that this backwardness is imported. Again, value judgements are thus sneaked in as shared knowledge.

In the following example from Swedish there is a reversed pseudo-cleft summing up what has been presupposed in the preceding context. The speaker is Per Unckel (line 1):

(27)   this is actually so self-evident that even line three ought to be able to agree//
we can use nuclear power being certain that in spite of its risks / it is safer than any other alternative which is at our disposal today// **and this is what is most important**

What is presupposed by the pseudo-cleft construction is that nuclear energy is safer than any other alternative type of energy. However the speaker cannot count on the audience's willingness to go along with the assumption that nuclear power is the safest source of energy and with the positive evaluation conveyed by the pseudo-cleft construction.

5.5   The expression of disagreement and the challenging of taken-for-grantedness

In general, disagreement is dispreferred in interaction. It has been shown that in ordinary conversation speakers will avoid disagreement and when it does arise they will try to soften it in various ways, including the use of delay devices, prefacing the disagreement with agreement expressions, and hedges (see Pomerantz 1984). In contrast, Clayman and Heritage (2002: 309ff.) have shown that disagreement is characteristic of panel interviews. By bringing together speakers known to represent different viewpoints the genre by definition invites disagreement. Further, the interviewers themselves frequently elicit disagreement by phrasing and rephrasing arguments and confronting interactants with the opposition's viewpoints. Also in contrast with ordinary conversation is the practice in panel interviews of voicing disagreements straightforwardly rather than hedgingly. Mitigating elements are almost always absent. Clayman and Heritage also show that disagreement in that genre may easily shift into confrontation, and that such "escalation" is signaled by a shift from mediated address (through the interviewer) to direct address (Clayman & Heritage 2002: 315). All of these features are indeed found in a very salient way in the Flemish data, which are from panel interviews. The following extract illustrates such an escalation. The topic is the decision to put the former Prime Minister, Dehaene (Christian Democrats), who is not a candidate in the coming elections, nevertheless on the list because he is expected to attract votes. The exchange becomes heated, with a great deal of overlapping talk, and very personal:

(28) I: Yes, Mr Daems, this is embarrassing for the Liberal Democrats, isn't it? He is not even on the list and yet he is in the limelight.

    RD: Well let me first say something about that tremendous call for Dehaene. I understand that Mrs Schauvliege has opened a website and she wanted a hundred thousand signatures, well, she's got five thousand. So that's a tremendous call, if you ask me.

    I: Yes, but in one week's time

    RD: [overlap] But apart from that ...

    I: [overlap] That's in one week's time.

    VR: [overlap] If you received five thousand if you received five thousand letters ...

    RD: [overlap] but apart from that...

    VR: [overlap] ... I would...I think you would...

    RD: [overlap] Oh but...

    VR: [overlap]... be happy with that.

    RD: [overlap] But colleague Van Rompuy...

    VR: [overlap] I think you would be happy with that.

    RD: [overlap] About the internet...

    VR: [overlap] I don't think you have recently received five hundred, have you?

    RD: [overlap] ... about the internet I know...

    VR: [overlap] I don't think you have received five thousand.

    RD: [overlap] You are extremely excited today, I think.

In the Flemish panel interviews disagreement is frequently voiced in very direct terms such as *that's not true, that's not correct,* or even *that's a lie.*

A similar situation obtains in the English data, where it is quite common for participants to forthrightly criticise, confront and nay-say each other. In the following extract, by way of example, the speakers, Scotland (S) and Howard (H) directly contradict and attack each other.

(29) S: But I think I want to add on to what David said because of course one has to acknowledge that schools facing the challenging circumstances with which many do in London are two and a half times better off now than they were. The improvements in the figures coming out now is

> clear, that they're doing two and a half times better. So those schools are really moving forward. And just to remind everyone that the Prime Minister does send his child and his children to state comprehensive schools and he hasn't opted out of this system.

H: Before – before Patricia lets her imagination run away with her let's remember that one in three of every child – one in three of our primary school children leave primary school unable to read, write and count properly and under this government the truancy figures.

S: That's not true.

H: . and truancy – oh I'm afraid it's true, I wish it weren't true but I'm afraid it's true, I know it's hard to believe but it's true.

In the Swedish data there is less open disagreement. Only occasionally does the speaker accuse his opponent of not telling the truth:

(30)   and when it is about oil Per Unckel says that it is quite clear that it is possible to replace the dependence on oil by nuclear power but to use your own words in an earlier context it is of course not true you know of course that in order to get rid of the total dependence on oil we would need fifty sixty power plants in this country (LD)

With regard to presuppositions, it has likewise been argued in the literature that interactants tend not to challenge them. Caffi points out that attacking presuppositions is not only difficult (because the implicit meaning must first be recognised before it is attacked) but also "highly polemical and aggressive" (Caffi 1998:753). Mey (1998:188–189) makes the same point in saying that in daily life we do not normally "go presupposition-hunting" and that we tend to take most presuppositions simply for granted. He goes as far as to claim that "metapragmatically questioning an interlocutor's presupposition is a dangerous sport, inasmuch as it may threaten the 'face' of my conversational partner" (1998:189). Sbisà (1999), too, ascribes the usefulness of presupposition as a persuasive tactic to the dispreferred nature of explicitation and challenging and hence to the default reaction of acceptance. However, at least one reason why presuppositions are typically left unchallenged may be that speakers violate the norms of discourse if the presupposed propositional content cannot be assumed to be part of the hearer's knowledge. Sbisà puts it as follows:

> Moreover, it is among the speaker's responsibilities to issue an utterance containing certain presupposition inducers only if the objective context really contains the presupposition they trigger. Thus we are describing presuppositions as assumptions that the speaker ought to make, or, however, assumptions for which he or she is responsible. (Sbisà 1999:503)

On the other hand, hearers "accommodate" to presuppositions:

> If at time t something is said that requires presupposition P to be acceptable, and if P is not presupposed just before t, then – ceteris paribus and within certain limits – presupposition P comes into existence at t. (Lambrecht 1994: 67)

This type of accommodation is, however, different from what takes place in the case of what Lambrecht refers to as "devious exploitation of presuppositional structure" (Lambrecht 1994: 70). As shown in the above extracts, presenting controversial propositions as to be taken-for granted is a strategy in political discourse. Such expressions are indeed manipulable because speakers use them for presenting non-shared and even highly contested propositions as if they were shared knowledge. The effect is on the one hand that solidarity is confirmed with those who share the speakers' viewpoint and on the other hand that those who hold alternative opinions are put into a position where more interactive work needs to be done if they want to challenge the speaker's views. The potential rhetorical usefulness of presupposition has been remarked upon by e.g. Verschueren (1999: 157) and Caffi (1998: 752). The question remains whether interactants in the types of data under investigation do make the efforts to challenge presuppositions.

It appears indeed that, in contrast with the rules of 'normal' interaction (cf. the "normative" nature of presupposition, Sbisà 1999: 502) the rules of media political debate do allow for and indeed seem to dictate the challenging of presuppositions. The challengers are the interviewer/moderator as well as the opponent in the debate. In several examples from the Flemish data given in the previous section speakers do challenge the presuppositions. In examples (19) and (23) given above, the challenges are put in bold.

The speakers in the English data demonstrate a similar willingness to challenge presupposed propositions, at least when they involve a point which is significant attitudinally or ideologically. The following exchange is illustrative of this tendency. The speakers, Peter Hitchens (H) and Maude (M) are discussing the recent resignation of the highly influential Conservative Party politician, Michael Portillo.

(31) H: Well I don't think it's a loss to the Conservative Party, in fact I wish he'd said it a long time ago because some years ago I suggested to the electors of Kensington and Chelsea that they should pick me instead because he wasn't – he wasn't a Conservative, which I don't think he is or was at the time. And what's interesting about Michael Portillo **is this strange journey that he's been on for some time away from Conservatism ... turning the Conservative Party into New Labour with a blue T-shirt on. ...**

M: ...Peter makes his point, I've heard him make before, about mod ernisation is all about making us like New Labour, it isn't at all. I mean a Conservative Party has been in existence for 200 years, it is actually, as Michael Howard said the other day, it's the most successful, the longest standing political party in the history of democracy.

Here, via the nominal structure, 'this strange journey ... away from Conservativ- ism ... into New Labour', the first speaker (Hitchens) presupposes that there has been a move, led by Portillo, to make the Conservatives more like the Labour Party. Despite the 'taken-for-grantedness' of the formulation, the second speaker unembarrassedly sets about turning an assumption into an arguable assertion and then forthrightly rejects it. Thus in his reply, he treats what was a presupposition as a 'point' which he asserts the speaker has made before.

The challenging of presuppositions was also frequent in the Swedish data:

(32)   RM: [with nuclear power] we would be able to provide forty thousand new beds/ we would able to get a hundred thousand new day care centre vacancies we would be able to get thirty thousand new jobs in child care we can improve the schools/all this is something we will find it difficult to do during the 80's anyhow/but it will be still more difficult with the rapid winding-up and the costs you impose on the citizens with your policy

LD: **yes I really protest** – the four hundred thousand billion that you men tioned are a sheer fabrication as well as the proportions of the crisis which you say will come about if we get rid of nuclear power

The relative clause in 'the costs you impose on the citizens with your policy' con- veys the presupposition that 'the line 3 policy' of winding up nuclear plants will impose costs making reforms possible. This presupposition is challenged by LD (the line 3 adherent) who claims that the costs are imagined.

The occurrence of challenges in this genre can be explained from the nature of the event itself. The rules of interaction in a media political debate are completely different from those in ordinary conversation with regard to norms of politeness and what is considered to be face-threatening (see Simon-Vandenbergen 1992; Simon-Vandenbergen and Aijmer 2005). These differences follow from more general differences on a number of parameters. Using Hymes's framework for the analysis of communicative events (1968) we can establish major differences along all parameters of the framework: setting and scene, participants, ends, acts, key, instrument, norms and genre. For instance, while conversations in daily life are geared towards creating and preserving solidarity and goodwill (Brown & Levin- son 1987), media debates are aimed at winning votes. The interaction is hence highly competitive and polemical. Further, participants in media debates are not

speaking in their own name but as representatives of groups and exclusively acting as 'we' (though ad hominem arguments may for instance change the footing:
the Flemish data contain a clear example of this (example (28) above), when one
politician says to his opponent in the debate "You are extremely excited today, I
think"). This means that in Goffman's terms (1981:147) the speaker as 'principal'
is communicating as a member of a political party and /or in a particular role (for
instance as a government minister). One of the consequences of this is that the
modesty maxim (Leech 1983) does not apply (Simon-Vandenbergen and Aijmer
2005). Another consequence is that attacks on the group are not felt as personal
attacks. Further, the norms of interaction with regard to turn-taking, interruption and overlap are regulated by the interviewer/moderator but participants in
their aim to persuade and score will frequently break them (cf. high frequency of
overlapping speech). All such differences create a genre in which presuppositional
manipulation is the rule, expected and recognised as such by the opponent. In
contrast with conversational partners in daily life, political opponents do go 'presupposition-hunting' as part of the game.

Another question is to whether *of course* and its equivalents in the Dutch
and Swedish data trigger any challenging. This would involve the denial by the
hearer that the information is to be taken for granted, an explicit rejection of the
'obvious' nature of the statement. As pointed out above, the markers of 'to-be-
taken-for-granted' are used in different contexts and with different functions. In
most of these functions they are left unchallenged simply because the proposition
is indeed not contested. These are cases where *of course* expresses agreement with
the interactant or where it signals concession. In the example below, from the
Flemish data, the interviewee uses *of course* ('natuurlijk') to convey agreement
with the interviewer:

(33) I: Wouldn't it have been better if Mr Van Rossem had been heard in the
           commission of inquiry? He could have said it then, I don't know
           why...
      RD: [overlap] Yes, as far as I'm concerned...
      I: [overlap] ... why
      RD: [overlap] well...
      I: [overlap]... he wasn't heard.
      RD: Yes, as far as I am concerned I wasn't in charge of the workings of the
           commission so that...
      I: [overlap] Would you ...
      RD: [overlap]... is his own affair.
      I: ... have found it a good thing if he had been heard?
      RD: I certainly wouldn't have had a problem with that.
      I: It's too late now.

RD: Yes, **of course** it's too late now. The commission of inquiry has finished its work but apparently Mr Van Rossem has still found other channels to vent his opinion.

The interesting cases are those where *of course* functions to convey concurrence on contentious issues. In such cases the speaker holding the alternative viewpoint will indeed deny the proposition, as in the example below. The speakers are Filip Dewinter (Flemish Bloc) and Robert Voorhamme (Socialist party, which is in the government coalition referred to as 'purple-green'). The topic is immigrant policy:

(34)   DW: Indeed, what Fortuyn said: full is full. And I don't think that we need still more new foreigners. No. We need to face the foreigners with the choice: adapt or return. In other words, a policy of integration for those who are here already. May I point out to you that for purple-green this is **of course** a bit of an alibi decree, isn't it? They have allowed 230 thousand foreigners to ...

      RV: [overlap] **Not true**

In the Dutch data 5 out of the 24 occurrences of *natuurlijk* get challenged. These are all cases where the proposition qualified by *natuurlijk* contains contextually highly polemical material.

In the English data, speakers also demonstrate a willingness to resist the rhetorical effects associated with *of course* and hence to challenge attempts by other speakers to construe particular propositions as entirely unproblematic and universally agreed upon. An example of such manoeuvring is provided in the following extract where the speakers, Phillips (P) and Oaten (O) are discussing a decision by the UN to end sanctions against Libya for the Lockerbie bombing, provided that compensation is paid to the victims' families.

(35)   P: Now to get to the actual question – should Libya, for example, be exempted by paying money? Personally I think no, I think this is blood money and ... I think it's all part of the way the West has over many decades now appeased terror, it's appeased terror by saying to the people who are committing terrorism – because you're committing terrorism we're now going to actually look at the root causes of this, we're going to have you to the UN, we're going to treat you as dignitaries, we're going to pay court to your cause. And that actually has incited more terror. And if one can say to people who have committed murder or have murder committed on their behalf – well all you have to do is pay a bit of money and then we can admit you to the family of nations, I think that is wrong, I think we would not do it, for example, if somebody committed murder in our civil society – you wouldn't say pay

money to the family and then we will admit you to the fact – to civilised society, we will expunge it from the record, **of course** we wouldn't. ...

O: ...if this situation that has emerged has meant that we now have Libya as part of the civilised world then this is a good thing. If this paying of the compensation is Libya's way of acknowledging that what happened was wrong this is a good thing. If it's a way of actually moving Libya forward in a positive way we have to accept this has to be on the whole a better thing than having Libya outside of the family of those civilised nations.

Here the first speaker employs *of course* to construe as 'taken-for-granted' that no-one in 'civilised society' would accept excusing murderers of their crime upon payment of money to the victim's family. The second speaker goes directly against this purportedly agreed-upon proposition as he develops his argument in support of excusing Libya.

Propositions with Swedish *ju* were not challenged to the same extent, probably because of the non-oppositional nature of this modal particle. On the other hand, *ju* itself was typically used to meet a challenge by explaining something as self-evident:

(36) PU: at last Lennart Daleus you still owe me the answer to the question/what governmental report was it that talked about the burning sun as an illustration of what you mean by nuclear power

        LD: **you know that poetry of course uses a different language** than we do in technical language for in the presentations we have made from the referendum we have prepared from the governmental reports which are the basis for the referendum

6. Discussion of the results and conclusions

In this article we have shown that 'taken-for-grantedness' is frequently manipulated in media political discourse. In doing this we have adduced further evidence of its importance as a rhetorical strategy. The advantages of the strategy mentioned in the literature are its construal of solidarity with like-minded viewers and the difficulty of challenging by those who hold alternative views. However, it has been shown that this strategy is recognised by the opponent for what it is, i.e. as a rhetorical ploy, and hence that the announcements of self-evidence and the presuppositions do get challenged. The question we can ask then is why speakers go on using the tactic anyway. One reason is of course that the first advantage still holds, viz. that the solidarity with the like-minded is confirmed and strengthened.

It is the like-minded in the first place who are addressed as the electors. Further, there is always the possibility that the yet-to-be persuaded will not recognise the tactic of taking-for-granted tactic as such and accept the implication of general knowledge. Most importantly however, the tactic has value as a rhetorical device which creates a forceful utterance and as such contributes to the image which politicians wish to project for themselves, i.e. that of someone 'in the know' (cf. Simon-Vandenbergen 1996). As such, the strategy becomes a way of making strong value judgements, likely to be challenged but nevertheless giving the speaker a temporary advantage in the battle for scoring with the audience. We may therefore conclude that such tactics are part of the professional discourse, and hence that interpersonal meanings are as much part of the genre as ideational ones.

Secondly, we have suggested that the engagement framework as developed by White (2003) needs to diversify its monoglossic option to more clearly allow for differences in rhetorical effect between presupposing and non-presupposing bare assertions. Our discussion has demonstrated the importance of noting the difference between bare assertions in which some point of contention is presented as new information (the non-presupposing option) and those in which it is presented as background, common knowledge (the presupposing option). As such presupposition has tremendous manipulative potential. White (2006) does introduce the notion "explicit attitudinal assessments" and places these in the framework as "unarguable and monoglossic". Our findings are in agreement with this, but we would argue that the pragmatic context may overrule the default effect of unarguability. The nature of media political debate reshapes presuppositional utterances into strong evaluative statements which cry out for challenging. As such presuppositions are two-faced in this genre. On the one hand, they present as presupposed judgements which the speakers know are not shared by their interlocutors and which they know will get challenged. The rhetorical effect is, however, in the saying itself. On the other hand, the presuppositions will work in the 'normal' way with at least part of the television audience, i.e they will simply be accepted.

Thirdly, we found that similar tactics were used in the British, Flemish and Swedish data. This suggests that the rules of interaction are largely similar in the genre in these cultural contexts. The Swedish data differed from the British and Flemish ones in that the debate was of a more formal and more strictly regulated type, and the rhetorical strategies differed accordingly. The similarities can partly be explained from similar views on linguistic ideologies and on how political debate works, what politicians are supposed to do and how the media handle political discussion. However, this aspect is in need of further study on the basis of more and culturally more varied data.

References

Bertuccelli Papi, M. 1997. "Implicitness". In *Handbook of Pragmatics*, J. Verschueren, J.-O. Öst-man, J. Blommaert and C. Bulcaen (eds), 1–29. Amsterdam: John Benjamins.

Blommaert, J. and Bulcaen, C. (eds). 1997. *Political Linguistics*. Belgian Journal of Linguistics 11. Amsterdam: John Benjamins.

Brown, P. and Levinson, S. 1987. *Politeness: Some Universals in Language Use*. Cambridge, Cambridge University Press.

Caffi, C. 1998. "Presupposition, pragmatic". In *Concise Encyclopedia of Pragmatics*, J. Mey (ed.), 751–758. Amsterdam: Elsevier.

Clayman, S. and Heritage, J. 2002. *The News Interview: Journalists and Public Figures on the Air*. Cambridge: Cambridge University Press.

Fairclough, N. 1995. *Media Discourse*. London: Arnold.

Fairclough, N. 2001. *Language and Power*. Second edition. Oxford: Blackwell.

Goffman, E. 1981. *Forms of Talk*. Oxford: Blackwell.

Greatbatch, D. 1992. "On the management of disagreement between news interviewees". In *Talk at Work; Interaction in Institutional Settings*, P. Drew and J. Hertiage (eds), 268–301. Cambridge: Cambridge University Press.

Grice, H. P. 1975. "Logic and conversation". In *Syntax and Semantics 3: Speech Acts*, Cole, P. and J. Morgan (eds), 41–58. New York: Academic Press.

Harris, S. 1991. "Evasive action: How politicians respond to questions in political interviews". In *Broadcast Talk*, P. Scannell (ed.), 76–99. London: Sage.

Hirsch, R. 1989. *Argumentation, Information and Interaction. Studies in Face-to-Face Interactive Argumentation under Different Turn-Taking Conditions*. Department of Linguistics, Göteborg University.

Holmes, J. 1988. "*Of course*: A pragmatic particle in New Zealand women's and men's speech". *Australian Journal of Linguistics* 2: 49–74.

Hymes, D. 1968. "The ethnography of speaking". In *Readings in the Sociology of Language*, J. Fishman (ed.), 99–138. The Hague: Mouton.

Kempson, R. M. 1975. *Presupposition and the Delimitation of Semantics*. Cambridge: Cambridge University Press.

Lambrecht, K. 1994. *Information Structure and Sentence Form*. Cambridge: Cambridge University press.

Lauerbach, G. 2004. "Political interviews as hybrid genre". *Text* 24 (3): 353–397.

Leech, G. N. 1983. *Principles of Pragmatics*. London: Longman.

Lewis, D. 2004. "Mapping adversative coherence relations in English and French". *Languages in Contrast* 5(1): 35–48.

Martin, J. R. 1997. "Analysing genre: Functional parameters". In *Genre and Institutions: Social Processes in the Workplace and School*, F. Christie and J. R. Martin (eds), 3–39. London: Cassell.

Martin, J. R. 2000. "Beyond exchange: APPRAISAL systems in English". In *Evaluation in Text: Authorial Stance and the Construction of Discourse*, S. Hunston and G. Thompson (eds), 142–175. Oxford: Oxford University Press.

Martin, J. R. and P. R. R. White 2005. *The Language of Evaluation: Appraisal in English*, Palgrave: London & New York.

Mey, J. 1998. *Pragmatics: An Introduction*. 2nd edition. Oxford: Blackwell.

Paulussen, H. 1999. *A Corpus-Based Contrastive Analysis of English 'on/up', Dutch 'op' and French 'sur' within a cognitive framework.* Unpublished PhD thesis. University of Ghent.

Pomerantz, A. 1984. "Agreeing and disagreeing with assessments: some features of preferred/dispreferred turn shapes". In *Structures of Social Action*, J. Atkinson and J. M. Heritage (eds), 57–101. Cambridge: Cambridge University Press.

Sbisà, M. 1999. "Ideology and the persuasive use of presupposition". In *Language and Ideology: Selected Papers from the 6th International Pragmatics Conference*, J. Verschueren (ed.), 492–509. Antwerp: International Pragmatics Association.

Simon-Vandenbergen, A. M. 1992. "The interactional utility of *of course* in spoken discourse". *Occasional Papers in Systemic Linguistics* 6: 213–226.

Simon-Vandenbergen, A. M. 1996. "Image-building through modality: The case of political interviews". *Discourse and Society* 7(3): 389–415.

Simon-Vandenbergen, A. M. 1997. "Modal (un)certainty in political discourse: A functional account". *Language Sciences* 19 (4): 341–56.

Simon-Vandenbergen, A. M. and Aijmer, K. 2003-4. "The expectation marker *of course* in a cross-linguistic perspective". *Languages in Contrast* 4 (1): 13–43.

Simon-Vandenbergen, A. M. and Aijmer, K. 2005. "The discourse marker *of course* in British political interviews and its Flemish and Swedish counterparts: A comparison of persuasive tactics". In *Beiträge zur Dialogforschung. Selected Papers from the 9th IADA Conference Salzburg 2003.* Part 2: Media: A. Betten and M. Dannerer (eds), 105–112. Tübingen: Niemeyer.

Stubbs, M. 1986. "A matter of prolonged fieldwork: Notes towards a modal grammar of English". *Applied Linguistics* 7(1): 1–25.

van Dijk, T. A. 1998a. *Ideology: A Multidisciplinary Approach.* London: Sage.

van Dijk, T. A. 1998b. "Opinions and ideologies in the press". In *Approaches to Media Discourse*, A. Bell and P. Garrett (eds), 21–63. Oxford: Blackwell.

Verschueren, J. 1999. *Understanding Pragmatics.* London: Sage.

White, P. R. R. 1998, *Telling Media Tales: The News Story as Rhetoric.* Ph.D dissertation, Sydney: University of Sydney.

White, P. R. R. 2000. "Dialogue and inter-subjectivity: Reinterpreting the semantics of modality and hedging". In *Working With Dialogue*, M. Coulthard, J. Cotterill, and F. Rock (eds), 67–80. Tübingen: Max Niemeyer Verlag.

White, P. R. R. 2002. "Appraisal – the language of evaluation and stance". In *Handbook of Pragmatics*, J. Verschueren, J.-O. Östman, J. Blommaert, J. and C. Bulcaen (eds), 1–27. Amsterdam: John Benjamins.

White, P. R. R. 2003. "Beyond modality and hedging: A dialogic view of the language of inter-subjective stance". *Text* 23 (2): 259–284.

White, P. R. R. 2006. "Evaluative semantics and ideological positioning in journalistic discourse – a new framework for analysis". In *Mediating Ideology in Text and Image: Ten Critical Studies*, Lassen, I. (ed.), 37–68. Amsterdam: John Benjamins.

Wodak, R., de Cillia, R., Reisigl, M., Liebhart, K., Hofstätter, K. and Kargl, M. (eds). 2000. *The Discursive Construction of National Identity.* Edinburgh: Edinburgh University Press.

Appendix: Examples in the original languages Flemish and Swedish

(8) I: Ja, mijnheer Daems, wat zegt uh mijnheer Van Rossem daar allemaal? Hij zegt de raad van bestuur was perfect op de hoogte van de plannen van de Zwitsers en blijkbaar wist ook VLD-voorzitter Karel De Gucht daarvan. Um... hebt u weet van dat scenario?

RD: Helemaal niet. Ik denk dat uh de onderzoekscommissie een aantal zaken heeft blootgelegd die belangrijk zijn. Ik denk dat we spijtig genoeg moeten vaststellen dat we wel in een partijpolitiek vaarwater zijn terechtgekomen waar op een bepaald ogenblik men zelfs uh zich heeft verlaagd tot persoonlijke aanvallen maar als je daar nu even afstand van neemt... dan denk je da je toch in dat rapport een aantal aspecten terugvindt...

I: Ja.

RD: ...hoofdzakelijk te weten ja financieel was het een bedrijf waar een aantal zeer slechte beslissingen vooral onder impuls van de Zwitsers zijn genomen en wat mij vooral is opgevallen is dat nu enkele dagen geleden vanuit het Ernst & Young-rapport uit Zwitserland is gebleken dat... ja eigenlijk met voorbedachten rade bedrog is gepleegd vanuit Zwitserland.

I: Ja, en volgens mijnheer Van Rossem...

RD: [overlap] Wat natuurlijk niet wegneemt...

I: [overlap] ...volgens mijnheer van Rossem wist wist de raad van bestuur dat, wisten sommige VLD'ers dat en is er niks tegen gedaan, zegt die.

RD: [overlap] Ja, Karel De Gucht is natuurlijk nog niet uh partijvoorzitter geworden in 1997 want daar gaat het dan over die die aankoop van die airbussen...

I: Hmm.

RD: Dus ik denk dat de dingen door mekaar worden gehaald en dat de heer Van Rossem...

I: [overlap] Vergist hij zich dan en kletst hij uit zijn nek, mijnheer Van Rossem?

RD: [overlap] Wel ik denk dat de heer Van Rossem natuurlijk nu hij politicus wil worden misschien daar toch ook wel een beetje door beïnvloed wordt maar de essentie van het verhaal, mijnheer Belet, is dat je de conclusies van dat rapport moet bekijken want wat voor mij belangrijk is, is dat we voor een stuk hebben blootgelegd waar dat de oorzaken liggen van een zo groot bedrijf dat stuk gaat: slecht management, verkeerde financiële beslissingen.

(9) VR: Ja, natuurlijk is de dreiging van oorlog iets iets verschrikkelijk en we moeten alles doen om dat af te wenden. Dat spreekt vanzelf. Dat vraagt de

bevolking. Dat vragen wij natuurlijk ook. Uh maar we moeten dan ook een consistente politiek hebben vind ik. Uh mijnheer Michel is einde januari in New York geweest. Hij is daar onder de indruk gekomen van wat hij daar gehoord heeft. Hij heeft begrip gevraagd voor het Amerikaanse standpunt. Men heeft zelfs van een bocht gesproken. Hij heeft dat . hij heeft dat gelogenstraft. Uh hij komt terug in Europa en dan nemen wij een standpunt in dat eigenlijk ja toch helemaal haaks staat op de indruk die hij in New York heeft gegeven.

(10)   (Rune Molin: line 2 postponing nuclear power)
// varför får vi så olika motstridiga besked // det kan ju inte vara för mycket begärt att väljarna ska få besked om / hur det ska gå med elförsörjningen hur ni ska ransonera hur ni ska höja priserna och så vidare / för det är ju det som kommer att bli följden när man ska dra ner / elförsörjningen under åttiotalet // < daleus > han ska ju själv lämna den här scenen efter den tjugotredje mars har jag läst i tidningarna // men skulle du inte dessförinnan kunna tala om på / vem vem som ska nu genomföra erat politiska budskap

(11)   VR: Het centrale thema: veiligheid. En men geeft massa's geld uit om minder mensen te hebben die voor veiligheid zorgen. Da's een onbegrijpelijk verhaal.

(14)   PU: om < ulla lindström > inte litar på linjerna ett och två så kan väl < ulla lindström > ändå lita på uländerna själva när dom skakar på huvudet och undrar hur vi i sverige kan överväga att avveckla kärnkraften / när detta innebär att trycket på knappa oljeresurser / som skulle kunna komma uländerna till del blir ändå hårdare

(15)   PU: / valet gäller om vi ovanpå den globala energikris vi redan i så hög utsträckning drabbats av / ska lägga ytterligare bördor som kan bli oss övermäktiga /

(16)   DH: [overlap]: Wel dat noem ik de het het debat verder zetten na de verkiezingen uh dus ik ik vond deze hype uh voor niets nodig uh totaal artificieel uh en sommige mensen zagen blijkbaar niet in dat ze daarmee de de de de schwung van de vernieuwing...
        I: [overlap]: Hmm.
        DH: ...en en en de campagne die rond de vernieuwing moet draaien, dat ze dit eigenlijk aan het ondermijnen waren.

(17)   DH: Maar als ik dan zie dat die stelling uh kwade . kwaad berokkent aan mijn partij, dat door de manier waarop dat men daarmee omgaat in mijn partij men zichzelf beschadigt bah dan moet ik daar paal en perk aan zetten.

(18)   (Lennart Dahleus, line 3)

ja <per unkel> vet ju att det finns fler möjligheter till stora olyckor än den som vi har diskuterat den här med / ångexplosioner och att kärnkraften / är en farlig energikälla och att den innehåller oerhörda risker allting från / uranbrytningen till avfallshanteringen det är vi nog överens om och att det är risker / som inte har någon motsvarighet i andra energikällor /

(19)   RD: Dit neemt niet weg dat natuurlijk de regering een investeringsplan op lange termijn heeft goedgekeurd, een kader waarbinnen de NMBS moet proberen gezond te worden, en één ding mag men zeker niet vergeten en dat is toch wel een heel belangrijk gegeven...

I: [overlap] Ja.

RD: ...binnen enkele maanden gaat die liberalisering van dat goederenvervoer in dus...

I: [overlap] Precies. Hmm.

RD: ...we moeten echt dringend hier gaan een aantal maatregelen die in...

I: [overlap] Ja.

RD: ...zovele jaren niet gebeurd zijn nemen want anders dan gaat de concurrentie wel hard toeslaan.

I: [overlap] Ja. Mijnheer van Rompuy. Het is de vorige regering weer geweest.

VR: Ja ja. 't Is uh we worden dat gewoon.

(20)   Rune Molin (line 2)

// det säger sig självt att använder vi våra kärnkraftverk ökar möjligheterna väsentligt att pressa ett oljeberoende som håller på att knäcka hela det svenska samhället /

(21)   PU: i den här kärnkraftsdebatten / har det funnits ett drag som / jag själv har uppskattat mycket // och det är ett drag hos många av dom som ändå stöder linje tre // som innebär ett krav på ett mjukare samhälle med utrymme för mera mänsklighet omtanke och närhet / om det var det här som folkomröstningen egentligen handlade om / tror jag ingen skulle behöva tveka om utgången

(22)   PU: ja < lennart daleus > var förvånad över att jag / talade om oljan i en folkomröstningskampanj om kärnkraften / skälet är ju / att vi har bestämt oss för att använda våra kärnkraftverk för att därigenom ge oss möjlighet att pressa ett oljeberoende som är på väg att gå oss alldeles ur händerna

(23) VR: Voelen ze zich veiliger?

RD: Ja maar natuurlijk als je in de politiek, collega Van Rompuy, belangrijke mensen zoals mijnheer Dehaene een belangrijk man is, krijgt, die de indruk willen wekken bij de bevolking dat het onveiliger wordt...

VR: [overlap] Oh, het is mijnheer Dehaene?

RD: ...dan vind ik het erg. Waar het om g...

VR: [overlap] Olala, mijnheer Dehaene die zorgt voor de onveiligheid.

RD: Waar het om gaat is de realiteit...

VR: [overlap] Dat is dat is...

RD: ...en ik geef u een ander voorbeeld.

VR: [overlap] ...zeer nieuw voor ons, dat is zeer nieuw.

I: [overlap] Ja, u moet afronden, mijnheer Daems.

VR: [overlap] dat is zeer nieuw.

(24) PU: // men det är klart att / om man nu bestämmer sej för att riva kraftverk / som motsvarar all den energi vi får från vattenkraften / så kan inte detta gå alldeles spårlöst förbi / och linje tre bekräftar väl också detta genom att själva hävda att det finns inget så kärnkraftsberoende land som < sverige >

(25) RV: [overlap] Het probleem van mijnheer Dewinter is dat hij alleen...

DW: [overlap] Het hangt eraan...

I: [overlap] Ja.

DW: ...vast.

RV: ...kijkt naar het verleden. En wij willen iets doen aan...

I: [overlap] OK

RV: ...de toekomst en daar weigert mijnheer Dewinter over te discussiëren.

I: Nee, hij heeft een duidelijke stelling. Zijn toekomst is: vol is vol.

DW: [overlap] immigratiestop.

(26) DW: [overlap] Wat u doet...

AD: [overlap] ...allez da kan niet. Da kan rechtelijk niet...

DW: [overlap] ...door de integratie

VR: [overlap] Mijnheer Dewinter?

DW: [overlap] ...door de integratie af te remmen...

AD: [overlap] ... de rechten van de mens...

DW: [overlap] is...

AD: [overlap] ...zeggen zeer duidelijk...

DW: [overlap]...de achterstand...

I: [overlap] Dit is onverstaanbaar. Laten we die...

DW: [overlap]...de achterstand importeren. En dat is een foute stelling.

(27)   PU: det är egentligen så självklart att till och med linje tre borde kunna hålla
med om det // vi kan använda kärnkraften i förvissningen om att den dess
risker till trots / är säkrare än varje annat alternativ som i dag står till vårt
förfogande / och det är ju detta som är det viktiga /

(28)   I: [overlap] Ja, mijnheer Daems, wel vervelend voor de VLD hé. Hij staat
niet eens op de lijst en toch staat hij centraal in de schijnwerpers.

RD: Wel ik wil het eerst eens hebben over die roep naar Dehaene. Ik heb
begrepen dat mevrouw Schauwvliege een website heeft geopend en
ze wilde honderdduizend handtekeningen, ze is al aan vijfduizend. Da's
ne geweldige roep als ge 't mij vraagt.

I: Ja, in één week tijd hé.

RD: [overlap] Maar los daarvan…

I: [overlap] Da's in één week tijd hé.

VR: [overlap] Als ge vijfduizend als ge vijfduizend brieven krijgt…

RD: [overlap] … maar los daarvan…

VR: [overlap] ik zou daar…ik denk dat ge…

RD: [overlap] Oh maar…

VR: [overlap] … content zoudt zijn hé…

RD: [overlap] Maar collega van Rompuy…

VR: [overlap] Ik denk dat ge content zoudt zijn.

RD: [overlap] Van internet…

VR: [overlap] 'k denk dat ge er de laatste tijd geen vijfhonderd gehad hebt
hé…

RD: [overlap] … van internet ken ik iets…

VR: [overlap] Ik denk dat ge er geen vijfduizend gehad hebt.

RD: [overlap] Ge zijt enorm opgejaagd vind ik vandaag.

(30)   och när det gäller olja så säger Per Unckel att / det är alldeles klart att det går
att ersätta oljeberoendet med kärnkraft men för att använda dina egna ord i
ett tidigare sammanhang / det är ju inte sant du vet ju att för att göra oss av
med hela oljeberoendet skulle det gå åt en femtio sextio reaktorer i det här
landet /

(32)   RM: vi skulle kunna skaffa hundratusen nya daghemsplatser vi skulle kunna
skaffa trettiotusen nya jobb i barntillsynen vi skulle kunna göra en
bättre skola // alltihop det här / är saker och ting som vi / får svårt att
göra under åttiotalet under alla förhållanden men det blir ännu svårare
med den snabbavveckling och dom kostnader som ni lägger på landets
medborgare med er politik

UL: ja det protesterar jag verkligen mot både de fyrahundratusen mil
jarderna som du här drog fram är gripna ur luften / liksom hela hela

den dimension du ger / den kris / som du påstår ska uppkomma / om vi avvecklar kärnkraften /

(33) I: Was het toch niet beter dat mijnheer Van Rossem gehoord was in de onderzoekscommissie? Dan had hij daar kunnen zeggen. Ik weet niet waarom heeft…

RD: [overlap] Ja, wat mij betreft…

I: [overlap] …waarom

RD: [overlap] wel…

I: …hij niet gehoord is.

RD: Ja, wat mij betreft ik heb niet de werking van de onderzoekscommissie gedaan, dus dat…

I: [overlap] Zou u het…

RD: [overlap] …is een zaak van hemzelf.

I: …een goede zaak gevonden hebben als hij gehoord zou zijn?

RD: Ik had daar absoluut geen enkel probleem mee gehad hoor.

I: Dat is nu te laat.

RD: Ja dat is natuurlijk te laat. De onderzoekscommissie is voorbij maar de heer Van Rossem heeft blijkbaar nog andere kanalen om zijn mening te ventileren.

(34) DW: Inderdaad, wat Fortuyn zei: vol is vol. En ik denk niet dat wij nood hebben aan nogmaals meer nieuwe vreemdelingen. Neen. Wij moeten de bestaande vreemdelingen voor de keuze plaatsen: aanpassen of terugkeren. Dus een inburgeringsbeleid voor degenen die er al zijn. Mag ik er toch op wijzen dat dit voor paarsgroen natuurlijk een beetje een alibidecreet is hé. Men heeft tweehonderd en dertigduizend vreemdelingen…

RV: [overlap] Niet juist.

(36) PU: till slut Lennart Dahleus du är mej fortfarande svaret skyldig på frågan / vilken statlig utredning var det / som hade talat om den brännande solen / så som en illustration till vad kärnkraft egentligen är

LD: du vet att poesin använder ju faktiskt ett annat språk än / vad vi gör i / fackprosa för dom framställningar vi har gjort från folkkampanjen / så har vi utgått ifrån dom statliga utredningar som ligger till underlag för den här folkomröstningen /

Metaphors in election night television coverage in Britain, the United States and Germany*

Rut Scheithauer

Johann Wolfgang Goethe-Universität, Germany

Based on Lakoff and Johnson's (1980) cognitive constructivist theory of metaphor, this paper presents a quantitative and qualitative analysis of the metaphors used by nine television stations covering the 1997 British general election, the 1998 German parliamentary election and the 2000 US presidential election. The analysis shows great similarities across cultures in terms of the occurring conceptual metaphors and their frequency. All channels use a lot of metaphors that intensify the controversial nature of elections (from the domains WAR, SPORT, and CONTEST), but there is also a considerable number of non-sensational metaphors (JOURNEY, NATURE). Clear differences exist between national channels and international channels. Differences between public-service stations and commercial channels are minor. The study also suggests that some metaphors are gender-biased.

1. Introduction

The purpose of this paper is to study the cross-cultural differences in the metaphorisation of elections in television discourse. Metaphors are a popular means of simplifying complex concepts. They enable us to make sense of abstract concepts by drawing parallels to concepts that are more easily accessible to us: "We

---

* This paper is part of the research project "Television Discourse", supported by the German Research Foundation (DFG) and directed by Gerda Lauerbach. The goal of the project is a comparative discourse analysis of election night (and, in the case of the US presidential election of 2000, post-election night) television coverage in the United States, Great Britain and Germany. For more information, see http://web.uni-frankfurt.de/zenaf/projekte/TVdiscourses/lauerbach.htm.
The author is indebted to Gerda Lauerbach, Anita Fetzer, Anne Barron, Annette Becker and Raimund Schieß for their encouragement and invaluable drafting suggestions.

typically conceptualise the nonphysical in terms of the physical" (Lakoff & Johnson 1980: 59). In our data, elections are for instance conceptualised as JOURNEY (e.g. "Were you happy with the *way* the campaign *went* all the *way* through?"), as WAR (e.g. "This would be a complete *massacre* if these polls are correct."), or as SPORT (e.g. "No rest for the Vice President this afternoon despite a 30-hour campaign *marathon*."). Yet beyond achieving easy comprehension, the use of metaphors also suggests a certain view of elections in particular and of politics in general which audiences are invited to share. Are there intercultural differences in the channels' use of metaphors? Do commercial channels differ from public ones? Do national channels differ from international ones? Can metaphors from certain source domains said to be gender-biased, as suggested by Howe (1988)? These are some of the questions this paper addresses.

Analysing the current British media culture, Cohen (1998: 18) found that events are often presented as exciting, controversial and sentimental. Is this trend evident in the present American and German media culture as well? Critical discourse analysts like Norman Fairclough have long pointed out that media texts of the informative genres increasingly contain elements of entertainment, incorporating features of conversation such as personalisation, dramatisation, emotionalisation (cf. Fairclough 1995; also see Lauerbach 2004). Cohen's excitement and controversy overlaps with Fairclough's dramatisation, Cohen's sentimentality with Fairclough's personalisation and emotionalisation. Do metaphors personalise, dramatise and emotionalise television broadcasts of elections? Are there cross-cultural differences in the ways this is done?

The remainder of the paper is organised as follows: Section 2 describes Lakoff and Johnson's cognitive constructivist model of metaphor and the functions of metaphor. It introduces the data and the context of the elections. Section 3 presents the findings of the qualitative analysis and compares how the various channels realise certain conceptual metaphors. It also provides a quantitative overview of the most frequent metaphor clusters. Section 4 discusses whether cross-cultural differences can be discerned in the use of metaphor, addresses the special nature of the international channels, and compares commercial channels to public-service ones. It also deals with the question of gender-bias.

2.   Theoretical framework

2.1 Cognitive metaphor theory

According to Eco (cf. 1984: 87), the term 'metaphor' defies precise definition. The difficulty lies in distinguishing metaphors on the one hand from literal language and on the other hand from other tropes, e.g. from similes. Beardsley (1967) and Searle (1979) identify metaphors as those utterances that would clearly be false if taken literally. Black (1979:35) points out that this test fails because "the negation of any metaphorical statement can itself be a metaphorical statement and hence possibly true if taken literally." Levinson (1983:271) suggests that if the context blocks the literal force of an utterance, this constitutes a trigger, not a proof, that the respective utterance might be a metaphor. For the purposes of the present analysis, metaphors are taken to be those cases of figurative language in which one concept is understood in terms of another and in which features are transferred from one domain to another. In the phrase "I've *invested* many months in this", 'time' is conceptualised through 'money'. The feature that is transferred is that of a resource that is perceived as valuable and limited.

There are two major approaches to metaphor: the constructivist and the positivist approach. Constructivists presume that the objective world is only accessible to us by applying our knowledge about the world and expressing it via language. They see metaphors as cognitive instruments that *create* reality. Non-constructivists assume that reality exists independently of human language and knowledge and that the world can be described perfectly well with literal language without the need for figurative speech (cf. Ortony 1979:1–2). Some scholars of the positivist approach hold that metaphors can easily be replaced by equivalent literal language. This is known as the *substitution view* of metaphor. A special case of this is the *comparison view* of metaphor going back to Aristotle (cf. Malmkjaer 2002:352). According to the comparison view, a metaphor is an implicit simile, i.e. an implicit comparison. It is argued that the metaphor "Richard is a lion" hardly differs from the simile "Richard is *like* a lion." Proponents of the comparison view of metaphor claim that a pre-existent[1] similarity between the two concepts that constitute the metaphor is the grounds for comparison. Constructivists, on the other hand, maintain that this similarity is decisively *established* by the creation or use of a metaphor, i.e. the perceived similarity between "man" and "wolf" can be minor before they are combined in the metaphor "MAN is a wolf". This post-construction similarity opens metaphors, especially creative ones, to polysemous interpretation (see Section 2.2).

The analysis of metaphors presented in this paper is based on Lakoff and Johnson's (1980) ground-breaking cognitive constructivist study *Metaphors we live by*. They challenge the traditional view of metaphor according to which metaphors are mere rhetorical flourish, "at best ornamental, and at worst, misleading" (Malmkjaer 2002:350). Lakoff and Johnson demonstrate that metaphor is not

---

1. 'Pre-existent' in the sense of prior to the construction or use of the metaphor.

only a characteristic of language, but above all of thought and action (cf. Lakoff & Johnson 1980: 4). As metaphors are not primarily a matter of verbal expression, they can also be realised in other modes, e.g. visually (cf. Forceville 1996). Some examples for visual metaphors are given in Section 3.

A metaphor consists of two subjects, the target domain and the source domain (Lakoff & Johnson 1980). In the metaphor "Man is a wolf", 'man' is the target domain and 'wolf' is the source domain. Through this metaphor, opinions shared by the members of our speech community about the nature of wolves determine our view of man. The metaphor thus *highlights* the features stereotypically perceived to be shared by both subjects and *hides* features of the target subject that the source subject does not have, or is not generally known to have.

Lakoff and Johnson distinguish between two levels of metaphor: metaphorical *concepts* that exist on the cognitive level, and metaphorical *statements*, i.e. linguistic surface realisations on the utterance level. Moreover, they differentiate between three main types of metaphors: (i) *orientational* metaphors with a spatial orientation, (ii) *ontological* metaphors in which abstract concepts such as events, activities, emotions or ideas are experienced in terms of concrete entities, substances, containers or persons, and (iii) *structural* or *conceptual* metaphors (cf. Lakoff & Johnson 1980: 14–32). "I'm feeling *up* today", a linguistic realisation of the concept HAPPY IS UP,[2] is an example for an orientational metaphor. "His ego is very *fragile*" (MIND AS A BRITTLE OBJECT) is an ontological metaphor. For the present study structural metaphors are the most important type of metaphor. They "use one highly structured and clearly delineated concept to structure another" less clearly delineated, more abstract concept (Lakoff & Johnson 1980: 61). When underlying metaphorical concepts materialise in many linguistic surface realisations pertaining to one semantic domain, we have a metaphorical *cluster*. For instance, "The exit polls can be two percent out *in either direction*", "Those results are about to *come* in" and "Were you happy with the *way* the campaign *went* all the *way* through?" are all realisations of the metaphorical concept ELECTION IS A JOURNEY. The terms 'metaphorical concept', 'conceptual metaphor' and 'structural metaphor' are used interchangeably throughout this paper.

2.2 Functions of metaphor

Contrary to the positivist belief (cf. 2.1), metaphors far exceed the ornamental function. They can be powerful rhetorical tools. It seems that it is often via anal-

---

2. Lakoff and Johnson (1980) initiated the convention to capitalise conceptual metaphors while individual realisations are written in normal upper and lower case.

ogy that we extend our understanding of the world. Just as stereotypes function by categorising people to reduce the unmanageable complexity of everyday life, metaphors are capable of boiling elusive matters down to a handy, expedient level. Analysing conversation, Levinson observed that speakers adhere to a *maxim of minimization*, i.e. they tend to "produce the minimal linguistic clues sufficient to achieve" their ends (Levinson 1987: 169; quoted in Wilson 1990: 124). Metaphors are linguistically very efficient: They communicate a lot with minimal linguistic effort, whereas attempts at literal paraphrases are often lengthy, clumsy and graceless.

The extensive use of metaphors in the present data indicates that metaphors are easily understood without the need to clarify meaning. This is indispensable because mass media communication is essentially one-way: no interactive negotiation and clarification of meaning is possible (cf. Wilson 1990: 125). However, as audiences are always heterogeneous, television channels have to allow for more than one understanding of their message in order to leave space for deviant, contrary interpretations. Fiske (1987: 40) proposes irony, jokes and contradictions as devices which open a text to polysemous readings (cf. Lauerbach 2004). As metaphors, especially innovative ones, may not trigger exactly the same connotations with everyone, it would seem that they are another device to allow for varying interpretations. The American channel NBC talks about New Hampshire having "changed its political *DNA*" from Republican to Democratic. Depending on a viewer's political leanings, this could either be interpreted positively as offering better evolutionary chances for survival or negatively as serious genetic malfunctioning. New, original metaphors might appeal to the recipient, but relax control over interpretation. Conventional metaphors, on the other hand, monotonous and uninspiring as they might be, are unambiguous, i.e. they prevent polysemous reading. It seems that the media have two ways of dealing with this dilemma: either (i) choosing conventional metaphors from different semantic domains to appeal to various sections of the audience, or (ii) striving for a balance between conventional and creative metaphors. An example of (i) is the way in which the American channel CNN depicts 'organised labour'. It is referred to firstly as the Democrats' "biggest *weapon*", secondly as a flexing "*muscle*" and thirdly as the "key *engine*" of Democratic turnout. In contrast to the *weapon* and *muscle* metaphors, the *engine* metaphor gives greatest credit to the unions as organisations in their own right. The *muscle* metaphor and especially the *weapon* metaphor might appeal more to conservative viewers, the *engine* metaphor more to left-of-centre viewers.

As visualised in Figure 1, metaphors have a wider range of meanings on the 'live', creative side of the continuum, i.e. polysemous readings are possible. The number of interpretations is restricted firstly by the local frame of the individual text and secondly by the global discourse environment, i.e. by the typical rhetoric

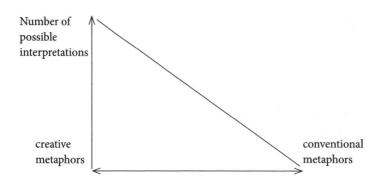

Figure 1. Metaphors and polysemy

employed by the speaker or institution in question. Conventional metaphors are located on the right side of the graph. They have a narrower range of meanings. The interpretation at the 'dead' end of the continuum is so habituated that such metaphors are perceived as 'literal'. Idioms are classical cases of 'dead' metaphors that allow for only one interpretation. Contrary to Wilson, Lakoff and Johnson (1980: 55) hold that metaphors are no less alive if they are conventional, i.e. they can influence our perception of the target domain, in our case elections, just as or even more powerfully than creative metaphors.

2.3 Previous studies of metaphor in media discourse on politics

In the past two decades, several studies have investigated metaphors in the domain of politics. Examining the metaphors used in the 1987 British general election, Montgomery et al. (1989) noted that ELECTION is mostly presented as WAR. Besides WAR, Howe (1988) and Beard (2000) found POLITICS often depicted as SPORT. Wilson came to the conclusion that single, isolated instances of metaphor do not affect our perception of reality. However, frequent repetitions of metaphorical concepts within and across local discourse practices are "directive evidence" (cf. Wilson 1990: 130) to the recipient for adopting the view of politics which the media are presenting. It is the task of critical discourse analysis to uncover processes of suggesting preferred interpretations, as attempted in the present paper.

2.4 Data

For the present study, the opening sequences of the coverage by BBC, ITV and CNN International of the 1997 British general election, the coverage by ARD, RTL, BBC World and CNN International of the 1998 German parliamentary election, and the coverage by NBC and CNN of the 2000 US presidential election were analysed. The opening sequences are approx. 20 minutes long. BBC1 and ITV are the leading British television stations. In the US, CNN was at the time the leading 24-hour news channel, and NBC a leading mixed channel. In Germany, RTL has been the market leader since 1993. ARD is the larger of the two German public channels (cf. Schulz 2004: 176–178). BBC World and CNN International are international 24-hour news channels. ARD and BBC are public-service stations, whereas the others are commercial.

All three elections led to a change in government: In the 1997 general election in Britain, 'New' Labour under Tony Blair ended eighteen years of Tory rule under Margaret Thatcher and John Major. Labour's victory had been predicted by the opinion polls but its extent came as a surprise. Similarly, the victory of Gerhard Schröder and the Social Democrats in the 1998 parliamentary elections in Germany put an end to the conservative Kohl era and shifted the majority in parliament to the 'Neue Mitte' (comparable to Blair's 'third way'). In the 2000 US presidential election campaign, then Vice President Al Gore, the Democratic candidate, was struggling not only against his Republican competitor George W. Bush, but also with the legacy of then President Bill Clinton who had been – unsuccessfully – impeached, charged with perjury and obstruction of justice in investigations of his relationship with White House intern Monica Lewinsky.

The analysis focuses on discursive contributions under the immediate control of the channel and its representatives, i.e. anchors, studio personnel and external reporters, but also takes into account contributions from the channels' interview partners.

3.   The most frequent metaphor clusters

A large proportion of all linguistic surface metaphors involve a rather small number of conceptual metaphors. This suggests that those metaphors are not arbitrary but systematic uses. The following metaphor clusters were the most frequent in the data: ELECTION IS A JOURNEY, ELECTION IS WAR, ELECTION IS CONTEST, ELECTION IS SPORT, ELECTION IS NATURE, ELECTION IS BUSINESS, ELECTION IS DRAMA, ELECTION IS LAW and ELECTION IS RELIGION as well as the meta-discursive COVERAGE IS JOURNEY, COVERAGE IS WAR, COVERAGE IS BUSINESS, COVERAGE IS DRAMA and COVERAGE IS SPORT. Metaphors from source domains that occurred only with very few isolated surface realisations were not considered in the analysis because they might arise from a speaker's idiosyncrasies whereas the large number of surface realisation from the above-mentioned source domains are assumed to be intentional and systematic uses.

The semantic categories are all conceived in a relatively wide sense. For example, the category BUSINESS includes economics, sales, trade and consumer terms; DRAMA embraces drama and other types of fiction; NATURE comprises matters of life and death, parts of the human body and natural phenomena; JOURNEY comprises various modes of transport and movement; and RELIGION comprises all matters metaphysical. If peaceful coexistence of political parties is doubted by the speakers, the underlying assumption seems to be that ELECTION (POLITICS) IS WAR.

Within each section (3.1–3.8), the findings are presented in chronological order, i.e. the 1997 British election first, then the 1998 German election, and finally the 2000 US election. Within each election, the national channels precede the international channels. The findings are visualised per metaphor cluster in Tables 1–12 for each individual channel. An overview of national, international and overall averages is presented in Table 13 in Section 3.9.

3.1   Election is a journey

ELECTION IS A JOURNEY is the most frequent conceptual metaphor across all analysed channels. Despite little pre-metaphorical similarity, it seems that ELECTION IS A JOURNEY (just as LIFE IS A JOURNEY) is so frequent because travelling, no matter how short the journey, is a universal experience that everyone can easily make sense of. 'Going' is so pervasive that (i) it has acquired an additional meaning, namely 'happening', as in "there was a lot of tactical voting *going* on", and (ii) it has even been grammaticalised in the *going to*-future. Its meaning has expanded from a movement in time *and* space to a development in time only. JOURNEY metaphors are very common and as such not restricted to political or media discourse. They do not seem to lend themselves as much to sensational reporting as WAR or DRAMA metaphors.

In the BBC's coverage of the British 1997 elections, "We *set out* to winning those ninety seats", stated in an interview by Deputy Labour Leader John Prescott, is one of the clearest cases of describing a political activity as a journey. The metaphor "the exit polls can be 2 percent out *in either direction*", voiced by election analyst Peter Snow, is another example. The verbal metaphor in Snow's question "How many seats will the parties get in that contest to *cross* Downing Street and *open the door to* Number Ten?" is visually reinforced by a simultaneous animation which takes the viewers into Number 10 and through the door to a virtual picture gallery of previous prime ministers.

Remarks such as "The exit poll is in line with what the national polls have been giving us right the *way* through the campaign" made by ITV's political editor Michael Brunson are both literal and metaphorical because a campaign actually involves physical touring of the candidates around their constituencies. However, whereas in many journeys travelling or arriving at the destination are ends in themselves, the ultimate aim of elections lies beyond the end of the campaign. For the government-to-be, another long journey starts only once they have won office. Other examples of highly conventional journey metaphors are ITV anchor Jonathan Dimbleby's comments "If this exit poll is correct, it really is the most astonishing *turn-around*", "We will *explore* all this on the assumption that the exit poll is right" and "The counting is about to get *underway*."

CNN International's anchor Richard Blystone announces that the first results of the British election will not be "*coming* in for another hour", thus personifying the results as if they were on a little journey of their own. Correspondent Christiane Amanpour states that the old ideological divides have "*gone*".

On public-service channel ARD regarding the 1998 German elections, Green politician Kerstin Müller states that her party wants "den Atom*ausstieg*" (to *get out of* nuclear energy) as if nuclear energy was a vehicle they wanted to get off before it crashed. Presenter Marion von Haaren asks SPD politician Christine Bergmann: "Mit wem werden Sie denn in Zukunft *zusammengehen*?" (With whom will you '*walk* together' [down the road of governing] in the future?) Phrases such as "Die CDU *kommt* auf 36%" (The CDU *arrives* at ...) and "in den Bundestag *kommen*" (*enter* parliament) are very typical of both German channels.

By saying that the Green Party is not a "*steuerungsfähige* Fraktion" (*steerable* group), RTL's political expert Johannes Groß implies that party members should be manageable like a vehicle that does not have a mind of its own. He thereby depersonalises the MPs. Groß acknowledges that the Social Democrats did well in the election because they followed "einem *gradlinigen* Plan" (a *straight* plan).

On BBC World, political guest expert Heinz Schulte uses the phrase "coalition with the SPD in the *driving seat*" which highlights the fact the SPD will be in control of the coalition-vehicle. The metaphor hides that the junior coalition partner will not be a passive passenger but demand their share in the decision-making process. Reporter Angus Roxburgh refers to the CDU's poll results, which improved during the campaign, as "*creeping up*".

CNN International's anchor Bettina Lüscher asks what "*went* wrong at the CDU". By campaigning in a certain way, the German conservatives made a mistake, they took the wrong road. "Either *way* it looks as if Mister Kohl is out of a job."

In their coverage of the 2000 US elections, CNN's political expert William Schneider explains that Americans "want a change of *leadership* but not a change of *direction*". Senior political correspondent Wolf Blitzer is "*following* two congressional races".

NBC reporter Tim Russert states that if Bush can win certain states, he will be "*on his way towards*" 270 electoral votes. Anchor Tom Brokaw notes that the

Table 1. Journey metaphors in percent of all metaphors (%)

	BBC	ITV	CNN Int. 97	ARD	RTL	BBC World	CNN Int. 98	CNN	NBC
Election is a journey	24	21	25	44	37	33	34	14	13

states on the map have "*so far* [...] *gone* the *way* we expected them to". Simultaneously, there is a caption on screen showing the words "The *Road* to 270" together with a picture of the White House. This visual element reinforces the verbal message. Correspondent Katie Couric reports that "voters who were most concerned about honesty and strong leadership *went* heavily for Bush." Curiously, they went both literally to the polls to vote for Bush, as well as metaphorically choosing the Republican over the Democratic way of governing.

As Table 1 illustrates, JOURNEY metaphors are particularly abundant in the German coverage while their number is somewhat lower for the British channels and considerably lower for the American channels.

3.2 Election is controversy

WAR, SPORT and CONTEST metaphors share one salient characteristic: they all highlight controversy. Therefore, metaphors from these domains are grouped in a more generic super-category labelled *controversy*. CONTROVERSY metaphors dramatise elections beyond their inherently exciting nature. In reality, however, political co-operation, consensus and compromise are possible, necessary, and especially in multi-party systems indispensable. As Howe (1988:99) and Beard (2000:22) have demonstrated, these aspects of politics are often concealed by using SPORT and WAR metaphors. However, it has to be pointed out that the media only *intensify* the antagonistic nature of elections by using confrontational metaphors; they do not *create* it. Given their long-term consequences, elections really *are* very exciting moments in politics. Before turning to the aggregate figures for the super-category CONTROVERSY, the findings for the three sub-categories are presented.

3.2.1 *Election is war*
There is a certain connection between the domains of politics and war. In practice, war is an instrument for solving international conflicts when diplomacy has failed, and it is politicians who decide about going to war. WAR metaphors paint a violent, destructive, uncompromising picture of elections.

In their coverage of the 1997 British elections, the BBC uses notably more WAR metaphors than any other channel under investigation. Calling the passive process of being elected to "*occupy* Number Ten" suggests a very hostile act, the use of military force by the Labour Party. It hides that the electorate is the decisive actor on election day. Similarly sensational is interviewer Jeremy Paxman's description of politicians as "*victors, vanquished* and *walking wounded*" and anchor David Dimbleby's saying that Peter Snow "will illustrate what's happened on the *battlefield*." Later during the night, the BBC visualises the battleground metaphor by blowing up building blocks representing target seats to the sound of explosions (cf. Schieß, this volume). The intensification through the visual metaphor makes the verbal metaphor all the more drastic. The other channels use less confrontational terms like 'critical', 'core' or 'marginal' constituency instead of the dramatising 'battleground' metaphor. The frequent use of the 'battlefield' metaphor by the BBC shows how high a premium they place on controversy (cf. Section 1).

ITV reporter Adrian Britton states that the returning officer in a Scottish constituency has been "*rallying the troops* saying [...] we've got to *beat* the English" in declaring the result first. In the same context, "*Brave Heart warrior spirit*" is not only a WAR metaphor but also an allusion to a Scottish national hero in Scotland's historical battle against the English. Moreover, there is talk of "*fighting* spirit" and "political *bloodshed*". The high concentration of five WAR metaphors within one minute of coverage is a strong indicator that irony is used here to open the text to polysemous interpretation (cf. Section 2.2).

On CNN International, correspondent Siobhan Darrow calls the Conservatives' loss of seats a "complete *massacre*" among Tory MPs. This is one of the sharpest metaphors in the entire data. It suggests that the electorate ruthlessly slaughtered the Tories. Anchor Richard Blystone declares that "you could make *enemies* but no friends" with the topic 'Europe' during the campaign. Here it is the voters who are depicted as the enemy, not the opposing party as is the case with most WAR metaphors.

Both in the English and German language the preparation for elections is referred to in WAR terms: English uses the word 'campaign' and German 'Wahlkampf' (election fight). ARD anchor von Haaren's question to Green politician Kerstin Müller if they would endure a coalition with the Social Democrats "*im Frieden*" (in peace) reveals the common notion that politics is a war-like pursuit in which peace is the exception. Apart from the harmless JOURNEY metaphor 'ins Parlament *kommen*' (to *enter* parliament), both ARD and RTL use the military phrase 'in den Bundestag *einrücken / einziehen*' (to *march* into parliament).

RTL anchor Peter Kloeppel dramatically refers to the German election as "die *Schlacht der Schlachten*" (the *battle* of *battles*). "Eine *Schlacht* an der Wahlurne" (a *battle* at the polls) inadequately suggests that voters are fighting each other in the polling stations.

BBC World uses the metaphor "*alliance*" to refer to (i) the permanent CDU-CSU union and (ii) the coalition of these two with the FDP, the German liberals.

Table 2. War metaphors in percent (%)

	BBC	ITV	CNN Int. 97	ARD	RTL	BBC World	CNN Int. 98	CNN	NBC
Election is war	27	19	19	18	14	17	17	21	14

CNN International uses the less militaristic term "*coalition*" to refer to the same fact. BBC World reporter Angus Roxburgh's feeling that the election was very much "a *fight* between two big personalities" personalises the election and hides how important party loyalties are in German voting.

In their coverage of the 1998 elections in Germany, CNN International's reporter Jim Bittermann describes Helmut Kohl as "one of the longest *serving* democratic leaders in history". The parallel between soldiers serving in the army and politicians is that they both serve their country. *Serving*, however, is not unambiguously a WAR metaphor. It could alternatively be understood in the non-ideological sense of *working for* or *waiting on* the people (as in a restaurant). Reporter Jonathan Mann and anchor Bettina Lüscher recount that Schröder has a "*commanding* lead" over this party, which hides that party members are not as obedient as soldiers.

While the BBC uses the *most* WAR metaphors, CNN uses the *fiercest* ones of all analysed channels. Their political expert Jeff Greenfield reports that the Democrats "*dispatched*" advisers and supporters as if they were troops. CNN also talks about a party "carry[ing]" or "tak[ing]", i.e. conquering a state. As so often in the data, the active-passive role distribution of politicians and voters is reversed by such phrases. Correspondent Candy Crowley's claim that the Republicans have "*zeroed in on* Florida" depicts Florida as a target they want to hit. With regard to electing a Democratic speaker of the House of Representatives, Stuart Rothenberg calls some Democrats "possible *defectors*" who betray their own side and help the enemy.

NBC reporter Tim Russert suggests that elections are a matter of life and death by reporting that a candidate is "*fighting for his life*" or that "John McCain *shot* George W." in the primaries. As usual, it is the opponent that is presented as the agent although it is of course the electorate that is responsible for the outcome of the election. Most strikingly, in an interview Harvard historian Doris Kearns Goodwin quotes John F. Kennedy as describing the significance of victory on election day in 1960 by saying that "at least it's not how the soldiers felt on D-Day. It's not of that dimension!" This statement puts the import of elections and war into perspective.

Table 2 shows a high number of WAR metaphors across all channels with above-average figures for BBC and CNN. The national average is the highest for

Britain followed by the US and Germany. The international channels use notably less WAR metaphors than the national channels.

3.2.2 *Election is sport*

Elections and sport do not seem to have much in common at first glance. Sport metaphors convey an image of a game that may be highly significant for individual sports people and their fans but remains without serious consequences for the society at large. Voters are much more powerful in democratic elections than a referee or an umpire in sport: They are the sovereign; they are the players, not the audience. Nonetheless, the competitive nature of both elections and professional sport seems a sufficient basis for frequent metaphorisation of elections through sport. Howe (1988: 95) observes that in contrast to WAR metaphors, SPORT metaphors suggest "fair play" and the chance for "peaceful resolution". The most frequent SPORT metaphor found in our data is 'race/running'. The reason for this could be that 'running' is the most basic, prototypical sport of all, as well as being one of the most straightforward forms of motion in general. There is little evidence in our data that sport metaphors differ substantially cross-culturally according to the types of sport most popular in each country.

The BBC's sport metaphors are unusual in that they refer to boxing, a very tough, aggressive confrontation between two individuals. Presenter David Dimbleby has "watched the politicians *slugging it out* together". Boxing metaphors like that hide that it is the electorate who are decisive on election day. ITV anchor Jonathan Dimbleby introduces the competition between constituencies to declare their results as a "*race* to be first". ITV correspondent James Mates replies that election aides in Sunderland are determined to be the fastest ever "*beating a record* set in Billericay back in 1959 of 57 minutes."

Referring to the expected struggle for Tory leadership after the projected defeat of the Tory party, CNN International's anchor Richard Blystone states that "that *race* is just about on."

The ARD's SPORT metaphors are mostly race-related. They talk of a "*Kopf-an-Kopf-Rennen*" (*head*-to-*head* race) and of "*Hürden* für die Volksbefragung senken" (lowering the *hurdles* for referendum). Apart from the chess metaphor "*ein Patt*" (*stalemate*), RTL's sport metaphors are also race-related.

BBC World anchor Nik Gowing states that there is "resentment against Chancellor Kohl and all [...] those who have been *running* the country." The concrete 'running' seems to be preferred over the abstract 'governing' or 'ruling'. In their programme on the election in Germany, CNN International use five 'running' metaphors, the non-specific "*scoring*" and the wrestling metaphor "*locked* in a campaign".

Table 3. Sport metaphors in percent (%)

	BBC	ITV	CNN Int. 97	ARD	RTL	BBC World	CNN Int. 98	CNN	NBC
Election is sport	6	6	3	10	10	10	14	20	25

Reporting on the US election, CNN use only three metaphors that are *not* race-related, one of them being the baseball term "home base". This reference to one of the most popular American sports occurs only once in CNN's opening sequence and is as such far from being *a* tyical, let alone *the* most typical SPORT metaphor. Not surprisingly in view of the frequent race metaphors, the candidate for the American vice presidency is called "running mate", a metaphor originating from horse racing[3] that has been lexicalised. CNN's most arresting race metaphor, however, is calling Gore's campaign a "*marathon*". A marathon runner evokes awe and admiration, i.e. positive connotations which are often absent in the context of professional politics.

All but one of NBC's sport metaphors are instances of racing. The frequent phrase 'a *race* that is *too close to call*' refers to the finish of a race which is so close that it is impossible to say who has won.

As Table 3 indicates, the American channels use far more sport metaphors than the British and the German ones.

3.2.3 *Election is contest*

This category includes metaphors that pertain neither clearly to the domain of WAR nor SPORT but have in common that they highlight and intensify the confrontational nature of elections – and thereby hide the potential and need for cooperation in politics. A contest between two adversaries, a fight between good and evil, between right and wrong simplifies such a complex process as politics.

Reporting on the 1997 British elections, BBC election analyst Peter Snow describes the Liberal Democrats as "*chasing*" seats. Once again, the party is portrayed as the decisive actor instead of the voters. Snow goes on to depict the election as a "*contest* to cross Downing Street". There are also many other parties "*contesting* this time like the Referendum Party." ITV anchor Jonathan Dimbleby envisages that Labour will "*win* with a massive majority of 159 seats." The author of this paper feels that the terms 'winning' and 'losing' are metaphors in the context of elections; they are already an interpretation of the most neutral way of referring to the results, i.e. 'getting' a certain percentage of the vote or a certain number of seats in parliament. To say that then Foreign Secretary Malcolm Rifkind faces a

---

3.   'Running mate': a horse used to set the pace for another horse in a race.

serious "*challenge* from Labour" hides that it is the electorate who are the decisive actor, not the opposition.

CNN International's Siobhan Darrow depicts then Defence Secretary Michael Portillo as a potential "big *contender*" for the Tory leadership – a fairly mild term compared to 'opponent', 'challenger' or 'adversary'.

ARD anchor Marion von Haaren portrays the German Social Democrat Gerhard Schröder as "*Herausforderer*" (*challenger*). Exit poll analyst Ulrich Deppendorf depicts the parties in terms of physical strength: "die *stärkste* Partei" (the *strongest* party). This common way of presenting election results in German is somewhat different from presenting the strongest party as the *winner* in countries with majority voting systems. Both German channels talk considerably less about '*winning*' and '*losing*' than their British and American counterparts.

RTL's political expert Groß presents the campaign as a "reiner *Personalwettbewerb* zwischen den beiden Spitzenkandidaten" (a mere personality *competition* between the two top candidates). This hides the fact that party affiliation may have played a central role for many voters. This verbal metaphor is visually mirrored in RTL's title sequence: Schröder and Kohl are shown on a split screen as opposing poles without mentioning parties (cf. Schieß, this volume). It would seem that the major parties in Germany and Britain have, at least up to the 1990s, had a fair percentage of loyal supporters whereas in the US the candidates' personalities seem to be more important. The "*Personalwettbewerb*" metaphor suggests that similar forces are at work in German politics, too. RTL anchor Peter Kloeppel further personalises the election by calling it a "*Duell* zwischen diesen beiden *Kontrahenten*" (a *duel* between these two adversaries).

Reporting on the German elections, BBC World uses the lowest number of CONTEST metaphors of all analysed channels. Reporter David Shukman thinks that the Conservatives will try to "*challenge*" the political dominance of Gerhard Schröder after the election. CNN International's anchor Bettina Lüscher uses a metaphorical mix from the domains of WRESTLING, WAR and CONTEST: "Kohl has been *locked* in a tough *campaign* with [...] *challenger* Gerhard Schröder."

Regarding the elections in the US, CNN correspondents Candy Crowley and John King talk about the parties having a state "*in the bag*" – a hunting metaphor based on the fact that the prey, once killed, is put in a bag for the ease of carrying it home. The analogy holds in so far as hunters (presidential candidates) compete against one another for the highest quantity of prey (number of electoral votes); hunting the largest quantity is rewarded with the highest prestige; and the hunters are traditionally men. One might argue with Howe (cf. 1988:92) that depicting elections in terms of the male-dominated activity of hunting denies women fair and equal participation in and experience of elections. On the other hand, 'having something in the bag' has become so conventional that it is not necessarily

Table 4. Contest metaphors in percent (%)

	BBC	ITV	CNN Int. 97	ARD	RTL	BBC World	CNN Int. 98	CNN	NBC
Election is contest	18	13	12	19	25	4	9	21	32

Table 5. Controversy metaphors in percent (%)

Election is...	BBC	ITV	CNN Int. 97	ARD	RTL	BBC World	CNN Int. 98	CNN	NBC
war	27	19	19	18	14	17	17	21	14
contest	18	13	12	19	25	4	9	21	32
sport	6	6	3	10	10	10	14	20	25
total controversy	51	38	33	47	48	31	40	61	71

associated with hunting anymore. It has come to mean 'having achieved, secured something'. However, the hunting analogy ultimately fails to hold in the domain of elections because voters are the decisive actors in democratic elections, not politicians.

Apart from 35 uses of 'winning' and 'losing' in NBC's opening section, correspondent Katie Couric and anchor Tom Brokaw refer to the election as a "*contest*" and a "hotly *contested* race".

Table 4 shows that the American channels and RTL use the highest number of CONTEST metaphors, followed by ARD and the British channels. The international channels use remarkably less CONTEST metaphors than the national channels.

We now return to the super-category CONTROVERSY and its aggregate figures for the sub-categories WAR, SPORT and CONTEST. As Table 5 shows, the US channels use by far the most CONTROVERSY metaphors. One possible reason for the many controversy metaphors in the American data is the use of the majority voting system in the US. Majority voting systems (also called first-past-the-post or winner-take-all) tend to be two-party systems. As in the prototypical war and in many sport encounters, there are two parties opposing each other. Under majority voting systems, victories tend to be clearer than under proportional representation. If governments were formed solely on the basis of proportional representation, parties might be seen less as opponents and more as co-operators becoming part of one team. However, although the British electoral system is also a majority voting system, the CONTROVERSY total of BBC and especially of ITV is considerably lower than the American average.

3.3 Election is nature

It lies in the nature of nature that it has positive as well as negative effects on people – just as elections. Accordingly, NATURE metaphors are used both positively and negatively, the latter often being catastrophe-like.

Frank Skinner, a well-known stand-up comedian hired by the BBC as a roving reporter for comic relief (cf. Schieß, this volume), exemplifies what it means to open a text to polysemous reading by saying that he is "gonna supply a sort of *low-brow*, down-at-heel counterpoint to your intellectual analysis in the studio." Some people will be more attracted by the intellectual analysis in the studio, others less so. BBC anchor David Dimbleby refers to the election result as a *"landslide"*. Later during the programme, this verbal metaphor is visually reinforced through computer animations "that bury hapless candidates" (Schieß, this volume). ITV uses slightly more dramatic NATURE metaphors than BBC, for example *"ero[sion]"*, *"flooding"*, *"tremor"*, *"seismic shift"* or *"disaster"*. Such catastrophe metaphors hide the fact that elections do not just occur; they are deliberate man-made decisions by the electorate.

CNN International refers to the Tory defeat as a *"melt-down"*, thus equating it with the potentially disastrous melting of fuel rods in a nuclear power station. By saying that Blair has realised that it is time for the Labour Party to "adapt or *die*", correspondent Christiane Amanpour also makes elections a matter of survival. Andrew Neil, editor of *The European*, states on CNN International that John Major was going to put Britain in the *"heart"* of Europe but that it is "nowhere near the *heart*, [it is] not even the big *toe"*. This neatly exemplifies how elusive concepts like European politics can be boiled down by using analogies to the human body that are immediately accessible to everyone. The "toe" metaphor is a playful, creative extension of the very conventional "heart" metaphor.

The German channels ARD and RTL use very few NATURE metaphors: ARD uses none at all and RTL just two. RTL reporter Carsten Mierke refers to the conservatives' defeat as *"Erdrutschartigkeit"* (like a landslide), which is more of a simile and thus milder than the outright "landslide" metaphor used by BBC and ITV. BBC World uses some very positive and some fairly mild NATURE metaphors. The dominant position of the conservatives "is *evaporating"* especially in the East because the *"blooming* economy" that Chancellor Kohl promised has not materialised. Compared to the high number of NATURE metaphors in their coverage of the British election, CNN International use very few in their reporting on the German election. Jonathan Mann states that many SPD supporters feel that Kohl has become *"tired"* after 16 years as chancellor.

Christian Coalition President Pat Robertson states on CNN that "the moral *climate"* of the nation was the decisive factor in the 2000 US election, thereby

Table 6. Nature metaphors in percent (%)

	BBC	ITV	CNN Int. 97	ARD	RTL	BBC World	CNN Int. 98	CNN	NBC
Election is nature	11	16	17	–	3	13	7	7	1

making it sound natural that the Republicans should do well – and hiding that the electorate makes a calculated decision. CNN correspondent John King quotes Al Gore's father saying that his son was "*born* to be president". Of course, this is impossible in a democracy but we infer that being the son of a "legendary Tennessee senator" gave Gore a head start into politics.

NBC anchor Tom Brokaw says that New Hampshire has "changed its political *DNA*" from a faithfully Republican state to one in which the Democrats have a true chance. This suggests that voting patterns are biologically determined, and not ideologically, psychologically, economically or socially. If New Hampshire's change of DNA is interpreted as a mutation, it carries ambivalent associations, either of serious genetic malfunctioning, or of better evolutionary chances for survival. How it will be interpreted depends on the political preferences of the audience. It is thus another example for opening a text to polysemous reading.

Table 6 shows that the British channels use a lot more NATURE metaphors than the German and US channels.

3.4 Election is business

The spheres of politics and business are linked through a government's interests in a nation's economic well-being and through companies' dependence on an administration providing a necessary minimum framework to do business, and last but not least through old-boy networks. The world of business is complex, but apparently perceived to be less abstract than politics; otherwise it would not be illuminating to depict elections in terms of business.

There are hardly any business metaphors in the British and in the US data. The BBC talks about "a busy night in *store*" for the returning officers. Similarly, ITV has a "huge night of drama in *store*". Reporting on the UK election, CNN International's anchor Richard Blystone states that "people are going to want their *pay-off*" and that according to John Major, Blair would "*sell* British sovereignty" in Maastricht. The illuminating aspect about the pay-off metaphor is that it highlights that the electorate does not vote for a party out of altruism but because they expect something in return, just as you have the right to good service in a business transaction.

Table 7. Business metaphors in percent (%)

	BBC	ITV	CNN Int. 97	ARD	RTL	BBC World	CNN Int. 98	CNN	NBC
Election is business	1	1	8	6	3	6	5	1	2

ARD and RTL '*rechnen* mit' (literally: *calculate* ('reckon') that there will be) certain majorities. This highly conventional metaphor is also used a lot in everyday talk. RTL moreover refers to political agreements between coalition partners as "*Geschäfte*" (*deals*). In their coverage of the German election, BBC World refers to politicians "*deliver[ing]* promises" and doing "a *deal*" with a coalition partner. Similarly, CNN International talks about a "tall *order*" being difficult to "*deliver*" for Schröder.

CNN's metaphor about Al Gore "looking for one last *promotion* after eight years in the House, eight in the Senate, and eight as the Vice President" is an analogy to a common business process which is often dependent on performance. As opinion polls showed, capability was not the decisive quality for the majority of voters in the 2000 US election, but that might not always be the case in business promotions, either.

NBC presenter Tom Brokaw reports that both parties made an enormous "*investment*" in Florida – which is certainly literally true but has an added metaphorical truth to it, as financial commitment alone does not ensure success on election day. Correspondent Katie Couric describes the voters as consumers by saying that "according to the exit poll, neither candidate was a *complete package* voters really wanted." Although this metaphor depersonalises the candidates, it adequately reflects who makes the decision on election day: the people.

As shown in Table 7, the international and the German channels use more business metaphors than the British and US channels. This is counterintuitive as the free market economy is commonly associated with Britain and the United States. However, the figures might be misleading due to the low absolute number of business metaphors in our data.

3.5 Election is drama

Elections and theatre have little in common – unless you believe that all the world is a stage. The decisions of politicians have far more serious consequences for the well-being of the country and the international community than those of actors. What politicians and actors have in common, however, is that their success is determined to a large extent by how much people like and support them.

Table 8. Drama metaphors in percent (%)

	BBC	ITV	CNN Int. 97	ARD	RTL	BBC World	CNN Int. 98	CNN	NBC
Election is drama	1	7	1	–	4	2	–	1	1

Out of all examined broadcasters, ITV uses the most DRAMA metaphors to sensationalise elections, e.g. "the *drama* of election night", "the election *story*" and "*subplots* in the election". The BBC uses only one drama metaphor. During CNN International's 1997 broadcast, interviewee Ian Hargreaves, editor of the *New Statesman* magazine, talks about Britain becoming "an active negotiator on the European *stage*". The German ARD does not use any drama metaphors at all. RTL uses the highly conventional "(k)eine *Rolle spielen*" (to play a (or: no) role), which is also used by BBC World. Referring to the presidential election in the US, Jeff Greenfield from CNN's election desk states that there is something about long-term senators that does not "*play* on the presidential *stage.*" NBC anchor Tom Brokaw announces that "a late and unexpected development [...] adds to the *drama* of this evening."

As Table 8 shows, the number of drama metaphors in the data is fairly low. However, it seems that the commercial channels ITV and RTL use more drama metaphors than their public-service counterparts BBC and ARD. ELECTION IS DRAMA is the only category where tendencies towards entertainment and dramatisation seem more pronounced with the commercial than with the public-service stations (cf. Section 1). However, due to the low absolute number of drama metaphors in the data, these findings should not be overinterpreted.

3.6 Election is law

The domains of politics and law are linked through the legislative process. LAW metaphors hide the fact that there can be (and frequently are) more than two parties running for presidency or for seats in parliament, whereas in court, there are always only two sides to the argument: prosecution and defence. However, under the British and American majority voting system, and for that matter also under the German mixed system, only two parties stand a true chance of making their leader head of government.

The LAW metaphors used by BBC are remarkable, particularly as they are hardly used by the other analysed channels, and when used by the latter, they are not very illuminating. BBC anchor David Dimbleby opens the programme by announcing that we are about to hear "the voters' *verdict*". In an interview with the BBC, Tory Chairman Brian Mawhinney declares that they put their "*case* to the people" and refuses to speculate about the outcome of the election because nobody knows what *"judgment"* the people "have *passed"*. Unlike SPORT or WAR metaphors, these metaphors give just credit to the people's vital role in the electoral process.

Jonathan Dimbleby invites viewers to *"witness"* one of the great moments in British post-war politics on ITV. This does not only refer to the election itself but also to ITV's reporting about it. Secondly, 'witnessing' history does not have quite the same legal force as 'judgment' or 'verdict'.

During CNN International's coverage of the British election, Andrew Neil, editor of *The European,* talks about Labour MPs who might "not *sign on* to the Blairite view" and Blair not *"sign[ing]* on" to the French and German way with regard to European affairs. In both contexts, 'signing' does not entail a legal obligation but a political commitment. Reporting on the US elections, CNN correspondent John King likewise describes the election day as "a *signature day* in the life" of Al Gore. This metaphor suggests that Gore himself can decide whether to 'sign on' to an existence as president, but it is the voters who make that decision.

ARD does not use any LAW metaphors. RTL's political expert Johannes Groß explains Schröder's attractiveness for the voters by saying that he has one *"Tatbestand"* (aspect; literally: *element of offence*) speaking in his favour: his age. *"Tatbestand"* is an odd and possibly unintentional lexical choice and should therefore not be overinterpreted.

BBC World reporter David Shukman states that there is not much *"precedent"* in post-war German electoral history for the exit poll being wrong. Though chiefly used as a law term, 'precedent' has long found its way into everyday talk. In our context, it would not have any legal relevance even if there *were* a precedent for an exit poll being wrong. "Unprecedented" is used in a similar way by CNN correspondent John King who states that organised labour showed "an *unprecedented* turnout drive" in support of the Democratic Party.

By speculating whether Bush can *"steal"* away Tennessee and Arkansas (the home states of Al Gore and Bill Clinton), NBC reporter Tim Russert implies that these two states belong to the Democrats and that a Republican has no right to win there. Another possible interpretation of "stealing" is that it is really clever of Bush to be able to do so, i.e. "stealing" allows for diverging interpretations. Moreover, as so often, the candidates are assigned the active role by this metaphor which the electorate actually has.

Table 9 indicates that the BBC stands out from the other channels in its use of law metaphors, not only qualitatively, as presented above, but also quantitatively.

Table 9. Law metaphors in percent (%)

	BBC	ITV	CNN Int. 97	ARD	RTL	BBC World	CNN Int. 98	CNN	NBC
Election is law	5	1	3	–	1	1	–	3	1

3.7 Election is religion

Today, the domains of politics and religion are far less closely related in most contemporary Western societies than in the Middle Ages. But still nowadays, religious and moral issues cannot be ignored by candidates running for high political office. In some countries they can even decide elections.

The BBC uses no religion-related metaphors at all. ITV, BBC World and CNN International reporting on the German election use RELIGION metaphors that can be considered equally relevant to all faiths and thus do not put viewers from any religious community at a disadvantage. Metaphors such as "a *ritual* part of the drama of election night" (ITV anchor J. Dimbleby), the "*fate*" of fellow candidates (ITV reporter Caroline Kerr), and "*destined* for many years in opposition" (BBC World reporter David Shukman) are culturally impartial in that they are not restricted to the Christian faith. Such neutrality is particularly important for international channels addressing trans-cultural audiences with viewers of many different creeds.

During CNN International's coverage of the British elections, interviewee Andrew Neil, editor of *The European,* puts Blair on a par with Jesus by saying that the election result would allow him to "*walk on water*". This metaphor (after the Bible, Matthew 14) magnifies how extraordinary the election result is and that it will give the Prime Minister superhuman powers. It thus personalises, dramatises and emotionalises the coverage.

ARD reporter Wolfgang Kenntemich quotes Hans-Olaf Henkel, President of the *Bundesverband der deutschen Industrie* (Germany's Federal Industrial Association), as hoping that "der *Kelch* Rot-Grün an uns vorübergeht", i.e. that the country be spared the ordeal (literally: the *cup*) of a coalition between Social Democrats and the Green party. The phrase "der *Kelch* / the *cup*" is originally from the Bible (Matthew 26) where Jesus, worried that he might be killed, prays: "My Father, if it be possible, let this cup pass from me." Although originating from the Bible, "der *Kelch* / the *cup*" has long been conventional in everyday talk.

NBC anchor Tom Brokaw also uses a metaphor deeply ingrained in the Christian faith when asking "whether Governor Jeb Bush in Florida is *his brother's keeper*". Curiously, the phrase is used affirmatively by Brokaw, while originally in

Table 10. Religion metaphors in percent (%)

	BBC	ITV	CNN Int. 97	ARD	RTL	BBC World	CNN Int. 98	CNN	NBC
Election is religion	–	2	3	1	–	2	–	–	1

the Bible (Genesis 4) it reads: "I do not know, am I my brother's keeper?" This is what Cain replies to God's question about his brother's whereabouts who he has just slain. With hindsight, in view of the Florida recount, the metaphor gains a certain delicacy; on election day it was probably no more than a pun.

As Table 10 shows, religion metaphors are not very frequent at all in the analysed data. No clear pattern is discernible.

3.8 Meta-discourse: Coverage is…

COVERAGE is partly conceptualised through the same source domains as ELECTION. By using the same metaphorical concepts for the depiction of their own coverage, the media liken the importance of journalism to that of elections.

3.8.1 *Coverage is journey*

JOURNEY is not only the most frequent source domain for ELECTION, but also for COVERAGE. JOURNEY metaphors are mainly used to give the floor to other speakers, but also to tell the audience how the programme continues, e.g. "*Stay* with us – we're about to *take you on an exciting and bumpy ride*" (Tom Brokaw, NBC). BBC election analyst Peter Snow promises to illustrate "this battle for power in a more adventurous and inventive *way* than we've ever done before."

In English, the transition between anchor and other channel staff is commonly achieved via JOURNEY metaphors as in 'Let's *go* to…' or '*Joining* us now….'. 'Let's *go* to…' *in*cludes the viewer in the process. In German, turn-taking is handled via the plain ontological metaphor "und jetzt *geben* wir *zurück* ins ARD-Wahlstudio" (literally 'we *hand* [the floor] back to the studio). The term 'zurückgeben' *ex*cludes the viewer from the action. Yet sometimes phrases similar to the English JOURNEY metaphors are used in German, too: "weiter mit Marion von Haaren" is short for "weiter *geht* es mit …" (we *go on* with …). The German channels use only one COVERAGE IS JOURNEY metaphor each while the British and American stations use a lot more. Twelve minutes into their coverage, RTL "*schreite[t]* zu unserer ersten Prognose [...] dieses Abends" (*proceed[s]* with our first exit poll of the night). By using the elevated term "*schreiten*" rather than the plain "weiter *geht* es mit..." or "Wir *kommen* jetzt zu" (We now *go* on with), RTL makes itself part of an important political ritual. ARD has invited "hochkarätige Gäste" (high caliber guests) into the studio who will "*begleiten*" (accompany) them through the election night.

NBC uses noteworthy COVERAGE IS JOURNEY metaphors that imply the need to guide the audience through the complicated events of the election night. Tom Brokaw invites the audience to travel through the night with NBC by saying teacher-like "We'll *take you through* what it all means" and tourist guide-like "We're about to *take you on an exciting and bumpy ride*." Especially the latter is a clear move towards exciting politainment.

3.8.2 *Coverage is war*

The only channels that use COVERAGE IS WAR metaphors are BBC, ITV and NBC. By talking about "two *battle-hardened* correspondents back at the *frontline*", the BBC makes itself part of the election battle. Anchor Tom Brokaw calls two NBC reporters "*veterans* of the long *march* of the *campaign*". Likewise, ITV presenter Jonathan Dimbleby introduces election analyst David Butler as "a *veteran* of programmes like this".

3.8.3 *Coverage is business*

RTL is the only channel that talks about their coverage in business terms: „Haben wir noch 'ne Variante *auf Lager*?" (Do we have another variant in *store*?), and "eine Einstellung *liefern*" (to *deliver* a shot). It seems quite apt for a commercial channel to present its coverage as business. What is RTL if not an enterprise selling its product? Such metaphors only hide that RTL is not selling messages to an audience but audiences to advertisers (cf. Lauerbach 2004).

3.8.4 *Coverage is drama*

ITV is the only channel that depicts its coverage as drama. Anchor Jonathan Dimbleby declares that "part of the *drama* of election night is to see how close our forecast is to the actual results." ITV is also the channel that uses the most ELECTION IS DRAMA metaphors.

3.8.5 *Coverage is sport*

CNN is the only channel to describe its coverage in sport terms. Anchor Judy Woodruff is "gonna *touch base*" with outside reporters. This is the second baseball metaphor used by CNN (cf. Section 3.2.2).

Table 11 shows that COVERAGE IS JOURNEY is the only meta-discursive concept used by all channels. The other meta-discursive metaphors are rare.

Table 11. Meta-discursive metaphors in percent (%)

Coverage is...	BBC	ITV	CNN Int. 97	ARD	RTL	BBC World	CNN Int. 98	CNN	NBC
journey	6	8	9	1	1	10	14	12	9
war	1	2	–	–	–	–	–	–	2
business	–	–	–	–	3	–	–	–	–
drama	–	1	–	–	–	–	–	–	–
sport	–	–	–	–	–	–	–	1	–

Table 12. Overview of metaphorical concepts in percent (%)

	Britain 1997			Germany 1998				USA 2000	
	BBC	ITV	CNN INT.	ARD	RTL	BBC World	CNN INT.	CNN	NBC
Election is...									
journey	24	21	25	44	37	32	33	14	13
controversy	51	38	33	47	48	32	40	61	71
– war	27	19	19	18	14	17	17	21	14
– contest	18	13	12	19	25	5	9	21	32
– sport	6	6	3	10	10	10	14	20	25
nature	11	16	17	–	3	14	7	7	1
business	1	1	8	6	3	6	5	1	2
drama	1	7	1	–	4	2	–	1	1
law	5	1	3	–	1	1	–	3	1
religion	–	2	3	1	–	2	–	–	1
Coverage is...									
journey	6	8	9	1	1	10	14	12	9
war	1	2	–	–	–	–	–	–	2
business	–	–	–	–	3	–	–	–	–
drama	–	1	–	–	–	–	–	–	–
sport	–	–	–	–	–	–	–	1	–

3.9   Quantitative overview

Table 12 presents an overview of all conceptual metaphors per channel. It should be pointed out that the findings have not been tested for statistical significance because the number of channels is too small to calculate the standard deviation. Given that previous studies of metaphor found politics depicted mostly in terms of WAR (and SPORT), it is important to stress that in our data election is most frequently conceptualised through the far less sensational JOURNEY metaphors – at least if the sub-categories WAR, CONTEST and SPORT are considered separately (the sub-categories are indented for ease of reference in Tables 12 and 13). Across all

Table 13. National, international and overall average in percent (%)

	British average	German average	US average	National average	Internat. average	Overall average
Election is...						
journey	23	40	13	23	31	25
controversy	45	48	66	55	35	49
– war	23	16	18	19	18	19
– contest	16	22	26	22	8	18
– sport	6	10	22	14	9	13
nature	13	2	5	7	13	8
business	1	4	1	2	6	3
drama	4	2	1	2	1	2
law	4	1	2	2	1	2
religion	1	–	–	1	2	1
Coverage is...						
journey	7	1	11	7	11	8
war	2	–	1	1	–	1
business	–	2	–	–	–	–
drama	1	–	–	–	–	–
sport	–	–	–	–	–	–

channels, 25% of all metaphors are JOURNEY metaphors. They are followed in frequency by WAR, CONTEST, SPORT and NATURE metaphors. JOURNEY is also the most common meta-discursive conceptualisation of coverage.

What could be the reason why we counted so many JOURNEY metaphors in our data while Howe, Montgomery et al., Wilson and Beard found politics mostly metaphorised as WAR and SPORT? Given that JOURNEY metaphors are very frequent in everyday talk (e.g. LIFE IS A JOURNEY, LOVE IS A JOURNEY), it is almost hard to imagine that texts comparable to ours should not use any JOURNEY metaphors at all. One possible reason why WAR and SPORTS metaphors were discussed more in previous studies could be exactly the frequency of JOURNEY metaphors in everyday conversation. JOURNEY metaphors are so conventional that they may not catch the eye quite as much as the often very striking and sensational WAR and SPORT metaphors.

Table 13 presents the national averages, i.e. the British average (BBC and ITV), the German average (ARD and RTL), the US average (CNN and NBC), the average of all national channels (i.e. BBC, ITV, ARD, RTL, CNN and NBC), the average of all international channels (i.e. CNN Int. UK 1997, CNN Int. FRG 1998, and BBC World), and the overall average of all channels.

4. Discussion

This section addresses the questions if there are (i) cross-cultural differences, (ii) differences between national and international channels and (iii) between public-service and commercial stations in the use of metaphors. (iv) Finally it is discussed if the metaphorical concepts that were identified are gender-neutral.

4.1 Great similarities across cultures

There is a notable similarity in the use of metaphors across channels and cultures in the analysed data. Not only do the same metaphorical concepts occur with all channels; also the quantities are alike in a lot of cases. The super-category CONTRO-VERSY is by far the most frequent. If the sub-categories are considered individually, JOURNEY metaphors are the most frequent with an overall average of 25%, closely followed by WAR (19%), CONTEST (18%) and SPORT (13%). JOURNEY metaphors are the only meta-discursive metaphors that occur across all channels.

The fact the metaphorical concepts and even their quantities are remarkably similar across all investigated channels and cultures may be explained by the fact that all channels are based in post-industrial western societies with similar cultural identities rooted in Christianity, a lot of common history and high economic interdependence. Furthermore, English and German are closely related languages that express many concepts including highly idiomatic metaphors in very similar ways. You could reasonably expect greater differences of linguistic features if you compared election night broadcasts from a European or western culture to those from Asian or African cultures, which also differ greatly on a socio-cultural level. For instance, Wei's (2003) analysis of metaphors in Taiwanese election campaign discourse shows not only the use of metaphors from domains she calls COSTUME and FINANCIAL TRANSACTIONS, the latter being close to our category BUSINESS, but also that election is frequently presented in terms of the compromise-oriented domain of MARRIAGE. Wei (2003: 128) explains that, unlike in western culture, marriage does not "stress free will or the maximization of individual satisfaction" in Chinese culture. Rather "the primary importance of marriage is the fulfilment of obligations to ancestors by ensuring the continuance of the family" (Thornton & Lin 1994: 36; quoted in Wei 2003: 129). MARRIAGE metaphors in Taiwanese politics reveal the expectation that even conflicting political parties are obliged to resolve tensions and friction cooperatively (cf. Wei 2003: 127–128).

Across all channels, a considerable number of metaphors reverse the active-passive role distribution between politicians and electorate. As if politicians did not have enough power once elected into office, they are presented as the key players even on election day on which they cannot do much apart from passively awaiting the electorate's decision. This reversal may arise partly because candidates provide a face to abstract party politics, whereas the electorate are an anonymous, intangible mass. The active-passive reversal occurs mostly with metaphors from the domains of WAR, CONTEST and SPORT: Parties having a state *"in the bag"*, parties *"carrying"* or *"taking"* a state, John McCain *"shooting"* George W. Bush – all these metaphors hide that voters are the decisive actors in democratic elections. When elections are portrayed as DRAMA (see Section 3.5), and politicians are presented as actors on stage, this turns the electorate into mere spectators – another distorting twist. Bush *"stealing"* Tennessee and Arkansas from Gore is the only LAW metaphor in the data that reverses the role of electors and elected. Other LAW metaphors such as 'the people's *verdict*' or 'the people's *judgment*' as used by the BBC, seem to be the only metaphors that give just credit to the people's vital role on election day. ITV's NATURE metaphors (*ero[sion], flooding, tremor, seismic shift, disaster*) do not reverse the active-passive roles, but hide that election results are deliberate decisions by the voters.

However, there are also some differences between cultures. Both US channels use by far the most SPORT metaphors, namely 22% compared to the low German average of 6% and a British average of 10%. The US channels (66%) also clearly outnumber the German (48%) and British ones (45%) in the use of CONTROVERSY metaphors. The German channels (40%) use a lot more of the non-sensational JOURNEY metaphors than the British (23%) and US (13%) channels. NATURE metaphors are used much more frequently by the British channels (13%) than by the German (2%) and US (5%) channels.

4.2 Clear differences between national and international channels

As Table 13 shows, the international channels (35%) use considerably fewer CONTROVERSY metaphors than the national channels (55%). The fact that across all channels 49% of all metaphors are CONTROVERSY metaphors clearly demonstrates that harmony is generally not newsworthy. On the other hand, the *inter*national average for non-sensational metaphors such as ELECTION IS A JOURNEY (international average 31%, national average 23%), ELECTION IS NATURE (int. average 13%, nat. average 7%) and COVERAGE IS JOURNEY (int. average 11%, nat. average 7%) is much higher than the national average.

It is suggested that these differences may be explained by the fact that international audiences are usually not directly affected by election results in other countries, which in turn reduces the pressure on the international channels to spice up their coverage with sensational metaphors. National audiences, on the contrary, who presumably overlap to a very large extent with the electorate, have a high stake in the election result as they are immediately affected by it. The national channels may compete more directly against each other than the international stations amongst each other, the former trying to attract larger audiences by using highly confrontational metaphors to make their coverage captivating.

4.3 Minor differences between public-service and commercial channels

Contrary to what intuition may have suggested, it is not discernible from the examined data that tendencies towards controversy and entertainment are generally more pronounced with the commercial channels than with the public-service ones. If anything, the BBC places a higher premium on controversy and excitement than commercial ITV through its numerous WAR and CONTEST metaphors. The German public-service channel ARD is hardly less controversy-oriented in its use of metaphor than RTL.

4.4 Are some metaphors gender-biased?

Following Howe's (1988) postulation that the depiction of politics through WAR and SPORT denies women equal participation in and experience of the political process, the present analysis looks at whether the metaphors found in our data are gender-neutral. Compared to past decades and centuries, there might be more women in LAW, BUSINESS, SPORT and even the military nowadays, but these are still male-dominated social domains. Likewise, open competitiveness (category CONTEST) is stereotypically associated with male rather than with female behaviour. Metaphors from these domains could therefore be considered gender-biased. JOURNEY, NATURE and DRAMA, on the other hand, seem gender-neutral source domains the use of which should make the election coverage equally accessible to both sexes. With metaphors from the realm of RELIGION, the case is not so clear: while positions in the church hierarchy are mostly held by men, faith can be expected to be practiced more or less equally by women and men.

Counting WAR, SPORT, CONTEST, BUSINESS and LAW metaphors as potentially gender-biased, the following picture emerges: As shown in Table 14, the overall average of all channels' gender-biased metaphors amounts to 55%, ranging from a low 38% on BBC World to a high 75% on NBC. Both US channels use considerably more gender-biased metaphors than all other channels, which leads to a US average of 70 % (CNN 65%, NBC 75%). The British and German averages are 52% and 54% respectively. Given the large number of CONTROVERSY metaphors within the category of gender-biased metaphors, the difference between the national and

Table 14. Percentage of gender-biased metaphors

	Gender-biased metaphors	Anchor
BBC	59	David Dimbleby
ITV	42	Jonathan Dimbleby
CNN Int. UK 97	44	Richard Blystone
ARD	53	Marion von Haaren
RTL	55	Peter Kloeppel
BBC World	38	Nik Gowing
CNN Int. FRG 98	45	Bettina Lüscher
CNN	65	Judy Woodruff and Bernard Shaw
NBC	75	Tom Brokaw
British average	52	
German average	54	
American average	70	
National average	60	
Internat. average	42	
Overall average	55	

the international channels is similar to the that of the CONTROVERSY metaphors, the international channels using far less gender-biased metaphors (42%) than the national channels (60%). For reasons of scope, the question of gender-bias can not be discussed exhaustively here. One example shall suffice to demonstrate what is meant by gender-bias: Anchor Tom Brokaw refers to NBC reporters as "*veterans* of the long *march* of the *campaign*". For men – at least for those who have served in the army – it will be much easier to identify with those veterans than for women who have not.

The question arises if the frequency of gender-biased metaphors is in any way related to the sex of the anchor. As shown in table 14, six out of the nine investigated channels employ male anchors to present such high-profile events as election nights. Like the predominantly male professional politicians, male anchors have the opportunity to perpetuate traditional power structures by the frequent use of metaphors from traditionally male-dominated social domains. The two broadcasts presented by women – on ARD and CNN International covering the German election – use a below average percentage of gender-biased metaphors. Marion von Haaren hosts ARD's election night 53% of their metaphors are gender-biased, which is only just below the overall average of 55%. CNN International's coverage of the German election is presented by Bettina Lüscher; their gender-biased metaphors add up to 45%. CNN has a mixed anchor duo, Judy Woodruff and Bernard Shaw: An above average figure of 65% of gender-biased metaphors occurs in their programme's opening sequence. This is a high figure, but still 10 percentage points lower than that of their national rival NBC, whose election night is hosted by Tom Brokaw. However, it has to be said that the three broadcasts with the lowest percentage of gender-biased metaphors are presented by men: BBC World by Nik Gowing (38%), ITV by Jonathan Dimbleby (42%) and CNN Int. UK 97 by Richard Blystone (44%). This suggests that the percentage of gender-biased metaphors and the sex of the anchor are not related.

5.   Conclusion

The analysis of metaphors during television election nights reveals that there are remarkable similarities across channels and cultures regarding metaphorical concepts and their frequency. The use of metaphors does also not differ very much between public-service and commercial channels, i.e. the differences between the British BBC and ITV and between the German ARD and RTL are minor. The study also reveals that across all channels a fairly large number of metaphors portray the politicians as the decisive actors on election day and thus reverses the active-passive role distribution between electors and elected. There is a large percentage of metaphors across all channels that is perceived to be gender-biased, but no relation can be established between the number of gender-biased metaphors and the sex of the anchor. The most striking difference among the investigated channels arises in the super-category CONTROVERSY: the average of the national channels (55%) is considerably higher than the average of international channels (35%).

Across all channels, nearly 50% of the detected metaphors fall into the super-category CONTROVERSY. This shows that metaphors contribute considerably to the tendency of increasingly dramatised infotainment observed by Fairclough (1995) and indicates that Cohen's (1998) finding that the media currently place a high premium on controversy is not only true for the British media culture but also for the German and even more so for the US channels. However, the single most frequent metaphorical concept in our data, i.e. ELECTION IS JOURNEY (overall average 25%), does not dramatise events at all, on the contrary it rather softens them. The same holds true for the less frequent ELECTION IS NATURE metaphors (8%) and COVERAGE IS JOURNEY metaphors.

As has been demonstrated, a fair number of metaphors allow for more than one interpretation. Our hypothesis that metaphors may serve as a device which opens a text to polysemous readings has thus been confirmed.

In future research, it would be interesting to investigate whether the use of metaphors differs with regard to the various political parties, i.e. whether conservatives are depicted differently from liberals. More attention could also be paid to the distinction between creative and conventional metaphors. No figures have yet been established for the active-passive role reversal between the electorate and the elected politicians; this would be another area for more in-depth analysis. Moreover, it might prove fruitful to investigate the effects metaphor usage in more detail.

References

Beard, A. 2000. *The Language of Politics*. London/New York: Routledge.

Beardsley, M. C. 1967. "Metaphor." In *Encyclopedia of Philosophy*, vol. 5, P. Edwards (ed.), 284–289. New York: Macmillan.

Black, M. 1979. "More about metaphors." In Metaphor and Thought, A. Ortony (ed.), 19–45. Cambridge et al.: CUP.

Cohen, N. 1998. "The death of news." In *New Statesman* 22nd May.

Eco, U. 1984. *Semiotics and the Philosophy of Language*. London / Basingstoke: Macmillan.

Fairclough, N. 1995. *Media Discourse*. London: Edward Arnold.

Fiske, J. 1987. *Television Culture*. London / New York: Routledge.

Forceville, C. 1996. *Pictorial Metaphor in Advertising*. London / New York. Routledge.

Howe, N. 1988. "Metaphor in contemporary American political discourse." *Metaphor and Symbolic Activity* 3: 87–104.

Lakoff, G. and Johnson, M. 1980. *Metaphors We Live By*. Chicago: University of Chicago Press.

Lauerbach, G. 2004. "Political interviews as a hybrid genre." In *TEXT: Special Issue: Media Discourse – Extensions, Mixes, and Hybrids*, J.-O. Östman and A. Simon-Vandenbergen (eds), 24 (3): 353–397. Berlin et al.: Mouton de Gruyter.

Levinson, S. 1983. *Pragmatics*. Cambridge: CUP.

Levinson, S. 1987. "What's special about conversational inference." In *Course Material for the Pragmatics Seminar 11 274*, L. Horn and S. Levinson (eds), Stanford: Linguistics Institute.

Malmkjaer, K. 2002. "Metaphor." In *The Linguistic Encyclopedia*, K. Malmkjaer (ed.), 350–354. London: Routledge.

Montgomery, M., Tolson, A. and Garton, G. 1989. "Media discourse in the 1987 general election: ideology, scripts and metaphors." *English Language Research* 3: 173–204.

Ortony, A. 1979. "Metaphors: a multidimensional problem." In *Metaphor and Thought*, A. Ortony (ed.), 1–16. Cambridge et al.: CUP.

Schieß, R. this volume. "Information meets entertainment: a visual analysis of election night TV programs across cultures."

Schulz, T. 2004. "Was ist RTL?" *Der Spiegel* 26: 176–178.

Searle, J. R. 1979. "Metaphor." In *Metaphor and Thought*, A. Ortony (ed.), 92–123. Cambridge et al.: CUP.

Thornton, A. and Lin, H. (eds). 1994. *Social Change and the Family in Taiwan*. Chicago: University of Chicago Press.

Wei, J. M. 2003. "Politics is marriage and show business. A view from recent Taiwanese political discourse." In *New Media Language*, J. Aitchison and D. M. Lewis (eds), 126–135. London/New York: Routledge.

Wilson, J. 1990. "Power to the people: political metaphors." In *Politically Speaking*, J. Wilson, 104–130. Oxford: Blackwell.

PART III

Discursive practice in political interviews

"Are you saying ...?"

A cross-cultural analysis of interviewing practices in TV election night coverages

Annette Becker
Frankfurt am Main, Germany

During election night coverages, TV channels make extended use of talk-in-interaction through interviews with politicians and experts. This paper examines and cross-culturally compares the form and function of question-answer-routines in political and expert interviews. The methodology employed is informed by pragmatics, conversation analysis, and appraisal theory. The study shows that the choice of linguistic strategies is closely connected to the function of an interview within the overall context of the media event. This can be observed across cultures.

1. Introduction

Election night broadcasts on television usually contain a multitude of monologic genres, such as reports, and dialogic genres, such as interviews. In *The Media Interview: Confession, Contest, Conversation*, Bell and van Leeuwen (1994) outline the general role of the interview in the broadcasting media as follows:

> The interview has become a dominant mode of conveying information in the broadcasting media. Much of our news and current affairs show us, not what happened, but what people say about what happened (or might have happened, or will happen), and makes us eye- (and ear-) witnesses, not of events that would have occurred if no microphones and cameras had been present, but of events specially created for the purpose of being reported, such as press conferences and interviews. (Bell and van Leeuwen 1994: 1)

Within their election night broadcasts, television channels stage a vast array of news genres, including interviews, for the above-mentioned "purpose of being reported" (Bell and van Leeuwen 1994: 1). In doing so, they present the process of nation-wide decision-making as a dynamic live event. Interviewing practices play an active part in the discursive construction and reproduction of a channel's identity. Generally, interviews conducted within election night broadcasts belong to two distinct sub-genres. Depending on the social and discursive identities of the interviewees, these two sub-genres are, firstly, interviews with politicians and, secondly, interviews with experts. This paper combines qualitative and quantitative methods for a cross-cultural analysis of British, German and U.S.-American interviewers' questioning practices. Data is taken from the videotaped and transcribed opening phases of nine national and international election night broadcasts.[1]

2. Theoretical background

Research from various disciplines such as sociology, critical discourse analysis and pragmatics has shown that it is advisable to adopt a dynamic view on cultures. Cultures can be interpreted as sets of practices shared by members of a society, or members of a social group. Most of these practices are discursive in nature. Speakers and writers employ them in order to produce or exchange meanings. (Hall 1997) Producing and exchanging meanings also includes the discursive production and exchange of social meanings, such as interpersonal relationships. Across cultures, discursive practices may vary considerably. Such differences are one of the main concerns of researchers from cross-cultural pragmatics and contrastive discourse analysis (e.g. Blum-Kulka, House and Kasper 1989; House 1996). Within critical linguistics and pragmatics, discursive practices have also been described as rhetorical styles (Fairclough 2000), or as communicative style (Selting 1999). For instance, Fairclough (2000:96) observes that "(a) rhetorical style is not an invariable way of using language, it is rather a mixture of different ways of using language, a distinctive repertoire". This "mixture" is not at all at random. Speakers and writers choose between linguistic options in a purposeful, goal-oriented way. As Selting (1999:1) suggests, styles are "meaningful choices made in order to achieve particular effects or to suggest particular interpretations". In spoken communication, the choice between styles is at its most dynamic:

---

1. This paper is part of the research project "Television Discourse", supported by the German Research Foundation (DFG) and directed by Gerda Lauerbach. The goal of the project is a comparative discourse analysis of election night (and, in the case of the US presidential election of 2000, post-election night) television coverage in the United States, Great Britain and Germany. For more information, see http://web.uni-frankfurt.de/zenaf/projekte/TVdiscourses/lauerbach.htm.

> Styles in spoken natural language have been shown as having the following proper-
> ties: Rather than simply applying pre-fabricated styles, speakers actively construct
> communicative styles as dynamic, flexible and alter(n)able linguistic structures,
> i.e. styles of speaking and styles of conversation. These styles are constructed and
> interpreted as contextualisation cues in relation to contextual stylistic norms and
> expectations as well as to fit the recipient design for the particular recipient(s) and
> their reactions in the context of social interaction. (Selting 1999: 2)

However, as mentioned above, choosing between stylistic options is not merely a
matter of individual taste:

> In relation to an activity type or genre that can be kept constant as tertium com-
> parationis, meaningful different ways of constituting this activity type or genre
> can be described as different communicative styles. Styles suggest additional
> social or interactional meanings which often have to do with self-presentation,
> definition of the situation, defining of the relationship between speaker and re-
> cipient, framing of activities and situations, etc. (Selting 1999)

When examining communicative styles in media interviews, one has to bear in
mind that such media interviews belong to the realm of what is known as "institutional talk", a term introduced by researchers from Conversation Analysis
(CA). Most CA studies set off institutional talk against ordinary conversation.
(e.g. Drew and Heritage 1992) This is criticised by authors like McElhinny who
warn against constructing an ideologically biased dichotomy between ordinary
and institutional talk (McElhinny 1997, quot. in Thornborrow 2002: 3). Therefore,
Thornborrow (2002) formulates a more neutral definition of institutional talk:

1. Talk that has differentiated, pre-inscribed and conventional participant roles,
    or identities, whether it takes place in a school classroom, in a TV or radio
    studio or in a police interview room (…).
2. Talk in which there is a structurally asymmetrical distribution of turn types
    between the participants such that speakers with different institutional iden-
    tities typically occupy different discursive identities; that is, they get different
    types of turns in which they do different kinds of things (for example, in-
    terviewers conventionally ask questions, interviewees answer them; teachers
    nominate which pupil will speak next, pupils respond).
3. Talk in which there is also an asymmetrical relationship between participants
    in terms of speaker rights and obligations. This means that certain types of
    utterances are seen as legitimate for some speakers but not for others (…).
4. Talk in which the discursive resources and identities available to participants
    to accomplish specific actions are either weakened or strengthened in relation
    to their current institutional identities.

In short, institutional discourse can be described as talk which sets up positions for people to talk from and restricts some speakers' access to certain kinds of discursive action (Thornborrow 2002: 4).

All these criteria are valid for election night interviews on television, too. But how can the discursive practices employed by interviewers from different cultural backgrounds be analysed and compared in more detail? For the critical analysis of discourse in general, various researchers have argued in favour of multi-disciplinary approaches (cf. e.g. the contributions in Wodak and Meyer 2001). Within such multi-disciplinary approaches, linguistic analysis is seen as one important tool among others. However, it has been suggested that linguistic research itself should be multi-dimensional. As to the linguistic analysis of political discourses, Chilton and Schäffner (1997) postulate that "(a)n analyst of political discourse needs to refer to:

1. *pragmatics* (interaction among speakers and hearers)
2. *semantics* (meaning, structure of lexicon)
3. *syntax* (the internal organisation of sentences) (Chilton and Schäffner 1997: 214)

Observations on these linguistic levels should be linked to the strategic political functions of "coercion, resistance, opposition, protest, dissimulation, legitimisation and delegitimisation" (Chilton and Schäffner 1997: 226). News interviews have been analysed from various theoretical perspectives such as pragmatics (Jucker 1986) and Conversation Analysis (Clayman and Heritage 2002). Other forms of interviews have been examined as well (e.g. Stax 2004). Cross-cultural analysis of news interviews may yield valuable insights as to how differently interviewers and interviewees construct and negotiate their discursive identities within various sub-genres of interviews and their hybrids (cf. Lauerbach 2004; Becker 2005). While no approach, be it mono-disciplinary or multi-disciplinary, will be fully able to analyse all these aspects in depth, it has proven fruitful for the cross-cultural analysis of TV election night interviews to combine tools from different research perspectives, and to evaluate the results quantitatively, as quantitative methods have yielded valuable insights for the analysis of linguistic resources within other genres as well (cf. Ford and Thompson 1996; Reaser 2003). The dimensions of communicative style examined for this paper are outlined in Section 4 "Method and Analysis" below, following a brief survey over the data in Section 3 "Data".

3. Data

Data for the analysis presented in this paper is taken from the videotaped and transcribed opening sections of six national and three international TV election night broadcasts from the 1997 U.K. General Election, the 1998 German *Bundestagswahl* (Parliamentary Election), and the 2000 U.S.A. Presidential Election: BBC, ITV and CCN-I on the U.K. General Election; ARD, RTL and CNN-I on the 1998 German *Bundestagswahl*; and NBC and CNN on the 2000 U.S.A. Presidential Election. Opening sections are defined as the first approximately 20 minutes of an election night broadcast. Within these 20 minutes, all channels introduce their studio, their most important studio personnel and their most relevant external reporters e.g. in the party headquarters. As national and international channels differ significantly in their choice of either politicians or experts as interviewees, these two sub-sets of data are examined separately for each channel.

National channels usually interview representatives of as many political parties as possible. During the opening sections of their election night coverages, they tend to concentrate on representatives of the most relevant political parties, depending on the election system. For instance, after the 1997 U.K. General Election, anchor David Dimbleby from the BBC interviewed only representatives from the two major parties during the opening section of the election night broadcast, whereas German ARD also conducted several brief interviews with representatives of the minor parties who may, due to the German election system, substantially influence the outcome of a German *Bundestagswahl*.

International channels tend to concentrate on interviews with political experts. Many of these experts are professional journalists themselves. Information delivered by such experts often supplies background explanations about facts that are possibly unfamiliar to an international audience. For instance, in the opening section of the German election night 1998, anchor Nik Gowing from BBC World extensively interviewed expert Heinz Schulte about the complicated German voting system.

During the opening sections of the nine election night broadcasts analysed for this paper, 11 television journalists interviewed nine politicians and seven experts. Two channels showed two different interviewers. Seven channels showed only one interviewing person. On all channels, the anchors themselves did at least some if not all of the interviewing. The majority of interviewees was interviewed only once. One of the politicians was interviewed twice, and one of the experts was interviewed four times. All in all, 11 interviewers conducted 19 interviews, nine with politicians, ten with experts. The number of interviews within an opening section varied from one to four. Interviews contained between two and seven questioning turns. The total number of interviewing turns per opening section

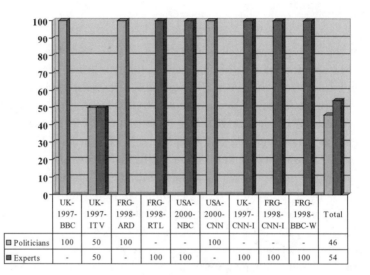

Figure 1. Politicians and Experts – Distribution [in %]

varied from two to 20. Politicians were interviewed by four out of six national channels, and not at all by the international channels. BBC, ARD and CNN showed interviews with politicians only, ITV interviewed one politician and one expert, RTL and NBC and all international channels only interviewed experts. Figure 1 illustrates the nine channels' choices of interviewees.

All interviews were transcribed and analysed firstly qualitatively, then quantitatively as outlined in Section 4 "Method and Analysis".

4.   Method and analysis

This paper seeks to cross-culturally compare aspects of communicative styles that are characteristic of individual television channels. Therefore, the analysis of interviews with politicians and experts focuses on discursive contributions under the immediate control of the channels and their representatives, i.e. on interviewers' linguistic strategies for the construction of interpersonal meaning. For this analysis, the framework outlined in Becker (2005) was slightly modified. 65 questioning turns from the opening sections of nine election night broadcasts were qualitatively analysed with respect to *addressee orientation* (Section 4.1), *complexity* (Section 4.2), *question type* (Section 4.3), *appraisal* (Section 4.4), and *discursive functions* (Section 4.5). The results were evaluated quantitatively, and represented in bar charts for a preliminary comparative overview. The most frequent patterns of *feature combinations* were evaluated separately (Section 4.6). The analysis of

both single features and feature combinations was summed up in nine preliminary channel profiles (Section 5). These profiles are, in the long run, to be worked
out in more detail on the basis of a larger data corpus with interviews from the
entire national and international election night broadcasts. Therefore, the analysis
based on the openings of the election night coverages also serves as a test run for
this combination of qualitative and quantitative methods. For the sake of clarity,
the presentation of results proceeds from macro to micro and back, starting with
the discursive construction of interpersonal relationships (Section 4.1 "Addressee
Orientation").

4.1 Addressee orientation

How do speakers establish their interpersonal relationship in discourse? As House
(1996) observes, English and German native speaker discourse tends to show characteristic phenomena in five central dimensions of cross-cultural difference:[2]

Table 1.

English		German
Indirectness	↔	Directness
Orientation towards Other	↔	Orientation towards Self
Orientation towards Addressees	↔	Orientation towards Content
Implicitness	↔	Explicitness
Verbal Routines	↔	Ad-Hoc-Formulation

This paper combines the dimensions of "Orientation towards Other / Self" and
"Orientation towards Addressees / Content", distinguishing between *high, medium and low addressee orientation*. These three categories were developed by
Becker (2005) to faciliate cross-cultural empirical analyis regarding the degree to
which interviewers linguistically orient towards their addressees, which is indicated by their use or avoidance of *nominal* or *pronominal terms of address* in their
questions. Jucker and Taavitsainen (2003) define terms of address as follows:

> Terms of address are linguistic expressions that speakers use to appeal directly to
> their addressees. In English, for instance, Sir is used in addressing only, but other
> words used in addressing like you, Helen, daddy, darling or Professor Braun have
> other functions as well as they are used to talk about other persons rather than
> talk to them, and you can be used generically. Address terms can take the form
> of pronouns, nouns, verb forms and other affixes. (Braun 1998: 2; see also Braun,
> Kohz and Schubert 1986: xv–xvi)

---

2.   House (1996) uses the term 'English' with reference to British English.

> Pronominal forms of address often distinguish between a familiar or intimate
> pronoun on the one hand and a distant or polite pronoun on the other. (...)
> Brown and Gilman (1960: 254) introduced the conventions of using T and V to
> talk about the choice between these two pronominal forms of address in many
> European languages. (...)
> Nominal forms of address include a wide range of nouns. Typical examples are
> names (Peter, Sally), kinship terms (mom, granny), titles, (Sir, Your Excellence),
> military ranks (officer) and occupational terms. (teacher). (...)
> Terms of address may differ according to the formality of the situation, the social
> relationship between the speaker and the addressee, the politeness or deference
> that the speaker wants to extend to the addressee, to name a few of the most im-
> portant underlying motivations for choosing an option. (Jucker and Taavitsainen
> 2003: 1–2)

Becker (2005) assumes that *high addressee orientation* is represented in discourse
by both nominal and pronominal forms of address, as highlighted in (1):

(1)   Well, **Mr Prescott**, it looks as though **you**'ve done it this time! [UK 1997,
      BBC, anchor David Dimbleby in his first questioning turn addressed to John
      Prescott, Labour Deputy Leader]

Similarly, the term *medium addressee orientation* is associated with either nominal reference (2) or pronominal reference (3), i.e. only one of the two reference
types relevant for high addressee orientation:

(2)   **Doris**, this is almost a mirror image because, in that race, it was Richard
      Nixon who closed fast at the end. In this race, it does appear that Al Gore
      has been closing some at the end. [USA 2000, NBC, anchor Tom Brokaw in
      his first questioning turn addressed to Doris Kearns-Goodwin, expert on
      history]

(3)   First reaction! What do **you** think of the numbers? [FRG 1998, CNN-I,
      anchor Bettina Lüscher in her first questioning turn to political expert Stefan
      Baron]

Finally, *low addressee orientation* is associated with the lack of any kind of address
terms (4):[3]

---

3.   Cf. Simon-Vandenbergen (2000) on the "power/solidarity function of pronominal choices"
in talkshows. I do not use the term *involvement* (Eggins and Slade 1997; Martin 1997) for this
dimension of interpersonal meaning, because involvement is more complex and includes resources like swearing, slang or anti-language, which are rare to non-existent in the election
night interviews.

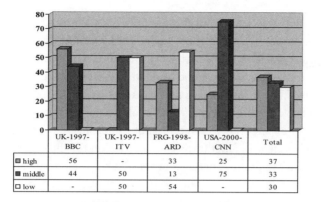

	UK-1997-BBC	UK-1997-ITV	FRG-1998-ARD	USA-2000-CNN	Total
□ high	56	-	33	25	37
■ middle	44	50	13	75	33
□ low	-	50	54	-	30

Figure 2a. Addressee Orientation – Interviews with politicians [in %]

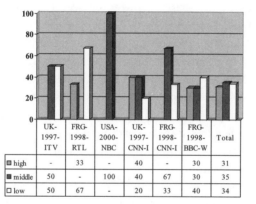

	UK-1997-ITV	FRG-1998-RTL	USA-2000-NBC	UK-1997-CNN-I	FRG-1998-CNN-I	FRG-1998-BBC-W	Total
□ high	-	33	-	40	-	30	31
■ middle	50	-	100	40	67	30	35
□ low	50	67	-	20	33	40	34

Figure 2b. Addressee Orientation – Interviews with experts [in %]

(4)   Die Zukunft für die Koalition sieht nicht gut aus nach dieser Prognose. (The coalition's future does not look good, according to this forecast.) [FRG 1998, ARD, interviewer Wolfgang Kenntemich in his first questioning turn addressed to Jürgen Rüttgers, the CDU's former Minister of Future]

Figures 2a and 2b show the distribution of the different types of addressee orientation exhibited by journalists interviewing either politicians, or experts. "Total" refers to the percentage of turns carrying a particular feature within the 30 questioning turns addressed to politicians (Figure 2a), and within the 35 questioning turns addressed to experts (Figure 2b).

As these figures show, interviewers used high addressee orientation slightly more frequently when interviewing politicians (37%) than when interviewing experts (31%). Middle addressee orientation was used in nearly equal frequency (questioning turns addressed to politicians: 33%, to experts: 35%), whereas low addressee orientation was used more frequently with experts (34%) than with politicians (30%). At first sight, this might lead to the hypothesis that interviewing politicians generally involves more face-work than interviewing experts, either because a larger social distance has to be bridged, or because such interviews are often about potentially face-threatening topics, like losing an election. At the same time, as the number of politician interviews analysed for this paper was higher than the number of expert interviews, one might interpret the correspondingly higher number of sequence-initial turns as a motivation for the higher frequency of high addressee orientation, because in these turns the interpersonal frame (Scollon 1998) is established. But, apparently, this is not the case in the three of the four channels covering the German election 1998. On the ARD, low addressee orientation is used in more than half of the interviews with politicians (54%). This is only surpassed by the share of low addressee orientation in the expert interview broadcast by German RTL (67%). Interestingly, the proportion of low addressee orientation on BBC World is above average, too (40%). At first sight, one might be tempted to assume that this might suggest a kind of accommodation process (Giles, Coupland and Coupland 1991) for the communicative style an interviewer from an international channel chooses when interviewing native speakers from another country, as it is the case here. Findings from the examination of other linguistic features seem to corroborate this hypothesis, such as the distribution of different types of turn complexity (Section 4.2). However, taking a closer look at the discursive functions of the turns containing low addressee orientation reveals that there are other relevant factors determining this choice. This will be discussed in Sections 4.5 and 4.6. All in all, the results of the qualitative and quantitative cross-cultural analysis of addressee orientation in election night interviews with politicians correspond closely to House's findings: Both British and U.S.-American interviewers oriented more explicitly towards their political interviewees than German interviewers, using more high and middle instead of low addressee orientation.

In the expert interviews, a slight majority of interviewer turns was uttered with medium addressee orientation (35%), closely followed by low addressee orientation (34%), whereas high addressee orientation was used in 31% of the turns. This is mainly due to the striking frequency of low addressee orientation in the German channel RTL (67%), and in BBC World on the German election (40%), as interviewers from the other channels tend to prefer middle addressee orientation, or a combination of middle and high addressee orientation. Thus, both the results from interviews with politicians and interviews with experts correspond closely to House's (1996) observations regarding an English tendency in favour of "Orientation towards Other" and "Orientation towards Addressees", and a German tendency toward "Orientation towards Self" and "Orientation towards Content".

Regarding House's observations on directness, or indirectness, the question arose how these two criteria could be effectively coded for empirical evaluation. Politeness theory suggests that directness and indirectness are closely related to the amount of linguistic effort put into an utterance (Brown and Levinson 1978). Therefore, Section 4.2 examines the dimension of *complexity*.

4.2 Complexity

Questioning activities within turns may come singly or in a series. They may be prefaced and/or postfaced. For the purpose of this analysis, the terminology of Linell, Hofvendahl and Lindholm (2003) was adopted. They distinguish between *single-unit questioning turns* as in (5) and *multi-unit questioning turns* (MUQTs) as in (6):

(5)   Heinz, what do these figures now tell us? [FRG 1998, BBC World, anchor Nik Gowing to Heinz Schulte, political expert]

(6)   Looking back on the campaign, Dr Mawhinney, were you happy with the way it went all the way through, are there things you like to have done differently? [U.K. 1997, BBC, anchor David Dimbleby to Brian Mawhinney, Conservative Party Chairman]

MUQTs are defined as a family of turn types that fulfil the following conditions: Firstly, they consist of "two or more turn-constructional units (TCUs), which are delivered together, either in one single turn or in a close-knit turn sequence with no intervening substantial responder" (Linell, Hofvendahl and Lindholm 2003: 540). Secondly, "one or more of the TCUs are formally designed as questions, or, more precisely, interrogatives, that is, such a TCU is marked by one or several interrogative indicators" (Linell, Hofvendahl and Lindholm 2003: 540). The structure of MUQTs may vary considerably. MUQTs may consist of various combinations of interrogative and non-interrogative elements, such as a series of interrogatives, or prefaces and/or postfaces to interrogatives. Sometimes, like in (6), it is hard to impossible to decide whether a MUQT is to be interpreted as a series of interrogatives, or as prefaced/postfaced. Therefore, this analysis distinguishes only between single-unit questioning turns and multi-unit questioning turns, assuming that the use of these turn types corresponds to House's dimensions of "directness" and "indirectness".

Research from Conversational Analysis suggests that the choice between single-unit questioning turns and multi-unit questioning turns may serve as a strategic linguistic option for both confrontational and cooperative goals:

Clayman and Heritage (2002) argue that in the sometimes confrontational context of press conferences, single-unit questioning turns are neutral and information-seeking, whereas MUQTs are assertive and opinionated. Yet, the distribution of MUQTs is similar in the maternal health care encounters of Linell and Bredmar (1996), which is a conversationalized and cooperative activity, in which parties seek to develop mutual rapport. Here too, new agenda points are preferably delivered in multi-unit designs, whereas other information gathering questions are single-unit turns. (Linell, Hofvendahl and Lindholm 2003: 541)

Multi-unit questioning turns often serve to accomplish conflicting communicative goals at the same time (for details see Linell, Hofvendahl and Lindholm 2003). For instance, communicative effort of this kind may serve to mitigate the negative impact of a face-threatening-question (Brown and Levinson 1978; Fraser 1990; Eelen 2001; Watts 2003). Further major functions, especially in media interviews conducted with an overhearing mass audience, are the contextualisation of an interviewer's question, e.g. by the more or less neutral rendering of background information, or the more or less subtle suggestion of candidate answers. In expert interviews, interviewers often use multi-unit questioning turns to collaboratively co-construct the news story. Quantitative analysis shows that most multi-unit questioning turns appear in expert interviews (Figure 3b), whereas most interviews with politicians make use of both types (Figure 3a).

In interviews with politicians, single-unit turns and multi-unit turns appear in equal shares, whereas the majority of questioning turns addressed to experts are multi-unit turns (74%). ITV is the only channel that uses single-unit turns throughout. BBC World is the only channel using both single-unit turns and multi-unit turns in its expert interviews. This may lead to the rash conclusion that interviewers generally put more quantitative communicative effort into their questioning turns addressed to experts, whereas less communicative effort is invested in interviews with politicians. However, one must not overgeneralise the

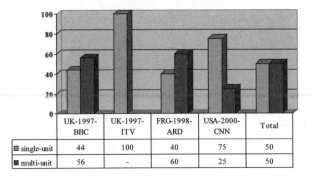

	UK-1997-BBC	UK-1997-ITV	FRG-1998-ARD	USA-2000-CNN	Total
single-unit	44	100	40	75	50
multi-unit	56	-	60	25	50

Figure 3a. Complexity – Interviews with politicians [in %]

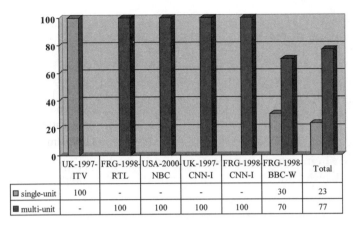

	UK-1997-ITV	FRG-1998-RTL	USA-2000-NBC	UK-1997-CNN-I	FRG-1998-CNN-I	FRG-1998-BBC-W	Total
single-unit	100	-	-	-	-	30	23
multi-unit	-	100	100	100	100	70	77

Figure 3b. Complexity – Interviews with experts [in %]

neutrality of seemingly straightforward *single-unit turns*. In all kinds of turns, interviewers also strategically employ further discursive resources to control an interviewee's answers. One of their most important linguistic means of control is the choice of *question type* (Section 4.3).

4.3 Question type

All types of questions aim at answers of a particular kind. Whereas closed questions like *yes-no-questions* (7) and *alternative questions* (8) only allow for a limited range of answers, open questions like *wh-questions* (9) seek to elicit more elaborate answers (cf. Quirk et al. 1985; Friedrichs and Schwinges 1999; Beard 2000; Rost-Roth 2003):[4]

(7)   Frau Müller, Gleichstand Bündnis 90/Die Grünen mit der F.D.P., theoretisch kann es jetzt sein, dass Sie mitregieren werden. Sind Sie denn bereit? (Ms Müller, a tie between the Green Party and the F.D.P., theoretically you might now be in the government. Are you ready for that?) [FRG 1998, ARD, anchor Marion van Haaren to Kerstin Müller, speaker of the Green Party]

(8)   Well, Heinz Schulte, what about the reasons why chancellor Kohl has done much worse than anyone would have expected? Can anyone put their fingers on – you are a political analyst – and say "was it his arrogance, was it his belief in himself, was it the fact that he didn't take the party with him" or just simply

---

4. Subtypes, like echo questions or elliptical questions, were subsumed under these headings, depending on the expected answer. In case of doubt, the subsequent answer, e.g. the recipient's interpretation, was used for orientation.

that he was out of touch after sixteen years in the chancellery? [FRG 1998, BBC, anchor Nik Gowing to Heinz Schulte, political expert]

(9)   Was hat dieser Schröder, was Kohl nicht hat? Was macht ihn so attraktiv für die Wähler? (What has this Schröder got that Kohl lacks? What makes him so attractive for the voters?) [FRG 1998, RTL, anchor Peter Klöppel to Johannes Groß, political expert]

Figure 4a and 4b show the distribution of the different types of questions used by interviewers in interviews with politicians and experts.

More than half of all questioning turns directed at politicians and experts were closed questions of the yes-no-type. Experts were asked a comparatively high share of wh-questions as well (37%), whereas politicians were asked the highest share of yes-no questions (67%). Alternative questions were asked only by BBC,

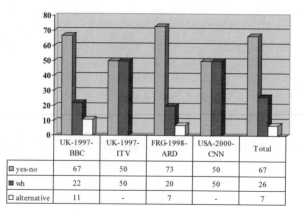

	UK-1997-BBC	UK-1997-ITV	FRG-1998-ARD	USA-2000-CNN	Total
yes-no	67	50	73	50	67
wh	22	50	20	50	26
alternative	11	-	7	-	7

Figure 4a. Question Type – Interviews with politicians [in %]

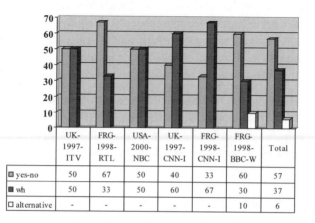

	UK-1997-ITV	FRG-1998-RTL	USA-2000-NBC	UK-1997-CNN-I	FRG-1998-CNN-I	FRG-1998-BBC-W	Total
yes-no	50	67	50	40	33	60	57
wh	50	33	50	60	67	30	37
alternative	-	-	-	-	-	10	6

Figure 4b. Question Type – Interviews with experts [in %]

ARD and BBC World. Apart from these quite explicit means of discourse control, interviewers frequently used various kinds of *appraisal resources*, as explained in Section 4.4.

4.4 Appraisal

Appraisal theory is a theoretical approach developed during the last fifteen years by systemic-functional linguists, and one of the theoretical orientations of the Frankfurt TV Discourse Analysis Project. *Appraisal theory* seeks to describe the linguistic resources speakers or writers use for evaluative purposes, always bearing in mind at least one real or virtual person as a co-active recipient. Central to *Appraisal theory* is the Bakhtinian perspective that all texts, either written or spoken, are dialogic in nature. This dynamic perspective has been adopted amongst others by Eggins and Slade (1997), Martin (1992, 1997), and White (2001a, 2001b). As *appraisal theory* is constantly being cross-checked against empirical data, it is currently undergoing noticeable changes (for an overview and recent updates see White 2002; Martin 2003; Martin and White 2005). This paper analyses how interviewers make use of the three main systems of appraisal resources as outlined by White (2001a, 2001b). These are *engagement* (4.4.1), *graduation* (4.4.2), and *attitude* (4.4.3).

4.4.1 *Engagement*
The appraisal system of *engagement* "includes values which have been analysed in the literature under headings such as attribution, modality, hearsay, concession, polarity, evidentiality, hedges, boosters and metadiscursives" (White 2001b). "Engagement covers resources that introduce additional voices into a discourse, via projection, modalisation, or concession; the key choice here is one voice (*monogloss*), or more than one voice (*heterogloss*)" (Martin and Rose 2003: 54). Originally, these categories were developed for the analysis of monologic genres, not for dialogic genres like interviews. However, questions are not per se heteroglossic. When interviewers use declaratives as questions, they choose between increasing (10), or limiting the number of voices in the discourse (11):

(10) Well, Mr Prescott, it looks as though you've done it this time! [UK 1997, BBC, anchor David Dimbleby in his first questioning turn addressed to John Prescott, Labour Deputy Leader

(11) Sie wählen Schröder. (You will vote for Schröder.) [FRG 1998, ARD, anchor Wolfgang Kenntemich to Heidi Knake-Werner, PDS Parliamentary Party Deputy Leader]

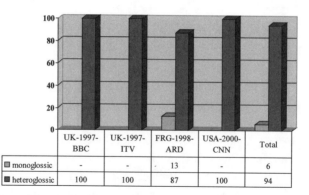

	UK-1997-BBC	UK-1997-ITV	FRG-1998-ARD	USA-2000-CNN	Total
▢ monoglossic	-	-	13	-	6
▪ heteroglossic	100	100	87	100	94

Figure 5a. Engagement – Interviews with politicians [in %]

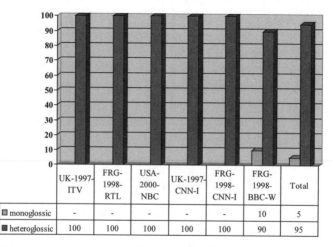

	UK-1997-ITV	FRG-1998-RTL	USA-2000-NBC	UK-1997-CNN-I	FRG-1998-CNN-I	FRG-1998-BBC-W	Total
▢ monoglossic	-	-	-	-	-	10	5
▪ heteroglossic	100	100	100	100	100	90	95

Figure 5b. Engagement – Interviews with experts [in %]

Only a "'bare' declarative" (White 2001a/b) as in (11) is labelled as *monoglossic*. This option was chosen very rarely within the corpus, as Figures 5a and 5b show.

Monoglossic engagement only appears in the ARD interviews with politicians and in the BBC World expert interviews. This may be interpreted as an accommodation process (Giles, Coupland and Coupland 1991) as outlined in Section 4.1 "Addressee Orientation", an adaptation of German discursive strategies with their bias towards the direct and straightforward (House 1996). In both *monoglossic* and *heteroglossic turns*, interviewers may choose to further modify their questions by using resources from the *appraisal system* of *graduation* (4.4.2).

4.4.2 *Graduation*

If a question is modified by items like 'a little' or 'certainly', this belongs to the appraisal system of *graduation*. Graduation refers to "[v]alues by which speakers

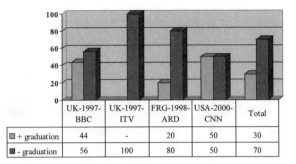

Figure 6a. Graduation – Interviews with politicians [in %]

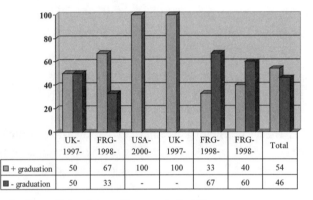

Figure 6b. Graduation – Interviews with experts [in %]

graduate (raise or lower) the interpersonal impact, force or volume of their utterances, and by which they graduate (blur or sharpen) the focus of their semantic categorisations" (White 2001b). This appraisal resource was only coded as being either activated (12) or neutral (13), but without any further differentiation regarding its subtypes.

(12)   Mike, if this exit poll is correct, it really is the most astonishing turnaround.[U.K. 1997, ITV, anchor Jonathan Dimbleby to Michael Brunson, political expert]

(13)   Heinz, what do these figures now tell us? [FRG 1998, BBC World, anchor Nik Gowing to Heinz Schulte, political expert]

Figure 6a and 6b show whether interviewers used graduation resources when questioning politicians, or experts.

Graduation was used to a higher extent in interviews with experts (54%) than in interviews with politicians (30%). This parallels roughly the distribution of single-unit turns and multi-unit turns as outlined in Section 4.3 "Complexity". Whereas graduation can be seen as a mainly quantifying resource, qualitative evaluations, on the other hand, are the objectives of the appraisal system of *attitude* (4.4.3).

4.4.3 *Attitude*

Attitude is concerned with evaluative positioning on an ethical, aesthetic, or emotional level. The corresponding sub-types of attitude are labelled *judgement, appreciation*, and *affect*. *Judgement* is associated with the evaluation of persons and their actions according to normative values. *Appreciation* refers to the evaluation of objects or facts according to aesthetical values, whereas *affect* is a resource for expressing subjective emotional reactions to either persons or facts (White 2001a, 2001b). For this paper, the appraisal resource of attitude was only coded as being either activated (14) or neutral (15), but without any further differentiation regarding its three subtypes.

(14)   On these voter guides, have you put to rest people's criticism that you're violating campaign law? [USA 2000, CNN, anchor Bernard Shaw to Pat Robertson, Christian Coalition President]

(15)   Ist das Thema Beteiligung an einer SPD-Grünen-Regierung ein Thema für die F.D.P.? (Is the topic of participating in a SPD-Green government an issue for the F.D.P.?) [FRG 1998, ARD, anchor Wolfgang Kenntemich to Jörg van Essen, Parliamentary Executive Director]

Figure 7a and 7b show whether interviewers used resources from the appraisal system of attitude when questioning politicians, or experts.

These figures show that more than half of all questioning turns contain some kind of evaluation to which a reaction is sought, with a slight majority on the side of the questioning turns addressed to politicians (60%). And again, BBC World seems quite "German" in its profile, with a striking parallel in the 1998 election night broadcast by CNN-I.

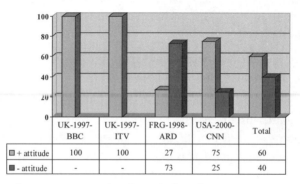

	UK-1997-BBC	UK-1997-ITV	FRG-1998-ARD	USA-2000-CNN	Total
▣ + attitude	100	100	27	75	60
▉ - attitude	-	-	73	25	40

Figure 7a. Attitude – Interviews with politicians [in %]

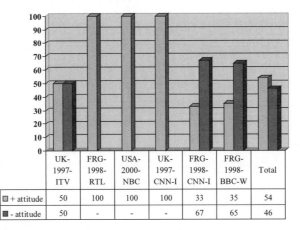

	UK-1997-ITV	FRG-1998-RTL	USA-2000-NBC	UK-1997-CNN-I	FRG-1998-CNN-I	FRG-1998-BBC-W	Total
+ attitude	50	100	100	100	33	35	54
- attitude	50	-	-	-	67	65	46

Figure 7b. Attitude – Interviews with experts [in %]

So far, analysis has concentrated on potential features of interviewer turns taken out of their discursive contexts. Within their discursive contexts, interviewer turns may have several *discursive functions*. These are explained in Section 4.5.

4.5 Discursive functions

Strategic sequencing of questioning activities is an important discursive resource for interviews (Lauerbach 2001; Clayman and Heritage 2002). It is also explicitly recommended in handbooks for journalists by authors like Friedrich and Schwinges (1999). Within a sequence of questioning turns, turns are used to accomplish different goals. Most questioning activities within the corpus were *questions* in the sense of "[a]ny topic-initiating turn by IR, asking for information or yes-no-response" (Lauerbach 2001: 201) It is important to state that the term question is used strictly functionally here, not in a grammatical sense. Questions usually take the grammatical form of an interrogative as in (17), but other grammatical forms are possible as well, e.g. declaratives such as in (18):

(17)   Frau Bergmann, noch steht das Ergebnis nicht fest, aber es sieht alles danach aus, dass es einen Regierungswechsel geben wird. Hatten Sie mit einer so deutlichen Führung gerechnet? (Ms Bergmann, there is no result yet, but a change of government is apparent. Did you respect such a clear leadership?) [FRG 1998, ARD, anchor Marion van Haaren to Christine Bergmann, SPD]

(18)   Well, Mr Prescott, it looks as though you've done it this time! [UK 1997, BBC, anchor David Dimbleby in his first questioning turn addressed to John Prescott, Labour Deputy Leader]

Follow-ups are requests for clarification, or interviewer activities "[c]ontinuing" (Lauerbach 2001:201) or elaborating a previous question on a topic (19):

(19)   Frau Bergmann, die wichtigste Frage in diesem Zusammenhang ist ja, mit wem werden Sie denn in Zukunft zusammengehen? (Ms Bergmann, the most important question in this respect is, who are you going to co-operate with?) [FRG 1998, ARD, anchor Marion van Haaren to Christine Bergmann, SPD]

Formulations are used by interviewers to "preserve relevant features of a previous utterance while also recasting them" (Heritage and Watson 1979:129) Thus, they provide "a candidate reading for a preceding stretch of talk" (Heritage and Watson 1979:138) and may serve as an efficient tool "to control the direction of the talk" (Thornborrow 2002:97) (20):

(20)   Are you saying you accept that Labour has won? [U.K. 1997, BBC, anchor David Dimbleby to Brian Mawhinney, Conservative Party Chairman]

Like formulations, *challenges* are also responding turns, with the interviewer "questioning aspects of IE's response" (Lauerbach 2001:201).[5] This is typically indicated by discourse markers like 'but' (21):

(21)   But are you saying you think there's a chance Mr Major has won, surely your own polls are telling you that's not possible, are they? [U.K. 1997, BBC, anchor David Dimbleby to Brian Mawhinney, Conservative Party Chairman]

Figure 8a and 8b show the distribution of the different types of discursive functions of interviewers' turns in interviews with politicians and experts.

Within the corpus, only politicians' answers are either formulated or challenged. This suggests that, generally, interviews with politicians tend to be more confrontational, whereas expert interviews are conducted in a more co-operative way. Is it possible, then, to identify any generally preferred feature combinations for either sub-genre? Section 4.6 discusses four patterns that indeed appeared most frequently.

4.6   Feature combinations

Out of 579 potential feature combinations, a small group of only four patterns occurred in 24, 62% of the 65 questioning turns. These patterns were grouped into Type 1 and Type 2. Type 1 (13,85%) refers to questioning turns in which an

---

5.   Some researchers also use "challenge" for interviewees' reactions to interviewer questions (e.g. Koshik 2003), or for any potentially face-threatening utterance within an interview (e.g. Blum-Kulka 1983).

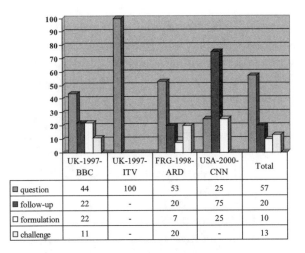

	UK-1997-BBC	UK-1997-ITV	FRG-1998-ARD	USA-2000-CNN	Total
▣ question	44	100	53	25	57
■ follow-up	22	-	20	75	20
☐ formulation	22	-	7	25	10
☐ challenge	11	-	20	-	13

Figure 8a. Discursive Functions – Interviews with politicians [in %]

	UK-1997-ITV	FRG-1998-RTL	USA-2000-NBC	UK-1997-CNN-I	FRG-1998-CNN-I	FRG-1998-BBC-W	Total
▣ question	50	67	100	80	100	40	57
■ follow-up	50	33	-	20	-	60	43
☐ formulation	-	-	-	-	-	-	-
☐ challenge	-	-	-	-	-	-	-

Figure 8b. Discursive Functions – Interviews with experts [in %]

interviewer exhibits high addressee orientation in a multi-unit turn which contains either a yes-no question (10,83%) or a wh-question (4,62%), heteroglossic engagement, elements expressing graduation and elements expressing attitude, and is used in the discursive function of question (22).

(22)   Dr Mawhinney, er, it's not a very good exit poll for you, it does look as though you've lost. [UK 1997, BBC, anchor David Dimbleby to Brian Mawhinney, Conservative Party Chairman]

Type 1 shows up to five of the five features identified by House (1996) as typical of "English" communicative style, namely indirectness, orientation towards other, orientation towards addressees, implicitness and verbal routines.

Type 2 (10,77%) refers to questioning activities in which an interviewer exhibits low addressee orientation in a single-unit turn which contains either a yes-no question (7,69%) or a wh-question (3,08%), heteroglossic engagement, but no markers of either graduation or attitude, and is used in the discursive function of follow-up (23):

   (23)   From East Germany? [FRG 1998, BBC World, anchor Nik Gowing to Heinz
          Schulte, political expert]

Type 2 shows up to four out of the five features identified by House (1996) as typical of "German" communicative style, namely directness, orientation towards content, explicitness and ad-hoc-formulation.

Interestingly, data shows that both types of feature combinations mainly appear in characteristic discursive contexts, and almost regardless of interviewers' nationalities, with only a slight tendency towards House's (1996) observations on English and German conversation in general. The majority of Type 1 questioning turns occur in sequence-initiating or topic-initiating turns of interviews with either politicians or experts on the British and German public channels BBC and ARD, as well as in the interviews with the German expert on BBC World, and also twice in sequence-initiating or topic-initiating turns of the debate-agenda interview which CNN-I conducts with two opposing British political experts. As to Type 2, all questioning activities of this type occur in non-sequence-initiating and non-topic-initiating turns, mainly in the four interviews with the German expert on BBC World, but also once in one of the politician interviews conducted by the ARD. Hence, one should be wary of jumping to conclusions concerning cross-cultural differences, or cross-cultural accommodation processes.

But what is it, then, that influences interviewer's linguistic choices most strongly? Analysis has shown that there is a highly complex interaction between the influences of cultural styles in general and discursive goals, both institutional and individual. More often than not, at least in the data, institutional and individual discursive goals openly outweigh what is generally seen as culture-specific at least for ordinary conversation. And what about the differences between public and commercial channels? Does the analysis of interviewers' questions yield any results that correspond to the much-quoted difference in seriousness versus sensationalism?

Summing up the results from quantitative and qualitative analysis presented in Sections 2 to 4, Section 5 "Channel Profiles" attempts to formulate preliminary profiles for the interviewing strategies practised by the nine channels.

5.   Channel profiles

5.1 National broadcasts

5.1.1 *UK 1997 – BBC*
Of all interviewers, BBC anchor David Dimbleby shows high addressee orientation most frequently, i.e. three times within the question-answer sequences of his
three politician interviews. As he does so each time within the initial turns of these
sequences, this can be interpreted as his strategy for the opening, or re-opening, of
interpersonal frames (Scollon 1998). This is corroborated by the observation that
two out of three sequence-initial turns are of the Type 1 pattern which is frequently
found in sequence-initial turns of interviews with politicians. Dimbleby's ratio of
single-unit and multi-unit questioning turns corresponds to the average, as does
his choice of question types. All his questions are heteroglossic. Graduation and
attitude are employed more frequently than average. All four discursive functions
are used. All in all, the BBC interviewing practices can be seen as prototypical examples of what House (1996) has identified as British English style.

5.1.2 *UK 1997 – ITV*
The British commercial channel ITV is the only national channel which shows interviews with both an expert and a politician. Both interviews are conducted with
medium addressee orientation in their sequence-initial turns and low addressee
orientation in the subsequent turns. They both contain only single-unit turns, an
equal share of yes-no and wh-questions, and heteroglossic engagement throughout. Whereas the politician interview contains no resources of graduation, the
expert interview shows an equal share of turns with and without graduation. At
the same time, all turns addressed to the politician contain resources from the appraisal system of attitude, whereas there is an equal share of turns with and without attitude in the expert interview. This corresponds to the discursive structure
of these interviews. The politician is asked two separate questions, whereas the
second question to the expert serves as a follow-up to the first question-answer
exchange. The second question does not introduce new resources of graduation
or attitude but draws implicitly on resources previously used, as this is frequently
the case in follow-ups. In spite of this, the interviewing practices of the commercial channel ITV appear in general to be more direct, more content-oriented and
more explicit than the practices of the public channel BBC.

5.1.3 *FRG 1998 – ARD*
The German public channel ARD is the only channel out of all channels which
employs two different political interviewers during its opening section. In turn, a

male interviewer and a female interviewer question five German politicians from
the three major and two smaller political parties. At first sight, nearly all linguistic
features analysed correspond to the average found in interviews with politicians.
But closer inspection reveals that the male interviewer displays e.g. significantly
lower addressee orientation than average. He is also the only national interviewer
who uses monoglossic engagement. His style could be regarded as prototypical
German style in the definition of House (1996), other than the female interviewer's style. She counterbalances her colleague's ratio in low addressee orientation
and monoglossic engagement by frequently using medium and high addressee
orientation and heteroglossic engagement throughout. This could (and should)
also be discussed from a gender perspective (Giora 1995; Mills 2003).

5.1.4 FRG 1998 – RTL

The German commercial channel RTL is one of the two national channels which
do not interview politicians in their opening sections. In this respect, RTL has
more in common with the U.S.-American channel NBC than with the German
public channel ARD. Addressee orientation in the expert interview is quite German, i.e. significantly lower than the average. Graduation and attitude are more
predominant, whereas all other features are within the range typical of expert
interviews.

5.1.5 USA 2000 – NBC

In his only expert interview during the opening section, the anchor of the U.S.-
American channel NBC uses middle addressee orientation, multi-unit turn structure, heteroglossic engagement and graduation as well as attitude throughout. In
its use of appraisal resources, this channel shows significant parallels to German
commercial channel RTL, and even more so to CNN-I 1997. All turns are questions. Due to the high amount of interviewer talk, this interview can be interpreted as a typical example of a co-constructed news story.

5.1.6 USA 2000 – CNN

In the opening section of the U.S.-American channel CNN, a politician is interviewed with a mix of linguistic resources often found at the more confrontative
end of this sub-genre. Addressee orientation is middle to high, yes-no questions
and wh-questions appear in equal shares, engagement is heteroglossic, but turns
are mainly single-unit and spiced with resources from graduation and attitude. In
contrast to the NBC anchor in his expert interview who uses only single questions,
the CNN anchor also uses the strategic discursive resources of follow-ups and even
formulation, just as BBC and ARD do in their interviews with politicians.

5.2 International broadcasts

5.2.1 *UK97 – CNN-I*

In its coverage of the 1997 U.K. General Election, CNN-I is the only channel which shows a so-called debate-agenda interview. Both interviewees are professional journalists from the U.K. As they are not only there to co-operatively enrich the news story with their expertise, but also to utter their opposing views, it is not surprising that this expert interview differs from the other expert interviews in that it shows several features more typical of interviews with politicians than of expert interviews. The high share of turns with high or medium addressee orientation or turns bearing the Turn 1 pattern is clearly motivated by the interviewer's communicative task to explicitly select the next speaker after an interviewee's answering turn. Multi-unit turns prevail. Graduation and attitude are used in all turns. All in all, this interviewer's style shows some similarities to the CNN interviewer's style described in 5.1.6, but also to the style of the BBC interviewer. This suggests an accommodation process towards the style associated with the interviewees' culture.

5.2.2 *FRG98 – CNN-I*

After the German election in 1998, CNN-I does not aim at confrontation, which is rather a British delight, but, at the interpretation of current tendencies and the forecast of potential coalitions. A German expert is invited and interviewed in a co-operative but at the same controlling manner, with the anchor delivering most of the relevant information herself. Addressee orientation is middle to low. All turns are heteroglossic multi-unit turns in the discursive function of question. The share of wh-questions is higher than average in expert interviews, the ratio of graduation and attitude is lower.

5.2.3 *FRG98 – BBC World*

The four BBC World interviews with a German expert are possibly the expert interviews stylistically closest to interviews with politicians, and, at the same time, the interviews with the highest degree of accommodation towards the native expert's national style. Like in CNN-I, all three types of addressee orientation are used, possibly also because of the recurring need for next speaker selection. There are more single-unit turns than in most expert interviews, whereas the distribution of question types corresponds to the average. The BBC World interviewer is the only international interviewer who uses monoglossic engagement, just as the German ARD interviewer is the only national interviewer using this kind of engagement. Graduation and attitude are lower than average. This may be due to the fact that the share of follow-ups is higher than average, as follow-ups often

implicitly refer to the resources of graduation and attitude in the previous utterances (cf. 5.1.3). In fact, the share of follow-ups is second highest of all nine
channels. The only interview with a higher share of follow-ups is the political interview conducted by the national channel CNN. All in all, the expert interviews
by BBC World on the 1998 German *Bundestagswahl* have structurally more in
common with the politician interviews by German ARD during the same election, or with BBC's political interviews during the 1997 U.K. General Election,
than with CNN-I's expert interviews during these two elections.

6.   Conclusion

Cross-cultural qualitative and quantitative analysis of interviewing practices from
the opening sections of nine election night broadcasts has shown that there is no
such thing as a clear national interviewing style, at least not in the examined data
corpus. Firstly, interviewers' stylistic choices depend strongly on the sub-genre.
Sub-genres are defined by the social and discursive identities of interviewers, i.e.
by their social and discursive roles as politicians or experts. Secondly, within sub-
genres, channels' interviewing practices sometimes differ more strongly within
the same culture than across cultures, depending on whether a channel is public or commercial. For instance, the German commercial channel RTL seems to
have more in common with CNN and CNN-I than with the ARD. Thirdly, even
within channels, and even within the same election night broadcast, there may be
different interviewing styles, depending on an interviewers' sociocultural identities, e.g. on factors like gender. And, last but not least, data from the international broadcasts suggest that international interviewers tend to accommodate
their interviewing style towards a tacitly assumed native interviewee's style. This
means, indirectly, that it is highly probable that the same interviewers might use
other communicative styles in other contexts. Still, it is not recommendable to
refrain from attempts at cross-cultural comparison altogether and to concentrate
on single interviewers' styles instead. There is no such thing as an invariable individual style. Even if such an individual style could be identified, critical linguistic research would try to measure it against styles already known. All in all, the
combination of qualitative and quantitative methods for the analysis of a small
set of data has proven a useful tool for cross-cultural comparison of interviewing
practices in televised election night interviews and for the formulation of first
hypotheses. In a next step, the relationship between forms and functions shall
be investigated in more depth and on the basis of a larger corpus. Fairclough's
observation that "(a) rhetorical style is not an invariable way of using language,
it is rather a mixture of different ways of using language, a distinctive repertoire"

(2000:96) has proven true not only for the analysis of individual styles, but also for the analysis of discursive practices employed by TV channels.

References

Beard, A. 2000. *The Language of Politics*. London: Routledge.

Becker, A. 2005. "Interviews in TV election night broadcasts: a framework for cross-cultural analysis". In *Dialogue Analysis IX – Dialogue in Literature and the Media. Selected Papers from the 9th IADA Conference, Salzburg 2003*, Betten, A. and M. Dannerer (eds.), 61–75. Tübingen: Niemeyer.

Bell, P. and van Leeuwen, T. 1994. *The Media Interview: Confession, Contest, Conversation*. Kensington NSW: University of NSW Press.

Blum-Kulka, S. 1983. "The dynamics of political interviews". *Text* 3(2): 131–153.

Blum-Kulka, S., House, J. and Kasper, G. 1989. *Cross-Cultural Pragmatics: Requests and Apologies*. Norwood, N.J.: Ablex.

Braun, F. 1998. "Terms of address". In *Handbook of Pragmatics 1998*, Verschueren, J. et al. (eds.), 1–18. Amsterdam: Benjamins.

Braun, F., Kohz, A. and Schubert, K. 1986. *Anredeforschung. Kommentierte Bibliographie zur Soziolinguistik der Anrede*. Tübingen: Narr.

Brown, P. and Levinson, S. 1978. "Universals in language usage: Politeness phenomena". In *Questions and Politeness: Strategies in Social Interaction*, Goody, E. (ed.), 56–311. Cambridge: Cambridge University Press.

Brown, R. and Gilman, A. 1960. "The pronouns of power and solidarity". In *Style in Language*, Sebeok, T. (ed.), 253–276. Cambridge, Mass.: MIT.

Chilton, P. and Schäffner, C. 1997. "Discourse and politics". In *Discourse as Social Interaction*. (= *Discourse Studies: A Multidisciplinary Introduction* 2), van Dijk, T. A. (ed.), 206–230. London: Sage.

Clayman, S. and Heritage, J. 2002. *The News Interview. Journalists and Public Figures on the Air*. Cambridge: CUP.

Drew, P. and Heritage, J. (eds.) 1992. *Talk at Work. Interaction in Institutional Setings*. Cambridge: CUP.

Eelen, G. 2001. *A Critique of Politeness Theories*. Manchester: St. Jerome.

Eggins, S. and Slade, D. 1997. *Analysing Casual Conversation*. London: Cassell.

Fairclough, N. 2000. *New Labour, New Language?* London: Routledge.

Ford, C. E. and Thompson, S. A. 1996. "Interactional units in conversation: syntactic, intonational, and pragmatic resources for the management of turns". In *Interaction and Grammar*, Ochs, E., Schegloff, E. and S. Thompson (eds.), 134–184. Cambridge: CUP.

Fraser, B. 1990. "Perspectives on politeness". *Journal of Pragmatics* 14(2): 219–236.

Friedrichs, J. and Schwinges, U. 1999. *Das journalistische Interview*. Opladen: Westdeutscher Verlag.

Giles, H., Coupland, J. and Coupland, N. 1991. *Contexts of Accommodation – Developments in Applied Sociolinguistics*. Cambridge: CUP.

Giora, R. 1995. "Female interviewing styles in the Israeli media". In *Form and Function in Language. Proceedings of the First Rasmus Rask Colloquium, Odense University, November 1992*, Millar, S. and J. Mey (eds.), 171–191. Odense: Odense UP.

Hall, S. 1997. "Introduction". In *Representation: Cultural Representations and Signifying Practices*, Hall, S. (ed.), 1–11. London: Sage.

Heritage, J. and Watson, D. R. 1979. "Formulations as conversational objects". In *Everyday Language. Studies in Ethnomethodology*, Psathas, G. (ed.), 123–162. New York: Irvington.

House, J. 1996. "Contrastive discourse analysis and misunderstanding: The case of German and English". In *Contrastive Sociolinguistics* (= *Contributions to the Sociology of Language* 71), Hellinger, M. and U. Ammon (eds.), 345–361. Berlin: Mouton de Gruyter.

Jucker, A. H. 1986. *News Interviews. A Pragmalinguistic Analysis*. Amsterdam: Benjamins.

Jucker, A. H. and Taavitsainen, I. 2003. "Diachronic perspectives on address term systems. Introduction". In *Diachronic Perspectives on Address Term Systems* (= *Pragmatics and Beyond New Series* 107), Taavitsainen, I. and A. H. Jucker (eds.), 1–25. Amsterdam: Benjamins.

Koshik, I. 2003. "Wh-questions as challenges". *Discourse Studies* 5(1): 51–77.

Lauerbach, G. 2001. "Implicit communication in political interviews: Negotiating the agenda". In *Negotiation and Power in Dialogic Interaction*, Weigand, E. and M. Dascal (eds.), 197–214. Amsterdam: Benjamins.

Lauerbach, G. 2004. "Political interviews as hybrid genre". *Text* 24(3): 353–397.

Linell, P. and Bredmar, M. 1996. "Reconstructing topical sensitivity: Aspects of face-work in talks between midwives and expectant mothers". *Research on Language and Social Interaction* 29: 347–379.

Linell, P., Hofvendahl, J. and Lindholm, C. 2003. "Multi-unit questions in institutional interactions: Sequential organisations and communicative functions". *Text* 23(4): 539–571.

Martin, J. R. 1992. *English Text. System and Structure*. Philadelphia: Benjamins.

Martin, J. R. 1997. "Analysing Genre: Functional Parameters". In *Genre and Institutions. Social Processes in the Workplace and School*, Christie, F. and J. R. Martin (eds.), 1–39. London: Cassell.

Martin, J. R. 2003. "Introduction". *Text* 23(2): 171–181.

Martin, J. R. and Rose, D. 2003. *Working with Discourse. Meaning Beyond the Clause*. London: Continuum.

Martin, J. R. and White, P. R. R. 2005. *The Language of Evaluation. Appraisal in English*. London: Palgrave Macmillan.

McElhinny, B. 1997. "Ideologies of public and private language in sociolinguistics". In *Gender and Discourse*, Wodak, R. (ed.), 106–139. London: Sage.

Mills, S. 2003. *Gender and Politeness*. Cambridge: Cambridge University Press.

Quirk, R., Greenbaum, S., Leech, G. and Svartvik, J. 1985. *A Comprehensive Grammar of the English Language*. London: Longman.

Reaser, J. 2003. "A quantitative approach to (sub)registers: the case of 'Sports Announcer Talk'". *Discourse Studies* 5(3): 303–321.

Rost-Roth, M. 2003. "Fragen – Nachfragen – Echofragen. Formen und Funktionen von Interrogationen im gesprochenen Deutsch". *Linguistik online* 13, http://www.linguistik-online.de/13_10.html.

Scollon, R. 1998. *Mediated Discourse as Social Interaction – A Study of News Discourse*. Harlow: Longman.

Selting, M. 1999. "Communicative style". In *Handbook of Pragmatics 1999*, Verschueren, J. et al. (eds.). Amsterdam: Benjamins.

Simon-Vandenbergen, A. M. 2000. "Towards an analysis of interpersonal meaning in daytime talk shows". In *English Media Texts Past and Present. Language and Textual Structure*, Ungerer, F. (ed.), 217–240. Amsterdam: Benjamins.

Stax, H.-P. 2004. "Paths to precision: probing turn-format and turn-taking problems in standardised interviews". *Discourse Studies* 6(1): 77–94.

Thornborrow, J. 2002. *Power Talk. Language and Interaction in Institutional Discourse*. Harlow: Longman.

Watts, R. 2003. *Politeness*. Cambridge: CUP.

White, P. R. R. 2001a. "An Introductory Tour Through Appraisal Theory" In http://www.grammatics.com/appraisal/AppraisalGuide/Framed/Frame.htm.

White, P. R. R. 2001b. "Appraisal. An Overview". In http://www.grammatics.com/appraisal/AppraisalGuide/Framed/Frame.htm.

White, P. R. R. 2002. "Appraisal". In *Handbook of Pragmatics 2002*. Verschueren, Jef et al. (eds.). Amsterdam: Benjamins.

Wodak, R. and Meyer, M. (eds.) 2001. *Methods of Critical Discourse Analysis. Introducing Qualitative Methods*. London: Sage.

Represented discourse in answers

A cross-cultural perspective on French and British political interviews

Marjut Johansson
University of Turku, Finland

This contribution examines the communicative function of represented discourse from a cross-cultural perspective in a dialogic framework. It focuses on its different functions and contexts of use in French and English political TV interviews, where it is used in different contexts: French speakers prefer descriptive settings while British speakers prefer an argumentative setting. In the British data represented discourse is used as a device to construct an oppositional stance in negatively loaded contexts. In the French data, it is used to give an opinion and to construct agreement. Thus British political discourse seems more polarized, focusing on the process and on the products of decision-making, while its French counterpart concentrates on description and explanation, thus embedding their political action in a wider public context.

1. Introduction

In recent studies of *reported speech* a new perspective has emerged, especially in analyses concentrating on spoken language or interactional talk. From traditional lexico-grammatical approaches to different *forms* of reported speech – direct, indirect or free indirect speech – there has been a shift in various aspects of its use. When examining the *functional aspects* of reported speech, several factors can be considered: contextual, cognitive, textual, discursive and evaluative, to name but a few. These factors can be investigated in various types of situational contexts as well as in various genres (Linell 1998b; Holt 2000; Sakita 2002). At the same time, the term used to designate this linguistic object has changed in a number of studies: it may be referred to as *voice, reporting discourse* or *represented discourse* (RD). In this contribution, the last term has been adopted.

In this chapter the functions of RD are studied in one interactional media genre, namely the *political interview*. Politicians are speakers who frequently quote their colleagues, opponents, supporters – and, not least, themselves. In previous studies of this phenomenon (Johansson 2000, 2002), the functions of RD were found to be linked to the different textual and discursive functions of talk. Politicians use RD when they are engaged in cognitive-discursive activities, such as telling, describing, and in particular explaining or arguing. In these various linguistic contexts, instances of RD can have different functions. These vary considerably: from anchoring a topic from public debate to an ongoing interaction, to introducing a point that allows the development of a counter-argument (ibid.). In studying the occurrence of RD in a politician's responses in an interview, the interactional organization of this activity type (Levinson 1992) is an essential issue.

In the political interview the main relationship between the social actors – the journalist and the politician – is asymmetrical: the institutional power to organize the talk is held by the interviewer (IR) in the first frame interaction (Fetzer 2002). While the starting-point is based on questions, and the interviewee (IE) has a genre-specific constraint to answer them, s/he may have a certain freedom in answering and developing the topic – or s/he may seize it. In the second frame interaction both speakers orient themselves towards the audience, but their goals differ: the interviewer is trying to reveal interesting information, while the politician seeks to influence and persuade (Charaudeau & Ghiglione 1997). In other words, the way the politician tries to position her/himself in this social context is a result on the one hand of how the politician presents her/his experience and values and imposes a certain vision of the social world, on the other of how these are shared with her/his discourse community (cf. Charaudeau 2002: 162).

The approach I adopt here is based on distinctions between different types of contexts and on the meaning of RD in them. In this study, instances of RD will be examined in four different contexts: cognitive, linguistic, social and sociocultural (Fetzer 2004). First, it is in the cognitive context that the basic type of RD can be determined (see Section 4.2). Secondly, the RD is used in linguistic and social contexts: this genre and activity type follow genre-specific constraints of turn-taking, and certain genre-specific cognitive-discursive activities are carried out by the speakers which unfold in certain types of textual sequences (see 4.3). It is the way in which the speaker constructs her/his talk and how s/he contextualizes the RD that reveals how RD represents, or reflects, the sociocultural context of her/his discourse community (see Section 3).

The object of the study is to contrast instances of RD in the answers of French and British politicians in political TV interviews. In other words, the social and linguistic contexts of the political interviews are similar, but the sociocultural contexts differ. The objective is to find out what the functions of RD tell us about sociocultural differences. My main research questions are based on the axes of similarity and difference:

1) What are the functions of RD in linguistic context?
2) What are the differences between instances of RD with regard to sociocultural contexts?

The political interview is a genre in which the construction of meaning occurs at the intersection of two institutional discourses, both of which are culturally produced: the discourse of the media and that of politics. A certain variation is therefore to be expected regarding the functions of RD. I base this hypothesis on a pilot study (Johansson 2005), focusing on the functions of RD in a narrative linguistic context that can be characterized by causal and temporal markers. In the French data, almost all narrative RD appeared in stories that focused on conflictual issues where the politician had to explain some questionable action of her/his own. In the British data, occurrences of RD were more problematic to categorize: they contained narrative features, i.e. temporal or causal characteristics, but they were not used to tell stories; rather, they were embedded in different types of textual sequences, for instance argumentative ones. In other words, their use was more incidental and hybrid.

In this chapter, I first present the data and a description of the instances of RD in the corpus (Section 2). I then discuss the perspective of cross-cultural pragmatics in Section 3 and define the notion of RD in Section 4. The analysis is presented in Section 5.

2. Data and method

2.1 Political interviews

The data are derived from British and French political TV interviews. In compiling data for intercultural comparisons, one has to ensure that the situations to be analysed are comparable (Traverso 2000b: 34). The case studied here is a single genre, namely the political interview. The French and British political interviews examined belong to different sociocultural contexts, but share features of the same activity type. In the data investigated, all the interviews are dyadic. The data was collected during approximately the same time period, and in fact some of the topics discussed are the same: social exclusion and the European Union.

The French TV interviews used here were recorded at the end of the 1980s and in the mid-1990s. These political interviews are from programmes called *L'heure de vérité* (Moment of truth) and *7 sur 7* (Seven days a week), both produced by French public broadcasting. These programmes were very popular; the French TV audience watched them for over a decade. *L'heure de vérité* was on for thirteen years, from 1982 to 1995; *7 sur 7* started two years later in 1984 and was broadcast until 1997.

The broadcast formats of the French interviews, however, were different. Normally, in both *L'heure de vérité* and in *7 sur 7* one politician was invited at a time. The difference was created by the interviewers. In the former there were three journalists, who took turns interviewing the guest for ten to twenty minutes each. In *7 sur 7* there was only one interviewer, Anne Sinclair, who talked to her guest – a politician or other celebrity – throughout the programme. The politicians interviewed in the present data represented different political parties, but all had occupied the position of minister in the past. The politicians were Martine Aubry (MA), Jack Lang (JL), Michèle Barzach (MB) and Bernard Tapie (BT). All the politicians who appear in these interviews share the same political position: they were in the opposition at the time of the interview.

These data will be contrasted with four British interviews with the leader of the Labour Party, Tony Blair, interviewed by different interviewers on different programmes, such as *On the Record* and *Newsnight* on BBC.[1] The first of the programmes, *On the Record*, is a political one, while *Newsnight* presents various topical issues in the news and in interviews. In these interviews, Tony Blair is interviewed by David Dimbleby, David Frost, Jonathan Dimbleby and Jeremy Paxman in 1997 and 1998.

In other words, the corpus consists of four French and four British interviews. The length of the French interviews varies from 36 to 47 minutes; the British interviews are somewhat shorter, from 24 to 30 minutes. In presenting the data a minimum of transcription conventions is used. Excerpts from the French material are presented side by side with an English translation made by the author. The translations have been made in order to help the reader follow the argument, and do not include the transcription conventions.

2.2 Description of the data and method

The analysis of the instances of RD starts with identification of the linguistic object by its formal features: the syntactic form of direct or indirect RD and the explicit voice. The syntactic forms taken into consideration here are direct and indirect forms. In the examples, the underlined words refer to the introductory part and the words in italics to the recontextualizing part:

---

1.   I thank Anita Fetzer for the use of her data.

(1) direct form
   IE: **vous** <u>l'avez rappelé à l'instant</u>.. **You** <u>recalled that a moment ago</u>
       deux fois cinq ans ministre   *twice the period of five years as a*
                                              minister

(2) indirect form
   IE: <u>euh</u> **il** <u>a dit</u> *que* c'était abominable Uh **he** <u>said</u> *that* it was horrible that it
       que ça ne correspondait pas du   *did not correspond at all to the facts*
       tout aux faits

In the direct form, the introductory and recontextualized parts are linked without any specific linguistic element at the boundary between the parts. In spoken language, however, there may be some kind of extralinguistic marking, as in example (1) above: the introductory part is followed by a fairly long pause marked by two dots (..). The indirect form is identified by the inclusion of connector *that* in English or *que* in French as in example (2).

By *voice*, I mean a proper or common noun that refers to a person or group of people or to the source of the voice (*Jacques Chirac, the specialist, the Conservatives, a rumour*). In the examples, the voice is marked in boldface as in the cases above (1–2). According to these criteria, there are 53 instances of RD in the French data and 43 in the British.

In the analysis the context of emergence of RD was examined. This was done first along two main lines of *sequentiality*, namely *turn-taking* and *topic progression*. The main examination focuses on the *textual sequences* of answers and the speaker activity in them. In other words, the positioning of RD in answers was examined, together with the kinds of textual sequences in which RD emerges and how speaker meaning is constructed in a linguistic context. The notion of *textual sequence* is used here in the sense defined by Adam (1992) (see Section 4.3 and 5.1–5.2). As some of these instances have already been examined in narrative sequences (Johansson 2005), in this study the functions of RD are investigated in sequences that are descriptive, explanatory and argumentative. Secondly, the functions were investigated in order to find different sociocultural functions (5.3).

3. Perspective of cross-cultural pragmatics

3.1 Point of departure

In the field of pragmatics, a number of different terms are used to label approaches that focus on the cultural dimension or on cultural differences in communication. However, there are few very significant differences between the more traditional terms *contrastiveness, cross-linguistic, cross-cultural* and *intercultural*. In order to clarify their meaning, I discuss these next.

Contrastiveness is a term that has been used especially in translation studies in comparisons between two languages that start with description, juxtaposition and end up with comparison (Krzeszowki 1989: 57). According to Chesterman (1998: 54–61), *comparison* usually starts with a perceived similarity of some kind between languages and leads to a problem that can be formulated as follows: what is the nature of this similarity? In pragmatic studies a broad variety of different types of pragmatic categories have been studied, such as requests, apologies, complaints and invitations. But, as Verschueren (1996) says, they are not stable phenomena and there is no fixed form-function relationship. In this sense this analysis is also contrastive as it starts with *cross-linguistic* differences between two languages: that is the linguistic forms of RD in French and in English.

In this study, the meaning of *cross-cultural* and *intercultural* is understood to be the same. Hinnenkamp (1995: 2) sees intercultural – or cross-cultural – communication as a broad relation between language and culture, which focuses on "the confrontation of one language-culture link with another". Scollon and Scollon (1995: 123) share this view of the term 'intercultural' as referring to cultural differences in communication and the problems that arise from these differences. In these definitions a broad perspective is adopted, but the focus is placed almost exclusively on problems of communication. Traverso (2002: 322), in contrast, distinguishes two major types of study in the field of intercultural studies of interaction: on the one hand there are analyses that take as a starting point interactants who belong to different cultures and who are involved in interaction with each other (Traverso 2000a: 5–6), on the other hand studies that focus on one culture in a given situation and compare it to the same kind of situation in another culture (ibid.). In such cases the approaches postulate a linguistic element and examine similarities and differences in its use in different cultural contexts (Traverso 2002: 323).

The second view mentioned by Traverso is the same as that in cross-cultural pragmatics. In approaches like Wierzbicka's (1991) or that of Blum-Kulka, House and Kasper (1989), the starting point is the above-mentioned linguistic element; in other words, the comparisons in these studies are usually between different expressions and speech acts. This is my starting point as well; to my mind, however, comparison – or contrastiveness – has to be understood in a very broad sense.

3.2 Contextual approach

Here the focus will be on language users in certain linguistic and social contexts and how they relate to the sociocultural context. The *linguistic context* has to be understood as certain contextual constraints and requirements of an activity type and a genre: the way the activities take place in it (Fetzer 2004:6). The *social context* is not only that of the situational speech event. In this case, it is a question of the political interview as an institutional and media genre that designates certain genre-specific institutional roles to the participants. In this the participants have their own objectives in relation to the audience (Johansson 2006). The social context is also that of the co-construction of the meaning between the speakers. In this it is important to analyze the complex and multiple ways by which the speakers display their interactive and discursive roles, not to mention their identities (Fetzer 2004:7). Fetzer (2004:9) sees the social context as the default one and the sociocultural context as a marked type of context. Instead of speaking of the cultural context, as is done in several cross-cultural approaches, I prefer to use a more precise notion of sociocultural context, as seen from a certain perspective on culture (ibid.) and examined through socially and culturally situated human (verbal) interaction. Moreover, here it is a question of the French and the British political discourse – two different discourse communities of sociocultural contexts.

The approach will not be contrastive in traditional terms, as Krzeszowki (1989:5) describes it, concentrating solely on similarities and differences between two languages. Rather, as explained above, the approach adopted has to be understood as pragmatic, focusing on the use and functions that are being compared between the sociocultural contexts.

4. Represented discourse

4.1 Definition of represented discourse

In my previous work I have studied speech and thought representation in interaction (Johansson 2000). For these, I proposed the notion of *represented discourse*, for the reason that this approach integrates several dimensions of analysis. How does this notion differ from reported speech? In order to understand this, the notion of reported speech has to be examined critically. It has been adopted as such in many recent studies on various types of spoken language or interaction, where it is used to investigate its functions. Despite this widening of its application, and even though these studies shed light on this linguistic phenomenon in language use, to my mind this does not change the meaning of the concept. Ontologically, it is derived from traditional literary, grammatical and context-independent approaches to language, in which it is seen as *reproducing* something, usually *spoken*, from previous speech situations and giving it a fixed meaning designated by the term 'reported speech'. The notion thus reflects the monologic and unidirectional theories of language and communication on which it is based; therefore, it is in my view inadequate for a dialogical approach to language. Some studies have suggested ways to overcome its shortcomings: Tannen (1989), for instance, proposes *constructed dialogue* and Sakita (2002) *reporting discourse*.

The notion of RD is based on a different theoretical framework, namely on dialogical, cognitive and pragmatic approaches to language and communication. In other words, there is a significant change in the conceptual basis and meaning compared to reported speech, in that the notion refers to a context-dependent and pragmatic object (for a detailed definition, see Johansson 2000: 78–81). It is a form of mediated action, a cultural, discursive and linguistic tool that creates a link between mental action, interaction and action situated in context (Johansson 2002: 13).

There are several levels of definition. First, the object is seen as being created by the speaking actor. In the cognitive process the speaker can make a recontextualization from other discourses. According to Linell (1998a: 154), recontextualization is a dynamic process between discourses and texts in contexts. In this the speaker mediates different meanings from these other discourses and texts to the present one s/he is engaged in. Secondly, every instance of RD contains a voice that stages an *other* and thus creates a polyphonic dimension to the utterance (Johansson 2002: 12). The voice links the speaker to these other contexts, as it functions as a trace in the consciousness of the speaker (ibid.). Thirdly, it is also textual, as it is used sequentially. In other words, its contextual placement is important, as it allows its functions in discourse to be discovered. This is shown in Table 1.

Table 1. Represented discourse (RD) (Johansson 2002)

A form of recontextualization in which speaker constructs		
THE LINGUISTIC OBJECT		A RELATION WITH
(explicit) voice trace in the consciousness of the speaker	⇔	Texts and other speakers intra- and intertextual and interdiscursive chaining
Positioning of RD in discursive and interactional context	⇔	Co-speaker negotiation with the co-speaker

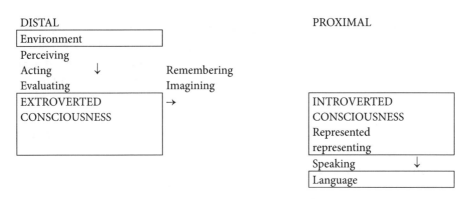

DISTAL   PROXIMAL

Environment

Perceiving
Acting   ↓   Remembering
Evaluating   Imagining

EXTROVERTED →	INTROVERTED
CONSCIOUSNESS	CONSCIOUSNESS
	Represented
	representing

Speaking   ↓

Language

Figure 1. Speaking in the displaced mode (according to Chafe 1994: 199)

The notion of RD emphasizes the cognitive, linguistic and pragmatic activity of the speaker. In the following, I take up the basic types of RD and the cognitive context of their formation.

4.2 Basic types of RD

There are two basic kinds of RD based in the cognitive context that can be explained on the basis of how the speaker constructs them. In Johansson (2000: 43–47), I made the first distinction between the types of RD, using Chafe's (1994) cognitive model of displaced and immediate context of speaking. According to this model, there are two main categories of speaking: the *immediate mode* and the *displaced mode*. Here I concentrate on the latter, which is described as follows (Figure 1).

The displaced mode reflects the position of the speaker towards other contexts (Chafe 1994: 195–201), which s/he relates in her/his speech by the acts of remembering or imagining. The latter has to be understood in a broad sense: it can constitute different types of activities, such as evaluation, appreciation and so on (cf. Chafe 1994). By these cognitive activities the speaker relates what s/he has perceived, acted and evaluated in other contexts.

Adapted to RD, the speaking actor recontextualizes for instance utterances from these displaced contexts and thus creates intertextual or interdiscursive links between her/his texts and discourses, as in the following example:

(3)   TB: <u>It's been **John Prescott** who said</u> *let's get private finance into the railway system*

In this example, the introductory part of RD contains a voice that is a proper noun, referring to another politician in the sociocultural context of British politics in an unspecified spatio-temporal context. There are no exact indications of time and place in the introductory part; the verbs in the past tense place the utterance in the past. The recontextualizing part presents the opinion of the person mentioned. This type of RD is a recontextualization from the shared sociocultural context of the interlocutors, the IR and the IE; it constructs event-related and existential types of recontextualizations, in that it is based on an act of remembering.

Occurrences of the other basic type of RD, based on imagining, are not rare. They are constructed of several linguistic elements, which characterize the recontextualization as possible, impossible, hypothetical, future-oriented or collective. These may resemble those in the following introductory parts:

(4)   **You** could say to him
      He didn't say
      If **she** says to you
      He will say
      They say

In other words, a RD of this type presents an interpretation of some kind of speaking actor, with no clear evidence of a speech event that has taken place. This interpretation may be based on the use of a connector (*if*), a verb form (conditional, future tense), a negative form, or a collective voice. In these types, the RD mediates ideas, issues and points of view to the ongoing interaction. The next theoretical point to be explained is how the RD does this.

4.3   RD in the linguistic context

In determining the function of RD, it is necessary to examine the way it is contextualized in the sequential organization of the answers. For this purpose, the local and global discursive, textual and interactional organization has to be taken into account. By this I mean, first of all, genre-specific constraints on turn-taking, on topical episodes and on the type of textuality unfolding in the answers. In other words, the placement of RD in the linguistic context has to be accounted for.

In the interaction it is the interviewer who has the power to organize the turn-taking as well as to propose the topics to be discussed (Charaudeau & Ghiglione 1997: 46–52; Johansson 2000: 63). The politician has the obligation to answer. From a textual point of view, the interview contains two types of questions: those that open topical sequences and those that develop the topic. In the topical opening the questions usually have a complex structure (Greatbatch 1988; Heritage & Greatbatch 1991; Léon 1999, 2004; Johansson 2000: 151; Heritage 2002). The complex question turn usually contains a presequence that prepares the topic, followed by an interrogative (Johansson 2000: 153). The politicians can answer the interrogative or can adopt other strategies in answering, which take up specific elements of the whole question turn (id.: 107–108). The question turn may be oriented towards agreement or disagreement: in the first case the question has an embedded assertion, in the second a negative orientation in the interrogative (Léon 1999: 109, 2004). Here I consider the occurrence in the data of both topic-initial complex questions and those that develop the topic.

In a political interview, topical episodes can be easily distinguished. Here I focus on the types of textual sequences used in topical episodes. In questions which open topical episodes, the IR proposes certain types of cognitive-discursive tasks to be executed by the IE. In this genre, the questions are usually information- or opinion-seeking questions; in the answers, the politician is therefore expected to develop an explanation, a description or an argument. In the analysis, I use the typology proposed by Adam (1992), who posits five prototypical textual sequences: dialogical (interactional), narrative, descriptive, explicative and argumentative. The basic and dominant type of textual sequence in a political interview is naturally interactional; the other types are embedded in it. Here I focus on descriptive, explicative and argumentative sequences (for narrative sequences, see Johansson 2005).

According to Adam (1992: 85–95), a *descriptive sequence* consists of four operations. The first is a referential anchoring of the topic. The second operation is that of illustration or aspectualisation, designating the qualities and characteristics of the object of description. Thirdly, there is an operation in which the relations are shown, and, finally, an embedding into another sequence.

In a textual *sequence of explanation* (see Adam 1992: 32), the main features are the following: presentation of a problem or an issue to be explained, an internal structure that follows a certain order of dealing with the problem or issue, and finally a conclusion or evaluation.

In an *argumentative sequence*, textual organization is created according to a certain order of argumentation (id.: 104). This order may be progressive, starting from an argument and following its development towards a conclusion, or the other way round, from a result towards a reason for it. To put it simply: this textual sequence is based on a basic pattern of *argument → conclusion* (the arrow means how the conclusion is reached from an argument). Its objective is to influence opinions and attitudes. In the following, the analysis starts with this point.

5. Analysis

5.1 Distribution

I first describe the distribution of occurrences according to their emergence in
different types of textual sequences. Table 2 shows all types of textual sequences,
even though narrative sequences are not included in the analysis (see Johansson 2005). As Table 2 indicates, the differences in the data are not significant,
only more or less indicative. However, the following observations can be made.
In the British data, more than half of all occurrences are found in argumentative sequences, with only a few in descriptive (and narrative) sequences. In the
French data the RD was used frequently – in a quarter of all cases – in descriptive
sequences, while not quite half of the cases were located in argumentative sequences. The analysis of the linguistic context of the RD will be taken up in 5.2.

The data have also been analyzed to find out whether or not the voices in RD
have a clear reference. The references vary in fact from named individuals, or the
author of a literary quotation, to plural or otherwise anonymous voices. In the
British data the categories of recontextualized voices are the following (Table 3).

Table 2. Distribution of RD in the textual sequences

	narrative	descriptive	explanative	argumentative	*total*
British	4	4	10	25	*43*
French	9	14	10	20	*53*
Total	13	18	20	45	*96*

Table 3. Voices in the British data

Categories	Examples	Total
identified person (noun or personal pronoun)	Mr. Major, Margaret Thatcher, Ian, Robin, my father, he	9
party	Labour party, Conservatives, they, conservative propaganda	12
identified plural voice or source of plural voice indicated	they, parents, British telecom, independent studies, studies in the newspapers, government or opposition	6
unidentified person	a woman [a supporter], no one, person who has studied	3
unidentified plural voice or type of RD	people, dogma, doctrine, myth, you know [hearsay], it is to say	13
		43

The identified persons are actors in the British political scene. The plural nouns are different: there is one firm, parents presented as actors in the public sector of education, and several references to various anonymous authorities (*studies*). The unidentified persons and plural voices are also presented as actors in the public sphere. The types of RD indicated by *doctrine, dogma* and *myth* present an argument to be refuted. What is characteristic of the British data is the use of political parties as a voice as well as the unidentified plural voice. One fourth of voices are proper nouns or personal pronouns referring to an identified person. There are as many plural nouns that refer to a political party. Nearly half of the voices are the type whose reference is not very clear; in other words, these are cases based on an act of imagining, that is, they do not have a clear reference in any past context (see example (4) in 4.1), bringing out the evaluation of the speaker.

In the French data the distribution of voices is somewhat different (Table 4).

The French data similarly contain a number of references to individuals, named political actors, but also several literary quotations with references to their authors. As for the plural, a large part of the voices refer to groups that can be identified such as *the Europeans* and *the French*. It has to be noted that more than half of the voices refer to plural voices whose reference is not clear, but designates an unidentified group of people or the type of RD in question (*argument, fantasme*). These cases include the use of the indefinite pronoun *on*. In other words, there are again several cases of the type of imaginative RD.

According to these tables, the type of RD that is clearly anchored to the public sphere is evenemential and factual, and is used similarly in both sociocultural contexts. The main difference lies in references to political parties; this occurs only once in the French data, but is more frequent in the British data. The use of

Table 4. Voices in the French data

Categories	Examples	Total
identified person (noun or personal pronoun)	le Premier Ministre, François Mitterrand, le président, Shakespeare, il [he]	14
party	gauche [the left]	1
Identified plural voice or the source of the plural voice indicated	les Français, les Européens, les spécialistes, ils [they], jeunes [young people]	12
unidentified person		0
unidentified plural voice or the type of RD	gens [people], certains [some], argument, fantasme, on [indefinite pronoun indicating unspecified actor]	26
		53

the French indefinite pronoun *on* is used fairly often in the combination *on dit que* ('*it is being said*', '*it is said*', '*it is to say*'). The French data also contain more references to a collective voice, which can be identified as referring to actors in the private sphere.

5.2 Functions of RD in linguistic context

As the previous Section 5.1 suggests, there are some differences between the British and French politicians in the use of RD in different types of textual sequence. In this section I examine the different types of textual sequence and the way RD emerges in them, from descriptive (5.2.1) and explanative (5.2.2) to argumentative (5.2.3) sequences.

5.2.1 *Descriptive sequence*

The use of RD in descriptive sequences is more frequent in the French than in the British data. Here the RD functions as a part of description, frequently serving as an example. The politician describes the social or the political situation of her/his country as in the following example, where the topic is social exclusion:

(5) IR: est-ce que ça veut dire que c'est seulement dans les banlieues qu'on trouve l'exclusion / does this mean that exclusion only exists in the suburbs

MA a) **non** pas du tout **il y a** bien sûr. les banlieues cumulent un certain nombre de difficultés qui permettent qui entraînent euh une masse de personnes qui sont en voie d'exclusion ou en exclusion / not at all of course the suburbs accumulate a certain number of difficulties which allow which draw a large number of people who are becoming excluded or are already excluded but <u>then</u>

b) **mais** <u>il y a aussi tous ces hommes ou ces femmes qui sont en chômage depuis très longtemps et qui se disent</u> *finalement est-ce que j'ai une chance.. de rentrer* / <u>there are all these men and women who have been unemployed for a long time and who say to themselves</u> *do I finally have a chance to re-enter society* I am

c) *dans la société* **je** pense notamment à tous ceux de plus de 50 ans (…) / thinking especially of all those who are over 50 years old

The politician disagrees with the proposed question, beginning her answer with a negation (*non pas du tout*). The first part of her answer, marked by (a), contains the referential anchoring of the same topic as proposed in the question (*exclusion in the suburbs*). The beginning of part (b) is marked by the connector *mais* (*but*). In this part the speaker shifts the topic (from *exclusion in the suburbs* to *unemployed people*). The RD also functions as a description: it shows the situation of one group of people. In the words of Adam (1992), it is an aspectualisation, illustrating the characteristics of the object of description (*unemployed people*). It contains a plural voice (*tous ces hommes ou ces femmes qui sont en chômage*), and a verb (*se dire*); this is not a reporting verb, but one indicating inner speech, an imaginative or evaluative type of RD. In part c), the speaker further specifies the unemployed people, adding age to the aspectualisation.

5.2.2 *Explicative sequence*

The second type of textual sequence, explanation, contained occurrences of RD in both sets of data. These sequences emerge when the topic of the talk is a social or political issue focusing on current events. In these sequences the function of RD is to anchor a fact from other contexts in the ongoing discourse. These other contexts are mainly other public-sphere discourses. In the following example, Tony Blair explains how certain issues have been handled, and his own and his party's attitude towards it:

(6) IR: **well you're selling off assets**
     TB: oh for goodness sake David
     IR: **well what is it**
     TB: no course it's not asset stripping we're compiling a register
     IR: it's selling the silver
     TB: a) **No** we're compiling a register of those assets that are in the public sector in order to see if there are those that can be better off in the
         b) private sector and raise finance (...) **we** had very strong objections to the way that it was being done and the deal that was being secured for
         c) the public sector **we** didn't object in principle on the railways <u>indeed</u>
         d) <u>it's been John Prescott who said</u> *let's get private finance into the railway*
         e) *system* **and** the reason that we have had to stay in relation to rail as with water we oppose the privatisation for perfectly good reasons (...)

Here, in the middle of a topical sequence in the IR's turns, there is a negatively oriented assertion and an interrogative focused on it (*well what is it*). The IR's interrogative can be considered as proposing a cognitive-discursive task of explanation. The politician's (Tony Blair) answer is direct and negative, starting with *no*. In other words, it marks a clear disagreement with the orientation proposed by the IR. The RD contains a voice that is identified by a proper noun, referring to a person who has presented a proposal for handling the issue under discussion.

    The answer contains an initial schematisation of the problem in part (a) – here the pronoun *we* refers to the IE's party. Part (b) consists of a reference to a past opinion on the problem. This is followed by a negative utterance (*we didn't object in principle on the railways*) in part (c). Here the politician specifies the domain (*railways*). The RD emerges in the middle of this turn, in part (d) which develops the topic. This constitutes the point in the explanation supporting the standpoint of the politician's party, expressed previously in part (c). In other words, parts (c) and (d) form a pair, with the latter part supporting the former one. Part (d) also allows the politician to give an evaluation, typical of the end of an explicative sequence, in part (e).

5.2.3 *Argumentative sequence*

The third kind of textual sequence to be taken up here is the argumentative sequence. Cases where the RD is part of some form of argumentation – whether in agreement or in counter-argumentation by the politician – occur in both sets of data. Here I distinguish two different types of use: one where the politician comments on the discourse of the public sphere in some manner, the other where the RD is a point in counter-argumentation.

One frequently occurring topic in political interviews is indicating what other politicians have said and expressing opinions about it. In the following examples the RD is used to bring out the opinions of other politicians, followed by an evaluation and the IE's self-positioning towards the voice. The French data include the following example:

(7)	MB:	c'est comment adapter un enseignement alors qu'il y a l'apport de la télé d'un certain nombre d'autres modes de communication et c'est oui euh c'est c'est	How to adapt teaching under pressure from TV and a certain number of other means of communication and it is yes uh it is it is
	IR:	adapter un enseignement et que l'enseignement soit aussi fait dans des conditions euh. au minimum de confort <incompréhensible>	to adapt teaching and that it would also be done in conditions uh where there is a minimum of confort <incomprehensible>
	MB:	c'est le grand de confort mais aussi adapter	in the maximum confort but also adapt
	IR:	et d'efficacité	and effectiveness
	MB: a)	mais aussi adapter à à la société. **alors** je voudrais juste dire que.	But also to adapt to society so I would just like to say that I this

b) je/.. ce/ la réaction du gouverne- the reaction of the government
ment à la fois m'a surprise et je suprised me and I think that it
pense que c'était un élément ex- was an extremely strong new and
trêmement fort nouveau et posi- positive element <u>the Prime Min-</u>
c) tif <u>le Premier Ministre capable</u> <u>ister capable of saying the follow-</u>
<u>de dire le lendemain matin</u> *je* <u>ing morning</u> *I was wrong* for me
d) *me suis trompé* **pour** moi c'est un it is a new element in political
un élément nouveau dans la vie life suddenly and it is very strong
politique c'est tout à coup et c'est (...)
très fort hein (...)

This occurrence is also from the middle of a topical sequence, in which the IR is not asking questions but offering comments on the topic (*teaching*). This can also be seen in the amount of overlapping speech in the excerpt. The orientation of the IR's comments is positive, and the IE (Michèle Barzach) does not disagree. The IE's last turn in the excerpt completes the elaboration that has been going on, and the politician moves on to give her own opinion on the topic of part (a). She initiates it in part (b), which is marked by the connector *alors* (*so*). This is followed by the first-person pronoun *je* (*I*) and by modality markers by which the IE expresses her (surprised) opinion towards the announcement of the Prime Minister in a certain political situation. Here, in part (c), the RD is an utterance which recontextualizes an example of a new type of political behavior, which is appreciated by the politician being interviewed. The evaluation is given before and after (b, d) – in other words, it frames the RD with several adjectives and is also underlined by the emphasis of certain words.

In the British data the Prime Minister's comments on the opposition do not receive a positive evaluation:

(8) IR: and er if in fact the **single currency** was to be accepted as an idea by the by the Labour cabinet not in nineteen-ninety-nine I think Robin Cook's made clear erm but if it was erm in those circumstances **would you be tempted to** er to do as the Conservatives have said they'll do and in fact allow a free vote of your MPs

TB: a) **no** as we said at the time when this was raised a few weeks ago by <u>the</u>
b) <u>Prime Minister who said</u> *it was a possibility* **and** then it appeared un-
c) clear whether it was or it wasn't **and no** if a Government decides that
d) the Government's got to get its legislation through **but** there would be a referendum of the British people if there is any question at all of
e) a single currency arising in the next parliament **then** I give you my absolute personal guarantee there would be a referendum of the Brit-
f) ish people **I** would not have a single currency imposed by a Government on Britain

Here, the IE is Tony Blair and the voice is that of John Major, at the time the Prime Minister. In the question turn, and in its presequence, the IR develops the topic (*single currency*) and in its interrogative part, there is a yes-no question (*would you*) proposing a comparison between the possible actions of Tony Blair and those of the Conservatives. In his answer in part (a), the IE first disagrees – the answers begin with a clear negation (*no*). The RD emerges here at the beginning of this answer in part (a), referring to the words of the Prime Minister. The RD is followed by the politician's opinion in part (b): he states that the Prime Minister's utterance did not give a clear answer on the topic. In part (c), he repeats his disagreement as to the possible actions of the government. This is followed in parts (d), (e) and (f), by a statement of the IE's position. The politician announces his standpoint and possible future actions on the issue, marked by hypothetical markers (*would, if*). In (e) he produces a speech act of promise (*I give my absolute personal guarantee*).

5.3 Functions of RD in different sociocultural contexts

5.3.1 *British political discourse*
In this part of the analysis I take up the functions of the RD in the British data, to examine its use in the linguistic context of political talk. First of all, Tony Blair uses voices that refer to political actors in the public sphere, as in the following excerpt:

(9)   TB: a) well what is important actually is to make sure that the schools that
      b) we have are schools of decent high standards for all our children **and**
      c) I want to say this to you and make it very clear **if** there are local edu-
         cation authorities that aren't performing well we want to raise their
      d) standards too **but I don't believe** that the Conservatives can turn
         round after eighteen years of Government and say *it's all the fault of
         local authorities*

In example (9) the RD is situated at the end of the turn. In part (a) the politician anchors the topic (good schools); in part (b) he makes a promise, which is emphasized by the use of a metapragmatic utterance focusing on the way of saying (*and I want to say this to you and make it very clear*). In part (c) he continues the topic. In part d), which begins by a connector but indicating an opposing stance, the RD recontextualizes a critique of the IE's political opponent. In the next example he defends his own agenda:

(10)   TB: (...) you know we can argue about Labour's position in the past but
              let's argue about what Labour is saying now...

IR: |
                                        okay now let me ask you

TB: <u>what labour is saying now is</u> *that it should be done in consultation*
        with business including small businesses since they may be those that
        are affected most by it (...)

Here, at the end of his turn, the politician begins to present the agenda of his political party, and the IR gives him permission to do so. The RD refers to a position
his party is taking vis-à-vis the social issue in question.

These two cases (9) and (10) present the most obvious cultural characteristics
of the functions of RD: the politician uses RD to build up polarized positions.
In the first case he presents the real or imagined sayings of his political opponents, in the second he announces his own or his political party's position on a
certain matter. Both are linked to discourse, emphasized with the frequent use of
metapragmatic utterances, indicating how the utterances are to be understood (*I*
want make myself perfectly clear), and to the speech act of promise. In these instances the RD is embedded in talk in which the politician is either explaining or
arguing a social or political issue. The RD functions as a starting or emphasizing
point to an agreement, as a supporting argument, or – most often – as a disagreement and counter-argument embedded in a negative linguistic context.

5.3.2 *French political discourse*

What types of RD functions characterize French political talk? First of all, the
use of a third person singular voice, as in example (7) above (*Premier Ministre*),
is common when accounting for actors and speech events in the French public
sphere. Contrary to the British data, however, in the French data the RD is not
always used to signal an opposing position; the IE may agree with the other politician, as in example (7) above. As in the British data, the politician may construct
instances where he opposes another political person, a party or an idea, but less
frequently than in the British context.

Secondly, what characterizes the opposition in these cases is that the RD is
directed towards the audience and its function is to show what to think about a
certain issue, as in the following excerpt:

(11) IR: vous n'avez pas l'impression que   Don't you have the impression
              c'est un peu de la mise en scène   that it is a little bit of staging to
              ça faire défiler la coordination   put agricultural associations and
              rurale et Isabelle Huppert en-   Isabelle Huppert together [in a
              semble   demonstration to oppose GATT]

JL: a) **c'est pas** de la mise en scène.   it is not staging a play it's an ex-
     b) **Non** c'est l'expression d'un cri   pression of a cry it's an expres-
        c'est l'expression d'un espoir.   sion of a hope you know <u>if the</u>
     c) vous savez <u>si les Français. et les   French and the Europeans do</u>
        <u>Européens ne se battent pas bec   not fight tooth and nail and say</u>
        <u>et ongles et ne disent pas avec   firmly no... we do not accept this</u>
        <u>fermeté</u> *non... nous n'acceptons   treaty so* we will be tarred and
     d) *pas cet accord.* **alors** nous serons   feathered and personally I dont
        roulés à la farine et je n'ai aucune   have any confidence in Sir Leon
        confiance personnellement dans   Brittain who like his predeces-
        Sir Leon Brittan qui comme des   sors is a Trojan horse
        prédécesseurs est un cheval de
        Troie. (…)

In the middle of the topical sequence the IR's question has a negative orientation, which the politician (Jack Lang) rejects at the beginning of his answer (a). Instead, in part (b) he gives his own interpretation of the action he is taking. This is continued in part (c) by a RD that constitutes the first part in an argument *si – alors* (*'if – then'*). This hypothetical utterance is a rejection of the proposal that has been presented in the political sphere (a treaty on GATT) – the politician does not say that he opposes it, but instead prefers to speak in the name of all Frenchmen and Europeans. There is a first person plural pronoun *nous* ('we'), referring to them and to the politician, not to his political party. In the *alors* ('then') utterance he announces the consequences if his advice is not followed. In other words, in this type of case the voice is plural or otherwise unidentified, without a clear reference, as explained (see Table 4). In such cases the politician is sharing her/his thoughts or giving advice.

Thirdly, the RD can also serve to describe or explain a certain political or social state of affairs, as in this last excerpt:

(12) MA: (...) aujourd'hui on est quand   (…) today we live in a paradox.
        a) même dans un paradoxe. **les**   the people who are under 25 do
        b) **moins de 25 ans** n'arrivent pas   not succeed in entering the labour
           à entrer sur le marché de travail.   market and those who are older
        c) **les plus de 50 ans** <u>on leur dit</u> *ça*   than 50 <u>are told</u> *that's enough uh*
           suffit hein euh   *uh*
      IR·   [Incomprehensible]   [Incomprehensible]

Here again the politician (Martine Aubry) is not constructing an opposing position, but describing a social situation and how, in her view, it should be understood. In part (a) she states an assertion concerning French society, followed by its aspectualisation in parts (b) and (c). In part (b), the grammatical subject is the people who are under 25 (*les moins de 25 ans*). This part of the description is contrasted with the situation of those who have to leave the labour market, those who are older than 50 (*les plus de 50 ans*). This case and excerpt (5) are examples of several of this type of use of RD in the French data. These are not clearly connected to other types of speech acts, such as promises. Rather, they describe and give an opinion on a certain matter.

6.   Conclusion

In this study a cross-cultural perspective was adopted. The starting point was the linguistic element of RD, whose functions were examined in one genre, the political interview, in two different political sociocultural contexts: the French and the British. RD is a linguistic device used to recontextualize something from other contexts in the social context of the ongoing speech situation. In other words, it is understood as a pragmatic, context-dependent object. In this study the functions of RD were compared in order to see whether and how they differ in French and British political talk.

First of all, RD is used in different types of cognitive-discursive activities that unfold in different types of textual sequences in political interviews. Where RD was found to be embedded in French political talk in some cases of description, the British hardly use it this way at all. Instead, in British political talk, RD is used in more than half of cases in argumentative sequences. The cultural differences are the following: in the British data, RD was first used to create an oppositional stance towards rival politicians and political party; secondly, to inform the audience about the position of the politician her/himself and the political party on a certain political or social issue. Moreover, it was noted that the linguistic context was frequently negatively loaded, and the saying was emphasized with metapragmatic utterances and speech acts of promises.

The French sometimes did this too, but opposition towards rival politicians appeared less often, as did mentions of other political parties. Instead, the French politician might take up her/his agreement with the political opponent. Morever, the French politicians used RD to give an opinion or advice on a political matter. Finally, they described the social situation, giving their opinion about it.

This suggests that the way of responding in these two sociocultural contexts differs even though the discourse topics are the more or less the same. It also suggests that the role played by the politician also affects the realization of represented speech. The politicians interviewed here were ex-ministers in the opposition, whereas Tony Blair was leader of the Labour Party in 1997 and Prime Minister in 1998. The political systems also differed, the French having several political parties and being less polarized. In any case, based on the analysis we are able to say that British political talk is more polarized, clearly signalling the politician's way of thinking about actions, focusing on positions in the public sphere of political decision-making, while the French discussed the issues more widely. The French politicians might state the same type of opinions, but their focus was rather on explaining and describing how to understand the society and political life, without clearly connecting every issue to their role in the decision-making process.

Transcription conventions

IR	interviewer
IE	interviewee
|	overlapping talk
[ ]	explanations, translations
.	pauses of different length from short . to longer ones ...
( )	omitted parts in the excerpts
bold	emphasizes linguistic elements in the examples other than represented discourse
<u>underlining</u>	introductory part of represented discourse
italics	recontextualized part of represented discourse
a), b), c)	shows different parts in the answers. They are most often identi fied by the use of different connectors (*and, but, so* etc.) or lin guistic subject of the utterance, also marked by bold type

References

Adam, J.-M. 1992. *Les textes: types et prototypes. Récit, description, argumentation, explication et dialogue*. Paris: Nathan.

Blum-Kulka, S., House, J. and Kasper, G. (eds.) 1989. *Cross-Cultural Pragmatics Requests and Apologies*. Norwood, NJ.: Ablex.

Chafe, W. 1994. *Discourse, Consciousness and Time. The Flow and Displacement of Conscious Experience in Speaking and Writing*. Chicago & London The University of Chicago Press.

Charaudeau, P. 2002. "A quoi sert d'analyser le discours politique? "In *Anàlisi del discurs polític. Producció, mediació i recepció*. C.U. Lorda and R. Monserrat (eds.), 161–176. Barcelona: Universitat Pompeu Fabra.

Charaudeau, P. and Ghiglione, R. 1997. *La parole confisquée. Un genre télévisuel: le talk show*. Paris: Dunod.

Chesterman, A.1998. *Contrastive Functional Analysis*. Amsterdam/Philadelphia: John Benjamins.

Fetzer, A. 2002. "Put bluntly, you have something of a credibility problem. Sincerity and credibility in political interviews". In *Politics as Talk and Text: Analytic Approaches to Politi-*

cal Discourse, P. Chilton and C. Schäffner (eds.), 173–201. Amsterdam/Philadelphia: John Benjamins.

Fetzer, A. 2004. *Recontextualising Context. Grammaticality Meets Appropriateness.* Amsterdam/ Philadelphia: John Benjamins.

Greatbatch, D. 1988. "A turn-taking system for British news interviews". *Language in Society* 17: 401–430.

Heritage, J. and Greatbatch, D. 1991. "On the institutional character of institutional talk: the case of news interviews". In *Talk and Social Structure. Studies in Ethnomethodology and Conversation Analysis,* D. Boden and D. H. Zimmerman (eds.), 93–137. Cambridge: Polity Press.

Heritage, J. 2002. "The limits of questioning: negative interrogatives and hostile question content". *Journal of Pragmatics* 34: 1427–1446.

Hinnenkamp, V. 1995. "Intercultural communication". In *Handbook of Pragmatics,* J. Verschueren, J.-O. Östman and J. Blommaert (eds.), 1–20. Amsterdam/Philadelphia: John Benjamins.

Holt, E. 2000. "Reporting and reacting: concurrent responses to reported speech. *Research on Language and Social Interaction,* 33(4): 425–454.

Johansson, M. 2000. *Recontextualisation du discours d'autrui. Discours représenté dans l'interview médiatique politique.* Université de Turku.

Johansson, M. 2002. "Sequential positioning of represented discourse in institutional media interation". In *Rethinking Sequentiality,* A. Fetzer and C. Meierkord (eds.), 249–271. Amsterdam/Philadelphia: John Benjamins.

Johansson, M. 2005. "Represented discourse as a form of mediation from a contrastive point of view". In *Dialoganalyse IX / Dialogue Analysis IX – Dialogue in Literature and the Media. Referate der 9. Arbeitstagung der IADA, Salzburg 2003 / Selected Papers from the 9th IADA Conference, Salzburg 2003. Vol. 2,* A. Betten and M. Dannerer (eds.), 61–70. Tübingen: Niemeyer.

Johansson, M. 2006. "Constructing objects of talk in the broadcast political interview". *Journal of Pragmatics* 38(2): 216–229.

Krzeszowki, T. P. 1989. "Towards a typology of contrastive studies". In *Contrastive Pragmatics,* W. Oleksy (ed.), 55–72. Amsterdam/Philadelphia: John Benjamins.

Léon, J.1999. *Les entretiens publics en France. Analyse conversationnelle et prosodique.* Paris: CNRS Editions.

Léon, J. 2004. "Preference and "bias" in the format of French news interviews: the semantic analysis of question-answer pairs in conversation". *Journal of Pragmatics* 36: 1885–1920.

Levinson, S. 1992. "Activity type and language". In *Talk at Work. Interaction in Institutional Settings.* P. Drew and J. Heritage (eds.), 66–100. Cambridge: Cambridge University Press.

Linell, P. 1998a. *Approaching Dialogue. Talk, Interaction and Context in Dialogical Perspectives.* Amsterdam/Philadelphia: John Benjamins.

Linell, P. 1998b. "Discourse across boundaries: on recontextualizations and the blending of voices in professional discourse". *Text* 18(2): 143–157.

Sakita, T. I. 2002. *Reporting Discourse, Tense and Cognition.* Oxford: Elsevier.

Scollon, R. and Wong Scollon, S. 1995. *Intercultural Communication. A Discourse Approach.* Oxford: Blackwell.

Tannen, D. 1989. *Talking Voices. Repetition, Dialogue and Imagery in Conversational Discourse.* Cambridge: Cambridge University Press.

Traverso, V. (ed.). 2000a. *Perspectives interculturelles sur l'interaction*. Lyon: Presses universitaires de Lyon.

Traverso, V. 2000b. "Autour de la mise en oeuvre d'une comparaison interculturelle". In *Perspectives interculturelles sur l'interaction,* Traverso, V. (éd.), 33–51. Lyon: Presses universitaires de Lyon.

Traverso, V. 2002. "Interculturel". In *Dictionnaire d'analyse du discours*, P. Charaudeau and D. Maingueneau (eds.), 322–324. Paris: Seuil.

Verschueren, J. 1996. "Functioning in a multi-cultural world. Contrastive ideology research: aspects of a pragmatic methodology". *Language Sciences* 18(3–4): 589–603.

Wierzbicka, A. 1991. *Cross-Cultural Pragmatics. The Semantics of Human Interaction*. The Hague: Mouton de Gruyter.

Challenges in political interviews
An intercultural analysis

Anita Fetzer
University of Lüneburg, Germany

Native and non-native discourse can never be 100% explicit, but rather is characterized by a high degree of implicitness, which is not only true for ordinary talk but also for media discourse. This is of particular relevance for the communicative act of a challenge, which represents a face-threatening act par excellence. This study examines the linguistic realization of challenges in British and German political interviews from the general elections in Britain (1997) and Germany (1998). It demonstrates language- and culture-specific preferences for communicating, interpreting and contextualizing challenges. Particular attention is given to different sociocultural practices in the context of media communication, in which coparticipants with different cultural backgrounds communicate and in which the media interview is watched by an audience with heterogeneous cultural backgrounds.

1. Introduction

Culture and context represent extremely complex phenomena, which are difficult to define since they refer to our knowledge of the world and to our knowledge about the world. Some approaches to culture are carried out in a framework based on the dichotomies nature versus culture and chaos versus order (Sonesson 1989), while other investigations employ a paradigmatic approach based on mental, social and material artefacts (Posner 1989). In linguistic pragmatics, the linguistic realization of particular speech acts has been examined with regard to language- and culture-specific preferences (Gass and Neu 1996; Blum-Kulka et al. 1989). All of the frameworks presuppose the existence of culture, which is seen as something already given and assigned the status of a product. Thus, there is no need for an explicit discussion of the question of how culture is constructed or reconstructed.

Unlike the rather static frameworks, the sociological field of ethnometholdol-ogy investigates social reality from micro and macro perspectives by focussing on the questions of how the two realms are interactionally organized and how they interact. Social reality entails different cultural and intercultural configura-tions, which are conceived of as subsets of social reality. Social actions and com-municative actions are embedded in and connected with cultural context which is embedded in and connected with social context. Regarding the conception of an interviewer, for instance, this means that the social role of an interviewer is a more general notion than the sociocultural role of a British or Hebrew inter-viewer (Blum-Kulka 1987). Ethnomethodologists have introduced a radically dif-ferent approach to the investigation of society, culture and context by highlighting the individual's role as a social actor, who reconstructs social reality in the micro realm through their social and communicative actions.

The connectedness between social reality, social action and communicative action is based on the premise of indexicality of social action. Thus, the analysis of the social structures of everyday-life activities has become of importance not only for ordinary language philosophers, such as Grice (1975), Austin (1980) or Searle (1969), but also for the social sciences. According to Garfinkel, the pioneer of ethnomethodology, ethnomethodologists have to undertake "an investigation of the rational properties of indexical expressions and other practical actions as contingent ongoing accomplishments of organized artful practices of everyday life" (Garfinkel 1994: 11). Against this background, verbal and nonverbal com-munication, institutional and non-institutional discourse, private and public dis-course, and mediatized discourse are key to the reconstruction of culture and interculture.

2.   Culture and interculture

Context and culture have long been conceived of as separate from the commu-nicative act whose environment they represent, and there has neither been a dif-ferentiation of context with regard to micro and macro domains, nor has there been a contextualization of culture. Unlike the discrete settings, which look upon context, culture and communicative act as bounded entities, ethnomethodology interprets communicative action as indexical action which interacts with socio-cultural context and context, and thus is dynamic.

The premise of indexicality requires a context-dependent investigation of ver-bal and nonverbal communication, of their constitutive communicative acts and of the linguistic system. As a consequence of the inherent connectedness between context, communicative act and language, meaning can no longer be assigned the status of an independent category. Rather, it is the interpretative result of the interaction between an object, such as a linguistic item or a communicative act, and its immediate and more remote linguistic, sociocultural and social contexts. Because of that, the interpretative result is one of the most important sources of intercultural miscommunication. But how do context, culture and communicative act interact?

In a traditional framework, communication is described as a speaker coding internal messages into external signals, which the hearer decodes. That setting does not accommodate the requirements resulting from the interaction of context, culture and language: it neither accounts for the contextualization of the coding process and the contextualization of the decoding process, nor does it take the contextual constraints and requirements of the sociocultural contexts into consideration. That is to say, the production and interpretation of an utterance require relevant contextual information regarding a possible explicit or implicit linguistic realization. In the framework of speech act theory, explicit utterances are referred to as direct speech acts. Their interpretation does not require the retrieval of a huge amount of contextual information. Unlike a direct speech act, an indirect speech act depends strongly on its immediate contexts.

So far, the discussion of the interactive processes between the language system and context has not taken into consideration the contextual constraints of the cultural system. The results of intercultural-communication research (Hall and Hall 1994; Wierzbicka 1991) show that the accommodation of language-external constraints on language production and language interpretation may be a universal phenomenon, but their linguistic realizations in context are definitely not universal. This is due to the fact that the question of whether a communicative contribution is realized explicitly or implicitly is interdependent on a speech community's preferred and dispreferred modes of realizing communicative intentions. The knowledge about possible linguistic realizations is part of a coparticipant's sociocultural competence, which is anchored to a speech community[1] (Gumperz 1977; Hymes 1974).

Different speech communities employ different contextualization practices, and it is those differences which lead to intercultural miscommunication. To investigate the differences more thoroughly, the functional-grammar concept of markedness (Givón 1993) is of relevance: the marked format is structurally more complex, while the unmarked format is structurally less complex; the marked format is less frequent with regard to distribution, while the unmarked format is more frequent with regard to distribution; the marked format is more difficult to process

---

1. With bilinguals or multilinguals, sociocultural competence categorizes into different subsets of sociocultural competence.

and requires more cognitive work, while the unmarked format is less difficult to process and requires less cognitive work. If the concept of markedness is adapted to the investigation of communicative contributions, this means that a contribution which is interpreted as adhering to the cultural modes of verbal performance is attributed to the unmarked format and does not require any extra cognitive work. In this setting the "et cetera" strategy applies and the status quo is confirmed (Garfinkel 1994: 21). That is to say, the linguistic realization – or interpretation – of a challenge, for instance, is "such as is required" (Grice 1975: 45) in a particular context, where it confirms and reinforces the coparticipant's background knowledge regarding the sociocultural practice of a prototypical challenge.

If a contribution is interpreted as a deviation from a sociocultural practice, but only a minor one, the strategy "let it pass" is employed and the procedure also follows the "et cetera" pattern (Garfinkel 1994: 21). Here, the minor deviation is interpreted as irrelevant as it is looked upon as idiosyncratic and accounted for accordingly. Should a contribution deviate from the expected cultural mode of behaviour in an unreasonable manner, the coparticipants need to account for the degree of deviation and they may either employ the "unless" strategy or practice "ad hocing" (Garfinkel 1994: 21). The "unless" strategy regulates the acceptance of a particular contribution under specified conditions, for instance psychological stress. "Adhocing" allows the coparticipant to look upon the contribution as an odd-one-out which is accounted for accordingly, for instance as not being of any immediate relevance.

In general, a contribution is contextualized in the unmarked format. That is to say, a speech community, which may comprise a national culture or one of its subsets, for instance a particular social, ethnic or gendered group, has an unmarked or preferred mode of realizing and interpreting the communicative act of a challenge, for example. Of course, that very general frame of reference needs to be broken down into further constitutive frameworks, that is communicative genres (Luckmann 1995), activity types (Levinson 1979) and communicative projects (Linell 1998). Those intermediate (meso) frames constrain the linguistic realization of communicative strategies and categorize them into marked and unmarked formats. While a directly realized challenge may be assigned an unmarked status in a British political interview, for instance, it tends to be assigned a marked status in its German counterpart. Should the interpretation of a contribution and its classification as marked or unmarked be inconsistent in a particular context and not hold, its status needs to be reevaluated. Again, clashes between speaker-intended meaning and hearer-intended interpretation are a rich source for a marked interpretation in intercultural communication.

If we accept the ethnomethodological premise that social reality is reconstructed in and through the process of communication and is both process and product – or is both brought to the interaction and brought out in the interaction, to employ interactional-sociolinguistics terminology (Gumperz 1977), we also have to accept the entailment that the social construct of culture as well as its subsets are reconstructed in a similar fashion. Their analyses should, according to Garfinkel, give special reference to "recognizing, using, and producing the orderly ways of cultural settings from "within" those settings" (Garfinkel 1994: 31). This means that culture and its subsets are structured constructs, which are interactionally organized. However, we do not generally communicate culture in an explicit mode, but rather presuppose it, or to employ Garfinkel's own words: "much ... of what is actually reported is not mentioned" and yet the "unstated understandings" are "required" for the production and interpretation of "recognizable sense" (Garfinkel 1994: 10). That is to say, a contribution's presuppositions are part of the sociocultural knowledge of a speech community and therefore do not need to be realized explicitly in everyday life discourse.[2] Again, there is variation with regard to the degree of explicitness in individual cultures, and it is those differences, which may cause a marked interpretation. But how do coparticipants interpret the unstated understandings, and how do they know what unstated understandings apply in a particular context?

In an ethnomethodology framework, the knowledge about when, where and how to fill in the gaps is part of the coparticipants' sociocultural competence (Gumperz 1977; Hymes 1974). Not only do coparticipants know when, where and how to employ the strategy of gapping, but they also know when, where and how to retrieve the contextual information required in order to make the gaps meaningful. Furthermore, they know how to formulate and interpret messages in a culturally appropriate manner, for instance the speaker-intended meaning of a challenge. Thus, a speech community's conventions regulate the degree of explicitness required for the appropriateness of a contribution. And it is up to the coparticipants to act in accordance with the recommended degree of explicitness, or to act in disaccordance with it. Acting in disaccordance, however, is assigned the status of deliberate action for which the coparticipant need to take responsibility.

Conventionalized modes of communication are also referred to as communicative strategies, and are examined in the following.

---

2.   Generally, presuppositions and conversational implicatures are only explicated in critical situations, e.g. infelicities and other forms of nonsuccess.

3.   Communicative strategies: Preferred and dispreferred modes

Communicative strategies contain information about how to express a communicative intention, for instance a challenge, in the most efficient and effective
manner. From an economy-of-speech perspective, the most effective way of challenging a contribution is realized something along the lines of *I challenge your
contribution* or *I do not accept what you have been saying*. In reality, however,
the most efficient way of saying something is not necessarily the most effective
one. Thus, challenging a contribution does not only need to take into account the
level of propositional information, it also has to consider interpersonal aspects
anchored to the coparticipants' face needs.

In general, natural-language communication involves a sequence of contributions. For this reason, communicative strategies have to be investigated in a
discursive framework (Fetzer 2002) which accommodates the results of preference organization (Levinson 1983; Pomerantz 1984), which have been refined by
Lauerbach (1993), who explicitly relates the coparticipants' face needs in the dispreferred format to additional semiotic and language material.[3] Since the additional semiotic and language material indicates an upcoming challenge, it can also
be assigned the status of an inference trigger. Since the realization and interpretation of the dispreferred format is not universal, but rather culture-specific, this
may again lead to intercultural miscommunication. Communicative strategies do
not only apply to language output and thus to the most efficient and appropriate
mode of realizing a communicative intention, but they also apply to language
input and the most efficient and effective interpretation and contextualization
strategies. Communicative strategies do not only describe the effective and efficient employment of the linguistic code, they also regulate and prescribe a socially
accepted mode of verbal and nonverbal performance. They do not necessarily
represent the most efficient way of transmitting information by adhering to the
Gricean maxims of quantity, quality, relation and manner, but they certainly describe the most habitual, the most appropriate and thus the most accepted mode
of communicative performance.

Communicative strategies also have a prescriptive function and thus stabilize
a speech community's sociocultural values. Should a coparticipant not adhere to
the preferred format, s/he will not generally suffer any sanctions, for communicative strategies do not have a normative, but a conventional status. Yet any deviati-

---

3.   The category of additional semiotic and language material is referred to as plus-language
in Fetzer (1996), where a socio-semiotic approach to language is applied to a second-language-
learning context.

on from a speech community's preferred format needs to be accounted for since communicative action is looked upon as deliberate action.[4]

Communicative strategies are connected with social and cultural aspects of language use and therefore offer a very promising field for the investigation of culture and interculture. From a preference-organization viewpoint, there are preferred and dispreferred modes. This entails that there exist less efficient and less appropriate modes of communication. Regarding their connectedness with context, communicative strategies are allocated to the micro-macro interface. Their connectedness with the micro domain is reflected on the utterance level, and their connectedness with the macro domain is reflected in the micro communicative intention's production and interpretation in accordance with culture-specific production and interpretation rules. Communicative strategies are not only characterized by internal factors, e.g. cognitive effort and structural complexity, but also by external factors, e.g. the sociocultural aspect of face and the contextual constraints and requirements of institutional communication. This is of particular relevance for the analysis of communicative strategies in the domain of media communication with its dual frame of reference, the first-frame communication on screen and the communication between the first-frame coparticipants and the second-frame audience. Here, the first-frame coparticipants produce and interpret meaning for the direct first-frame communication partner and for the indirect second-frame communication partner, the audience. Because of the multilayered setting, the interpretation of media communication represents a rich source of miscommunication, especially in an intercultural setting.

In the following, those configurations which count as challenges are examined in detail, and particular attention is given to their connectedness with culture-specific and media-specific modes of linguistic realization.

4.   Challenges in context

Challenging a communicative contribution is intrinsically connected with denying its truth and/or rejecting its appropriateness and sincerity. A communicative contribution can be rejected completely or partially, it can be disagreed with completely or partially, it can be denied, and other contextual references can be non-accepted, such as its degree of politeness or its sequential status. The frame of reference adopted in this contribution is a sociopragmatic approach, which

---

4.   Goffman's (1974) concept of virtual offence states that the non-communication of a friendly attitude indicates a hostile attitude. Edmondson (1983) claims that any surface (and non-surface) is communicatively significant.

conceives of language as a tool for communicative action. Adopting the theoretical outline and terminology of Habermas (1987), rational coparticipants negotiate the communicative status of validity claims in communication. This means, a speaker postulates a validity claim and directs it towards an addressee, who ratifies the act by accepting it and assigning it the status of a plus-validity claim, or by rejecting it and assigning it the status of a minus-validity claim. A non-acceptance initiates a negotiation-of-validity sequence, in which the non-accepted references of the postulated claim are made explicit and in which their communicative status is negotiated in order to reach some kind of agreement, which is acceptable to the coparticipants.

A negotiation-of-validity sequence is of particular relevance to the analysis of challenges in political interviews because it demonstrates how meaning is negotiated in a dyadic setting, and how meaning is negotiated in a mediated frame of references in front of an audience. In a media-communication setting, such as a political interview, Habermas's conception of communication as an inherently dyadic endeavour is refined with respect to the first-frame interaction between interviewer and interviewee, and with respect to the second-frame interaction comprising the first-frame interaction with the media frame. In order to adapt Habermas's macro approach to a micro setting, the notion of context is made explicit.

Context comprises social context and sociocultural context, linguistic context and cognitive context, which are conceived of as an onion with constitutive layers, metaphorically speaking (Sperber and Wilson 1996). Naturally, the different sets of contexts are administered in their own particular ways. Adapting Habermas's frame of reference, a validity claim is anchored to three worlds: the subjective world, the social world and the objective world. Since a validity claim denotes a process-oriented concept which requires ratification, it entails both a plus- and a minus-validity claim. In natural-language communication, validity claims are anchored to social and sociocultural contexts represented by the social world, they are anchored to linguistic context represented by the objective world, and they are anchored to cognitive context represented by the subjective world. The tripartite system is schematized in Figure 1.

In the framework of plus/minus-validity claims, challenges can be explicated as follows:

–   The objective world is defined by the guiding principle of truth, which is based on reference and predication, and on their presuppositions. False validity claims comprise a challenge of reference, predication or of their presuppositions.

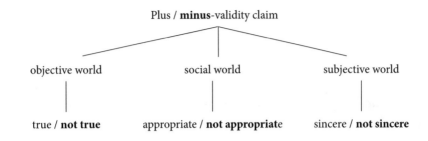

Figure 1.

-   The subjective world is defined by the guiding principle of sincerity, which
    is based on a coparticipant's communicative intention, which is meant as ut-
    tered and interpreted as meant. Insincere validity claims comprise the chal-
    lenge of the speaker's or hearer's sincere intentions.
-   The social world is defined by the guiding principle of appropriateness, which
    subcategorizes into another tripartite system of interpersonal, interactional
    and textual presuppositions, which is defined as follows:
    -   The textual system inherits the overall guiding principle, the Gricean co-
        operative principle (CP), which is the fundamental premise of the defini-
        tion of a plus/minus-validity claim. Here, the maxims of quality, quantity,
        relation and manner, and the conversational implicature (Grice 1975) are
        of prime importance. Inappropriate validity claims are defined as chal-
        lenges which claim that a contribution is in disaccordance with one or
        more of the maxims, or that its conversational implicature has not been
        calculated accordingly.
    -   The interpersonal system is based on Brown and Levinson's conception
        of a model person, their face needs and face wants (Brown and Levinson
        1987), and on Goffman's conception of footing (Goffman 1974, 1981). In-
        appropriate validity claims are defined as challenges which claim that a
        contribution is in disaccordance with the contextual constraints and re-
        quirements regarding face and participation.
    -   The interactional system is based on sequentiality and sequential organi-
        zation. Inappropriate validity claims are defined as challenges which claim
        that a contribution is in disaccordance with the premise of adjacency and
        that a contribution is in disaccordance with the contextual constraints
        and requirements of the turn-taking system (Atkinson and Heritage 1984;
        Levinson 1983).

Challenges may communicate that a communicative contribution is looked upon
as inappropriate, untrue or insincere on the micro domain, and they may commu-

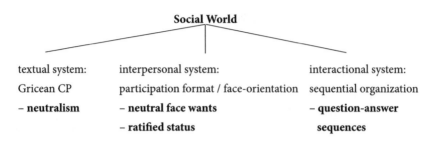

Figure 2.

nicate that the macro contribution of a communicative genre (Luckmann 1995) is seen as inappropriate or insincere. From a top-down perspective, a communicative genre is conceived of as a macro validity claim, in which the cognitive-context, linguistic-context and social-context references are specified. No specification is required for the objective world anchored to objective context, because the objective context never changes – not even in other possible worlds. Regarding the subjective world, the premise of communicative intention meant as uttered and interpreted as meant is specified with respect to the macro communicative intention anchored to the macro category of genre. Regarding the social world, which is a context-dependent notion par excellence, specification is required for all of its constitutive systems, as is reflected in genre-specific constraints and requirements of a political interview, namely question-answer sequences and neutralism, which is schematized in Figure 2.

Challenging the macro validity claim of a political interview indicates an inappropriate performance with regard to the guiding principle of neutralism (Greatbatch 1992), the constitutive coparticipant-specific question-answer sequences, the genre-specific ratified participation statuses, and the media-specific constraints and requirements. For instance, an interviewee might choose to ask questions instead of answering them, an interviewer might ask questions about the politician's personal domains, or an interviewer and interviewee might only talk amongst themselves and not to the audience. From the markedness perspective introduced above, inappropriate communicative performance is assigned a marked status, which tends to reflect negatively on the coparticipants.

In the following, the linguistic realization of challenges in the British election-night interviews is examined in detail.[5]

---

5. This paper is part of the research project "Television Discourse", supported by the German Research Foundation (DFG) and directed by Gerda Lauerbach. The goal of the project is a comparative discourse analysis of election night television coverage in the United States, Great Britain and Germany. For more information, see http://web.uni-frankfurt.de/zenaf/projekte/TVdiscourses/lauerbach.htm.

5.   Challenges in the British election-night interviews

The data investigated comprises forty-one short dyadic interviews (2 to 5 minutes) between professional journalists and leading political figures. There are twenty-eight interviews with members of the conservative party, ten interviews with members of the labour party, two interviews with members of the liberal democrats and one interview with an independent candidate. The focus of the analysis lies on the politician's employment of communicative strategies for performing a challenge and, for this reason, I neither take differences between public-broadcasting styles (BBC1, BBC2) and commercial-broadcasting styles (ITV), nor particular interviewer styles into consideration. Instead, I concentrate on the communicative strategies employed in the particular context of an election night and account for the different strategies used by the winners and losers of the general election.

The interviews with leading members of the conservative party, the losers of the 1997 general election, display numerous negotiation-of-validity-claim sequences. This is due to the fact that the conservatives do not focus on the present moment of the interaction which entails their defeat and loss of power. Instead, they talk about the merits of their former government. The negotiation-of-validity-claim sequences show a higher frequency of markers of the dispreferred format, such as verbs of cognition used with an epistemic function, cohesive links, references to media-specific constraints and requirements and to the inappropriateness of questions and presuppositions. The verbs of cognition signify subjectification and reduce the pragmatic force of the argument, and the cohesive links function as textual signposts and indicate some kind of incoherence. While textual-meaning references to one's own argument have the communicative function of boosting the pragmatic force, textual-meaning references to other's argument indicate that the argument has not been fully conclusive. This also holds for references to media-specific constraints and requirements, which are frequently used as a reason for opting out (Fetzer 2006; Lauerbach 2004). The interviews with the winners display less lengthy negotiation-of-validity sequences, but also a high frequency of verbs of cognition and a high frequency of negative contextualization cues (Fetzer 1997), which are used to attenuate the pragmatic force. While there is a lot of variation in the interviews with the losers, the winners tend to use only one strategy.

In the following, the challenges identified in the election-night interviews are systematized with regard to their referential domains, namely challenges indexing the inappropriateness of a validity claim's content, challenges indexing the inappropriateness of a validity claim's force with a negative evaluation, challenges indexing the inappropriateness of a validity claim by explicitly opting out, challenges indexing the inappropriateness of a validity claim by avoiding the question and challenges indexing the inappropriateness of the macro validity claim.

5.1 Challenging the appropriateness of a validity claim's content

All of the following examples[6] are responses to interviewer questions, through which s/he intends to elicit a statement about who is to blame for the defeat of the conservatives. All of the conservatives' responses display metapragmatic devices, which intensify the pragmatic force of the argument. In example (1), Stephen Dorell (SD), the Health Secretary, boosts the pragmatic force of his challenge with the adverbial phrase *by any means* and explicitly rejects the interviewer's (IR) implicit presupposition that the outcome of the general election has already been decided:

(1) IR   Do you agree with Edwina Currie that it was the divisions in your party and particularly the behaviour of the eurosceptics that did it for you?

   SD   **I don't accept** *by any means* that the results of the election has yet been decided or at least that it is yet known. Erm I do agree with Michael Portillo saying earlier ...

In (2), the IR's request for information about who is to blame for the defeat is challenged by SD who again refers to the *unknown result*. Unlike the boosted force in (1), the challenge is attenuated by the negated verb of cognition *don't think*:

(2) IR   If a party cannot be forced into unity by one leader isn't it time to change the leader?

   SD   **No I don't think** that we need to get into speculations about what the lessons are from a result we don't know yet.

William Hague's (WH) challenge in (3) is attenuated by the negated verb of cognition *don't think* and by the discourse marker *well*, which signifies a change in context (Smith and Jucker 2002):

(3) IR   Nicolas Winterton you see says that Kenneth Clarke was the fault and that he lost the campaign?

   WH   *Well* **I don't think** we should **I don't think** there is any point in apportioning blame around the party ....

Challenging the appropriateness of a validity claim's content is frequently anchored to a negotiation-of-validity sequence, in which the challenged presupposi-

---

6.   To facilitate readability, the transcription follows orthographic standards.

tions are made explicit. In (4), the IR requests Malcolm Rifkind (MR) to comment on the validity of the claim about him being *confident* that he will keep his seat:

(4)   IR   **Are you confident** you'll hang on to your seat?

       MR   **I'm extremely hopeful** ....

       IR   **Being hopeful isn't quite the same as being confident is it**?

       MR   **Well**, it's because **you're asking me to** predict it, **I mean** are you just wanting me to use the usual optimism that all candidates use or are you trying to find out if I have some privileged access to information? **I haven't counted the ballots yet so I don't actually know any more than you do** but I'm very happy to sound optimistic.

MR's response indirectly challenges the IR's lexical choice *confident* and corrects it with the more moderate term *hopeful*. The IR does not accepted that and spells out the inappropriateness of MR's response by saying *being hopeful isn't quite the same as being confident is it*. In the follow-up move, MR gives reasons for why he prefers the term *hopeful*, and his account is introduced with the discourse marker *well*, the other-reformulation *you're asking me* and the self-reformulation *I mean*, which all signify that he intends to terminate the negotiation-of-validity sequence. The rather elaborate move contains a number of explicit references to the IR, namely *I haven't counted the ballots yet so I don't actually know any more **than you do***. This extends the negotiated domain of validity from MR to the IR thus including him and his propositions in the argumentation.

A reference to the not-yet-decided election is also used by other conservatives. In (5), the verbal exchange between Michael Heseltine (MH) and the IR is more confrontational:

(5)   IR   .... do you accept **it** hasn't quite worked out?

       MH   **Well the opinion polls** haven't worked out .....

       IR   Michael Portillo says that it's disunity that was the problem for the Tory party would you agree with that?

       MH   **Well I think** it's important to have a mature period of reflection ....

       IR   **Does this imply** that the prime minister will resign as leader of the party

       MH   **Well I hope not** I've spent .....

MH challenges the IR's validity claim *it has not worked out* by making the indeterminate reference *it* explicit with the determinate meaning *the opinion polls*, which was not intended by the IR, who intended the pronoun *it* to refer to the conservatives' election campaign. The deliberate mis-retrieval of contextual information is introduced with the discourse marker *well*. The IR does not explicitly comment on the mis-retrieved reference. Instead he takes up the previously introduced discourse topic and specifies it in a subsequent question, in which he explicitly refers to another conservative politician and his reference to the disunity of the conservative party. MH indirectly challenges the IR's claim. This is manifest in the discourse marker *well* and the verb of cognition *I think*, which both attenuate the pragmatic force of the response. The response is rather vague and refers to another indeterminate concept, viz. *a period of mature reflection*. Again, the IR takes up MH's vague response and requests him to be more precise and spell out his implications (*does this imply*). MH does not comply but remains vague. This is manifest in the discourse marker *well* and in the marker of subjectivity *I hope*.

The interviews with the winners of the election, the labour party, also contain a number of challenges. Like the conservatives, the majority of the labour politicians refers to the not-yet-decided election. Gisela Stuart (GS) is one of the few who presupposes labour's victory. In (6), her challenge of the IR's question is attenuated by the verb of cognition *I think* and the more-fuzzy hedge *kind of*:

(6)   IR   Yes. Gisela Stuart erm congratulations. Why do you think you won this seat which has been a conservative seat since nineteen twenty-two? Was it just that people were fed up with the Tories?
      GS   No **I think** it meant much deeper. It was **a kind of** total disillusionment but also they had lost trust and I see the labour victory ....

Alastair Campbell (AC) is less explicit in his responses (7), (8) and (9), which challenge the IR's presupposition that labour has won the election. Again, we find the discourse marker *well*, the verbs of cognition *I think* and *I doubt*, and the appreciation device *if you don't mind*. All of the metapragmatic devices attenuate the pragmatic force of the challenge, and all of AC's responses indicate a possible victory which is implicit in the references *a pretty good night* and *we'll get through tonight which seems to be a success*:

(7)   IR   Well, David, a moment or two ago, about half an hour ago actually, er Tony Blair came here, he wouldn't say anything, but with us at the moment for any informal chat I'm told is is Alastair Campbell, his press spokesman. Alastair, y/you/you've won, haven't you?
      AC   **Well** Mr Blair's constituency is not yet declared but erm **I think** we're having a pretty good night

(8)   IR   Well, I would doubt that but I think that it's fair to say we've had a very good campaign, we're having a very good night.
      AC   **Well I would doubt that but I think it's fair to say** ...

(9)   IR   It's gonna be a problem, though, isn't it, all governments with big majorities have problems?

> AC **Well I think if you don't mind** we stick on one night and we'll get through tonight which seems to be a success and then ...

In (10), Peter Mandelson (PM) challenges the IR's claim that he is the architect of new labour. In spite of the attenuation device *well*, the challenge is assigned a strong pragmatic force because of the explicit negative operator *not* and the directly negated proposition *I'm not the sole architect of anything*:

> (10) IR Now you are of course the architect of this whole campaign and
> PM **Well** I'm one of them, **I'm not the sole architect of anything.**

Another winner of the general election are the liberal democrats. In (11) and (12), their leader Paddy Ashdown (PA) challenges the IR's validity claim in a rather explicit manner. Even though his challenge is attenuated by the discourse marker *well* in (11), the IR's claim is directly denied by the explicit negative operator *not* and the corrected proposition *the liberal democrats are not on the left*. The pragmatic force is further boosted by a direct reference to the IR with title and last name, viz. Mr. Dimbleby, and a reference to common ground, namely *as you well know*. In (12), the challenge is attenuated by the verb of cognition *I doubt*:

> (11) IR So erm Mr. Ashdown, you/you were saying in your speech, when you er when you had the count, er that you looked to the liberal democrats to influence the changes in the nature of politics and the constitution and all that. There's going to be obviously a hefty labour majority. Do you think that Tony Blair will still stand by that commitment he gave to try and bring other parties in on the left into a sort of new corporative agreement or some such?
> PA **Well the liberal democrats are not on the left** Mr. Dimbleby **as you well know** we're a radical party but we're an independent and distinctive one...

> (12) IR Isn't it a difficulty for you that you get this strength, this new strength in the House of Commons , something like two and a half or maybe three times what you had before at the very moment labour roars ahead and gets a vast majority er for itself, thus diminishing any influence you may have
> PA **I doubt that** but let's wait and see how the results play out and in particular ...

In (13), the liberal democrat David Steele (DS) challenges the IR's claim in an explicit manner by the denial *I did not say that* while providing the corrected formulation introduced by the reformulation marker *what I said was*:

(13)   IR   even better had you abandoned the pantomime that you were contesting every seat in Britain and hoping to form a government.

DS   We had that argument I seem to remember during the campaign

IR   Yeah, you were maintaining stalwartly

DS   stalwartly well, we did-

IR   that you were hoping to form a government.

DS   But we no it was **no no I didn't say that what I said was** we had to fight all the seats ..

Analogously to the straightforward challenges by the liberal democrats, the independent candidate Martin Bell (MB) employs rather explicit challenges. In (14), he boosts his challenge with the booster *absolutely* and with the straightforward denial *I did not campaign*, and in (15) he uses the direct denials *he can't be vindicated* and *its's just not possible*, which are attenuated by the discourse marker *well*:

(14)   IR   Now you claim you stood as the Independent candidate for higher standards in public life. Have you smeared and wrecked the reputation of Neil Hamilton?

MB   **No I absolutely have not. I did not campaign** at all on er on the charges that are not yet resolved. ...

(15)   IR   If he should be vindicated, as he says he will, by Sir Gordon Downey, what will you do by then as elected MP who replaced him.

MB   **Well he can't be vindicated** on what is already out there on the record. **It's just not possible**.

Challenges of the appropriateness of a validity's content are performed by all politicians, whether they have won or lost the election. While both labour and the conservatives tend to attenuate their challenges, the liberal democrats and the independent candidate boost their challenges, which might be due to their particular position in the British election system. In that configuration, smaller parties, such as the liberals, hardly stand a chance of wining the election.

Challenging the appropriateness of a validity claim can be further boosted by attributing a negative evaluation to its force, which is examined in the following.

5.2   Challenging the appropriateness of a validity claim's force with a negative evaluation

In the data investigated, only the losers of the general election challenge the appropriateness of a validity claim with an explicit negative evaluation. Unlike the challenges of an inappropriate content, challenges with a negative evaluation do not accept the IR's communicative action performed though the claim. The force and the implied sequential status of the validity claim tend to be referred to in a rather general and thus indeterminate manner. The general references are evaluated with strong negative adjectives, such as *ridiculous* by Alan Clark (AC) in (16), *not sensible* by Michael Howard (MH) in (17), Stephen Dorrell (SD) and John Redwood (JR) in (18), respectively (19). Another negative evaluation, *secondary*, is used by SD in (20):

(16) AC Oh that's a **ridiculous question**

(17) MH I do**n't** think that's **a very sensible question**

(18) SD ... and I do**n't** think it's **very sensible** to speculate about **it** when we all know that the result, the true result ..

(19) JR ... I do**n't** think **it's sensible** to rush off tonight with all sorts of explanations ...

(20) SD Well I think the **leadership** question is frankly **a secondary question**

All challenges with a negative evaluation are produced by the conservatives. This may be due to their particular position of not having anything else left to lose, and it may be due to their frustration.

In the following, challenging the appropriateness of a validity claim by explicitly opting out is examined.

5.3 Challenging the appropriateness of a validity claim by explicitly opting out

In the data investigated, only the conservatives use the strategy of *opting out*. The strategy is adopted from the Gricean CP, which is the fundamental premise of the definition of a plus/minus-validity claim and which is inherited to the social world's constitutive textual system. Against this background, coparticipants can opt out locally if higher-order principles provide good reasons for doing so. The good reasons over-rule the fundamental requirement that coparticipants should make their contribution "such as is required, at the stage at which it occurs, by the accepted purpose of direction of the talk exchange" (Grice 1975: 45). In the British data, the strategy is quite frequent and it is often based on the claim that one should not speak on behalf of a colleague. Implicit in the strategy is the premise that the moral principle of loyalty overrules ordinary conversational requirements, as is the case with John Redwood (JR) in (21):

(21) IR Do you think John Major can survive this result?

JR **I'm not commenting on anything like that.** John Major is the leader of the conservative party and you should allow him time to consider what is best for the conservative party

(22) IR What is your reaction to the defeat of Neal Hamilton in Tatton?
   MH **Erm well I think that's best up for the history books.**
   IR **Why do you say that?**
   MH Because I don't see why you think I should comment on something like that which is for Neal a personal tragedy. It's happened, you can have a judgement, I can have a judgement but **I'm not going to be drawn on that.**

In (22), the IR challenges the legitimate motives of Michael Heseltine (MH) and his reference to the *history books* and requests him to spell them out in more detail. MH complies by making his reasoning explicit in the closing remark *I'm not going to be drawn on that*, which is accepted by the IR, who does not ask any further questions.

Interviewees can also opt out by simply stating that they are not commenting on a validity claim thereby implicating that the claim in question lacks validity, as is the case with JR in (23) and Ian Lang (IL) in (24):

(23) IR Do you think leadership talk during the campaign damaged the cam paigning effort?
   JR **I have no further comments** on the campaign. I'm just very pleased that in Wokingham people have backed me again and I will work very hard over the next five years to earn that trust.

(24) IR I mean you you were seen as a possible leadership contender of course after this election erm obviously not in position to contend for the leadership now, I mean, who who would you like to see succeed John Major?
   IL **I'm not gonna talk about that now**
   IR Erm would you would you have run had you still been in Parliament?
   IL **I'm not gonna talk about that either** that's a hype a hype a hypothesis on top of another one

The strategy of opting out is only used by the losers of the general election, and it is used in order terminate the negotiation-of-validity sequence of a particular discourse topic. Opting out can be anchored to a higher-order moral principle or to an individual who voices her or his preferences for closing the encounter.

In the following, a less explicit strategy is examined, the strategy of avoiding the question.

5.4 Challenging the appropriateness of a validity claim by avoiding the question

The strategy of challenging the appropriateness of a validity claim by avoiding the question represents a truly dyadic scenario with a lengthy negotiation-of-validity sequence, which becomes more and more confrontational. Because of this, it has a very strong face-threatening potential for both coparticipants who do not intend to give in by accepting the other's evasiveness or by complying with the request for more precise information. In the data examined, only the conservatives use the strategy of avoiding the question in order to challenge the appropriateness of a validity claim. In (25), Edwina Currie (EC) challenges the appropriateness of the IR's validity claim, in which he requests her to confirm a former standpoint by saying *is that still your view*. EC does not comply with the request but talks about her *pro-European colleagues'* positions. The IR challenges the rather general answer by repeating his question *your view* thus indicating that EC has not provided an appropriate answer. But EC does not go along with the IR's request and provides another vague answer. At that point, the IR changes his strategy of challenging her contributions by requesting her to state her own viewpoint. He introduces the anticipated candidate *Mr Michael Portillo* as a discourse topic and requests EC to comment on it. But she does not give in and remains vague, which is reflected in the attenuation devices *I think* and *well* and in the rather general references *this area in the Midlands* and *very good and honourable people*:

(25)   IR   …. is that still **your view?**

EC   **Well** I know some of my pro-European colleagues feel that that John Major ought to hang on and perhaps even stay until October or November for the sake of party unity.

IR   **Your view?**

EC   But I think I'm going to su/ I think it would be a tragedy for the man who is an honourable decent man who's uh I think who been very battered …. My preference ….

….

IR   **Mr Michael Portillo** has been mentioned …. Your reaction to him as a potential leader?

EC   **Well I think** in **this area in the Midlands** …..

IR   And that's **Mr Portillo as far as you're concerned.**

EC   Uh, they're all **very good and honourable people** …

Challenging the appropriateness of a validity claim by avoiding the question seems a very common strategy in political interviews (Bull 2003), and if the interviewer is not very persistent, the interviewee can get away with it. In confrontational settings, there are explicit references to the non-appropriateness of answers and questions, but they only occur in marked interviews (Fetzer 2000). Avoiding the question is necessarily anchored to longer sequences. Here the interviewee blatantly fails to respond thus signifying that s/he does not intend to respond in the interviewer-intended manner, not even if challenged in a follow-up move.

In political interviews, validity claims are not only rejected on the micro, but also on the macro domain of genre with respect to genre- and media-specific constraints and requirements. This is examined in the following.

5.5 Challenging the appropriateness of the macro validity claim

Since political interviews are both public discourse and media event (Fetzer 2000), the appropriateness of a validity claim can be challenged with regard to the two domains. In the election-night interviews, there is not a single instance of challenges referring to the public domain. Media-specific references and constraints are only challenged by the conservatives. Brian Mawhinney (BW) and Michael Heseltine (MH) challenge the appropriateness of the macro validity claim as follows:

(26)   IR   Have you spoken to John Major, are you urging him to stay on?

BM   I have spoken to the prime minister er on a number of occasions during the course of the evening and you would erm expect me to give him any advice that he might or might not seek in private **not in front of the television**

(27)   IR   And why should the electorate have sleep-walked, in your words, to disaster?

MH   Well those are the sort of questions we'll have to ask ourselves and, as I said, I don't myself go for the sort of pealing technique within hours of the polls closing I think these will require mature reflection .... **a way which is very fascinating to the media** but it is not the best interest of the conservative party

In both cases, the appropriateness of a communicative act as mediated communicative action, such as giving advice in (26) and analysing an election defeat in (27), is challenged. In general, a reference to the macro validity claim's contextual constraints and requirements does not initiate a negotiation-of-validity sequence. This may be due to the fact that the type of challenge implicates a criticism of the IR, who is portrayed as having performed a request for inappropriate information.

In the short election-night interviews investigated, challenges are classified with regard to their domains of non-acceptance, namely a validity claim's content and a validity claim's force with a negative evaluation. Furthermore, challenges are performed through the communicative strategy of opting out, which is anchored to the social world's textual system, and they are performed through the strategy of avoiding the question. However, challenges are not restricted to the local domain of discourse. There is also the strategy of challenging the macro validity claim and its contextual constraints and requirements. Here, a challenge of the media-specific requirements signifies an inappropriate interviewer performance. In the British data, a challenge initiates a negotiation-of-validity sequence, in which the appropriateness of lexical items, pronominal references and presuppositions is negotiated. While challenges anchored to the macro domain and to the micro domain of opting out are brief, challenging the appropriateness of a validity claim's content and avoiding the question tend to initiate rather lengthy negotiation-of-validity sequences in the media event of a political interview.

In the following, communicative strategies for challenges are examined in the German data.

6.   Challenges in the German election-night interviews

The German data comprise twenty short dyadic interviews (2 to 5 minutes) between professional journalists and leading political figures broadcasted on the ARD, the first public broadcasting channel. There are seven interviews with members of the conservative party, the christian democrats and their Bavarian sister party, the christian social union, who lost the general election in 1998. There are seven interviews with members of the social democrats and three interviews with members of the green party, who won the general election in 1998. There are two interviews with members of the socialist party and one interview with a member of the liberals. Unlike the Britain system, the German election system is based on proportional representation and on the first-past-the post system. For this reason, smaller parties stand a good chance of being a coalition partner as neither the conservatives nor the social democrats tend to have overall majorities. Adopting the same procedure as above, the focus lies on the politician's employment of communicative strategies for challenges.

Analogously to the British conservatives, the German conservatives talk about the merits of their former government rather than commenting on their defeat; and like the British labour party, the German social democrats and the greens avoid talking about their victory. In spite of the content-based similarities between the British and German data, the challenged domains of reference and the strategies employed differ significantly. In the German sociocultural context, the linguistic realization of challenging the appropriateness of a validity claim's content is different; the same is true for the communicative strategies of opting out, avoiding the question and challenging the appropriateness of the macro validity claim. Not only is there variation with regard to the strategies employed, there is also a significant difference in the length of contributions and sequences. In the British data, there are numerous rather lengthy negotiation-of-validity-claim sequences, while the German data do not only display less negotiation-of-validity sequences, but also briefer ones. While the British negotiation-of-validity sequences show a high frequency of verbs of cognition and other metapragmatic devices, the German negotiation-of-validity sequences display a high frequency of impersonal constructions, such as passives or the *man-muss Konstruktion* ('one-has-to construction'), which attenuate the pragmatic force of a challenge by shifting responsibilities in context.

In the following, challenges of the election-night interviews are systematized with regard to their referential domains, namely challenges indexing the inappropriateness of a validity claim's content, challenges indexing the inappropriateness of a validity claim by implicitly opting out, challenges indexing the inappropriateness of a validity claim by avoiding the question and challenges indexing the inappropriateness of the macro validity claim.

6.1   Challenging the appropriateness of the validity claim's content

In the following, responses to the interviewer's questions about the outcome of the general election and about who is to blame for the conservatives' defeat are examined in the German interviews. In the British data, the pragmatic force of the politicians' challenges is intensified, and challenging the appropriateness of a validity claim's content is realized quite explicitly and sometimes boosted with an explicit negative evaluation. In the German data, the challenges are realized explicitly and implicitly. The conservative Peter Hinze (PH) challenges the IR's validity claim in an implicit manner by referring to his notion of democracy thus indirectly criticizing the IR's concept. The challenge is further attenuated by the discourse marker *now*:

(28)   IR   Lassen Sie uns mal spekulieren. Es gibt ja noch 'ne Möglichkeit, dass es doch für Rot-Grün nicht reicht und eine Große Koalition ins Haus stünde. Wären Sie bereit, da mitzumachen? (*Let us speculate for a bit. There is still the possibility that there are not going to be enough votes for the SPD and the greens so that there could still be a coalition between the CDU and SPD. Would you be prepared to take part in that?*)

   PH   **Also mein Demokratieverständnis** ist, dass die erste Frage an den Gewinner geht, das sind die Sozialdemokraten, hier sich zu entscheiden, mit wem sie sprechen wollen .... (*Now my conception of democracy is that the first question ought to be directed at the winner, that is the social democrats. And it is up to them to decide with whom they want to speak ...*)

The winners, the green politician Jürgen Trittin (JT) and the social democrats Gerhard Schröder (GS), Oskar Lafontaine (OL) and Franz Müntefering (FM) challenge the IRs' validity claims without any explicit interpersonal devices. They use impersonal constructions, such as *one has to* in (29) and (30), which attenuate the claim's force, to some extent:

(29) IR Eine letzte Frage mit der Bitte um 'ne kurze Antwort. Sie werden heute Abend feiern, haben Sie gesagt,gibt's einen Fahrplan für die nächsten Tage? (One *last question. Would you answer briefly, please. As you said, you will celebrate tonight, is there a timetable for the next few days?*)

      GS Den gibt's, aber den **muss man** jetzt nicht ausbreiten (*That exists, but **one does not have to** make it explicit now ...*)

(30) IR Sie haben für einen neuen Politikanfang in diesem Land geworben; sie wollten einen Politikwechsel, der sieht im Augenblick noch äußerst knapp aus, denn Rot-Grün ist noch lange nicht ausgemacht. Oder haben sie bereits en Signal von Gerhard Schröder? (*You have courted for a new beginning in politics in this country. You wanted a change in politics, which still looks rather vulnerable at the moment, because the social democrats and the greens will have a long way to go. Or, have you already had some indication from Gerhard Schröder?*)

      JT Sehen Sie wir haben noch keine Gewissheit an diesem Abend. Äh **man muss** das alles mit der nötigen Vorsicht sagen. Wir wissen aber äh .... (*Look, we do not yet have certainty tonight. Erm **one has to** say all that with the necessary caution. But we know erm ...*)

Another strategy of challenging the IRs' validity claims consists of the use of explicit negatives, such as ***not** going to* in (31) and (32), and *did **not*** in (31), which are frequently combined with impersonal constructions, such as *that is not going to be discussed*:

(31) IR Marion von Haaren, das ist der voraussichtliche neue Bundeskanzler. Voraussichtlich muss man sagen, Herr Schröder, weil Sie noch gewählt werden müssen, dazu werden Sie einen Koalitionspartner brauchen. Wer wird das sein? (*Marion von Haaren, this is probably going to be the new chancellor. We have to say probably, Mr. Schröder, because you still need to be elected, and for that you will need a coalition partner. Who is it going to be?*)

     GS   Das werden wir **nich** heute Abend entscheiden. Wir kennen ja noch nicht einmal die endgültige Zusammensetzung des Bundestages und deswegen ist darüber heute nicht zu diskutieren... (*We are **not** going to decide that tonight. We do not yet know the final composition of parlia ment und for that reason **that is not going to be discussed** tonight ...*)

     IR   Haben Sie mit diesem Wahlergebnis, mit diesem Vorsprung vor der Union selbst gerechnet? (*Did you yourself expect that lead over the conservatives?*)

     GS   Nein das habe ich **nicht**. Ich habe es deutlich knapper erwartet. Ich habe geahnt und gefühlt, dass wir äh wohl vorne liegen würden. Aber in dieser Deutlichkeit, wie es sich jetzt ankündigt, habe ich das Wahlergebnis nicht erwartet ... (*No, I did **not**. I expected it to be a lot closer. I have anticipated it somehow and I have had a feeling that we might lead. But I did not expect that clear lead ...*)

(32) IR   ... Äh nach dem derzeitigen Ergebnis geht Rot-Grün, wenn auch knapp. Heißt das, dass Sie dann zuerst mit den Grünen verhandeln werden, oder ist dies eine Marge, die Ihnen im Moment noch zu knapp wäre? (*... erm according to the present results a coalition between the SPD and the green party is possible, with a small majority though. Does that mean that you will negotiate with the greens first, or is that a majority that would be too small for you at the moment?*)

     GS   Ich habe ja schon deutlich gemacht, dass wir darüber **nich** heute entscheiden, das werden Oskar Lafontaine und i und ich morgen früh besprechen und dann sicher wird das auch in den in der Partei diskutiert werden ... (*I have already made it clear that we are **not going to** decide that tonight, Oskar Lafontaine and I will discuss that tomorrow morning and surely that is going to be discussed in the party ...*)

Another strategy of challenging the IR's validity claims consists of the use of inherently negative verbs, such as *wait* in (33) and (34). Since there are no explicit attenuation devices, the contributions are assigned a strong pragmatic force:

(33) IR   Ja, Herr Lafontaine, Sie haben die Hochrechnung mitgesehen. Äh es würde für Rot-Grün mittlerweile sogar relativ komfortabel reichen. Äh kann sich die SPD da eigentlich noch leisten, was anderes zu machen als Rot-Grün? (*Yes, Mr Lafontaine, you have watched the projections with us. Erm there would be a comfortable majority for the SPD and the greens in the meantime. Erm, can the SPD actually afford to enter into another coalition?*)

     OL   Also wir werden zunächst mal in Ruhe jetzt das wirkliche Ergebnis **abwarten**. Wir wissen ja auch nicht, ob die PDS im Bundestag ist oder ob sie nicht drin ist.... (*Now we will **wait** for the real result without any*

*rush. We also do not know whether the PDS is going to be in parliament
or not ...*)

(34)   IR   Können Sie jetzt schon sagen, mit welcher Koalition dieses dann pas-
sieren wird? Denn für Rot-Grün ist es ja noch verdammt knapp. (*Can
you already say with what kind of coalition that is going to happen?
Because for the SPD and the greens it is going to be dammed close?*)

FM   **Nein** das kann man noch **nicht** sagen da muss man **abwarten** ... (*No,
one cannot yet say that, one has to **wait**...*)

In the German data, there is no preference for an employment of cognitive verbs
when challenging the appropriateness of a validity's content. Instead, there is a
preference for explicit negatives and for impersonal constructions, which have
the communicative function of boosting the pragmatic force of a challenge. Even
the implicitly realized challenge in (28) does not use any markers of subjectivity.
Another difference to the British data is the German preference for first-person
self-references with verbs of action, through which the politician expresses determinate meaning and spells out what he or she intends to do, and what he or she
does not intend to do.

With regard to intercultural communication, the language-specific preferences are one source of potential miscommunication: the verbs of cognition and
the negative contextualization devices in the British data signify that a coparticipant is willing to negotiate the communicative status of their validity claim, which
does not seem to be the case with the communicative strategy of challenging the
appropriateness of a validity claim's content in the German data.

In the following, the communicative strategy of opting out is examined,
which – unlike the challenges of the appropriateness of a validity's content – is
performed implicitly.

6.2   Challenging a validity claim's appropriateness by implicitly opting out

In the British data, interviewees frequently opt out in an explicit manner. Or, they
simply state that they do not intend to comment on a particular discourse topic
any more thus closing it. In the German data, opting out is performed implicitly.
In (38), the conservative Norbert Blüm (NB), opts out non-verbally by shaking
his head thus signifying that he does not intend to respond in the requested manner. The implicit non-compliance is supplemented by an account, in which NB
provides reasons for not responding in the requested manner. At the same time,
he agrees with the IR on a very general position, namely that there exists no policy
which is flawless:

(38)   IR   Was haben Sie falsch gemacht? (*'What were your mistakes?'*)

     NB   [**kopfschütteln**] Also ich bin nicht jetzt der äh Besitzer der Gedanken der Wähler. Aber richtig ist, es gibt nie ne fehlerlose Politik .... ([**shaking his head**] *Now I do not erm own the electorate's thoughts. But it is correct there exists no flawless politics ...*)

In (39), the chair of the social democrats, Oskar Lafontaine (OL), opts out implicitly by referring to himself in his role as the party chairman (*der Parteivorsitzende*) and his /her particular responsibilities:

(39)   IR   Vollkommen klar, dass Sie feiern wollen. Aber ich meine, es gibt doch Erwartungen in der Partei, in der Bevölkerung, auch bei den Grünen. Sie haben gemeinsam, wenn auch in verschiedenen Rollen, für den Regierungswechsel gekämpft. Wie viel Mandate mehr braucht denn eine Rot-Grüne Koalition, damit Sie sagen, das geht auch stabil. (*It is perfectly clear that you want to celebrate. But I mean there are expectations in the party, in the population, also with the greens. You fought together, in different roles, for a change in government. How many more seats would a coalition between the SPD and the greens need so that you can say that it's going to be stable?*)

     OL   **Der Parteivorsitzende** hat eine besondere Verantwortung in der Partei und er kann nicht leichtfertig herumspekulieren ... (*The **chairman** has got a particular responsibility within the party and he cannot speculate just like that ...*)

In the German data, the communicative strategy of opting out in order to challenge the appropriateness of a validity claim is used by the winners and by the losers, which is not the case in the British data, where it is used by the losers only. In the German data, opting out is performed implicitly. It is not very frequent and therefore not the preferred strategy for performing a challenge.

In the following, the strategy of challenging the appropriateness of a validity claim by avoiding the question is investigated.

6.3   Challenging of the appropriateness of a validity claim by avoiding the question

At first sight, the communicative strategy of challenging the appropriateness of a validity claim by avoiding the question does not seem to query the appropriateness of a communicative contribution or of its constitutive validity claims. The postulated validity claim is being ratified, but the ratification move is neither an acceptance nor is it a non-acceptance. With respect to the follow-up move, it becomes apparent, that the ratification move does not count as an acceptance because acceptances are not challenged by following-up moves. For this reason, the strategy of avoiding the question counts as a challenge – but as a two-sided challenge. On the one hand, the interviewer takes the interviewee's response as a challenge, which requires another challenge. On the other hand, the interviewee takes the interviewer's challenge of their contribution as an inappropriate challenge, which does not have to be complied with. So, a negotiation-of-validity sequence with almost incompatible premises is initiated, which, for this reason, can only be controversial.

In (40) and (41), the conservatives Michael Glos (MG) and Peter Hinze (PH) employ the strategy of avoiding the question. Their responses are challenged by the IR. While MG seems to get away with responding on a rather general level referring to the voters' mentality when being asked to give reasons for the defeat of his party, PH's response in (41), in which he suggests to postpone his answer, is challenged by the IR. PH partially complies with the IR's request by making his previous implication explicit, which the IR accepts:

(40) IR .... warum hat das nicht geklappt? (*Why didn't it work out?*)

MG Es ist natürlich für uns eine Enttäuschung, dass dieser Schwung aus Bayern sich nicht ausgewirkt (*Of course it is a disappointment for us, that the support from Bavaria did not have any effect*)

IR Woran lag das Herr Glos? (*What was the reason for it Mr. Glos?*)

MG Es liegt (*It was*)

IR Am Kanzler? (*The chancellor?*)

MG Es liegt sicher ein ganzes Stück daran, dass die Mentalität .... (*It is certainly due to some extent that the mentality ...*)

(41) IR Ist das heute das Ende des Bundeskanzlers? (*Is this the end of the chancellor today?*)

PH Wir wollen jetzt mal den Wahlabend abwarten ...(*We want to wait what else will happen on this election night*)

IR Gut also die Antwort verstehen ich ... (*Good, well, the answer I understand ...*)

PH Das ist n bisschen verfrüht ... (*It is a bit too early*)

Compared to the British avoiding-the-question sequences, a politician's evasiveness seems to be more acceptable in the German context, where there is no real controversy and no lengthy negotiation-of-validity sequence. Most of the time, politicians seem to get away with rather general and rather vague answers when requested to provide specific information. In the German data, the follow-up moves are restricted to two or three turns, which again may lead to intercultural miscommunication. For instance, if a British journalist interviews a German politician and if the British journalist employs the strategies identified for the

British context by initiating a controversial negotiation-of-validity sequence, the German politician, who expects two or maximally three follow-up moves, will consider the interviewer to be rude and prejudiced. Should a British politician be interviewed by a German interviewer employing the strategies identified for the German context, s/he will consider the German interviewer to be rather lenient and not very professional.

In the following, challenging the appropriateness of the macro validity claim is examined.

6.4 Challenging the appropriateness of the macro validity claim

In the British data, challenging the macro validity claim's appropriateness is reflected in references to the media domain and its public status. In the German data, there is only one reference to the macro validity claim which refers to the genre-specific requirement of the turn-taking system. Like the strategy of opting out, the reference to the turn-taking system is realized implicitly. In (42), the conservative Theo Waigel (TW) asks the IR to let him finish his turn thereby implicating that he has been interrupted:

> (42) IR   Theo Weigel. Herr Weigel, ein herber Verlust für die Union, auch klare Verluste für die CSU, woran hat es gelegen? (*Theo Weigel, Mr Weigel, a dramatic defeat for the christian union, also a clear defeat for the christian social union, what was the cause?*)
>
> TW Das ist ganz klar eine Niederlage der Union. Was die CSU anbelangt, mit achtundvierzig Komma vier Prozent haben wir überproportional gut abgeschnitten. Normalerweise liegt die CSU etwa zehn Prozent über dem Bundesdurchschnitt CDU/CSU (*This is clearly a defeat of the christian union. What concerns the CSU, with 48.4% we have had a very good result. Normally the CSU is something like 10% above the federal average of the CDU/CSU*)
>
> IR   Aber es sind zwei Komma acht, Herr Weigel, (*But it is 2.8 Mr Weigel*)
>
> TW Ja, trotzdem (*Yes, but still*)
>
> IR   unter vierundneunzig und vier Komma fünf, unter dem Landtagswahlergebnis (*below 94 and 4.5 below the results of the state election*)
>
> TW Ja kleinen Moment. **Lassen Sie mich einen Satz nach dem anderen sagen**. Wenn wir nun die absoluten Zahlen nehmen. Und wenn wir nun die absoluten Zahlen nehmen, dann haben wir bei einer höheren Wahlbeteiligung etwa so viel Stimmen erreicht, wie bei der Landtagswahl, aber wir konnten bei der schwierigen Gesamtstimmung nicht noch Stimmen dazugewinnen ...(*A tiny moment. **Let me say one sentence after the other**. If we take the absolute figures. And if we now take the*

> *absolute figures, then we have reached almost as many votes as we had in the state elections, but with a higher turnout, but we could not win more votes in that difficult electoral climate...)*

There is no other instance of challenging the macro validity claim. For this reason, the communicative strategy of challenging the appropriateness of the macro validity claim is assigned a marked status as it is not the preferred mode for challenging the appropriateness of a validity claim in the context of a political interview. With respect to intercultural communication, the strategy can be another source of intercultural miscommunication. Again, British politicians might use the strategy to challenge the interviewer's validity claim and signify that s/he intends to close a negotiation-of-validity sequence, while German interviewers would not interpret and contextualize the reference in the speaker-intended way.

In the German data, the most prominent strategy for performing a challenge in the context of a short dyadic political interview is challenging the appropriateness of a validity's content. While the losers prefer an indirectly realized challenge, the winners tend to challenge the interviewer's contributions in a direct manner. With respect to their linguistic realizations, there is a preference for explicit negatives and impersonal constructions, which boost the force of the challenge. Another preference lies in first-person self-references employed in the context of verbs of action, through which the politician expresses determinate meaning and spells out what action they intend to perform, and what action they do not intend to perform. The strategy of challenging the appropriateness of a validity claim by opting out implicitly or by challenging the appropriateness of the macro validity claim are not very frequent; they are used by the winners and by the losers. The strategy of challenging the appropriateness of a validity claim by avoiding the question is more frequent but it is only used by the losers in the data examined.

7.   Challenges: An intercultural context perspective

Intercultural communication is defined as a communicative encounter, in which participants from different cultural backgrounds communicate. A necessary condition for intercultural communication is the premise that the ratified coparticipants do not share identical production, interpretation and contextualization strategies. The application of the functional-grammar conception of markedness introduced above allows for a differentiation between an unmarked production, interpretation and contextualization, which is performed in accordance with a speech community's conventions, and between a marked production, interpretation and contextualization, which is produced in disaccordance with a speech community's conventions.

In natural-language communication and in social interaction the general premise holds that coparticipants expect unmarked settings and thus similar production, interpretation and contextualization strategies. As a consequence of this, any deviation is considered to be a marked instance of communicative performance and is assigned the status of something that goes beyond ordinariness and therefore is strange. Expecting similar production, interpretation and contextualization strategies in intercultural communication is especially true for those settings, in which the non-native coparticipants have a rather high linguistic competence. Because of that, native coparticipants would expect native-like production, interpretation and contextualization strategies and thus a high sociocultural competence. With a low linguistic competence, deviations in a coparticipant's production, interpretation and contextualization of contributions are expected because the coparticipants' prime task lies in the production and the retrieval of factual information. Here, the deviations are accounted for with the practical-reasoning strategies of 'let it pass' or 'unless'.

The definition of intercultural communication also holds for the context of media communication, but needs further refinement with regard to the first-frame setting between direct coparticipants, such as interviewer and interviewee in the context of a political interview, and with regard to the second-frame interaction between the first-frame encounter and the second-frame audience, whose reception process differs significantly from the one of the first-frame coparticipants (Fetzer 2000). As a consequence of the multilayered encounter of media communication, interculture can be both a constitutive part of the first-frame encounter with coparticipants of different cultural backgrounds, and it can be a constitutive part of the second-frame encounter, where the cultural background of the first-frame coparticipants is different to the cultural background of the second-frame audience. To make the context even more multilayered, there might also be diverging cultural backgrounds with diverging production, interpretation and contextualization strategies between first-frame coparticipants, second-frame coparticipants and one or more of the second-frame audience's constitutive subsets.

Due to the ongoing process of globalization and internationalization, inter- and multicultural scenarios are becoming more and more common. It has to be pointed out, however, that the complexity of international and global communication is not necessarily a source of miscommunication or of misunderstanding. Should miscommunication occur, possible perlocutionary effects have to be differentiated with respect to effects anchored to the direct first-frame coparticipants and with respect to effects anchored to the indirect second-frame audience.

The multilayered intercultural setting may account for some of the rather negative perlocutionary effects resulting from the performance of challenges in the German-British context. That is to say, the German tendency to produce a challenge with a high degree of product orientation and a low degree of interpersonal orientation can, if transferred directly to the production, interpretation and contextualization of challenges in British English, have the perlocutionary effect of being perceived as unfriendly and uncooperative. This is due to the lack of the rather high degree of interpersonal orientation through which the British context communicates the possibility of initiating a process of negotiating the communicative status of a contribution.

Culture-specific production, interpretation and contextualization strategies are of great importance if culture and interculture are seen as interactionally organized in and through the process of communication. It is at that stage, where national stereotypes are confirmed through culture-specific production, interpretation and contextualization processes. Against this background, a German speaker talking British English will be allocated to a negative reference group and considered to be bossy, rude and narrow-minded, while a British speaker talking German while adhering to the British strategy of signalling that s/he is open for a process of negotiating the validity of a contribution is also allocated to a negative reference group and considered to be vague, unclear and uncommitting.

8. Conclusions

Challenges in political interviews have been investigated in the framework of a plus/minus-validity claim, where they are systematized with regard to their micro and macro contextual references. The tripartite system allows for a systematic investigation of language- and culture-specific communicative styles for both acceptances and non-acceptances. A challenge is defined as a non-acceptance and thus as a minus-validity claim. Depending on the non-accepted domains of validity, communicative strategies are identified for the German cultural context and for the British cultural context. Culture and interculture are conceived of as interactionally organized phenomena, and communicative strategies are seen as carriers of cultural information. The British and German short election-night interviews of the general elections have almost identical contents: the losers do not want to give reasons for their failure and talk about the merits of former governments instead, and the winners do not want to talk about a victory, which has not yet been assigned an official status. The contents are, however, formulated differently and German culture and British culture are done differently by the coparticipants. The culture-specific ways of expressing a challenge in the political interviews examined confirm the results obtained for unmarked everyday talk: first, the British sociocultural context makes more references to both interpersonal and information domains. Compared to the German sociocultural context, the interpersonal domain is stressed. Second, the British sociocultural context prefers a process-oriented setting, where the institutional identities of interviewer and interviewee are interactionally organized in a more dynamic manner and with more interpersonal needs. The German sociocultural context prefers a product-oriented setting, where the identities are interactionally organized in a less dynamic manner with less interpersonal needs.

The diverging communicative styles have predictable consequences for intercultural communication and for intercultural media communication, where British coparticipants speaking German in accordance with the British style for performing a challenge are perceived as diplomatically unclear by a German audience while German coparticipants speaking British English in accordance with the German style for performing a challenge are perceived as stiff.

References

Atkinson, J. M. and Heritage, J. 1984. *Structures of Social Action: Studies in Conversation Analysis*. Cambridge: Cambridge University Press.
Austin, J. L. 1980. *How to Do Things with Words*. Cambridge: Cambridge University Press.
Blum-Kulka, S. 1987. "Indirectness and politeness in requests: same or different?" *Journal of Pragmatics* 11: 131–146.
Blum-Kulka, S., Kasper, G. and House, J. (eds.). 1989. *Cross-Cultural Pragmatics: Requests and Apologies*. Ablex Publishers, Norwood.
Bull, P. 2003. *The Microanalysis of Political Communication: Claptrap and Ambiguity*. Routledge: London.
Brown, P. and Levinson, S. 1987. *Politeness: Some Universals in Language Usage*. Cambridge: Cambridge University Press.
Edmondson, W. 1983. "A communication course for German teachers of English". *Dialoganalyse und Sprechfertigkeit* (Amsterdamer Werkheft), 25–36. Geothe Institut, München.
Fetzer, A. 1996. "Preference organization und Sprechfertigkeit im engl.-dt. Kontext. Vom propositionalen Schlagabtausch zur interkulturellen Kompetenz". *GAL Bulletin* 24: 63–80.
Fetzer, A. 1997. "Negative contextualization: a socio-semiotic approach to language teaching". In *The Cultural Context in Foreign Language Teaching*, M. Pütz (ed.), 85–109. Lang: Frankfurt.
Fetzer, A. 2000. "Negotiating validity claims in political interviews". *Text* 20: 1–46.
Fetzer, A. 2002. "Communicative intentions in context". In *Rethinking Sequentiality: Linguistics Meets Conversational Interaction*, A. Fetzer and C. Meierkord (eds.), 37–69. Benjamins: Amsterdam.
Fetzer, A. 2006. "'Minister, we will see how the public judges you'. Media references in political interviews." *Journal of Pragmatics* 38(2): 180–195.

Garfinkel, H. 1994. *Studies in Ethnomethodology.* Polity: Cambridge.

Gass, S. and Neu, J. (eds.). 1996. *Speech Acts across Cultures.* Mouton: Berlin.

Givón, T. 1993. *English Grammar: a Function-Based Introduction.* Benjamins: Amsterdam.

Goffman, E. 1974. *Frame Analysis.* Harper and Row: New York.

Goffman, E.1981. *Forms of Talk.* Basil Blackwell: Oxford.

Greatbatch, D.1992. "The management of disagreement between news interviewees". In *Talk at Work,* P. Drew and J. Heritage (eds.), 268-301. Cambridge University Press: Cambridge.

Grice, H. P. 1975. "Logic and conversation". In *Syntax and Semantics. Vol. III,* M. Cole and J. L. Morgan (eds.), 41–58. New York: Academic Press.

Gumperz, J. 1977. "Sociocultural knowledge in conversational inference". In *Linguistics and Anthropology,* M. Saville-Troike (ed.), 191–211. Georgetown University Press: Washington.

Habermas, J. 1987. *Theorie des kommunikativen Handelns.* Frankfurt/Main: Suhrkamp.

Hall, E. and Hall, M. R. 1994. *Understanding Cultural Differences.* Yarmouth/ Maine: Intercultural Press.

Hymes, D. 1974. *Foundations in Sociolinguistics: An Ethnographic Approach.* University of Philadelphia Press: Philadelphia.

Lauerbach, G. 1993. "Conversation analysis and its discontent". In *Anglistentag 1992,* W. Goebel and H. Seeber (eds.), 427–436. Niemeyer: Tübingen.

Lauerbach, G. 2004. "Opting out of the media-politics contract. Discourse practices in confrontational television interviews". In *Selected Papers from the 8th IADA Conference Bologna 2000,* M. Bondi (ed.), 283–294. Niemeyer: Tübingen.

Levinson, S. 1979. "Activity types and language". *Linguistics* 17: 365–399.

Levinson, S. 1983. *Pragmatics.* Cambridge University Press, Cambridge.

Linell, P. 1998. *Approaching dialogue.* Benjamins: Amsterdam.

Luckmann, T. 1995. "Interaction planning and intersubjective adjustment of perspectives by communicative genres". In *Social Intelligence and Interaction: Expressions and Implications of the Social Bias in Human Intelligence,* E. Goody (ed.), 175–188. Cambridge University Press: Cambridge.

Pomerantz, A. 1984. "Agreeing and disagreeing with assessments: some features of preferred/ dispreferred turn shapes". In *Structures of Social Action,* J. Atkinson and J. Heritage (eds.), 57–101. Cambridge University Press: Cambridge.

Posner, R. 1989. "What is culture? Toward a semiotic explication of anthropological concepts." In *The Nature of Culture,* W. Koch (ed.), 240–295. AKS: Bochum.

Searle, J. 1969. *Speech Acts.* Cambridge University Press: Cambridge.

Smith, S. and Jucker, A. 2002. "Discourse markers as turns: evidence for the role of intersubjectivity in interactional sequences". In *Rethinking Sequentiality: Linguistics Meets Conversational Interaction,* A. Fetzer and C. Meierkord (eds.), 151–178. Benjamins: Amsterdam.

Sonesson, G. 1989. *Pictorial Concepts : Inquiries into the Semiotic Heritage and its Relevance to the Interpretation of the Visual World.* Lund University Press: Lund.

Sperber, D. and Wilson, D. 1996. *Relevance: Communication and Cognition.* Blackwell: Oxford.

Wierzbicka, A. 1991. *Cross-Cultural Pragmatics: the Semantics of Human Interaction.* Gruyter: Berlin.

Variation in interviewing styles

Challenge and support in Al-Jazeera and on Israeli television*

Elda Weizman, Irit Levi and Isaac Schneebaum
Bar Ilan University

This paper explores patterns of interviewers' challenge and support in TV news interviews conducted by two interviewers – Faysal al-Qasem in Arabic (on Al-Jazeera) and Ben Kaspit in Hebrew (Israel Television, Channel 1), focusing on topic introduction in the openings, explicit comments and elaborative reformulations in triadic interviews with two interviewees.

Based on a micro-analysis and on meta-comments, we argue that Faysal al-Qasem frames the interview from the outset as unbalanced, and the interviewer's identification with one of the interviewees at the expense of the other is further reinforced by explicit comments, as well as by elaborative reformulations. In the Hebrew part of the corpus, the opening is mostly informative and neutral, expressions of the interviewer's stance are qualified as deviations and do not necessarily converge with those of one of the interviewees, and reformulations are symmetrically distributed between the interviewees. These differences are interpreted in terms of challenge and support.

1. The conceptual framework

(1) ("Between the Headlines", Israeli Television, Channel 1, December 19th 2002)

    162 Lapid   You promised me equal time division, and you let him make speeches

* We wish to thank Dr. Mordechai Kedar and Mr. Richard Atrakchi for their important input about Al-Jazeera and the socio-political context; the anonymous referees, for their valuable contribution to the analysis; Dr. Miriam Shlesinger, for her enriching stylistic comments; and Dr. Hannah Amit-Kochavi, for her expert advice on transcription conventions in Arabic.

(2)   ("The Opposite Direction", Al-Jazeera, July 2nd 2002)
     228 Harb: [...] at first, you invent facts and then you believe them and bring
                        guests to confirm
     229 Ier: Eh
     230 Harb: the version you wish to promote, and you [dare] speak about
                        propaganda through media.

This paper explores patterns of interviewers' challenge and support in news interviews in Arabic and in Hebrew. Specifically, it focuses on triadic interviews with two interviewees each, and examines whether the examined patterns are distributed symmetrically between interviewees.

In line with previous discussions (e.g. Weizman 1997, 1998, 1999, 2003, 2006a), our notion of challenge is anchored in Labov and Fanshel's (1977) definition, suggested in the context of therapeutic discourse:

> When a person takes an action implying that another person did not perform some of these role obligations, he is necessarily heard as criticizing that other person's competence in that role. This applies to problems of initiating role performance, performing the role correctly, or terminating it appropriately. (ibid.: 95)

This view is very much inspired by Goffman's notion of roles, and mostly by the emphasis on the multiplicity of roles fulfilled by each person "in order to be seen as performing his normal role in society with full competence" (ibid: 95). As far as verbal behavior is concerned, Labov and Fanshel (ibid.: 96) go on to say: "If A asserts that B has not performed obligations in role R, then A is heard as challenging B's competence in R". More specifically,

> "If A asserts a proposition that is supported by A's status, and B questions the proposition, then B is heard as challenging the competence of A in that status" (ibid.: 97). Hence, "A challenge is a speech act that asserts or implies a state of affairs that, if true, would weaken a person's claim to be competent in filling the role associated with a valued status". (ibid.: 97)

Elaborating on this notion, challenge is conceived of here as *any verbal behavior which might be interpreted as saying or implying that the addressee has not fulfilled his or her role appropriately, or has failed to fulfill any component thereof.* A basic distinction is made between interactional and social roles.[1] Interviewees' *interactional role* consists, for example, in the obligation to answer properly, to provide information and express opinions, as well as in their right to be given the chance

---

1.   On various nuances in the notions of social role, identity and category membership as they are realized in talk, see, for example, Antaki and Widdicombe (1998); Chabrol (2006); Charaudeau (1995); Lochard (2002).

to do as required. Interviewees' *social roles* vary, and their rights and obligations depend on the social roles which are made relevant (Sacks 1995 [1979]; Schegloff 1991, 1992) in the interview, by virtue of which they were invited to the studio (politicians, experts, media figures, ordinary people). If the interviewees are introduced as politicians, their opinions and convictions are important components of their social role.

Interviewees may be challenged either at the interactional level, or at the level of their social role, or at both. Accordingly, interviewees are *interactionally challenged* if the interviewer says or implies that they have not fulfilled their interactional obligations properly, and they are *socially challenged* if their opinions are undermined (Weizman 2006a, b).

As has been previously argued, challenge potential may be embedded in the semantic meanings of the utterance, or in such discourse patterns as irony (Weizman 2001), reciprocity (Weizman 2003), terms of address (Weizman 2006b) and others, some of which might be culture-specific. Thus, for example, when an interviewee responds to an interviewer's question by saying "Dan, as I see it this is an insignificant question, and in a week from now we won't remember having discussed it" (Erev Xadash [=New Evening], Israeli Television Channel 1, 8.12.91), his response might plausibly be interpreted as challenging the latter's fulfillment of his interactional obligation to restrict the agenda to significant issues. This interpretation relies first and foremost on elements of the utterance meaning, such as the criticism in "this is an insignificant question"; but it is further anchored in the use of an address term (the interviewer's name, "Dan"), which has been shown to carry challenge potential in Hebrew (Weizman 2006b).

In this paper, it will be argued that in multiple-interviewee shows, an interviewee may also be challenged by an asymmetrical attitude of the interviewer. Thus, if the interviewees hold conflicting views, and if the interviewer identifies with one of them and systematically disagrees with the other, he may be perceived as challenging the latter, far beyond the expected 'playing the devil's advocate'. We will further analyze the implications to asymmetry to the positioning of the participants in the interview.

In a previous study of two sequential short interviews on Israeli television, conducted by a single interviewer with two interviewees holding opposing views on a highly emotional topic, it was shown that the host challenged each interviewee in turn, and that in each case he used the same challenge strategies. A symmetry between interviewees has been obtained (Weizman 1999). Judging by the two extracts quoted at the opening of the paper, no such symmetry is maintained in the interviews they are taken from: in the first, the interviewee accuses the interviewer of political bias; and in the second, the interviewer is blamed for establishing interactional asymmetry between interviewees. What are the discourse patterns which trigger these protests? Is there a variation in degree and type of asymmetry established by the interviewers examined here? These are the questions this paper proposes to answer, based on a micro-analysis of discourse styles of two interviewers: Faysal al-Qasem on Al-Jazeera, and Ben Kaspit on Israeli Television. A previous analysis of the same corpus explored the interviewers' meta-pragmatics comments on the management of the interview (turn-taking and agenda) and on the violation of Gricean maxims (Levi et al. 2006). In line with the overall purpose of this paper, we will explore other interviewers' patterns: topic introduction in the openings (Section 3), explicit comments (Section 4) and elaborative reformulations (Section 5) in the course of the interviews.[2] We will argue that through the use of these patterns, Faysal al-Qasem consistently favors one of the interviewees. Ben Kaspit, on the other hand, marks expressions of asymmetrical preferences as interactional deviations, makes attempts to compensate for them, and when he does take a stand on a political issue, it differs from that of either interviewee. This difference will be accounted for in terms of positioning. "The act of positioning [...] refers to the assignment of fluid 'parts' or 'roles' to speakers in the discursive construction of personal stories that make a person's actions intelligible and relatively determinate as social acts" (Harré & Langenhove 1999: 17). Positioning is dynamic, in that it changes in and through discourse; it affects the meaning and the illocutionary value assigned to a given utterance; it is determined in relation to other participants in the discursive event; and, most important for our purpose, a speaker can self-position him/herself, or be positioned by the other discourse participants (ibid.). Based on the proposed comparison, we will suggest that through his asymmetrical attitude, Faysal al-Qasem positions himself as the author of some of the political convictions he expresses. Ben Kaspit, on the other hand, positions himself as fulfilling the traditional interviewer's role of managing the interview.

This interpretation is supported by the interviewees' meta-comments on the interviewers' attitudes, discussed in Section 6. Note that while the analytic approach is of crucial methodological and conceptual importance, it is undoubtedly the overall combination of patterns that determines the nature of interviewers' positioning (Section 7).

---

2.   The coding scheme for the overall analysis includes additional patterns, such as flouting Gricean maxims (Grice 1975), turn taking qualifiers and terms of address.

2.   Context and methodology

The analysis draws on a corpus of evening news interviews in Al-Jazeera, broadcast from Qatar, and on Israeli Television, Channel 1. The programs in question are Al-Ittijah al-Mu'aakis (literally "The Opposite Direction"), and "Bein Hakotarot" (literally "Between the Headlines"), each having one interviewer and two interviewees, representing opposing political views. The two hosts are, respectively, Faysal al-Qasem and Ben Kaspit. The corpus consists of 4 interviews in each language, i.e. 3408 turns in Arabic, and 1157 turns in Hebrew.

The television channel Al-Jazeera is the first Arabic-speaking one to broadcast news and political shows all day long (Usembassy accessed 2003). Broadcasting from Doha, capital of Qatar, with offices all over the world, it is owned by the royal family of Qatar (Andreus 2003; Fandy 2002), and is financed mostly by the Qatar government (approx. 50 million dollars a year) (Barel 2003) as well as by commercials. However, the Emir of Qatar decided recently to turn the station into a self-sustaining private one (Hammad 2003). The channel's slogan is "Ar-Ray war-Ray al-Aaxar", literally: "an opinion and the opposing one". Channel One of the Israel Broadcast Authority (henceforth IBA or Israeli Television) is a public license-fee channel, partly financed by sponsorship ads. In addition to news and current events, it carries entertainment shows, movies, documentaries etc. Its general director is appointed by the Prime Minister and the Minister of Communications (Shalita & Meydan 2003).

The programs discussed here are weekly evening shows. For six consecutive years, Faysal al-Qasem has been awarded the title "the best host in the Arabic world" by the Association of Arab journalists (As-Safeer, January 28, 2003). Ben Kaspit is also a journalist in the Israeli daily Maariv. "The Opposite Direction" always has two interviewees; "Between the Headlines" has either one or two, but the study compares only 2-interviewee shows. The comparability of both programs has been assessed by four experts on Middle East Media. Similarities were pointed out in terms of the combinations between discussion and entertainment, the structure of the program, and the degree of explicitness and aggressiveness of the interviewers. The present discussion is based on the following:

(1)   "The Opposite Direction", Al-Jazeera, June 18th 2002. (999 turns)
Topic: The Palestinians in the lands of dispersion.
Interviewees: Dr. Ahmad 'Uwaydi al-'Abaadi, a former Jordanian Parliament member, and Dr. 'Ali Badwaan, member of the Central Committee of the Democratic Front for the Liberation of Palestine.

(2)   "The Opposite Direction", Al-Jazeera, July 2nd 2002. (724 turns)
Topic: American Media.

Interviewees: Dr. 'Abd al-Hay at-Tameemi, a media specialist from Thames Valley University in London, and Dr. Muwaffeq Harb, a specialist on U.S. affairs, and the Director of the American radio station Ash-Sharq al-Awsat, literally: "The Middle East".

(3)   "The Opposite Direction", Al-Jazeera, December 31st 2002. (1345 turns)
Topic: The vote of Israeli Arab citizens in the general elections in Israel.
Interviewees: Saleh Tareef, an Arab parliament member of the Israeli Labor party, and 'Abd al-Bari 'Atwan, Editor-in-Chief of the Arabic newspaper Al-Quds al-'Arabi.

(4)   "The Opposite Direction", Al-Jazeera, June 17th 2003. (340 turns)
Topic: Palestinian Resistance Movements.
Interviewees: Muhammad Nazzaal, a member of the political bureau of Hammas movement and 'Ahmad Subh, the Palestinian Deputy Minister of Information.

(5)   "Between the Headlines", Israeli Television, Channel 1, December 19th 2002. (314 turns)
The subject: Religious and secular parties in Israel.
Interviewees: Eli Yishay, the leader of the religious "Shas" party and Yosef (Tomi) Lapid, Head of the central anti-religious "Shinuy" party.

(6)   "Between the Headlines", Israeli Television, Channel 1, December 26th 2002. (160 turns)
Topic: The transfer of the Palestinians and political corruption.
Interviewees: Yossi Sarid, Head of the extreme left-wing Merets party and Avigdor Liberman, Head of the extreme right-wing party "Haixud Haleumi – Israel Beitenu".

(7)   "Between the Headlines", Israeli Television, Channel 1, February 20th 2003. (496 turns)
Topic: National Unity Government in Israel.
Interviewees: Minister Tzipi Livni of the right-wing Likud party and Member of Parliament Chaim Ramon from the left-wing Labor party.

(8)   "Between the Headlines", Israeli Television, Channel 1, May 29th 2003. (186 turns)
Topic: The ideology of Israeli Prime Minister Ariel Sharon.
Interviewees: Eyal Megged, a writer and Israel Har'el, a journalist.

The micro-analysis is based on the original texts in Arabic and in Hebrew, but the extracts discussed in this paper have been translated into English, for the sake of the presentation, Note that the gloss has been intended to convey the style of the source text, sometimes at the expense of acceptability in English.

3. Topic introduction in interview openings

Openings are usually intended to define the agenda of the interview, to frame it as newsworthy and to enhance the status of its participants (Blum Kulka 1983; Clayman 1991), and they usually include a statement of topic, background information and a lead-in to the interview (Clayman & Heritage 2002). This, indeed is the case in example (3) from the IBA Hebrew corpus:

(3)[3] ("Between the Headlines", Israeli Television, Channel 1, February 20th 2003)

    Ier: Hello and good evening to you, so tomorrow it will probably happen Amram Mitsna will sit again face to face with Ariel Sharon, in Tel Aviv, at noon, a third meeting and probably a decisive one, on the agenda, a unity government – yes or no, hello Member of Parliament Chaim Ramon, good evening minister Tsipi Livni.

Variations may result from editorial considerations or reflect the personal preferences of the interviewee. Consider the following opening:

(4)   ("Between the Headlines", Israeli Television, Channel 1, December 26th 2002)

    Ier: It is time to say good evening to the two of you, Member of Parliament Yossi Sarid eh, head of "Merets", hello, and Member of Parliament Avigdor Liberman aah, the le- leader of "Haixud Haleumi

---

3.   In the transcribed interviews, the punctuation stands for transcription signs, as follows:

, = a brief pause, the number of commas represents the length of the pause

. = falling intonation

? = rising intonation

(.) (?) = mixed intonation, with a tendency towards a falling or a rising intonation, respectively

{ } = overlap of two utterances

<u>word</u> = stress

word = increased volume

wo::rd = syllable lengthening

= at turn end and next turn opening – no intervening pause between the two

[laughs] = comments on paralinguistic features

In the transcribed Arabic words,

'= pharyngal vowel

aa, ee = phonemic lengthening

→   Israel Beitenu", good evening, you were both, eh, prettier when you
        were younger, that we've just seen on the short video clip".

Here, the topic is alluded to solely through reference to a previously shown video
clip. A humoristic comment ("you were both, eh, prettier when you were young-
er") probably purports to establish solidarity between the participants (Brown &
Levinson 1987) and ease potential tension, and seems to be in line with the use
of other solidarity markers later in the interview (note the use of slang in extracts
9,10 below). The concise, essentially informative pattern revealed in ex. (3) has
been found to be the norm (in 99.4% of the openings) in a 24-hour corpus of
short dyadic news interviews on Israeli television (Weizman 2006b).

    The openings in the Al-Jazeera interviews are different in three respects: they
are relatively long, they follow the formulaic pattern 'A but B', whereby A and B
present the pros and cons of the topic in question, and, most important for our
purpose, they convey the host's stance, which converges with that of one of the
interviewees, and diverges from that of the other. Example (5) is a case in point.
On the agenda – the credibility of the American mass media, mostly when they
report on events within the Moslem context:

(5)   ("The Opposite Direction", Al-Jazeera, July 2nd 2002. With Dr. 'Abd al-Hay
       at-Tameemi, a media specialist from Thames Valley University in London,
       and Dr. Muwaffeq Harb, specialist on U.S. affairs, and the Director of the
       American radio station Ash-Sharq al-Awsat)
       Ier: In the USA there is a liars' club, and each year one American wins
               the title 'The Most Famous Liar'. Last year, however, and in the
               current one, no American won it, not because ordinary Americans
               gave up lying but because this title has become a part of the American
               propaganda mechanism, as one of the satirists says, and the American
               media and political circles have proven that they are worthy of the
               title 'The Most Famous Liar', for the many manipulations and
               nonsense that they have given the world, starting with Muhammad
               'Ataa's passport inside the ruins of the world trade center through the
               Anthrax panic and finally blaming a simple person of planning the
               production of a radioactive bomb.
               Until when will the USA underestimate the world's intelligence? Does
               it really believe the world is that stupid, to believe the panorama of its
               lies, that wouldn't even fool children? Asked one writer. Why did
               American media become a means of deception, distortion of facts and
               fright, in a way that logic would not accept? Why does the USA try to
               arouse the world through the lie of fear and anxiety of an unknown
               amorphous enemy, and strive to make the world stupid? Why does
               Washington keep trying to spread constant panic, and whenever the

level of anxiety decreases, it would invent a dramatic story to evoke fear once more? Was it not totally obvious that behind these stories are purposes from hell?

However, what are the proofs of those who doubt American reports? Why are there people who laugh at the American media only because they disagree with its policy? Could it be that the Arabic non-recognition and revolt are nothing but an Arabic-Islamic means to revenge the USA? Why do we not say, that these constant American alertness and fear of terrorism are a proof of their strong sense of responsibility [and commitment] to protect their citizens' life and the world's security? Is it not of a great injustice to accuse American politics and media of such faults?

This opening has three parts. In the first one, the host tells his audience a short, amusing anecdote about a "liars' club" in the U.S., and in the others he addresses the main issue: the question whether American media are reliable. On the face of it, the second and the third paragraphs may be considered as balanced. Each section is formulated as a series of rhetorical questions, typically characterised by "the addresser's commitment to the answer implied by the question, which is meant to induce the addressee's recognition and acceptance of the message contained in this implicit answer" (Ilie 1995: 73, and see also Ilie 1999). The answers are implied via the background assumptions (Kiefer 1980)[4] which, in turn, support respectively a negative answer to this central question (in the second paragraph) and a positive one (in the third). In the second paragraph, for example, the WH-question "Why did American media become a means of deception, distortion of facts and fright, in a way that logic would not accept?" queries the reasons for the deceptive attitude of American media, while at the same time conveying the background assumption that 'American media have become a means of deception, distortion of facts and fright'; and the question "Why does Washington keep trying to spread constant panic[…]?" conveys the background assumption

---

4. Amongst the vast literature on the presupposition and assumptions embedded in questions, we have chosen to rely on Kiefer's (1980: 101) definition of "background assumptions", as follows:

"Let p be a proposition, ? the question operator (which forms yes-no questions out of p's) and F that part of p that is focused. By *background assumption* of $?p$ we shall understand the proposition p' which we get by replacing F in p by the corresponding Pro-element. By 'corresponding Pro-element' I mean 'somebody' or 'someone' for persons, 'something' for objects, 'some time' for time, 'somewhere' for place, etc." In this account, when asking 'who is leaving?' the speaker normally assumes that the proposition 'somebody is leaving tomorrow' is true.

that 'Washington keeps trying to spread constant panic'. In addition, the negative question "Was it not totally obvious that behind these stories are purposes from hell?", which closes the same paragraph, is conducive to a positive answer (e.g. Bolinger 1957),[5] i.e. 'It is totally obvious that behind these stories are purposes from hell'. Thus, the answers implied by these questions support the view of the US as deceptive and manipulative. The third paragraph, on the other hand, raises the possibility that this criticism is politically biased. The WH-question "Why are there people who laugh at the American media only because they disagree with its policy?" conveys the background assumption that such bias does exist, and the negative question "Is it not of a great injustice to accuse American politics and media of such faults?" is conducive to a positive answer. Both questions, then, support the view of the U.S. as an innocent victim of prejudice.

This balance, however, is only apparent. First, the background assumptions implied by the questions in the second paragraph seem to be more pronounced than those in the third, due to the use of more emotionally loaded expressions such as "distortion of facts", "the lie of fear and anxiety", "strive to make the world stupid" and "purposes from hell". More important, it is the second paragraph which further elaborates on the claim made in the first: "[...] the American media and political circles have proven that they are worthy of the title 'The Most Famous Liar', for the many manipulations and nonsense that they have given the world". In this statement, the use of "have proven" further suggests that the interviewer's subjective evaluations are in fact widely recognised, indisputable facts. Note that some of the accusations directed at the Americans are formulated as given information, in the form of grammatical subordination (e.g. "because ["the Most famous Liar"] has become a part of the American propaganda mechanism" and "not because ordinary Americans gave up lying"), and are thus less vulnerable to refutation. The jocular tone further drives home the host's criticism, establishing an in-group solidarity (Brown & Levinson 1987) between him and the audience. The close co-textual relations between the two first paragraphs undermine any apparent symmetry in the opening, and gives more weight to the implied accusations directed at the American media.

The opening in (6) has a similar structure.[6] The interview addresses the issue of the elections for the Israel Parliament, and, more precisely, questions the

---

5. For Bolinger (1957: 10), "a conducive or leading Q [=question] [is] one that shows that a given answer is expected or desired". It is of particular interest to mention Heritage's (2002) claim that in the context of news interviews, negative interrogatives favor 'yes' answers, and their recipients "respond to them in ways that deny their status as questions" (ibid: 1432).

6. A more detailed analysis of the openings (Levi, Weizman & Schneebaum 2004) supports the claim of implied asymmetry conveyed by a three-part apparently balanced structure.

legitimacy of the adherence of the Arabs citizens of Israel to the Labor party. In the background – a coalition of the Labor party with the right-wing Likud party in the last unity government led by Likud Chair, Prime Minister Ariel Sharon, as well as the election of Amram Mitsna, previously a General in the Israel Defense Force and the Mayor of Haifa, as new Chair of the Labor party. As is always the case, the opening is divided into three parts, which detail some of the pros and cons of the Arab vote. As will be shown later, this symmetry is only *prima facie*.

The opening paragraph consists of a series of rhetorical, WH- and negative questions. Consider the following extract from the opening paragraph:

(6)   ("The Opposite Direction", Al-Jazeera, December 31st 2002. With Saleh Tareef, an Arab parliament member of the Israeli Labor party, and 'Abd al-Bari 'Atwan, Editor-in-Chief of the Arabic newspaper Al-Quds al-'Arabi)

Ier: [...] How are we to bet on the Israeli left, in the coming elections, while it turned out, to be, a caricature of the Likud party, or rather its tail? [...] How are we going to bet on Mitsna now, as if his party left Sharon's party, for the sake of peace,, Do those who applaud the Labor party, not know, that it left the coalition only because of the budget? And, doesn't the Israeli left itself, incline to the right, in a shocking way? Has Israel not turned more fascist?

Here, a series of WH-questions convey through subordinate clauses *background assumptions* which favor a complete rejection of the Labor Party. Thus, the question "How are we to bet on the Israeli left, in the coming elections, while it turned out, to be, a caricature of the Likud party, or rather its tail?" conveys the speaker's criticism of the party's weakness, and the question "How are we going to bet on Mitsna now, as if his party left Sharon's party, for the sake of peace" suggests that Mitsna's Labor Party is not committed to peace. The following negative question further drives this point home, being conducive to a positive answer pointing to the greediness of the party ("Do those who applaud the Labor party, not know, that it left the coalition only because of the budget?"), and the two last negative questions are conducive to the claim that Israel in general, including the political left, has turned more fascist.

In the second part of the same opening, some of the pros are brought up, mostly through conducive negative questions of the type presented in (7):

(7)   ("The Opposite Direction", Al-Jazeera, December 31st 2002)

Ier: Didn't Mitsna show an exceptional experience of coexistence of Arabs and Jews while he was Mayor of Haifa? Does the new leader of the Labor party, not use the slogan, that there is no military solution, for the conflict with the Palestinians, and emphasize that negotiations should go on, from where they stopped? [...] asks Nawfal . Another

> Palestinian journalist thinks that the winning of the Labor party should, lead towards a full retreat from the Gaza strip, and the liberation of millions of Palestinians[...]

This apparent symmetry is compromised, however, by the difference in footing (Goffman 1981) between the two first parts: in the first paragraph, the questions are raised by the host himself; in the second, all of them are ascribed to a third party through voicing (Heritage & Greatbatch 2002; Lauerbach 2006). Thus, the two questions in (7) are attributed to 'Arafat's counselor Mamdooh Nawfal, and the last statement is attributed to an unidentified journalist (no name is mentioned). As a result, in terms of Goffman's (1981) distinction, the interviewer is positioned here as the *author* of the implied cons, and a mere *animator* of the pros. This positioning is further reinforced by the third part of the opening, which consists of a single question:

(8)   ("The Opposite Direction", Al-Jazeera, December 31st 2002)
      Ier: Why have Palestinians got to the <u>point</u> that they consider Mitsna, as trustworthy, although, he threatened a few days ago, to break their head?

This WH-question, which marks the shift from the opening episode to the interview itself, queries the reason for the background assumption that Palestinians unjustly trust the Chair of the Labor Party, thus supporting the interviewer's objection to Mitsna's candidacy.

In the two interviews discussed so far, an asymmetrical introduction of two conflicting stances and the host's subtly marked preference for one of them frame the interview as an unbalanced event whereby the interviewer establishes a kind of "coalition" with one of the interviewees, and positions the other as "less preferred". By so doing, he supports the former and challenges the latter, who is held from the outset accountable for views that are unacceptable to the two other parties.

As we saw, no such framing is manifest in the short, reformulated openings of the IBA interviews. It remains to be seen whether this difference has repercussions for the body of the interview.

4.   Explicit expression of interviewer's stance

In two of the four interviews in Al-Jazeera, the position conveyed in the opening is further confirmed explicitly in the body of the interview. Let us pursue our analysis of program 3. As demonstrated earlier, the host has conveyed some of his misgivings about the support of the Arabs citizens of Israel for the Labor Party in the first part and in the closing utterance of opening. Now he addresses an explicit criticism of the Labor candidate for Prime Minister, Amram Mitsna, at the interviewee Saleh Tarif, Member of Parliament of the Israeli Labor party, former Deputy Minister of the Interior and Minister without Portfolio, the first Druze Minister in the Israel government.

(9)   ("The Opposite Direction", Al-Jazeera, December 31st 2002)
    52 Tareef: When he was the commander [...] during the first Intifada in the days of the Lebanon war, he was the only one of the superior commanders in the Israeli army, and he [=who] addressed, and met, with Begin, and refused to go on, and said, I'll resign, and will not agree that such a war will go on, this was his position towards the Intifada, and he resigned from the army, this is Mitsna
    53 Ier: Eh
    54 Tareef: Eh, {the question is}
    55 'Atwan   {But he}
    56 Ier:→   {Just a minute} Mr. Saleh Tareef, what Intifada, the first Intifada, Mitzna you know, he is responsible for the destruction,, of tens, hundreds of {Palestinian houses}
    57 Tareef: he:y brother, e:h
    58 Ier:→   And for breaking the bones, of thousands of Palestinians,, I mean he he boasts of it now
    59 Tareef: No, {no, he did not – he doesn't boast}
    [...]

In (52), the interviewee brings to the fore Mitsna's active opposition to the Lebanon war while he served as an officer in the army, in an attempt to build a favorable image for him in the eyes of his host. The latter, in turn, is not convinced, and accentuates Mitsna's involvement in the military activities conducted by Israel against Palestinian during the first armed Intifada (56, 58).

The objections to Mitsna's candidacy are further corroborated by the use of highly emotional words such as "destruction of house" (tadmeer al-buyoot), (56) and "breaking bones" (takseer al-'izaam) (58), and through the ironic use of "glorious" (taleed) in the phrase "his glorious, military past and Palestinians' bone breaking" (62). Since this defiance is anchored in Mitsna's alleged aggressive activities against Palestinian Arabs, the interviewer thus challenges not only the interviewee's political stance as a member of Mitsna's party, but also the very essence of the latter's solidarity with his Arab brothers, namely – with the audience.

Later on in the same interview, the interviewer criticizes the Israeli Arabs who vote for the Labor party, by qualifying as "facts" (haq'aiq) his controversial evaluations concerning the reasons for their vote (i.e. the influence of "fundamental right-wing streams of thought and religion"), and then condemning the voters for ignoring them. He further qualifies their political convictions as "a reproduced cliché" (fikra mubtadhala), thus suggesting that they lack reasoned judgment:

(10)   ("The Opposite Direction", Al-Jazeera, December 31st 2002)
840 Ier: [33 words omitted] and it seems like the situation of the Labor party, and these groups, has been negatively influenced in Israel,, by the enormous rise, of fundamentalist right-wing streams of thought and religion,, also in the USA,, right? The question,, which one of the two is the origin and which is the echo is arguable,,[...] We say that some of the Arabs avoid, or ignore,,
→   these facts,, and this is what explains,, why they reproduce, the
→   cliché, that it is obligatory to help the camp of Israeli Labor party,, and the groups close to it,, so that they win,, the coming, elections

Obviously, the interviewer thus challenges Tareef's public role as MP of this very party, whose supporters are so severely criticized. This judgmental attitude is not counterbalanced by a similar approach to the second interviewee. It is therefore not conceived of as "playing the devil's advocate" (Clayman & Heritage 2002: 136–138). Rather, it further enhances the interviewer's bias implied in the opening.

Expressions of the interviewer's attitude have also been found in the IBA interviews. They mostly differ from the previous ones in two respects: they are explicitly marked by the host as deviations, and they do not necessarily side with either of the interviewees.

The following extract figures in an interview which addresses the issue of the establishment of a unity government under the leadership of Prime Minister Sharon. In (11) below, the interviewer expresses his enthusiastic support of such a government:

(11)   ("Between the Headlines", Israeli Television, Channel 1, February 20th 2003. With Minister Tzipi Livni of the right-wing Likud party and Member of Parliament Chaim Ramon from the left-wing Labor party)
269 Ier: to go to this government, I call it a historic government, I am not ashamed here to be now in the kind of a situation not only of an interviewer but also of a Zionist patriot, this is a historical government we have never had.

This stance, however, is explicitly marked by the host as a violation of his discursive role ("I am not ashamed here to be now in the kind of a situation not only of an interviewer"). To justify it, he positions himself in a widely accepted national script ("a Zionist patriot"), and alludes to the legitimacy of its co-existence with his interactional obligations ("not only of an interviewer but also of a Zionist patriot"). Of considerable importance for our discussion is the fact that by expressing his opinion, the host does not compromise the symmetry between the interviewees, since neither of them is in favor of the kind of unity he so enthusiastically opts for: Likud Minister Tsipi Livni supports unity with the religious parties, Labor MP Chaim Ramon refuses to have the Labor join a unity government, and the interviewer envisages an intermediate solution, i.e. a unity government with the Labor party and without the religious parties. The interviewer seems to be well aware of his interviewees' reservations, and enthusiastically proceeds to persuade them:

(12) ("Between the Headlines", Israeli Television, Channel 1, February 20th 2003)

> 74 Ier: If Ariel Sharon proposes a government,,,Labor,,Likud,,Shinuy ,, Mafdal maybe,, you'd agree with me, that this is, a government , unprecedented in the history of Israel, you'd agree with me, ,that this is not the government you come from,, this is a differ ent government, you go to,,,could you,, let yourself,,say,no,,,and leave the country,,with a natural Sharon government, Shas, Agudat Israel, Ixud leumi, Mafdal, which::let us say, according to evaluations will not ensure even the American guarantees

Other manifestations of the host's high involvement in the same interview are distributed evenly between interviewees. In (13), for example, when Likud Minister Livni criticizes her fellow-interviewee, MP Ramon of the Labor party, for his unwillingness to join a unity government run by the Likud (177, 179), the interviewer responds by reformulating and justifying Ramon's reservation (180). In (14), on the other hand, the host explicitly rejects Ramon's stance:

(13) ("Between the Headlines", Israeli Television, Channel 1, February 20th 2003)

> 177 Livni: [41 words omitted] As a matter of fact what does he say, he says I don't believe you
>
> 178 Ier: Correct
>
> 179 Livni: In other words, {the thing, just a minute,excuse me,,,in these two and a half years}
>
> 180 Ier: {But he has a case, we have had two and a half or three years, eh, believing}
>
> 181 Livni: there were some people of the {Labor}
>
> 182 Ier:[to Ramon]: →   {I am working for you}

(14) ("Between the Headlines", Israeli Television, Channel 1, February 20th
2003)

408 Ier: This is the government which Chaim Ramon **for some reason**,,,
and I think he is wrong, {does not want to join,, this is a secular
Unity government [...]}

Note, that in (13), the host jokingly marks his own involvement as a deviation ("I
am working for you", addressed to Ramon, turn 182). By so doing he excludes the
possibility of being ascribed the position he adopts, and thus reaffirms his discursive position as "playing the devil's advocate".

Symmetry seems to be also preserved, to an extent, in an interview confronting Members of Parliament Avigdor Liberman, of the right-wing party Haixud
Haleumi, and Yossi Sarid of the left wing party Merets. Here, each of the interviewees is being challenged by personal judgments pertaining to his behavior in
the public arena: Liberman is accused of corruption (ex. 15), and Sarid – of exces-
sive centralism (16):

(15) ("Between the Headlines", Israeli Television, Channel 1, December 26th
2002)

64 Ier (to Liberman):   [6 words omitted] Now to an issue which has both
ered he:re for quite some time very many people the corruption
in the Likud Avigdor Liberman **as a matter of fact**...you evaded
it at the last minute since it all started with you, the author Of
this method, of[...]is our Ivette Liberman, who is now making a
bundle

(16) ("Between the Headlines", Israeli Television, Channel 1, December 26th
2002)

99 Ier (to Sarid):   But the alte{rnative of Merets, is a one-person rule, of
Yossi Sarid}

100 Sarid: E:h, corruption,,,corruption,E::h}

101 Ier: Who, everyone says is a dictator, no one challenges his position,
getting votes is as easy as pie for you [...]

Indeed, Sarid notices the parallelism: faced with the host's criticism, he ironically
echoes[7] the words previously addressed at his fellow interviewee: "E:h, corruption,,, corruption, e:h," 100).

In both cases, the challenge is somewhat attenuated through the establishment
of solidarity by the use of slang (Brown & Levinson 1987): "making a bundle", Hebrew "gozer kuponim", in 14, and "as easy as a pie", Hebrew "lokeax bahalixa", in

---

7. For a discussion of ironic mentions in news interviews following Sperber and Wilson
(1981), Wilson and Sperber (1992), see Weizman (2001).

15. Still, this is one more place where symmetry seems to be compromised: the criticism addressed at Liberman is intensified by the ironic pretense (Clark & Gerrig 1984) conveyed by "our Ivette Liberman", as well as by the estrangement embedded in calling the interviewee by his non-Hebrew name (Ivette), which he had made a point of replacing by a Hebrew one (Avigdor). In addition, the symmetry is broken by the following comment, whereby the host speaks with Sarid about Liberman in the third person, thus establishing a kind of "coalition" between himself and the former, against the latter:

(17) ("Between the Headlines", Israeli Television, Channel 1, December 26th
      2002)
      138 Ier: Liberman the man, what do you think about him, not the politi
                 cian
      139 Sarid: I don't know him so well, but I guess, tha:t his intentions are
                 good, the problem is no:t,
      140 Ier: You showed me here some papers, in which it was written that
                 he was a hooligan
      141 Sarid: you know,, no no, look, what I:s written in here is that [...]

Note, that unlike the manifestations of political bias in the discourse of Faysal al-Qasem, here the interviewee reframes the episode as pertaining to the personal, rather than the political level ("what do you think about him, not the politician", turn 138), a shift willingly taken up by Sarid ("I don't know him so well"). By so doing, the asymmetry is collaboratively keyed (Goffman 1974) as relatively non-serious.

5. Elaborative reformulations

Reformulations are conceived of here as "[the procedure] by which speakers double back on their [...] interlocutor's speech to change or modify their words, thus producing a new (reworded) version that is offered as a more satisfactory one" (Ciapuscio 2003:211, following Gülich & Kotschi 1995). More precisely, in our corpus it is the interviewer who reformulates the previous interviewee's talk. In a conversational-analyst framework, Heritage and Watson (1979, 1980) observe that reformulations manifest the following properties: preservation, deletion and transformation. Any discussion of these attributes is related to such complex notions as 'sameness' and 'similarity' (Sovran 1992; Chesterman 1998:5–15). We have chosen the term *elaborative reformulation* in order to indicate a marked distance between the reproduced interviewee's utterance and its reformulation by the interviewer.[8] A prominent feature of these reformulations is that they elaborate on the original interviewee's words, and further press home the argument embedded in them. Consequently, they seem to position the interviewer as supporting the interviewee whose utterance is reformulated, thereby challenging the other.

In extract (18), the interviewee Badwaan, a member of the central committee of the Democratic Front for the Liberation of Palestine, indirectly accuses his co-interviewee, former Jordanian Member of Parliament Al 'Abaadi, of identifying with Israel (turn 114):

(18)   ("The Opposite Direction", Al Jazeera, July 2nd 2002)
 114 Badwaan: this is why I mean I request, that we not speak in the name [literally: language] of Israel
 115 Ier: =you mean [ya'ni, literally: it means]
   t- t- you mean Dr. {'Ahmad 'Uwaydi al-'Abaadi, speaks a Zionist dialect}
 116 Al-'Abaadi: {if you may, if you may, if you may}
 117 Badwaan: {eh,, hm,,, hm,,, yes}
 118 Ier: a Zionist language, {if you may [...]}
 119 Badwaan: {The point, a- a Zionist} language

He softens this accusation by formulating it as a direct request for a change in attitude, and hedges it by the use of we-perspective ("I request, that we not speak in the name [literally: language] of Israel"). The interviewer, in turn, reformulates the accusation, and intensifies it by explicitly naming the target of the accusation ("you mean Dr. {Ahmad 'Uwaydi al-'Abaadi, speaks a Zionist dialect"), as well as by replacing the relatively neutral word "Israel" with the more emotionally loaded qualifier "Zionist" (115, 118), which, signifying the ideology underlying the establishment of the state of Israel, carries negative connotations for the Arab speakers and audience. As can be seen in extract (19) below, a few turns later, the interviewer repeats the accusation (133), demands that Al-'Abaadi respond (131), and elaborates on it, blaming him for adopting not only Hebrew, but also English. All this time he avoids calling those languages by their accepted names (Hebrew and English), and qualifies them by their emotionally loaded national affiliation (the Israeli language, the American language):

(19)   ("The Opposite Direction", Al Jazeera, July 2nd 2002)
 131 Ier. [I would like}, you to answer him
 132 Al 'Abaadi: =First, {I'll answer, I}
 133 Ier:→ {you speak} the Israeli {and American}

---

8. In the context of her work on reformulations, see, for example, Blackmore's (1997) discussion of elaboration, including restatement and exemplification.

134 Al-'Abaadi: {No, firs-}
135 Ier: language I mean dialect
136 Al-'Abaadi: =First the Israeli
137 Ier: In this part
138 Al-'Abaadi: =First {the Israeli}
139 Ier: {aha}
140 Al-'Abaadi: Dialect, the Israeli dialect, we don't speak it, neither I nor
                          anybody in Jordan

Thus, the interviewer sides with Badwan in holding Al- 'Abaadi accountable for what seems to them an ideological misconduct. As suggested earlier, by maintaining this imbalance throughout the interview, the host positions himself as the author of the opinions he defends, and thus supports Badwan, and challenges Al- 'Abaadi.

The extract in the next example takes place after al-Tameemi, a media specialist, accuses the American media of deception, and Harb, manager of an American radio station, strongly objects to this criticism. In turn 120, the interviewer claims that Harb failed to answer all his colleague's arguments, and, urging him to provide an answer, reformulates the latter's claims:

(20)   ("The Opposite Direction", Al-Jazeera, July 2nd 2002)
        118 Ier: You said, that you wouldn't {like to answer}
        119 Harb: {I've heard some} of it, yes
        120 Ier: =aha, you wouldn't like to answer these lies, and it is very easy
                         for a- a person, to sit behind a table and talk about, about such
            →   things and fabrications, a- I mean Mr. Eh, Tameemi a short while
            →   ago, hasn't spoken only about lies, but, he said that the American
            →   administration and the American media do, political deception,
            →   that underestimates, people's intelligence and takes them for
            →   fools, as if they were a group of children, and these li- deception
            →   doesn't work on anyone anymore I mean, it became visible and
            →   there are statistics, I would like you to answer that
        121 Harb: I mean I know that there is journalistic deception, and Media
                         deception, and all that is pompous talking that have no no no
                         meaning, [but] there is reality, there are things that happened,
                         and events, there were on September 11th, 19 youngsters, young
                         sters, who bombed, and killed, no less than 3000, innocent
                         people

Here, the host rephrases Al-Tameemi's allegations against the US media at some length. In this reformulation, he uses indices of personal involvement ("these li- deception doesn't work on anyone anymore I mean"), makes additions to al-

Tameemi's words ("as if they were a group of children"), and even modifies them, replacing al-Tameemi's affirmation that the US underestimates the *Arab* nations ("us"), by a more general one, i.e. the US "underestimates, *people's* intelligence and takes them for fools".

In support of his disbelief in the American policy and media, al-Tameemi rejects the Americans' claim that they had found the passport of one of the bombers of the twin Towers, Muhammad 'Ataa. He does so through the use of irony ("I mean, the Americans, nothing, nothing other than Muhammad 'Ataa's passport came down from the plane and and got to the hands of the FBI?", 200) , and by providing what seems to him as scientific data supporting his refutation (196, 198):

(21)   ("The Opposite Direction", Al-Jazeera, July 2nd 2002)

190	Al-Tameemi:	I'll ask the the
191	Ier:	=OK
192	Al-Tameemi:	The respected brother in, in, in
193	Ier:	=Washington
194	Al-Tameemi:	In Washington, after, what is called the explosions, 9/11, they come out to us of course, eh e- in, the plane which, hit the world, trade center,, they haven't found in this plane anything but the pass, eh {e:h}
195	Ier:	{port} of Muhammad 'Ataa [in Arabic – "passport" is 2 words]
196	Al-Tameemi:	of Muhammad 'Ataa, Dr., before coming [here] I met a pilot,, I asked him I mean about about about the plane, he told me, and this information, may be scientific, eh, I mean clear
197	Ier:	=aha
198	Al-Tameemi:	He told me that the plane, weighs around 300 tons when it is in the air, that when it comes down, while it is landing physically it's 3 times heavier,, than its normal weight,, it carries no less than 20 tons of of of of of oil, and if it explodes, its heat level will be, 100 degrees, I mean if you put water, [as they say] in the vernacular, it will melt
199	Ier:	=eh
200	Al-Tameemi:	I mean, the Americans, nothing, nothing other than Muhammad 'Ataa's passport came down from the plane and and got to the hands of the FBI?

The host then reformulates Al-Tameemi's claims in the form of a question addressed to Harb ("he told you for example, that everything had melted, except for Muhammad 'Ataa's passport?", 217, 221) and adds another argument, i.e. the claim that the Americans' information about the plane's black boxes is no less misleading (221, 223), unduly attributing it to Al-Tameemi:

(22)   ("The Opposite Direction", Al-Jazeera, July 2nd 2002)

217 Ier:	For example,, or he told {you for example}
218 Harb:	{but, yes}
219 Ier:	Does it make sense
220 Harb:	=yes
221 Ier:	That everything had melted, except for Muhammad 'Ataa's pass port? OK brother where, are the black boxes, or two black boxes, in, on the two planes, is it possible, that the passport, didn't melt
222 Harb:	Is
223 Ier:	And I mean the passports, how to say it, the black boxes, which never, never melt, did melt? He wants you to answer that, I mean he considers it as nonsense
224 Harb:	Fir- first, I, I will answer you
225 Ier: Eh	
226 Harb:	=I'll give you, I'll give you, I don't know where you got this infor mation, the passport was found

Just as in examples (18) and (19), here too, by consistently reformulating the talk of one of the interviewees and by substantiating the reformulated claims through additions and indices of personal involvement, the host is positioned as asymmetrically supportive of Al-Tameemi, and challenging Harb. This asymmetry excludes a reading of his arguments as "playing the devil's advocate".

In the IBA interviews, there is one apparently comparable case. Discussing the possibility that the Labor Party join a unity government under the leadership of PM Ariel Sharon of the Likud Party, Chaim Ramon, Labor MP, expresses his disbelief in the Prime Minister's promises, and demands that he submit them to the Chair of the Labor Party, Amram Mitsna, in writing. The interviewer asks the co-interviewee, Likud Minister Tsipi Livni, if Sharon might agree to do this, and, since she avoids the question, he declares:

(23)   ("Between the Headlines", Israeli Television, Channel 1, February 20th 2003)

363 Ier:	{no time tables, I demand, I demand now on Mtsna's behalf,, I demand on-M}itsna's behalf, what he told him on Mon{day, in writing,}

By so doing, the interviewer represents Ramon's earlier demand. However, aware of the challenge embedded in this practice to the co-interviewee, he soon withdraws:

(24) ("Between the Headlines", Israeli Television, Channel 1, February 20th 2003)
380 Ier: Maybe we are making it {to:o hard, it is Chaim and I against you}

By acknowledging the unacceptability of the 'coalition' his reformulation has established, the host neutralizes his imbalanced positioning, and re-assumes the interactional obligations underlying interview-management.

6.   Meta-comments: Interviewees blame interviewers

So far we have seen that Faysal al-Qasem positions himself in and through discourse as being politically biased and consistently supportive of one of the interviewees, while Ben Kaspit is rather particular about marking any manifestations of asymmetrical attitude as deviations, and trying to compensate for them. These observations having been made from the researchers' viewpoint, we turn now to the interviewees themselves: does their discourse provide any evidence for the insights gained from our analysis? The corpus presents us with the following answer: both in Hebrew and in Arabic, interviewees explicitly challenge the interviewers for failing to fulfill the obligations pertaining to their role. For example, in (25) Kaspit is taken to represent the media's hunt for scoops, and in (26) al-Qasem is accused of unreliability and distortion:

(25) ("Between the Headlines", Israeli Television, Channel 1, December 26th 2002. With Yossi Sarid, Head of the extreme left-wing Merets party and Avigdor Liberman, Head of the extreme right-wing party "Haixud Haleumi – Israel Beitenu)
102 Sarid: { Listen, th:is}, I know you [in the plural],, you,, eh, and I do::n't God forbid,,,e:h you are more interested in a merchandise, another merchandise, absolutely, in confrontations, fights, quar rels,, in, in in dirt,,,[…]

(26) ("The Opposite Direction", Al-Jazeera, June 18th 2002. With Dr. Ahmad 'Uwaydi al-'Abaadi, a former Jordanian Parliament member, and Dr. 'Ali Badwaan, member of the Central Committee of the Democratic Front for the Liberation of Palestine)
152 Al-'Abaadi   {I,, no sir if} you would, {I don't, please}
153 Ier: {aha, yes}
154 Al-'Abaadi   If you please [Literally: May God protect you] Don't put words I haven't said into my mouth Mr. Faysal, {we are on the air and millions of people see me}

However, in Arabic the interviewer is consistently reproached for establishing asymmetry between interviewees, mostly at the political and ideological level, while in Hebrew the interviewer is blamed for asymmetry only once, and it is interactional asymmetry which is at stake.

This difference is well represented by the two examples quoted at the opening of the article. Lapid reproaches the interviewer for violating his interactional rights by establishing *discursive asymmetry*:

(1)   ("Between the Headlines", Israeli Television, Channel 1, December 19th 2002. With Eli Yishay, the leader of the religious "Shas" party and Yosef (Tomi) Lapid, Head of the central anti-religious "Shinuy" party)
162 Lapid   you promised me equal time division, and you let him make speeches

Harb, on the other hand, is concerned with the interviewer's unreliability and *political bias*, which, to his mind, affect the very selection of invited guests:

(2)   ("The Opposite Direction", Al-Jazeera, July 2nd 2002. With Dr. 'Abd al-Hay at-Tameemi, a media specialist from Thames Valley University in London, and Dr. Muwaffeq Harb, specialist on U.S. affairs, and the Director of the American radio station Ash-Sharq al-Awsat)
228 Harb: […] at first, you invent facts and then you believe them and bring guests to confirm
229 Ier: Eh
230 Harb: the version you wish to promote, and you [dare] speak about propaganda through the media.

Later in the interview, he elaborates on his accusations and explicates them (note the words "propaganda" [di'aayaat], and "distortion [of facts]" [tashweeh]):

(27)   ("The Opposite Direction", Al-Jazeera, July 2nd 2002)
236 Harb: = Whenever, each time I met with an official of Al-Jazeera I urged them, to translate, into English, the programs of Al-Jazeera, but what I have heard in some cases from Al-Jazeera, and some of the guests it has brought {and some of the propa ganda and the distortion of facts that you [in the plural] do}

More striking are Al-'Abaadi's allegations in (28) and (29), whereby the interviewer is accused of distorting the facts, misleading the audience, depriving the interviewee of his interactional rights and siding with his co-interviewee:

(28)   ("The Opposite Direction", Al-Jazeera, June 18th 2002. With Dr. Ahmad 'Uwaydi al-'Abaadi, a former Jordanian Parliament member, and Dr. 'Ali Badwaan, member of the Central Committee of the Democratic Front for the Liberation of Palestine)

957 Al-'Abaadi: respected brother, all of the entrances [of viewers through Internet] – it seems like they are all prejudiced against my stance, either because I am Jordanian, against Jordan's stance, or they can't understand me because of your interruption, you are a loud mouth, you twisted the picture and tired the viewer.

(29)   ("The Opposite Direction", Al-Jazeera, June 18th 2002)

813 Ier: {and these sayings you} a short while ago you blamed the, eh brother 'Ali of [using] rhetorical phrases, and these sayings of yours are the very <u>essence</u> of {contemptible Arabic rhetoric, I would like to ask you, 55, entrance 55, OK just, a minute

814 Al-'Abaadi: {No brother, brother, **because you didn't like it**, if you may,, no, Mr. Faysal, if you please [literally: may god be satisfied with you]} **because you didn't like it** when I said about him that he speaks rhetorically, that's true

815 Ier: Aha

816 Al-'Abaadi: =and I tell you

817 Ier: =eh

818 Al-'Abaadi: =if you may, let me complete my answer, first

819 Ier: =eh

No comparable accusations are made by the interviewees in the IBA interviews.

7.   Conclusion

Interviewers' neutrality, whether genuine or pretended, may be achieved in a number of ways, mostly by asking questions, formulating statements as if they were preliminaries to questions, and attributing statements to a third party via quotations and voicing (Clayman 1988; Clayman & Heritage 2002; Greatbatch 1988; Lauerbach 2006). In the view suggested in this paper, in multiple-interviewee events, (seeming) neutrality may be realized by the establishment of symmetry between the interviewees.

The comparative analysis of two-interviewee discourse events in Arabic and in Hebrew has yielded interesting differences in this respect. We have shown that in Al Jazeera, al-Qasem's interviews are framed from the outset as unbalanced, and the interviewer's identification with one of the interviewees at the expense of the other is compounded by explicit comments, as well as by elaborative reformulations. In Kaspit's interviews on Israeli television, on the other hand, the opening is mostly informative and neutral, expressions of the interviewer's stance are qualified as deviations and do not necessarily converge with those of one of the interviewees, and reformulations are symmetrically distributed between the interviewees. These preliminary findings, we have shown, are supported by the interviewees' own evaluations, manifest in their meta-comments.

In a deeper sense, we suggest that these differences affect the basic role-design underlying the interviews. Ideological and political asymmetry entail the interviewer's positioning as the author of a viewpoint rather than its animator; the framing of stances as deviations and the preservation of a relative symmetry, on the other hand, reinforce the interviewer's interactional power.

These differences may suggest that the search for neutrality is not a universal, and that cultures may differ in terms of their perception the interviewer's role. A larger corpus representing a large number of interviewers, a wider range of discourse patterns and topical variation may lead to deeper insights on this issue.

References

Andreus, Z. 2003. "Al-Jazeera" – another look. *Ha'ayin Hashvi'it*: Jerusalem, 36 (January 2002), 30–31.

Antaki, C., Widdicombe, S. 1998. "Identity as an achievement and as a tool". In *Identities in Talk*, Ch. Antaki and S. Widdicombe (eds.), 1–14, Sage: London.

Barel, T. 2003. "The Event in "Al-Jazeera"". *Ha'ayin Hashvi'it* 44 (May 2003), 18–20 (in Hebrew).

Blakemore, D. 1997. "Restatement and exemplification: A relevance theoretic reassessment of elaboration". *Pragmatics and Cognition* 5(1): 1–19.

Blum-Kulka, S. 1983. "The dynamics of political interviews". *Text* 3(2): 131–153.

Bolinger, D. L. 1957. *Interrogative Structures of American English*. University of Alabama Press: Alabama.

Brown, P. and Levinson, S. 1987. *Politeness: Some universals in language usage*. Cambridge University Press: Cambridge.

Ciapuscio, G. E. 2003. "Formulation and reformulation procedures in verbal interactions between experts and (semi-) laypersons". *Discourse Studies* 5 (2): 207–233.

Chabrol, C. 2006. "Des "identities" sociales et discursives: De L'analyse de discours à la psychologie sociale." *Questions de Communication* 2006: 15–28.

Charaudeau, P. 1995. "Rôles sociaux et rôles langagiers". In *Modèles de l'Interaction Verbale*, Charaudeau, P. (ed.), 79–96. Aix en Provence : Publication de l'Université de Provence.

Chesterman, A. 1998. *Contrastive Functional Analysis*. Amsterdam/Philadelphia: John Benjamins.

Clark, H. and Gerrig, R. J. 1984. "On the pretense theory of irony". *Journal of American Psychology* 113(1): 121–126.

Clayman, S. E. 1988. "Displaying neutrality in television news interviews". *Social Problems* 35: 474–492.

Clayman, S. E. 1991. "News interview openings: Aspects of sequential organization". In *Broadcast Talk*, P. Scannel (ed.), 48–75. Sage: London

Clayman, S. and Heritage, J. 2002. *The News Interview*. Cambridge: Cambridge University Press.

Fandy, M. 2002. "Al-Jazeera: News with an Agenda". *Middle East Insight: Washington* 17(2) (March-April 2002): 79–80.

Goffman, E. 1974. *Frame Analysis*. New York, Evanston, San Francisco and London: Harper.

Goffman, E. 1981. *Forms of Talk*. Philadelphia: University of Pennsylvania Press. Greatbatch, D. 1988. "A turn-taking system for British news interviews". *Language in Society* 17: 401–430.

Grice, P. H. 1975. "Logic and conversation". In *Syntax and Semantics 3: Speech Acts*, P. Cole and L. Morgan (eds.), 41–58. New York: Academic Press.

Gülich, E. and Kotsch, T. 1995. "Discourse production in oral communication". *In Aspects of Oral Communication*, U. Quasthoff (ed.), 30–66. New York: de Gruyter.

Hammad, M. 2003. "A new Directorate for "AL-Jazeera"" *Channel. Al-Quds al- Arabi*, 21/11/2003 (in Arabic).

Harré, R. and Van Langenhove, L. (eds.). 1999. *Positioning Theory: Moral Contexts and Intellectual Action*. Blackwell, Oxford.

Heritage, J. C. 2002. "The limits of questioning: Negative interrogatives and hostile question content". *Journal of Pragmatics* 34: 1427–1446.

Heritage J. C. and Watson R. D. 1979. "Formulations as conversational objects". In *Everyday Language: Studies in Ethnomethodology*, G. Psathas (ed.), 123–162. New York: Irvington.

Heritage J. C. and Watson, R. D. 1980. "Aspects of the properties of formulations in natural conversations: Some instances analysed". *Semiotica* 30 (3/4): 245–262.

Ilie, C. 1995. "The validity of rhetorical questions as arguments in the courtroom". In *Special Fields and Cases: Proceedings of the Third ISSA Conference on Argumentation*, F. H. van Eemeren, R. Grootendorst, J. A. Blair and A. Willard (eds.), 73–88. Sic Sat: Amsterdam.

Ilie, C. 1999. "Question-response argumentation in talk shows". *Journal of Pragmatics* 31: 975–999.

Kiefer, F. 1980. "Yes-no questions as WH-questions". In *Speech Acts and Pragmatics*, J. R. Searle, F. Kiefer, M. Bierwisch (eds.), 97–119. Dordrecht: Reidel.

Labov, W. and Fanshel, D. 1977. *Therapeutic Discourse*. Academic Press: London.

Lauerbach, G. 2006. "Discourse representation in political interviews". *Journal of Pragmatics* 38(2): 196–215.

Levi, I., Weizman, E. and Schneebaum, I. 2004. "Cultural variation in interviewing styles: News interviews in Hebrew and Arabic". In *Studies in Modern Hebrew*, Y. Shlesinger and M. Muschnik (eds.), 152–167. Tsivonim: Jerusalem (in Hebrew).

Levi, I., Weizman, E. Schneebaum, I. 2006. "Soutien et défi: Pour une étude comparée des interviews télévisées sur Al-Jazira et a la téleévision israélienne". Questions de Communication 9: 73–94.

Lochard, G., 2002, « Identités sociales, médiatiques et discursives à la télévision : de la mobilité à l'instabilité », Questions de Communications 2: 145–158.

Sacks, H. 1979. "Hotrodder: A revolutionary category". In *Everyday Language: Studies in Ethno-methodolgy*, G. Psatahas (ed.), 7–14. New York: Erlbaum.

Sacks, H. 1995. *Lectures on Conversation*. Blackwell: Oxford.

Schegloff, E. A. 1991. "Reflections on talk and social structure". In *Talk and Social Structure: Studies in Ethnomethodology and Conversation Analysis*, D. Boden and D. Zimmerman (eds.), 44–70. Polity Press: Cambridge.

Schegloff, E. A. 1992. "In another context". In *Rethinking Context: Language as an Interactive Phenomenon*, A. Duranti and C. Goodwin (eds.), 193–227. Cambridge: Cambridge University Press.

Shlita H. and Medan, I. 2003. "Kesher Bar'el. *Yediot Aharonot*, January 10th :16–20.

Sovran, T. 1992. "Between similarity and sameness". *Journal of Pragmatics* 18(4): 329–344.

Sperber, D. and Wilson, D. 1981. "Irony and the use-mention distinction". In *Radical Pragmatics*, E. Cole (ed.), 295–318. New York: Academic Press.

Usembassy. accessed 2003. http:// www.usembassy.at/en/download/pdf/al_jazeera.pdf

Weizman, E. 1997. "Journalistic discourse in modern Hebrew: Saturated environments". In *Shay la'Hadassa: Research in the Hebrew Language and in Judaic Languages*, Y. Bentolila (ed.), 211–227. Ben Gurion University: Beer Sheva (in Hebrew).

Weizman, E. 1998. "Individual intentions and collective purpose:The case of news Interviews". In *Dialogue Analysis VI*, S. Cmejrkova, J. Hoffmanova, O. Mullerova, J. Svetla (eds.), 269–280. Max Niemeyer Verlag: Tübingen.

Weizman, E. 1999. "Discourse patterns in news interviews on Israeli television". In *Hebrew: A Living Language*, G. Toury and R. Ben Shachar (eds.), 1–22. Haifa University Press (in Hebrew).

Weizman, E. 2001. "Addresser, addressee and target: Negotiating roles through ironic Criticism". In *Negotiations and Power in Dialogic Interaction*, E. Weigand and M. Dascal (eds.), 125–137. John Benjamins: Amsterdam/Philadelphia.

Weizman, E. 2003. "News interviews on Israeli television: Normative expectations and discourse norms". In *Dialogue Analysis 2000*, S. Stati and M. Bondi (eds.), 383–394. Niemeyer: Tübingen.

Weizman, E. 2006a. "Roles and identities in news interviews: The Israeli context". *Journal of Pragmatics* 38(2): 154–179.

Weizman, E. 2006b. "Positionnement par le défi : les négociations des rôles dans l'interview télévisée". *Questions de Comunication* 9: 135–149.

Wilson, D. and Sperber, D. 1992. "On verbal irony". *Lingua* 87: 53–76.

PART IV

Media events

From public address to election nights

Christmas Messages by heads of state

Multimodality and media adaptations

Christoph Sauer
University of Groningen

This chapter investigates the multimodal quality of Christmas Messages by European heads of state on TV from a functional-pragmatic and semiotic angle. It defines them as dealing with multiple types of materialities from different modes and sub-modes. Section 1 develops the central concept of discourse anchoring as (multimodal) ways through which discourse participants and TV viewers are guided towards and supported in their information processing. Section 2 discusses the discourse facets of Christmas Messages on TV as adaptation of a re-oralised written text to TV features and their media design potentials. Section 3 examines two addresses: the 'multimedia show' by the British Queen in 2003 and the 'sermon' by the Finnish President in 2004. Section 4 presents a synopsis of message materialities from nine countries giving particular attention to their multimodal 'grammar'. The Conclusion reflects on the growing need of visual representation within the political culture and the complex relationship between what TV viewers see and what they hear.

1. Introduction: Materialities of TV Christmas Messages

This chapter addresses the multimodal quality of Christmas Messages by European heads of state from the perspective of TV audiences. On the occasion of Christmas Day, New Year's Eve or New Year's Day, nations are used to seeing their highest representatives delivering special messages. Not included are speeches on the same occasions by heads of government, since they normally are more (party) political and programmatic in nature. I do neither discuss processes of speech writing and reviewing; their investigation needs access to presidential staff or to a royal institution I do not have (Jochum 1999; Neumann 2004). The paper is based on a corpus of nine televised Christmas Messages (see Table 3.1 below) suppplemented with the speech texts provided by official websites (including translations into English) or transcribed from the screen. In general, I concentrate on the visual and multimodal aspects of transmission, on what TV audiences *see* while listening to their heads of state.[1]

Heads of state are defined by their *representative* functions. Their duties include state visits, receptions of foreign guests on the same formal level, formal political (constitution-driven) acts and, in general, the representation of their own nation on different occasions throughout a year. Ritual communication is rampant at such moments. While their duties are fully absorbed by their main task of being present ceremonially and making the nation audible and visible, on Christmas or New Year's Day their Messages normally bear a *semi-official* character. Personal and individual considerations may amplify topical variation (Sauer 1999, 2000, 2001, 2002). Because Messages cannot only consist of Christmas and New Year's wishes, although they are a constitutive part, the question arises *what* is said, and which topics, also visual ones, evoke other types of discourse. For TV viewers also react to the delivery as such and pay attention to *how* heads of state are shown and *how* convincingly they perform. Media features and actualisations of recipient design count.

We therefore regard Christmas Messages, seen as a generic term referring to the corpus, as *communicative events* rather than as pure texts. This implies that communicative practices (of the delivery of public speeches) have to mingle with media practices (of their TV formats). The media practices of our corpus range from the footage of a person sitting at a desk and reading aloud from a manuscript to a person who is shown acting and chatting with other people, moving around while addressing and looking directly into the camera, using teleprompter technology. Besides, as is characteristic of TV settings, Messages are always *framed*. Their most general frame is the announcement by TV announcers, but music, national symbols, Christmas decoration and festivity signs add frames too. How these frames trigger special meanings and what their impact is in terms of the materialities the Messages draw upon is part of this investigation.

A Christmas Message as a communicative event employs two domains: with regard to its content, it embeds *other discourses* including the *personal voice* or *tenor* and, with regard to media potentials, it relies on *other practices*. A mini-

---

1.   I want to thank my anonymous reviewer who constructively commented on an earlier draft and enabled me to improve the argument of the present version. Special thanks are due to Gisela Redeker for discussing the text content and Anita Fetzer for supporting the style editing.

mal requirement, as we may assume from earlier investigations (Atkinson 1984; Sauer 2001, 2002, 2005; Tiemens 2005), would be an appropriate environment for its content that reflects the 'state of the art' concerning its media adequacy. It is these materialities that constitute the Message's impact. TV viewers are expected to fall back on them when processing and constructing their own meanings. Of course, this is not a radically new perspective. In political discourse analysis, however, the recipient-designed materialities are often neglected and sometimes not even mentioned. This chapter attempts to work out in detail how the materialities could be taken into consideration as relevant pieces of the meaning potentials that are offered to the public.

Our corpus and other publications (not in the least publications in the national press covering of the event) reveal what the Messages have in common. The addresses

- contain accounts (often narrations) of last year's events
- show certain episodes from the head of state's personal perspective
- accentuate developments of the public opinion during the last year
- invite the TV viewers to share social values that have been seen as 'problematic' or 'challenging' within the last year
- re-establish the common ground for public communication by contributing to the social fabric of the community
- provide a context for individually coloured Christmas or New Year's wishes

Such kinds of verbal actions, visual appearances and other discourse actualisations form the network of every Message. Their combination, however, is vast. Moreover, because heads of state tend to depend on public support, they have to provide visions, opinions or meanings that are both acceptable and plausible. Consequently, the Messages are 'neutral' rather than 'one-sided'. Yet they are controlled by ideological notions that delineate the national political culture (see also Clyne 1994). In order to avoid political arguments, which might be provoked by the political leaders, Christmas Messages are almost always restricted to those activities which the government as the actual centre of politics does not claim for itself (see Sauer 2001; Neumann 2004). Ideological work is rather done visually and musically than verbally. Considering the use of national symbols and culture-related pictures, and the reference in music and appearance to national customs and Christmas habits, it is very likely that common values are highlighted, or at least welcomed as a bonus.

What is at stake in general is the issue of a *televised* Message. This encompasses heads of state delivering their Messages directly from the screen. No public is visible in their vicinity. A Christmas Message therefore has a sermon-like appearance. Heads of state are shown on the screen reading aloud from teleprompter or manuscripts lying on a desk. So how does what you see contribute to what you hear? Undoubtedly, the viewers get more than what they hear, more than an articulated Message text. They also get heads of state in a specific environment (e.g., standing at a lectern), seen from a specific camera angle, with or without camera movements, and framed by symbols (like flags, candles, Christmas trees), flowers, props etc. as well as by music (before and/or afterwards). Thus, they get linguistics *and* semiotics. They get meaningful material of different kinds, in different layers and partaking in different practices. This is the reason why we call such Messages 'communicative events' rather than 'texts'. The event is of course text-related, but the text is also event-related, since it aims at communication *and* interaction. No text exists as such, it needs *modes* and *media* to come to life, to become communication. The challenge, then, is to track down these material meaning-making elements of spoken discourse fused with images, music and sounds. It is this *fusion* that calls for scrutiny.

In an early publication, Fiske and Hartley (1978: 85–100) suggest that TV, in general, has a "bardic function". Television as a "bard" articulates the established cultural consensus and implicates the members of the culture into its dominant value systems. It celebrates the position of socio-centrality by controlling eccentricity and assures the culture of its practical adequacy in the world. TV exposes potential ideological re-orientation, if needed, and convinces the audience that individual status and identity are guaranteed by the culture as a whole. By these means, TV puts forward a sense of cultural membership. It may be worth attempting to relate the general "bardic function" of TV to the head of state's representative voice. This entails that the head of state himself or herself is also a kind of "bard" and may be associated with traditional bards who rendered the central concerns of their days into verse. Although the highest representatives do not perform verse (with the exception of some quotes from poetic and literary texts), their performances clearly give room to the central concerns of that year and time. In such a way, a Christmas Message on TV is culturally positioned by specific discourse practices and sociocultural practices, and may therefore receive acclaim.

One such practice consists of the *doubling* of the bard: officially, heads of state possess the highest representative function, but when acting as such, they also act as natural persons. The latter are made explicit when they mention, or react to, personal circumstances like family relationships. Audiences are acquainted with this demeanour. It echoes the "King's two bodies" (Kantorowicz 1957), an (originally medieval) description of the preconditions of every representative public office: incumbents have in them the *body natural*, which is mortal, and the *body politic*, which is eternal. This mystification is necessary as well as useful, for it allows achieving political acts without provoking resistance against the political power that is executed by the office. The public, then, hears official words as belonging to its own repertoire. It responds to both bard and office. Against this background, descriptions offered by heads of state may become prescriptions. This is the price people pay for cultural membership. In Christmas Messages, the magic, to which the common ways of Christmas celebration on TV allude, pertains to this mystic fiction.

In order to gain access to the materialities of Christmas Messages, three lines of investigation are combined in this chapter: Functional Pragmatics, Critical Discourse Analysis and Multimodal Discourse Theory. In Functional Pragmatics, the constellation that is characteristic of Christmas Messages is seen as the *importation* of other discourses into the main discourse. One searches for propositions that bear ambiguous or vague meanings, or one considers other ambivalences and discrepancies throughout the text, in particular concerning discourse anchoring devices (see below) and rhetorical strategies (Ehlich 1994a, 1994b; Sauer 1996, 2002). In Critical Discourse Analysis, this constellation is seen as *intertextual* movement. One looks for what genres, voices and discourses are drawn upon, how they are articulated together and what relationships and identities are constructed (Fairclough 1995). In Multimodal Discourse Theory, the constellation is seen as resulting from the integration of several communicative practices. Its analysis has to reflect the different *semiotic resources* that establish the meaning-making potentials of the event (Fiske 1987; Fiske & Hartley 1978; Kress & Van Leeuwen 1996, 2001; Van Leeuwen 2005; Lemke 2002; Stöckl 2004; Lim 2004).

In Figure 1 (below), the relationship between the three approaches is shown. My basic assumption is that discourse needs to be distinguished from what I call "discourse shadow" (following Ehlich 1994b): the means of *discourse anchoring* in the ongoing communication, e.g. by deixis (i.e. focussing and re-orientation), morpho-syntax, operative procedures related to information chunking, control of mental actions, articulation and body language. Discourse anchoring operates as harmonisation of the information part of an ongoing discourse with its function and with the very needs of the processing in the reception situation. I link the means of the discourse shadow to semiotic resources that depend on media features.

The origin of this distinction is Bühler's "Language Theory" (1934, English 1990). Bühler developed the so-called "Organon Model" as a unity of every communicative exchange that consists of three general functions: *representation, appeal* and *expression*. Representation is considered to be delimited by the functions of expression (as related to the speaker's significative expressive phenomena) and appeal (as related to the hearer's perception and attitude). The three functions can be studied if one divides the discourse at hand into language external functions which aim at external goals, e.g. the illocution of speech acts, and language internal functions which aim at discourse anchoring by fostering the participants'

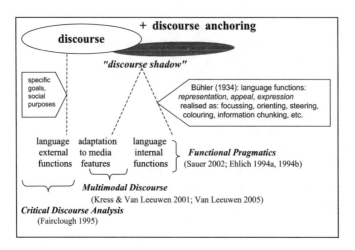

Figure 1. Discourse and its need of being anchored in the communicative situation: Three methods of analysis and their provenance

processing, e.g. concerning information clustering and focus movement, accentuation and concatenation of content parts. The latter ones form the discourse shadow and provide its recipient design. They depend also on media features and have therefore to be adapted to the semiotic resources used. The discourse shadow anchors the ongoing communication in the situation and combines language means with other semiotic resources. It bridges the gap between the speech text and multimodal practices that are characteristic of TV speeches.

In such a way, the materialities of Christmas Messages may be tackled. In the following section, I discuss the concept of multimodality by combining discourse anchoring, semiotic resources and more general concepts, such as secondary orality and literacy. In Section 3, Christmas Messages from GB (3.1) and Finland (3.2) are examined. They represent two extreme positions: one is very rich in semiotic resources while the other is more like a sermon-like address. In Section 4, a synopsis of the semiotic resources of the corpus will be developed. This is to serve as a first step towards a semiotic grammar of Christmas Messages. In the conclusion (Section 5), I relate my findings to cultural dimensions which are characteristic of Christmas addresses and their materialities.

2.   From orality to secondary literacy and its adaptation to TV

The starting point in analysing a modern Christmas Message on TV is to reflect on the change of political *rhetoric* from live oratory to media transmission (Atkinson 1984; Sauer 1996; Tiemens 2005). This change affects the speaker's role concerning their screen appearances; it is often referred to as a "decline" of rhetoric.[2] In classical antiquity, speaking meant personification, performance and content management at the same time by *live oratory*: organised spontaneity, catching applause and spellbinding eloquence. The semiotic resources classical orators had at their disposal consisted of place and time, body movements, dress, gaze, verbal craft and actors' skills. Nowadays, medium conditions determine the semiotic resources to a great extent. What was adequate in live oratory no longer functions appropriately when transmitted by television. Because the primary orality of oral culture has been influenced by the emergence of written communication and the development of other technical media (in particular TV), we now live in the age of secondary orality. To use Ong's own words: "It is essentially a more deliberate and self-conscious orality, based permanently on the use of writing and print, which are essential for the manufacture and operation of the equipment and for its use as well" (Ong 1982: 136).

This secondary orality governs the reality of modern political discourse. When politicians appear on TV, we may discern a range of realisations of this orality. As for some politicians, it is obvious that they act spontaneously, although their spontaneity is "cultivated and domesticated" (Ong 1982: 137). Others routinely formulate sentences that sound like written passages even if a manuscript is neither used nor memorised. Their routine is a result of education and instruction, which normally means learning from books and written examples. A third group produces well formulated oral texts which were indeed written in advance and therefore re-oralised for such an occasion. TV audiences mostly can see that the speakers rely on manuscripts. These three realisation forms of secondary orality, although there are of course more of them (Holly 1995), demonstrate that the concept of secondary orality is plausible, but needs to be further refined.

The routine and the text-dependent groups both echo an inclination towards old speech attitudes. Politicians on the screen often execute *declamations*, a term borrowed from rhetoric. They 'declaim' rather than 'do' speech acts. Moreover, it was declamations that formed the basis of Western education. People have had to learn written texts in order to be able to equip their ongoing or future oral communication. Without texts their oral skills would not increase. The speech habit of declamations still influences the way representative politicians act in public. When they represent the nation, they act as *declamators* – of texts written by others. The declamations are clearly script-bound since the ritual nature of a representative speech and the representation situation accentuate the need for a

---

2. But not so by MacArthur (1999) who only admits that eloquence remains necessary however modified, in order to actualise the general sense of "drama" needed by the "media democracy".

reliable text basis. If we compare a Christmas Message with, say, a spontaneous appearance, such as a reception or the like that shows heads of state acting and chatting with people, then their overtly script-bound character comes to the fore. In general, spontaneity shown by representatives and transmitted by mass media is normally carefully planned and often rehearsed. At least, it is a result of reflections and professionally supplied preparations (Holly 1995; Neumann 2004).

In the light of these considerations, a Christmas Message bears an 'overcultivated' air. The consequence of this practice (or, more precisely, "discourse practice", as Fairclough (1995) calls it) is that a Christmas Message uses a kind of *secondary literacy*, an overtly re-oralisation of a written text. This occurs in combination with a TV script or a planned footage. Its literacy is based on the fact that the written text provides the relevant content. Additionally, the availability of the Message text on official web sites or, as is the case, for instance, in the Netherlands, its publication by the national press, contributes to this air of literacy. Its secondariness shows in the sermon-like presentation style: speakers *enact* the text as if performing by memory, although they use the teleprompter technology or read from a manuscript. Seen this way, secondary literacy equals the oral re-articulation of a written text by a speaker reading aloud.[3] Accordingly, secondary literacy is re-oralised written text – whereas secondary orality is textualised (writing-oriented and medium-related) orality.

Christmas Messages are embedded in the nation's Christmas celebration. This embeddedness asks for more than declamations as it is unthinkable that heads of state 'declaim' the wish "Happy Christmas to you all". They must be more convincing – more 'live'. In such a decisive moment, they must be less script-bound, e.g. by smiling, putting their reading glasses down, looking into the camera, making an inviting gesture, articulating enthusiastically etc. The communicative practices applied in a Christmas Message, thus, borrow (and must borrow) from other practices that are less script-bound. The secondary literacy has to be mitigated by other ways of addressing and other semiotic resources used.

In general, TV viewers gather more than the re-oralised text alone. They *see* a speaker speaking and acting at the same time. TV audiences respond to meanings which are related to "televisuality" (Atkinson 1984). The medium features and their semiotic resources are predominant. It depends on the chosen realisation whether the Message is seen and heard along the lines, to take extreme cases, of a 'sermon' or a 'multimedia show'. On the one hand, a 'sermon' is characterised by the fact that speakers are alone on the screen and create a relationship with their recipients that depends more on the speech content than on the few other

3.   This is often supported by subtitles of the Message text, which is indeed a strong indication of secondary literacy. Deviations from the manuscript are practically impossible.

semiotic elements. When heads of state speak directly from the screen then only the variation of camera shot sizes (from medium via medium close-up to close-up) and camera movements may lower their intenseness. According to Atkinson (1984), this is a situation not convenient as far as TV features are concerned. The Finnish example (see below) belongs to the sermon-like Messages that are customary in most of the European countries. It urges the recipients to concentrate on the Message content, although the way of performing (concerning gaze, body language, articulation, dressing code, the use of props etc.) may cause a range of responses, from fascination to disappointment, from sympathy to compassion.

On the other hand, a Christmas Message as a 'multimedia show' presents not only an orator, but also video sequences of him or her in different environments, sometimes even other people who themselves contribute to the Message content by delivering statements. This last example refers to the style of the British Queen's Christmas Message from 1997 on. The British example (see below) demonstrates a strong inclination towards mass media expertise and expectations, at least preparedness for innovative media exposure and willingness for experiments. It is a long way from live oratory to the 'multimedia' approach.

Seen from this perspective, the challenge is to bring about more correspondence between words and pictures, what people hear *and* see. The semiotic resources have to be richer, with respect to either the performance itself or its frames. As for the frames, the audiences' expectations may depend on Christmas customs and thus be *culturally* determined. In Figure 2, the factors that influence the representation style and the use of medium features are summarised.

The written text of the Message is predominant in that it provides the very content. The first step is to re-oralise this text, i.e. to find a balanced way of its realisation in accordance with the speaker's oral style and body language. This is also what the rehearsal entails. The second step is the adaptation to the TV features in

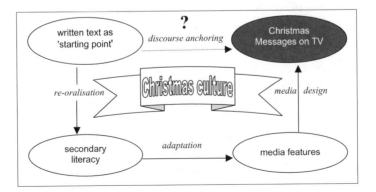

Figure 2. The discourse and media facets of a Christmas Message

order to achieve an apt performance. That means that the 'Christmas culture' has to be reflected, not only in the choice of topics, but also in the choice of music, room decoration, props, symbols and the like. The third step is the choice of media design and how the televisuality is realised. Camera movements, sequence of shots, montage, size, angle, dynamics and other means are called for. The fourth step is to consider both the cultural elements expected and the discourse anchoring means, for they have to be visually and verbally adequate in order to support the processing of the Message. Because Christmas Messages contribute to the head of state's representative function they use the sociocultural practice of public representation. And they allude to some other culture-related practices, such as evoking national traditions or appealing for (ideological) values. The "multi-layeredness" (Clark 1996) reflects the medium adaptation of the discourse anchoring as well as its semiotic resources. The question mark (in Figure 2) indicates that the anchoring might be questionable insofar as comprehension support in words *and* pictures *and* sounds is a risky business.

The point of view adopted in this paper is that the transcript of a Christmas Message, as provided on official websites, does not suffice as the only source of investigation. Access to its *multimodal* nature is indispensable. Accordingly, a description of the visual and acoustic quality of the performance is a minimum requirement. A Christmas Message has to be treated as a TV programme in the first instance. Its materialities are seen as providing the information design the recipients are facing when they listen *and* view.

It depends, however, on the concept of multimodality whether the fusion of spoken discourse, sounds and pictures may be approached. Multimodality often tends to 'add' another communication mode to an existing mode. Considering the complexity of modern mass communication, this is undesirable (Lemke 2002). It was the idea of "design" (Stöckl 2004), and more in particular "media design" as related to "semiotic resources" (Lim 2004), that was able to combine communicative and discourse practices, on the one hand, with multi-layered discourse, on the other hand. Both domains merge into a multimodal theory of communication (Kress & Van Leeuwen 2001: 111):

> A multimodal theory of communication ... concentrates on two things: the *semiotic resources*, the modes and the media used, and the *communication practices* in which these resources are used. These communicative practices are seen as multilayered and include, at the very least, discursive practices, production practices and interpretive practices, while they may also include design practices and/or distribution practices. ... The key point here is that meaning is made not only with a multiplicity of semiotic resources, in a multiplicity of modes and media, but also at different 'places' within each of these. ... In any one mode *all* realisational elements are available for the making of signs, and are used for that. From the

moment that a culture has made the decision to draw a particular material into its communicative processes, that material has become part of the cultural and semiotic resources of that culture and is available for use in the making of signs.

In such a way, the prospect of adaptation of a text to media features and the combination of different semiotic resources comes into focus (Lemke 2002). This is what multimodal discourse analysis is meant for. However, whereas Kress and Van Leeuwen (2001) treat multimodality, in general, as a range of semiotic resources related to communicative practices and discuss examples of different kinds and in a variety of designs (as does Lim 2004), a representative address transmitted by television is exactly the other way round. Its purpose is – more or less – fixed, although its realisation is flexible. Its text stands, but the other elements need to be constructed in an appropriate manner. The Message has to reckon with the complexity of TV meaning-making potentials. In this paper, multimodality is therefore seen as the *result* of the adaptation of a Message to TV features. The medium is TV, its modes depend on the meanings it is able to carry.

According to Stöckl (2004), language, image, sound and music are considered *core modes*. They are either realised in visual or auditory *sensory channels*, which have certain *medial variants*, like static vs. dynamic, or animated writing vs. text on screen, and speech. Furthermore, we distinguish *peripheral modes*, such as non-verbal means and para-verbal means, and *sub-modes*, such as size, angle (camera), lighting, colour, 2-dimensionality, rhythm and volume. TV as multimodal communication, then, applies the four core modes and their sub-types in full.

As for *communicative practices*, the way TV programmes are usually made determines what audiences may expect, already know or respond to when viewing and listening. Here, the live performance of a Christmas Message, although it is faked, is predominant. This entails specific *presentation practices* (*discourse practices*), such as live vs. recorded, but in particular spontaneous speech vs. written to be spoken, and their sub-types, like directly to camera/audience, to other participants, and voice-over during different images. Also the *distribution practices* have to be taken into consideration: the frames of the Message, its musical context as well as the Christmas-related props, that contribute to what viewers may manage to grasp. In general, the performance is furnished with *sociocultural practices* if the speakers succeed in relating its content to their "body politic" as well as "body natural" (Kantorowicz 1957) and if they confirm their very role by performing as a "bard".

The written text of TV Christmas Messages as prepared by the head of state's staff matters in that it is the basis of the address. Yet it is written with the aim of adequate re-oralisation. It is therefore the main facet of the speech delivery that all kinds of anticipations, which are characteristic of the "apparatus of literacy",

have to be "translated" (Lodge 1997:214–215) into re-oralised instances – and pictures. Thus, the anchoring of the Message in the reception situation (Ehlich 1994a,
1994b) has to be performed in conformity with medium features, in general, and
(socio)cultural determinations, in particular.[4] Accordingly, the discourse shadow
is not only actualised by words, body language, gaze, but also by pictures (Chandler 1994) and by sounds people may pick up on the way (Van Leeuwen 1999,
2005). Consequently, the significance of anchoring refers to the need to anticipate
what the audience may encounter – and to the fact that a TV Message is "immediate" and even "vivid" (Lodge 1997). Its evanescence challenges the nature of the
written text basis. Given this contradiction between secondary literacy and film
dynamics, it is likely that the adaptation to television features, while, at the same
time, referring to cultural expectations, will depend on fortuitousness. The multimodal nature of a Christmas Message carries too many indeterminate factors to
deal with easily.

In Figure 3 (below), a network of decision-sensitive points is developed which
influences the wording and structure of a Christmas Message as well as its adaptation to the medium features and its anchoring in the reception situation. Anchoring and TV adaptation are related to the discourse practices of the Message.
Furthermore, its sociocultural practices are acknowledged. We regard them as
related to the general cultural-political purpose of the construction of *social cohesion*. This is one of the most essential tasks a head of state has to fulfil (Ensink
& Sauer 2003). It is linked to his or her role as a bard in giving the community
a proper voice. It does not only concern the way the text is written, but also the
way its content is realised in accordance with the medium, cultural traditions of
the country and performance skills of the representative. Even certain "design
practices" (Kress & Van Leeuwen 2001, 5: "design stands midway between content
and expression") need to be taken into consideration, namely dressing, hairdo,
room decoration, lighting and colours, Christmas symbols, national symbols and

---

4. To be precise, *anchoring* is connected with knowledge operations. The discourse shadow
provides TV recipients with *cues* that are necessary in order to "know" what is new or already
known, what is part of a perception common to addresser and addressee (in verbal communication: deictic elements), what needs further clarification or not, what is already cognitively
accomplished or still has to be worked out, etc. The concept of anchoring therefore must not
be confused with "anchorage", the phenomenon that we see images (in the press) that are supported by words as "captions" (Barthes 1977). These captions function as reinforcements of the
intended meanings. Although a caption guides the looking, it is only some pieces of the caption – for instance, an "a" in place of a "the" that signals that the following verbal concept is not
yet known – and some pieces of the picture – for instance, a cultural icon – that enable viewers
to process the meaning of the combination. It is therefore anchoring that counts with regard to
understanding, and not anchorage alone, which needs anchoring too.

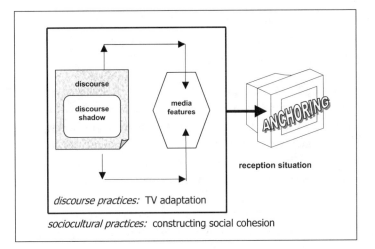

Figure 3. Sociocultural practices of Messages triggered by media adaptation and discourse anchoring

the like. It is likely that these practices underlie all decisions concerning *what* is depicted *in what way*.

In the following section, a Christmas Message from GB and one from Finland are investigated. The GB example (3.1) belongs to a multimedia show style, whereas the Finnish example (3.2) is sermon-like, as it would be in most other European countries. Both realisations reflect the use of semiotic resources, as related to TV medium potentials on the one hand, and to the speech content on the other hand. However, the solutions chosen vary. In Figure 3, I pay attention to the media design character of TV adaptation and anchoring, and to the sociocultural practices involved. To a certain extent, I also deal with the Message content in order to detect verbally conveyed sociocultural practices, such as certain topics. Due to lack of space, however, I cannot give a full analysis. Yet I try to combine the three methods of analysis as referred to in Figure 1 above. Moreover, because a Queen's representative role differs from the one of an elected President, the Messages may represent two ways of dealing with the highest public office and its eternal and temporal nature. This enables us to outline two cultural political settings ("cultural values", according to Clyne 1994) and to relate them to the actualisations of the recipient design means.

3. Two examples of Christmas Messages 2003

3.1 Queen Elizabeth II: Christmas Message 2003

As announced by the British press, the Queen's Christmas Message 2003 was broadcast for the first time from outside a royal residence.[5] At the usual time, at 3 p.m. on Christmas Day, the Queen appeared on BBC 1.[6] A transcript of the Message – of which the texts (and some photographs) are available from the official website – including descriptions of pictures and inserted footage is used in order to give an impression of its multimodal character.[7]

normal text	=	directly addressing from the screen
text in *italics*	=	*written text as appearing on screen*
• [text in brackets]	=	[descriptions and explanations of pictures and sounds]
text in white box	=	interruption of the delivery, footage showing the Queen and other people involved in different social activities.
M	=	medium shot
MCU	=	medium close-up shot
text in grey box	=	continuation: voice-over (v-o) by the Queen, while footage is shown

---

5. For the first time, too, people were able to listen to the Christmas Message on telephone, by dialling a special number (only until 6 January 2004). However, if one listened to the Message then the inserted footage might have been "strange" acoustic elements not easy to place within the context of the text. Without the information obtained by pictures, the audio text must have been quite confusing.

6. In order to avoid overlap with earlier investigations, I refer globally to other publications in which I have offered a comparative pragmatic perspective on those speeches (Sauer 2000, 2001, 2005). Like in the other publications, I do not apply a score-like transcript that treats all visual and auditory units in the same way. Instead, I concentrate on the few differences by working with boxes, grey and descriptions. If the readers see both transcripts from a distance they will immediately realise the different multimodal representation styles. Considering the aim of this paper, this degree of precision is sufficient.

7. http://www.royalinsight.gov.uk/output/Page2843.asp – with photographs (accessed 15 May 2004). For convenience of reference, sections in the written Message text – according to the website – are marked by capitals in brackets: "(A)", "(B)", etc.

- [Beginning sequence: National Anthem, played by the military band of the Household Cavalry, Windsor, in traditional uniforms, Queen's car arriving, Q stepping out, shaking hands with commander, anew the band, then text *The Queen*, Windsor flag]
- [Queen, in Combermere Barracks, Windsor, (after having come forward from behind) is now standing between two tanks, one of them decorated with red crosses, in blue dress; the camera zooms from M to MCU so that at least one tank could be seen. Talking directly into the camera]

(A) I am sure that most of you will be celebrating Christmas at home in the company of your families and friends, but I know that some of you will not be so lucky. This year I am speaking to you from the Household Cavalry Barracks in Windsor because I want to draw attention to the many Servicemen and women who are stationed far from home this Christmas. I am thinking about their wives and children, and about their parents and friends. Separation at this time is especially hard to bear.

- [voice-over Q (video footage from Iraq with original sounds underlying Q's words): soldier in battle dress, camouflage style, patrolling in the streets of an Iraqi city, friendly with children and other people)]

(B) It is not just a matter of separation. The men and women of the Services continue to face serious risks and dangers as they carry out their duties. They have done this brilliantly.

- [v-o Q (video sequence: control post in a desert landscape, soldiers controlling cars, searching through a house, giving food to children)]

I think we all have very good reasons for feeling proud of their achievements – both in war, and as they help to build a lasting peace in troublespots across the globe.

- [talking directly from the screen, MCU, standing in front of a tank]

(C) None of this can be achieved without paying a price. I know that all our thoughts at this time are with the families who are suffering the pain of bereavement. All those who have recently lost a close relative or friend will know how difficult Christmas can be.

- [Interruption: video footage from an aircraft carrier, meeting of soldiers with commander, then servicemen and women in different shots]

Commander:	In less than an hour's time this ship will be brought on four hours notice to execute operations in Iraq

- [v-o Q (video sequence: soldiers climbing up helicopter, climbing up jet fighter, preparing aircrafts)]

> **(D)** These individual Servicemen and women are our neighbours and come from our own towns and villages; from every part of the country and from every background. The process of training within the Navy, the Army and the Air Force has moulded them together into disciplined teams.

- [v-o Q (video footage: soldiers marching, tanks riding, control post controlling people, observation post from a tank)]

> They have learnt to take responsibility and to exercise judgement and restraint in situations of acute stress and danger. They have brought great credit to themselves and to our country as a whole.

- [Interruption: inserted video report of a reception of the Queen in Combermere Barracks, with several soldiers]

> Q: So how long have you been with them/ with the regiment/ have you been away and back again?

- [v-o Q (video footage: reception in the Barracks, Q chatting with different groups of servicemen and servicewomen, original voices can be heard softly)]

> **(E)** I had an opportunity recently at the Barracks to meet some of those who played their part with such distinction in the Iraq operations. I was left with a deep sense of respect and admiration for their steadfast loyalty to each other and to our nation.

- [Interruption: continuation of video report of a reception of the Queen in Combermere Barracks, with several soldiers]

> Soldier: I was in Iraq, yeah, where I made my service/ my job was to fix the-uh tanks.
> Queen: [...]
> Other soldiers: [...] [Length is nearly two minutes]
> Queen chats with 5 different men and women, focussing on the theme of "team building" and "teamwork", also on "regiment as family".

- [talking directly from the screen, MCU, standing, from a royal residence (Sandringham House, Norfolk)]

(F) I believe there is a lesson for us all here. It is that each of us can achieve much more if we work together as members of a team. The Founder of the Christian Faith himself chose twelve disciples to help *him* in his ministry.

(G) I was reminded of the importance of teamwork as I presented, for the first time last summer, the Queen's Awards for Voluntary Service by groups within the community.

- [v-o Q (video footage: reception in Buckingham Palace, Q presents the Awards to different groups of people, original noises can be heard softly)]

> I have been struck by how often people say to me that they are receiving their award on behalf of a team and that they do not deserve to be singled out. This annual award recognises the team rather than the individual.

- [Interruption: inserted video reports showing social activities by the Award-winning groups, accompanied by a short introduction of the kind of activity, interrupted by an direct talk into the camera by a representative of the Award-winners]

> Text: *Swansea Old People's Welfare*
> Voice by *Iris Aubrey*, later on for a short while also directly:
> In total we have 20 volunteers and they are worth their weight in gold. They work hard, they are good tempered, they are pleasant and without them we would have to close. Most of the people we deal with, about 90% of them live alone, have got some sort of infliction and they need to get out and to know that people really care about them. Winning the Queen's Jubilee Award was a great achievement for the volunteers to be recognised for what they do.
> Text: *Asian Blind Association, Coventry*
> Voice by *Bhanamuti Dabhi*, also directly:
> Being a visually impaired person in the Asian community it was hard for me to get help and support. We have got people from all religions and cultural backgrounds, they speak in different languages, we do social activities, we do counselling, fill benefit forms whatever. Without the help of the volunteers we won't be able to run the group.
> Text: *Ferryhill Town Youth, County Durham*
> Voice by *David Foster*, also directly:
> We first started 10 years ago in 1994, we started with one team. For us, in a deprived area, if the football wasn't here for the children, they would just be on the streets anyway getting into trouble and we felt that something needed to be done. We've very proud of it, I mean, 5 teams of boys and girls is a lot of children off the streets every weekend.
> Text: *Epsom and Ewell PHAB, Surrey*
> Voice by *Julia Giles*, also directly:
> We have disabled youngsters, we have able-bodied children we bring them together to have fun and they don't even know that they're integrating they are just having fun doing different activities. I think it would be quite difficult to describe a stereotypical volunteer because we have such a variety of people. We have people that come in from the city and take off their suit and change into their jeans, we have people that come and help from local hospitals, all walks of life help out here, which is fantastic. The feeling you get from helping other people is a great sense of achievement.

- [v-o Q (video footage from [text] *Gatehouse Oxford*, where obviously homeless people get food]

> **(H)** In this country and throughout the Commonwealth there are groups of people who are giving their time generously to make a difference to the lives of others.

- [talking directly, M to MCU to M, Queen is standing in room in Sandringham House, Christmas tree on the right, visible are also different family photographs on mantelpiece and Christmas cards, see photograph]

As we think of them, and of our Servicemen and women far from home at this Christmas time, I hope we all, whatever our faith, can draw inspiration from the words of the familiar prayer [pretending to read from the book but not doing so]:

Teach us good Lord
To serve thee as thou deservest;
To give, and not to count the cost;
To fight, and not to heed the wounds;
To toil, and not to seek for rest;
To labour, and not to ask for any reward;
Save that of knowing that we do thy will.

[Closing the book]
It is this knowledge which will help us all to enjoy the Festival of Christmas.
[With a shy smiling] A happy Christmas to you all.

- [Closing sequence: the same traditionally uniformed military band of the Household Cavalry playing the Christmas carol "Hark The Herald Angels Sing"]

For full comprehension, it is necessary to see the pictures, to pick up acoustic and visual signals, to listen to the speech and the different texts by other people, and to assimilate the different semiotic resources used. Thus processing its multimodal content and integrating different communicative practices seem to be an issue that is really at stake here.

At face value, the Christmas Message 2003 is organised symmetrically with respect to music, pictures and words. It comprises three parts. The first part establishes the topic of the *state* or *nation state* (A-F), the second one the topic of social activity by *voluntary work* (G) and the last part the *Christmas wishes* (H). All parts are linked by the Queen as the main actor in them and by the topic of "teamwork" that applies to the military and social side of the community. The three parts are ratified by the underlying Christian morality, since the Queen refers to Christ and his twelve disciples "as members of a team" (F) and uses this reference later on too (G, H).

The beginning is official: National Anthem, played by a traditionally uniformed brass band (beginning sequence), visit at the Barracks and starting the address standing in front of tanks (A, see also the first photograph), then meeting with servicemen and servicewomen (E), and of course the reference to the war in Iraq, also with inserted footage from Iraq (A-D), including the Queen's reference to the dead (C). In this section of the Message we also find a certain "dramatising strategy" (MacArthur 1999) insofar as the information the viewers are provided with has been turned into dialogue (E: Queen chatting with soldiers). In such a way, the practice of small talk and the discourse practice (by TV viewers) of overhearing such talk underpin the practice of representing the nation. The "body politic" merges into the "body natural" (Kantorowicz 1957), visually as well as acoustically.[8]

The second passage starts with the topic of Christianity ("I was reminded of the importance of teamwork", G, referring to F). It consists of video sequences of the presentation of the Queen's Awards for Voluntary Service and includes special transmissions in words and pictures by four award-winners. These sequences enact a *documentary* practice. They function as a *eulogy* of volunteers in Great Britain and of the community itself (G). The length of that part is nearly half of the whole Message. Even the fact that the long footage of volunteers' work might take the viewers' minds off things contributes to what may be called the Queen's serving role in society, i.e. having an open eye for social relationships. In this passage, it is the Queen's office that is foregrounded so that her "body politic" connected with social questions is acclaimed.

After this chain of volunteers' footage the Queen suddenly stands in Sandringham House (already for a short moment in F, but mainly in H). From a room, very well known from earlier Messages (see also the second photograph), she first *declaims* a prayer referring to the teamwork topic, then closes the prayer book and wishes her viewers a happy Christmas with a shy smile. The Christmas carol "Hark The Herald Angels Sing" in sound and pictures is the last sequence, played by the same military band as in the beginning and closing the frame.

Although the Message takes no more then nine and a half minutes, and although the speed with which the change of addressing from the screen, voice-over, film sequences and other people in words and pictures shown is very high, thus obeying the general requirements of modern TV, the main line is presented quite clearly: war in Iraq and official politics, social work and royal duties concerning the welfare sector, political morality and social achievements. Yet the semiotic resources used and the different frames applied (music, military, the topic of teamwork, volunteers, Christmas symbols, religious references) may cause a problem of integration. This comes especially to the fore, if one listens only once to the Message, as an ordinary audience would.[9]

The meaning making depends on the *anchoring* devices. Visually, there seems to be no problem, since it is the Queen who symbolises the nation in words and deeds. Even the bright blue of her dress contributes to the impression of the unity of discourse. As she wears the same dress in all the sequences, this signals to the viewers that the different activities happen within the same context. This is also

---

8. In earlier Messages the Queen mentioned family relationships explicitly or was shown as member of the royal family, which was also part of the "body natural" exposure.

9. However, the same night, on BBC 2, a repetition was broadcast, with sign interpretation added.

reflected in pictures which illustrate several formulations of her speech (see also Sauer 2001, 2005), thus supporting the meaning visually. Acoustically, however, the words of the address, the words to be picked up from the Queen's chatting with people and the words by several social welfare representatives do not match to that extent. It is even a bit cacophonous.

In sum, the documentary style of the Christmas Message, which results in its multimedia show style, relies on the written text, but is deliberately adapted to the needs of televisuality (*sensu* Atkinson 1984). The Queen interrupts her orator role and is shown chatting with people, which, together with report-like footage from Iraq, resembles a year's review rather than a Christmas Message (Sauer 2001). This functions as a form of intertextual discourse (Fairclough 1995) and makes the Message more political. From time to time, the TV features are predominant in that they may distract the viewers from the Message content. Its multimodal realisation goes much further than what the discourse shadow requires with respect to the anchoring concerning text cohesion, focus control and (speech) acts which are well supported. However, interruptions by video footage and other people may disengage the viewers' attention. Consequently, it is the Message's "media event" character (Wardle & West 2004) that has to be taken into consideration. The makers of the Message, who had already in advance taken care of press releases of the 'new' way of addressing, were obviously more interested in its innovative design than in its content. For them, the Queen appearing between tanks in the Barracks turned out to be more relevant since these pictures might stay longer on the viewers' retinas. Accordingly, the visual quality of the Message was their very concern notwithstanding the fact that the Message text did not go that far.

This becomes especially clear if we look at the closing part of the Message recorded from Sandringham House. It reminds us of the sermon style of a Christmas Message that prevailed before 1997 in the United Kingdom and is still widespread in the other European countries. However, because the room where the Queen delivers her last words – a conclusion, a prayer declamation and a Christmas wish (H) – is not a study and not related to work, the viewers are, so to speak, made welcome to her *home*. One sees a living room in Christmas time: a Christmas tree, Christmas cards on the mantelpiece and hanging on tape from it, a three-piece suite (style 'Chesterfield') with a coffee-table decorated with cards, and more cards on the dining table in front of the Christmas tree. This arrangement may be considered a 'material' expression of the *domesticity* which, according to Ong (1982), is characteristic of the era of secondary literacy: speech under TV influence that is dominated by pseudo-spontaneity. It induces a *pseudo-home*. This sense of domesticity has the advantage of mitigating the scandalous footage of armoured servicemen in Iraq and the Queen standing between tanks, although

they are curiously decorated with Red Cross flags. A certain degree of preposter-
ousness thus might be perceived in these arrangements.

On this Christmas Day, the Queen functions indeed as a bard. Her voice
states the concerns of the year 2003 that are reinforced and proved by relevant
footage. Moreover, the alternations between direct speech from the screen, voice-
over passages and footage of her chatting with soldiers bear a rhythmic character, a bardic manner too. They contribute to a vivid style and evoke national
pride in the British Army, the welfare institutions and the volunteers. It is all the
people who fulfil their duties, as the Queen does. Viewers are invited to respond
to these proud people, who are not only named, but also shown. Even the "Herald
Angels" sound proud. Pride, then, is part of the social fabric of the community
and suggests satisfaction in whatever way it may be achieved. It is at that stage
where the Message turns into the emotional side of the sociocultural practice of
social cohesion. The public may also become aware of traditional meanings of
the English culture (uniforms, flag, National Anthem) matched with intercultural
relationships represented by the award-winners by voice and look. The Christmas
Message is explicitly modern in form and media practices, but at the same time
traditional in content. The traditional impact naturalises the eternal office of the
Queen, who observes the hurly-burly of daily politics from a distance. It is her
role of being there which is demonstrated incessantly. These pictures are powerful in that they celebrate the Queen's divine omnipresence and bestow the "mystic
fiction" (Kantorowicz 1957) on her.

3.2 The Finnish President: New Year Message 2004

The Finnish President, Mrs. Tarja Halonen, delivers her New Year's Message 2004
on New Year's Day at 12 noon on TV first in Finnish, then in Swedish, the second
language of the country.[10] She sits at a desk in front of a movable wall to which a
great oil painting is attached which depicts several sailing boats and vessels approaching a coast, presumably Finland's. The mahogany desk is decorated with
four props: a small Finnish flag with Presidential coat of arms, a table bell belonging to her role as chairwoman, a bouquet of white flowers and a table lamp. A
speech manuscript lies on the desk, but she almost always looks directly into the
camera, obviously using the teleprompter. The room is separated from a much
larger hall since on the right-hand side of the screen (only for the few moments

---

10. The text of the message in both languages and in English translation is presented on the
Presidential website: http://www.tpk.fi/ – with photograph (accessed 15 May 2004). For conve-
nience of reference, sections in the English Message text are indicated by capitals in brackets:
"(A)", "(B)", etc.

when the shot size is M, see Figure 4, below) three windows and a few chairs can be seen that belong to the original hall furniture. The presentation style is calm; the shot sizes are, with the exception of the establishing long shot of the very beginning and the medium shot at the beginning and the end of the speech, only MCU and CU; the average length of the shots is nearly 1 min., but it can also be considerably longer. There is a certain tension between what is said and how it is pictured since the text content units (say: sections) do not clearly correspond to the sequence of shot transitions.

normal text	=	directly addressing from the screen (which is always the case)
• [text in brackets]	=	[descriptions and explanations, also transitions via searching for the next camera or looking at manuscript, despite the use of the teleprompter]
M, MCU, CU	=	medium shot, medium close-up shot, close-up shot
S-4 (46s)	=	shot number 4, length: 46 seconds (picture content and text

- [S-1 (20s) Beginning sequence: establishing long shot of the Presidential Palace in Helsinki, music of the National Anthem (partly), then zooming in on the Finnish flag on the top of the Palace tower.]
- [S-2 (33s) Superimposition: President in M sitting at a desk in a study-like part of a greater hall, in front of a wall with an oil painting attached to it. Then a short smile.]

(A) Citizens, elections are an important part of democracy. Following last spring's parliamentary elections, our country received a new coalition Government. After Prime Minister Jäätteenmäki's brief Government, the same parties formed a new Government. This Government headed by Prime Minister Vanhanen has now established its position.

This year is also an election year. Elections for the European Parliament will be held in June and local elections in October.

- [S-3 (29s) Looking at desk where the manuscript lies, which is obviously meant for searching the next camera, cut to MCU]

The significance of the European Union has increased in our daily lives. Co-operation is needed in more and more areas. The position of the European Parliament has been strengthened and its significance will continue to increase in the future.

Local authorities have a key task in arranging services in our welfare society, such as social services, health care and education. It is thus important for our daily lives whom we elect to make these decisions.

Let's exercise our right to vote!

- [S-4 (46s) Cut to CU (other camera)]

(B) International uncertainty and armed conflicts continued last year in different parts of the world. The situation in Europe and Finland's position have remained safe and stable, however, and our relations with all our neighbours are excellent.

During the past year security policy has been actively discussed in our country. Discussion has particularly concerned the development of co-operation in the European Union and the preparation of the Government's security policy report. The question is how we can best take care of Finland's and Finns' security in the future.

Co-operation between the Government and the President of the Republic in preparing the security policy report has gone well. Parliament will receive the report sometime this year.

* [S-5 (38s) Searching for other camera, cut to MCU]

I myself have emphasised the following points concerning our security policy: (a) Finland does not face any security threat which in itself would require us to change the basic structure of our security policy. (b) Finland's defence has always been primarily up to us, regardless of whether we belong to an alliance or not.

(C) The European Union's Intergovernmental Conference last year did not reach a consensus on a new Constitution. The Union still has its present treaty and there is plenty of time to negotiate a new one. Negotiations should continue without delay, however.

Finland wants to develop the European Union as an equal community of member states so that it corresponds to citizens' needs and wishes as well as possible. The Union's justification and acceptability depend on these things as well as the division of power, which is also important.

* [S-6 (79s) Cut to CU]

Membership of the European Union and active participation in every sector of it have promoted Finns' well-being and have also strengthened our security policy position.

Finland considers it important to develop the Union's civilian and military crisis management capability. The Union should promote peace and stability in Europe and other continents. The Union's ability to prevent and manage crises is above all political and economic, but military capability is also needed in crisis management.

Our point of departure has been that we are prepared to help other member states if they need help. On the other hand we assume that others will help us if we need help. The consensus achieved in the Intergovernmental Conference regarding this matter is a good compromise.

* [S-7 (111s) Looking at manuscript, cut to MCU]

Ten new members will join the Union at the beginning of May. This is a good thing for all Europeans, although enlargement still involves many challenges.

Finland is dependent on international trade. The efficiency of the Union's internal market is a precondition for our welfare. An efficient internal market will help us succeed in global competition.

(D) Finland has been regarded as a winner and success in globalisation – and even an example to others. With the reduction of barriers to international trade we have been able to export our products and services around the world. Of course we also have experience of the dark side of globalisation.

Important matters are of common interest around the world. Peace, stability and prosperity in our neighbourhood and farther away promote and strengthen Finns' prosperity and security.

* [S-8 (50s) Searching for other camera, cut to CU]

Finland works in the UN, the World Trade Organisation and other international forums to create rules and develop co-operation to govern globalisation. In its present form globalisation is not fair and does not ensure sustainable development. Everyone must return to the negotiating table to revise the rules of international trade and investment.

• [Looking at manuscript, without transition]

The nation-state must be strong to meet the challenge of globalisation. We know that our own success has been based above all on people - on expertise, innovation and co-operation.

Our social welfare net helps people but also supports participation in tightening international competition. Globalisation is about participating and adapting to changing circumstances.

• [S-9 (48s) Looking at manuscript, cut to MCU]

(E) We have done well, but we cannot become complacent. Our challenge is also to succeed in tomorrow's globalisation.

Our key success factors will remain education, research, expertise and entrepreneurship. We need active measures to spur innovations and to develop and market them. Smooth co-operation between the public sector, education and business is extremely important.

In my international tasks I have become even more certain that we must take care of ourselves. Finland must create a national globalisation strategy for the future. This requires co-operation between the Government and labour market organisations. On the basis of discussions I am convinced that this work is being approached with the necessary determination.

• [S-10 (56s) Looking at manuscript, cut to CU]

Unemployment is still our most serious social problem. In many workplaces people are worried about their jobs. Yet at the same time Finland faces a shortage of workers. We must continue to invest in properly educating our children and young people and helping adults develop new skills.

Work is the foundation for our national wealth and well-being. Success in tightening international competition requires continuity in working life and possibilities for lifelong learning. The modern working world requires flexibility. The basic point of departure, however, should still be people and their need to balance work and family life.

Children's welfare has been a common concern in recent years. Most children are better off than before. Still, all too many children need help. Parents' care is the primary way to ensure children's welfare and prevent mental health problems. We all have a shared responsibility for children and families as well.

• [S-11 (99s) Looking at manuscript, cut to MCU]

Deficiencies in mental health services have been repaired. A great deal has been achieved particularly in children's and young people's psychiatry. New prevention and treatment models have been created along with new co-operation networks.

I believe it is important to devote serious attention to preventing and treating mental health problems. Particularly resources should be available in children's psychiatric research and care and in different forms of social support.

(F) I have often talked about culture being people's spiritual home in our rapidly changing world. Culture also has a growing economic significance. Successfully combining artistic creativity and economic production has resulted in nationally significant products. We could even say that industrial design is part of our national identity.

Finnish architecture, design, music and other culture also have international appeal. In different fields of culture and the arts we have strong international successes.

Our challenge is to improve different dimensions of cultural expertise. This requires respect for our cultural heritage, attention to creativity and the development of cultural production. Finland has opportunities to make cultural production a significant national industry.

Our own culture is developing and receiving influences from outside. It would be good if our country could attract immigrants to start businesses and hold jobs. Immigration should not be viewed only on the basis of our own needs, however. Immigrants should be treated as neighbours who have equal rights and obligations.

- [S-12 (27s) Looking at manuscript, cut to M]

One of the most important values of a multicultural society is tolerance. Tolerance does not mean that we would approve, under the guise of cultural traditions or customs, violations of the principles of democracy, human rights and the rule of law. We must strengthen these together.

(G) Finally, I would like to thank you on behalf of my husband and myself for your co-operation and numerous contacts.

Thank you also for the greetings I received on my birthday. Your support and interest in the management of common affairs has been important.

I wish all of you a good year in 2004.

- [S-13 (3s) Fading out, dark screen]
- [S-14 (88s) Fading in, M, beginning of Swedish address]
- [S-15 – S-23 (645s=10min45s) Delivery of the Message in Swedish, with less speed than in Finnish, cuts to MCU en CU, more or less same transition pattern as during Finnish speech]

- [S-24 (35s) Looking at manuscript, cut to M]
- [S-25 (4s) Final sequence: picture fades out, coat of arms of the Finnish President on blue background, silence]
- [TV announcer]

The Message takes 11 min. in Finnish and 14 min. in Swedish, together 25 min., including beginning and final sequences. The text is organised in seven main topics. Each topic begins with a description in general terms and is then followed by a focus on Finnish contributions, reflections or problems, and finally a statement is made concerning what has already been done or still needs to be done in the future. There are only two exceptions. The first topic (A) begins with a direct address and the statement that "elections are an important part of democracy". It ends in a request formulated as an invitation: "Let's exercise our right to vote!" The last topic (G) is coloured personally. The President thanks for co-operation and birthday greetings, mentions her husband, smiles and finishes her speech with a New Year's wish.

The thematic organisation is a typical example of a representative speech in 'sermon' style, addressing the audience directly from the screen. Its overall rhetorical strategy is that of a *laudatory speech* (Sauer 2001, 2005). This entails that there is also some criticism in order to prepare the audience for measures that will be taken by the government in the future. Because the President's role is representative and not party political, the political dimension concerns general developments and expectations rather than government businesses. Consequently, she relates descriptions and advice giving to her task and experiences which she herself had gained during the last year in her office. In such a way, the problems which the Finnish have to deal with are formulated in such a manner which may involve the viewers in their solutions. This is, among other things, done by the change of I-clauses and we-clauses (see Ensink 1996). The I-clauses accentuate that she knows what she is formulating, and knows that the audience knows too. Moreover, by using I-clauses she brings to the fore her personal engagement in the issues she is dealing with. In such a way, the I-clauses link the actual speech content to previous discourse – her own or other. The we-clauses, however, have no such clear status. She uses them in order to speak about "we = the Finnish people" including herself (like in A, D, E) or to refer to the government's decisions (like in B, C). In other cases she simply treats Finland as a "person": "Finland wants ... Finland considers it important ..." (C).

The topics, the perspective of the descriptions and the form of advice are shown in Table 1. The Message is quite general in content and moderate in tone. As far as she is inclined to give advice, she formulates mainly approvingly rather than admonishingly, positively rather than negatively. She seems to be more interested in the future than in the past and obviously avoids the genre of a year's review, which could have been expected on such an occasion. The fact that there was a crisis in government and a change of the Prime Minister (A) is imparted but not assessed. Yet she mentions several earlier developments in different social and political fields that have to be picked up and improved in the new year.

There are, however, some peculiarities. The first point is the topic of security policy (B). It belongs obviously to the President's duties insofar as she plays a

Table 1. Thematic and rhetorical organisation of the Finnish New Year Message

section and topic	topic specification	rhetorical action: "advice"
A: elections coming	essential for democracy	please vote!
B: security policy	threads to national security	no changes, however!
C: Europe	consensus as working basis	but more efficiency!
D: globalisation	Finland is a winner	more innovation!
E: successes and deficiencies	tomorrow's challenges	more co-operation between public sector, education and business!
F: culture	people's spiritual home	more cultural expertise!
G: personal perspective	contact and co-operation	thank you and good wishes!

role in contributing to the national security report. Regarding this report, she pleads for continuation of the Finnish policy of neutrality concerning Finland's defence, although she avoids the word neutrality herself. The formulation of two essentials ("points") indicates that she desires to participate in the continuing discussion. Because there has been an ongoing debate on whether Finland should join NATO or not, this functions as a clear intertextual and interdiscursive tie to previous political discourse. It stimulates the TV viewers to mobilise their (political) memory.

The second point is related to culture (F). It begins with an I-clause: "I have often talked about culture being people's spiritual home in our rapidly changing world". This is again an intertextual link and concatenates the actual speech with her earlier discourses. It underlines her trust in the importance of cultural affairs. She favours the Finnish successes in industrial design abroad and emphasises them as part of the "national identity". Her appeal to make "cultural production a significant national industry" links influences from outside – which she considers necessary ("It would be good if our country could attract immigrants") – with the Finnish way to deal with ("Immigrants should be treated as neighbours"). In this context, however, the concept of tolerance is used in order to show that Finland does not tolerate violations of democratic principles. The idea of a multicultural society therefore is strongly focussed on Finnish values as parts of more general occidental values. In such a way, she claims and reassures at the same time; she claims that there is a need for immigrant workers and she reassures the audience that there exists no real threat to the Finnish culture.

The last point is connected with the President's personal situation. In her closing statements (G), she becomes a wife who has a husband, and a woman who had received birthday greetings. Furthermore, she considers her own work "the management of common affairs" and encourages the audience, also by smiling at last, to show interest in it and support her in her job. Finally the wishes for a good New Year 2004 follow. This is one of the rare moments that the "two bodies" (Kantorowicz 1957) appear explicitly.

Considerably little attention is paid to the anchoring of the Message and to the adaptation of the overtly script-bound text to TV features. The text topics are in principle realised in short sentences in the form of statements, but their coherence is not much supported by language means. The Message structure that may help to generate an outline of its complexity is neither made explicit nor clarified otherwise. The most characteristic feature of the text is that of a list. If recipients are distracted for a short moment, they cannot easily continue from where they were lost. Thus, the Message has the lulling effect of a litany. Maybe this is not inconvenient since she indeed acts like a preacher giving a sermon. Moreover, the discourse anchoring during the Finnish Message focuses the TV viewers repeatedly on the political role of the President in different discourses. In such a way, the Message content presupposes a certain political knowledge and experience.

This communicative practice, however, hardly takes into consideration that the screen presentation requires more than verbal content alone. Hence a poor practice, albeit well-known in representative speeches. As a matter of routine, the re-oralisation of the written text that can be seen as a manuscript lying at the desk dominates the style of the speech. What people see when they listen to the verbal content is a 'talking head'. The desk at which she speaks and its environment, in particular the background that is used (the painting, see the photograph), establish the impression of a study. Because the audience might be aware of the fact that this study is constructed by artificial props and clearly separated from a greater hall, it is a *pseudo-study* that frames the Message. What is depicted is a fictitious room in which the real President enacts her speech. Consequently, the public is invited to participate in this semi-real business. The transmission itself is oscillating between the serious content and its theatrical framing. This functions as an overt appeal to the audience's imagination. It may create a certain feeling of involvement, a mutual job done between public and President. Accordingly, the sociocultural practice of social cohesion is not so much related to the role of the bard, although the year's review style contributes to this a bit, but to a strong, even *authoritarian* voice that confronts the viewers with their need of being advised and coached. This treatment is quite rough. "We have done well, but we cannot become complacent" (E), is an appeal to political morality that might be associated with Protestant ideology, albeit mitigated by the claim of Finnish normality.

There is only one moment when pictures and words coincide. The emphasis on Finnish design (F) is linked with "respect for our cultural heritage". Apart from the fact that this passage equals the rhetorical strategy of *fishing for compliments*, it also draws the audience's eyes to the things that are pictured at this very moment. The mahogany furniture (the desk and the chair) harmonise on the one hand with the red colour of her hair and on the other hand with the colour of the vessels in the painting. Accordingly, the arrangement of the pseudo-study as well as her dress and hairdo signal interest in and attention to design. We do not know whether this impression is intended or not, what we do know, however, is how the TV viewers are treated. The colour harmony, the lighting, the things shown and the topic of Finnish design work together appetisingly. It is this multimodal quality that, albeit for a few moments, transcends the overall sobriety of the Message and produces the sense of hope and optimism that is inherent in a New Year's Message.

Whereas, in the British Queen's Christmas Message, the viewer is confronted with many vantage points by different cameras and video footage inserted, the Finnish New Year's Message works only, with the exception of the cover shot of the Presidential Palace, with one single vantage point. As Figure 4 (below) shows, this is done by two cameras that frame the Finnish President by turns in medium close-up shots and close-up shots. Only the beginning and the concluding shot of the address (in Finnish as well as in Swedish) is realised as a medium shot. But this means no change of the vantage point. Without any exception, the Finnish President remains in the centre of attention.

The medium close-up and close-up shots, in general, have a very slow cutting rate. The duration of the shots ranges between 29s and even 141s, which is exceptional slow in the context of modern television (Tiemens 2005). This increases the viewers' concentration on the speaker. There is nearly no possibility to see other picture content than the talking head. Even if the viewers are familiar with the speaker and her addressing style, the visual content they are provided with implies special attention for the *movements* the speaker is doing during her address. What we see is that the Finnish President performs generally two movements: she looks at her manuscript for a short moment, on the one hand, and she searches for the other camera (one of the two cameras that are present), on the other hand. Both movements obviously function as signals to the camerapersons to change the frame. What is more, as the transcript (above) shows, the change of camera frames does not correspond with the speech text. So speaker movements and change of camera frame tend to disengage the viewers, at least to contribute to a certain irritation.

There is another factor that contributes to the impression that the "televisuality" (Atkinson 1984) in the Finnish Message seems to be underestimated. The medium features neglect the potential semantic connections between picture content and speech text: "semantic connections refer to those instances in which the visual images are linked to the verbal text of the speech" (Tiemens 2005: 400). How could one choose visual images that would match or reinforce verbal references in the text? Above, I mentioned already the short coincidence between Finnish design props and the topic of design in the speech. But this lasted just for

S-1	(20s)	Establishing LS [long shot]: Presidential Palace in Helsinki, music of the National Anthem (partly, only two "lines"), zooming in on the Finnish flag on the top of the Palace tower
S-2	(33s)	Superimposition: President in M sitting at a desk in a study-like context, in a greater hall, in front of a wall with an oil painting attached to it, at the right side of the hall chairs are standing in front of windows. Short smile
S-3	(29s)	P looking at manuscript, searching the other camera, cut to MCU
S-4	(46s)	P cut to CU (other camera)
S-5	(38s)	P searching for other camera, cut to MCU
S-6	(79s)	P cut to CU
S-7	(111s)	P looking at manuscript, cut to MCU
S-8	(50s)	P searching for other camera, cut to CU
S-9	(48s)	P looking at manuscript, cut to MCU
S-10	(56s)	P looking at manuscript, cut to CU
S-11	(99s)	P looking at manuscript, cut to MCU
S-12	(27s)	P looking at manuscript, cut to M
S-13	(3s)	Fading out, dark screen
S-14	(88s)	Fading in, M, beginning of Swedish address
S-15	(77s)	P searching for other camera, cut to MCU
S-16	(56s)	P looking at manuscript, cut to CU
S-17	(50s)	P looking at manuscript, putting page aside, cut to MCU
S-18	(50s)	P looking at manuscript, cut to CU
S-19	(97s)	P searching for other camera, looking at manuscript, cut to MCU
S-20	(74s)	P looking at manuscript, cut to CU
S-21	(69s)	P looking at manuscript, cut to MCU
S-22	(81s)	P looking at manuscript, cut to CU
S-23	(141s)	P searching for other camera, looking at manuscript, cut to MCU
S-24	(35s)	P looking at manuscript, cut to M
S-25	(4s)	Coat of arms of the Finnish President, silence

Figure 4. Shot content, camera framing, shot length of the Finnish President's New Year's Message 2004

a few moments, the following topic change then caused a mismatch. This is, however, a very strong view of the situation. Concerning the structure of the address, its culmination point may be considered the good wishes at the end. An adequate match would be the speaker in close-up and smiling, as is the case in most of the speeches of our corpus. But this does not seem to be the case in Finland. Here the end of the New Year's Message is framed in medium shot! We do not know why, but it seems that the director has chosen a kind of formal *parallelism*: both the beginning and the end of the address in Finnish as well as in Swedish are framed in medium shots. Concerning the TV features and their meaning-making potentials, this is a surprising choice.

4.   Synopsis of Message materialities

4.1   Semiotic resources

In this section, the semiotic resources with which Christmas Messages and New Year's Messages are assembled will be documented.[11] No attention is paid to the speech content so that no interpretations will be given on how content and TV features may influence each other. According to the concept of multimodality as multimodal materialities developed in this chapter, the figures show how European heads of state are exposed when presenting their Christmas or New Year's Messages. Considering that the speakers (or their staff or government) might incline to enhance their means of recipient design, they have to select a certain presentation style and to link them to the semiotic resources available. In order to differentiate these resources and the corresponding communicative practices, we concentrate on the *core modes* of language, image, sound and music, the *sensory channels*, their *medial variants*, their *peripheral modes* and *sub-modes* (Kress & Van Leeuwen 2001; Stöckl 2004) as well as on the *discourse practices* (the frames that are used and the anchoring signals), *production practices* (the design of media features) and *sociocultural practices* (which also depend on the content that is not included here; Sauer 2005). First, the semiotic resources of the corpus identified on the occasion of Christmas 2003 or New Year 2004 (Table 2) are compiled. Secondly, a synopsis (Table 3.1–3.3) is given of specific elements based on a rough categorisation rather than a systematic empirical examination, which contribute to the 'syntactic' meanings that might be established by the corpus (Figure 5). The semiotic resources used and their combinations are seen as contributing to what in future may be termed a 'semiotic grammar of Christmas Messages'.

---

11.   What I propose here, is not really new. Several examples have already been developed (Barthes 1977; Fiske & Hartley 1978; Fiske 1987; Kress & Van Leeuwen 1996, 2001; Van Leeuwen 2000, 2005). However, they had a more general concern. They were either related to a specific medium, mainly photography, film or TV, in order to gain access to "readings" of such a representation. Or they propagated the idea of a semiotic approach of all media and resources, as a contribution to semiosis in general seen as generic concept of culture. Both lines are necessary, but here I cannot combine them satisfyingly. I feel the need for more moderate steps. I concentrate on *one* discourse genre and *one* medium (TV), and I try not to treat "language" as independent from other semiotic resources. If "language" is no longer the starting point, then one focuses really on how recipients process the combination of different semiotic resources.

4.2 Genre-specific elements

In Table 2 (below), the opening and closing frames are treated separately as they represent a traditional media practice. The *images* and the *music* and *sound* before and after the speech proper form a bracket which signals to the audience that the Message is an exceptional TV programme. The other appearances of the semiotic resources belong to what I want to call the message style of a speech, since they are based on choices by the speakers themselves, their staff, and their political and media advisers. Another domain of choices concerns the room from which the transmission takes place; traditions and traditional interiors may be of influence and personal considerations concerning how a head of state wants to be exposed as well. The message style elements are divided into *visual* and *auditory* ones. *Speaker-related and visual elements* are posture, body and hand movements, the dynamics of face, looking behaviour (in particular the use of teleprompter technology), tools, dress and desk. All these categories appear in different configurations. *The speaker's context* is also *visually* represented (context-related means): useful are distinctions, such as room, lighting, manuscript, props and background. *Audience-related visual elements* consist of looking into the camera and recipient-directed gestures. Also subtitles and a sign interpreter are regarded as visual supports of the audience's interpretation of the speech and therefore categorised here, although they add a layer to the transmission, a technical one. As for *speaker-related and auditory elements*, the quality of the speaker's voice and the use of one or more national languages matter. *Audience-related and auditory means* are forms of direct address, greeting formulas, the use of you-clauses, some speech acts, repetitions and of course the wishes at the end of a Message. *Recipient-directed* material articulation means, such as warmth or intenseness, also need attention.

The so-called interruptions by footage in documentary style play a specific role. They happen, as far as I can see, only in the GB Christmas Messages from 1997 onwards. They have to be treated as particular sequences: sometimes with the Queen's voice in voice-over format, sometimes as a short report of receptions or visits, sometimes in other combinations.[12] But they always add a meaning dimension, which hardly could have been articulated otherwise. Therefore they cre-

---

12. It is worth to develop a closer look at the British Messages. Later on, I hope to be able to study them more closely with respect to their "documentary" dimension that show a great degree in variation, content, culture-related activities and traditions. In particular, the representation of the "body natural" and the "body politic" (Kantorowicz 1957) is performed in sophisticated ways. It needs more scrutiny, especially with regard to the innovative use of TV features.

Table 2. Semiotic resources in Christmas and New Year's Messages

Opening frame:	*what is pictured*	palace, flag, coat of arms, other (band, guardsmen, traffic, etc.) text of anthem in subtitling, other text
	what is heard	music: religious, carol, anthem, other (classical or other) other: traffic, guard (military orders, marching, military signals)
Message style:	*what is pictured*	
– speaker-related:	posture:	sitting, standing
	body language:	hands: few movements, lot of movements body: discernible, nearly indiscernible, moving, not moving, other
	face:	serious, smiling, other (static, dynamic)
	looking behaviour:	directly into the camera (indicating teleprompter), other
	tools:	reading glasses (putting on, putting down), pen, other
	dress:	festive, official, evening dress, jewellery
	desk:	sitting at desk, no desk (sitting on chair, standing)
– context-related:	room:	study (real, pseudo), home (real, home), church, hall, library, other
	lighting:	natural colours, specific colours, "neutral"
	text as "thing":	manuscript (lying on desk, held in hands), other
	props:	flag, bouquet, Christmas tree, Christmas cards, candles, computers, desk lamp, ink set, other things
	background:	books, mantelpiece, photographs, paintings, "neutral", other
– audience-related:	addressing:	(no) looking into the camera, other
	recipient-directed:	gestures, turning, other
	interpreter:	sign language interpreter, no interpreter
	text on screen:	with running subtitles, without subtitles
Message style:	*what is heard*	
– speaker-related:	voice:	articulation, voice quality, rhythm, speed, pausing, other
	national language:	one language, more languages
– audience-related:	addressing:	direct address, no direct address, specific speech acts, wishes, "you" (and similar constructions), other
	recipient-directed:	heartily, intense, accentuated, other
Interruptions:	by pictures only:	video footage (voice-over by head of state)
	by pictures/voices:	video footage of head of state with other people video footage of other people in words, pictures and voice-over
	by pictures/sound:	video footage: original sound
Closing frame:	*what is pictured*	palace, flag, coat of arms, guard, band, traffic, landscape, other text of anthem in subtitles, other text
	what is heard	music: religious, carol, anthem, other (classical) other: traffic, guard (military orders, marching, military signals)

ate innovative *discourse practices* and may evoke specific *sociocultural practices*, like the one of modernism in monarchy.

Table 2 displays the recent repertoire of sign making in Christmas Messages under the conditions of mass communication. It presents an exemplary inventory of potential realisation forms, a vocabulary. The chart does not show all possible categories of the collection, since this depends on what one wants to categorise. Nor does it reflect all possible combinations, other than the ones I myself propose by distinguishing the frames before and after the speeches and interruptions. The following step therefore is the "concatenation" (Sauer 2002) of semiotic resources. In order to arrive at a syntax of these resources, we have to get grasp at their combinative potentials. The only way of doing so is to *compare* the speeches of the corpus with one another, and to pay specific attention to the resources used.[13] As the heads of state's choices verify *their* syntax, we might be able to find some patterns, which are characteristic of the genre. These syntactic means show which solutions are opted for in the European countries in order to expose the head of state to the public in Christmas time (for sermon-like transmissions, see Figure 5, below).

In Table 3.1 (below), the corpus is introduced. What is interesting from the point of view of multimodal discourse is the attention paid to the framing of the Message: structure, length and complexity of the *opening sequences*. The announcements by television presenters were left out since they are clearly separated from the Message itself. Most countries use the Presidential or Royal Palace as an *icon* in order to clarify what may be termed the centre of the nation. This is very often accompanied by the National Anthem (or, as is the case in N, a Royal Anthem) played or sung (sometimes with subtitles) and followed by flags or coats of arms. However, some countries have no real opening (A, DK) or a very short one (D). That means that Austria and Denmark start *in medias res*, i.e. both heads of state can be seen immediately on the screen. It is perhaps because of this sudden appearance that the Danish Queen begins with a smile which is connected with her putting on the reading glasses. In NL, the religious setting refers already to the content of the Message. It is realised by sacred music during which shots of the palace are shown. Only in GB the opening sequence is not only a salute to the Queen but also a kind of report, which functions as a communicative practice borrowed from journalistic genres. It marks the fact that the Queen delivers her Message outside her residence: she is shown arriving at an unusual place, the Combermere Barracks, so that recipients can see she is really outside and there-

---

13. The Christmas Messages of the corpus were available on cable television services in the Netherlands (where I live and work) and the WWW. As for A, DK, FIN and N, colleagues recorded them.

Table 3.1 Country, representative function, occasion (time) and opening sequences

country	head of state	time	opening sequence
Austria (A)	President	NY	no opening sequence
Belgium (B)	King*	C	Palace in different shots in daylight, then Belgian flag colours filling the screen, while National Anthem is played
Denmark (DK)	Queen	NY	no opening sequence: Queen smiling, visibly preparing herself and putting on reading glasses
Finland (FIN)	President[†]	NY	Palace in daylight, National Anthem played, flag on tower
Germany (D)	President[‡]	C	Palace at night, text *Die Weihnachtsansprache des Bundespräsidenten*, also as male voice-over, no music
Netherlands (NL)	Queen	C	Palace in daylight, different views from the park, religious music, text *Kersttoespraak van Hare Majesteit de Koningin* (female v-o), also in text the title of music piece, on tower royal flag with coat of arms (of the House of Orange)
Norway (N)	Crown Prince[#]	NY	Palace in snow at night, Royal Anthem sung, subtitles of the text of the Royal Anthem
Spain (E)	King	C	coat of arms, then Palace fading in on the blue screen, text *Mensaje de Navidad de S.M. el Rey*, National Anthem played
United Kingdom/Great Britain (GB)	Queen [✓]	C	Military band in dark red uniforms playing National Anthem, text *The Queen*, then footage: Queen's car arriving at Barracks, Queen stepping out, welcomed by commandant, shaking hands, appearing between tanks

* The record was taken from the Flemish TV. The King also delivers a Christmas Message in French, broadcast in the French speaking regions of Belgium.
† The Message is delivered first in Finnish, then after a very short pause in Swedish.
‡ The German President delivers his Message twice, at 7 p.m. (ZDF channel) and at 8 p.m. (ARD channel), both on prime time immediately before the TV news programme begins.
# Because the King was ill the Crown Prince took over.
✓ The Message was repeated at 9 p.m., added was a sign language interpreter standing at the right of the screen.

fore in the midst of society. The report dimension of this footage documents, as it were, that the Queen is 'moving'.

All opening sequences, as far as they had been produced, also reflect the time of the transmission. If it is at noon or later, daylight is shown; if it is in the evening, then the lighting is clearly artificial. The latter adds some magic to the delivery, in particular when a palace is illuminated in the snow (D, N). The opening sequences focus the audiences globally on the meaning of the speech: only in NL and GB where a certain tradition of variational realisations of the format exists, the relationship between the pictures (GB), the music (NL) and the speech content is developed in such a way that viewers may infer a general meaning. However, their potential assumptions concern rather feelings and sentiment than a clear indication of the content that will follow.

In Table 3.2, the semiotic resources of the place, the Message delivery style, the props on the head of state's desk or in his or her environment, and the closing sequences are compiled. Whereas the question whether or not to make use of the teleprompter technology and thus to dispense with the showing of the manuscript may depend on the experiences and preferences of the different heads of state, the room from which the Message is delivered and its decoration are clearly in the centre of decisions and arrangements.

The speakers and their appearances form the core activities. Everywhere we see festive clothes, albeit with some differences. The most remarkable examples are the Danish Queen, who obviously prefers *très chic* fashion and exclusive jewellery, and the Norwegian Crown Prince, who seems to be on his way to a New Year's Eve party immediately after the broadcast. The speakers usually sit at a desk so that only the upper part of the body is exposed. The Spanish King sits on a chair with no desk which turns out to cause a bit of discomfort, whereas the British Queen stands and moves around. The movements, in general, are restricted: hardly any hand motions (often combined with holding a manuscript), some hand motions in order to accentuate the tenor of a passage and a lot of hand motions (A, E) which obviously aim at encouraging the public's involvement. In such a way, *speaker-related resources* may comprise some clearly *audience-related* units produced by hand motions, gaze and looking into the camera.

Heads of state obviously prefer the atmosphere of a study in order to display their working context even on a festive occasion. The occasion itself is referred to by Christmas symbols, bouquets, candles or more general means that indicate a festive moment. The rooms are mainly arranged and decorated as though they were studies. We call them *pseudo-studies* since the audience may see that these rooms are not real offices (as workplaces). Sometimes however, the rooms have the air of a home and are therefore termed *pseudo-homes*. A pseudo-home looks like the head of state's home and gets the viewers to suppose that the speaker lives there (E, GB). Even family photographs contribute to this purpose. However, viewers cannot be sure that their impression is realistic. It is this oscillation between feeling invited and being part of the fabrication that is profited from.

Apart from Christmas-related props, national symbols, like flags and coats of arms, are used in general. Only Austria combines the national flag and the flag of the European Union. The Dutch and the British Messages use the flags of their royal families: the flag of the House of Orange flutters on top of the Palace in The Hague, whereas the kettledrums of the military band are decorated with the flag of the House of Windsor. The 'natural' context in which these national symbols are shown thus provides an air of self-evidence which avoids carefully the danger

Table 3.2 Delivery style, props used in room, closing sequences

country	Message delivery	props	closing sequence
A	study, sitting at desk, no manuscript, tele-prompter, many hand movements	Austrian flag, European flag, computer screen, mir-ror (reflecting a painting and a red silky wallpaper), baroque style elements	no closing sequence
B	pseudo-study, sitting at desk, teleprompter, hardly hand movements	Christmas tree, giant Christmas bouquet on floor, sideboard with photographs, painting de-picting first King between two lamps	Belgian flag, while National Anthem is played, then Palace in different shots, Christmas tree outside near stairs
DK	pseudo-study, sitting at desk, manuscript in hands, mainly reading from paper, subtitles	bouquets on the left and on the right, painting, can-dles, remarkable brooch in turquoise blue	guard of honour lining up, orders, rising flag, National Anthem is played, then end of ceremony, officers march-ing through Palace gate
FIN	pseudo-study separated from hall, sitting at desk, manuscript, however mainly teleprompter	bouquet, table lamp, table bell, flag, painting attached to movable wall	coat of arms on light blue background
D	study, sitting at desk, no manuscript, teleprompter	Christmas tree, candle, bouquet, wall behind shelves with many books	Palace, text and male voice-over *Die Weihnachts-ansprache des Bundespräsi-denten*
NL	no identifiable room, sitting at desk, manu-script reading and use of teleprompter	bouquets, through the window a Christmas tree outside with lights on in daylight can be seen	Palace, music (Dvořak), title as text, also text *Hare Majesteits Kersttoespraak is te lezen op www.koninklijkhuis.nl and www.nos.nl*, also by female v-o
N	study, sitting at desk, manuscript in hands, mainly teleprompter, subtitles	festive dress with bow-tie, bouquet, table lamp, ink pot set on desk, some paintings or etchings	Norwegian Anthem sung with subtitles, pictures from all over Norway and all seasons, in helicopter view, idyllic sunset
E	pseudo-home, sitting on chair crossing legs, no desk, many hand move-ments, teleprompter	flag, Christmas tree, crib with large nativity figures, table with two big photo-graphs to the left	coat of arms, then Palace fading in on the blue screen, text *Mensaje de Navidad de S.M. el Rey*, National Anthem played
GB	standing in Barracks, standing in footage, voice-over, interruptions, pseudo-home, tele-prompter	tanks, different videos, direct address with Christmas tree, cards and photographs, a three-piece suite, a prayer book in hand (at the end)	Military band playing Christ-mas carol "Hark The Herald Angels Sing", daylight, with dark red uniforms, text *BBC MMIII*

of bombastic nationalism, as is also the case with the Finnish President's mini flag. In sum, the props demonstrate an aloof style of the Message so that few distractions from its solemn content can take place. The compositions of the props unveil a certain relationship between the *production practices* and the *sociocultural practices*. They gently inform the audiences that the royal representatives are exposed to the mass public with reference to eternal traditions (often shown in paintings of predecessors), whereas the elected representatives incline to more specific discourses: education (indicated by books, D), technology (shown by computers, A) and business (demonstrated by the desk design, FIN). Regarding E and GB, the pseudo-homes are predominant. They demonstrate normality, at least in Christmas customs and family photographs that contribute to the "body natural" (Kantorowicz 1957). In NL, the room presents a fictitious environment; it is no-one's place, neither study nor home, and therefore evidently the result of a temporal arrangement.

The last category of this chart is devoted to the closing sequences. Do these sequences mirror the opening ones or do they add special meanings? Four closing sequences are symmetrical (A, B, D, E). The others represent either a variation (same pictures with another piece of music, NL; a short picture of the coat of arms, FIN; a Christmas carol, GB) or something completely different. The Danish Message comes to an end by a military ceremony: the guard of honour rises flags, salutes the National Anthem and marches through the Gate of the Royal Palace. This refers unmistakably to the official character of the Queen's role as head of state. Yet in Norway, the singing of the National Anthem with text in subtitles is accompanied by film pictures in helicopter view of the Norwegian landscape and its seasons all over the country, thus glorifying its beauty[14] and stimulating the audience to respond to this promotion of Norway.

4.3 Semiotic grammar

In Table 3.3, the camera work and the sub-mode of colour are taken into consideration as these constituents of TV media practices concern domains of meaning making which are both unavoidable and essential, such as number of cameras, their placement and their operations. They may even respond to the verbal content, e.g. a close-up shot at a crucial moment or the zooming in on the speaker in order to concentrate on the ongoing passage. The fact that audiences are not accustomed

---

14. In Norway, the National Anthem on TV, for instance on National Day, is always pictured this way. The role of the "bard" the Crown Prince personifies is taken over by "nature" that sings the praise of Norway as a cultural entity.

Table 3.3 Shot sizes, camera movements and general colour impression

country	shot sizes	camera movements	colour impression in general
A	M, MCU, CU	zooming in, zooming out, one camera	dark red, red, white, gold (mirror frame visible), daylight
B	M, MCU, CU	zooming in, zooming out, one camera (or two?)	brown, dark yellow, red, floral green, no daylight
DK	MCU, CU	hardly any movement, one camera	dark brown, dark yellow, floral green, no daylight
FIN	M, MCU, CU	no zooming, hard cuts, some dissolves, three (or two) cameras	mahogany, yellow, white, light red, daylight
D	MCU, CU	zooming in, zooming out, one camera	dark brown, dark yellow, floral green, many book covers in colour, no daylight
NL	MCU	no movement at all, one camera	light beige, nearly white, floral green, daylight
N	MCU, CU	zooming in (no zooming out), several cameras, several cuts, little change of angle and distance	dark brown, dark green, dark yellow, beige, no daylight
E	M, MCU, CU	zooming in, zooming out, several cameras, several cuts, also few changes in pan so that either the crib or the flag is depicted apart from the King	dark brown, dark blue, floral green, dark green, no daylight
GB	LS, M, MCU, CU, different sizes/angles in footage	many movements in direct address, also in inserted footage, many cameras, "documentary style"	Message from screen in daylight, dark pink, floral green, brown, in videos much olive-green (military colours), most videos in daylight

to expecting a lot of camera work in sermon-like addresses and that the shot sizes and movements tend to be modest, contains a political dimension. It contributes to the *solemnity* that characterises a public appearance of a head of state and it reflects the *dignity* this office possesses. A nervously or excitingly shooting camera would be completely out of place. Yet a nearly motionless picturing (like in NL or DK) might be associated with other meanings: tedium, old-fashioned ideas or respecting traditional values. Decisions concerning the camera work therefore resemble the conundrum of navigating between Scylla and Charybdis.

As for the sub-mode of colour, the colour scheme of a Message also needs to be accounted for. I see colour as a "sub-mode" (Stöckl 2004) or a "combinational not in itself existing mode" (Kress & Van Leeuwen 2002) that belongs to the *lighting* of an address. Apart from national colours in flags, which play a restricted role here, the combination of composition elements 'colours' a speech at hand. I distinguish daylight and no daylight Messages and seek for patterns which organise both transmission types. In the case of daylight transmissions, mostly different shades of white are used, in combination with beige, light yellow and the like. But there are also some clear contrasts, produced by red, brown, gold and the mahogany of furniture. The floral green of flowers and bouquets belong to both transmission types. It depends on the intensity of spotlights whether the floral green is contributing to a natural or artificial appearance. The night transmissions prefer a darker set of colours, which make contrasts appear more conspicuous and constructed. What is shown behind the speakers counts in particular. If a zooming out camera or a medium shot is used then one sees some open doors which allow insight into differently lighted rooms (B, N), thus giving an impression of depth. Globally speaking, the colour schemes applied in Christmas Messages tend to *harmonise* the exposure of the head of state with his or her representative function. They play down the strangeness of a speaker addressing her or his audience from the screen and *naturalise* the artificiality of the 'faked' live transmission.

4.4 The materialities of sermon-like Christmas Messages

After the examination of, first, the vocabulary of semiotic resources and, second, their potential syntactic relationships in the genre of TV Christmas Messages, I want to summarize the sermon-like transmissions. Their construction is simple: frame X, delivery of the speech, frame X or frame Y. Most of the frames are combinations of music (played, sung or both) and national symbols like palaces and flags. In these cases, the frames mark the representative function of the head of state so that there is no doubt that it is him or her who delivers the Message. As for the picturing of the Message itself, syntactic relations are only discerned if the camera work is related to the content of the speech or to other semiotic resources. There are only some moments, where a camera, mostly in medium close-up or close-up, depicts the speaker directly addressing the audience with a gesture or smile. Apart from these rare moments in which language, body language and camera operation coincide, no other syntactic relations have been established. Variations concern the decoration of the rooms and dressing style.

Figure 5 shows the materialities of the sermon-like Christmas Messages. As is characteristic of the secondary literacy of representative addresses, the performance of a *talking head* – or more precisely: a *talking upper part of the body* – sitting at a desk relies heavily on both the content of the speech and the re-oralisation by means of body language and articulated voice. The camera movements and the sizes of the pictures, which are presented in Figure 5 by the left part, oscillate be-

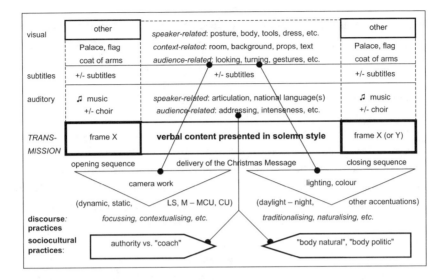

Figure 5. "Syntactical" relations of semiotic resources and their meaning-making potentials

tween focussing (the speaker as centre) and contextualising (the speaker within a visible context, the decorated room). The discourse anchoring therefore depends in part on the speech content. What is shown and how it is shown, which are presented in Figure 5 by the right part, may support these discourse practices. I distinguish between a naturalistic way, which accentuates the speaker's individuality, and a traditional way, which underlines the office (and its burden). The former denotes the way politicians act in public, and the latter contributes to the eternal quality of a monarch. The discourse anchoring then draws upon the ability of the audience to relate the ongoing performance to earlier speeches and appearances or to respond to the royal office and to produce loyalty anew. I consider these picturing modes linked with the "body natural" vs. "body politic" (Kantorowicz 1957) distinction. It makes political representation flexible in that it invites the viewers to take into account that a Christmas Message however heartily worded is a semi-official discourse. The speaker's body language as caught by the camera contributes to such an interpretation. Normally, the authority of a head of state is beyond doubt. But if he or she performs a Christmas Message then their hand motions, gaze and the articulation – in conformity with the content – may contribute to the sociocultural practice of 'coaching' rather than reiterating the status quo (Sauer 2001). The point is that such sort of considerations needs to be supported by the multimodality of the semiotic resources which are combined only to a certain extent syntactically. The material realisations of Christmas Messages as presented in this section yet open up the possibility of thinking and analysing them in terms of grammar.

5. Conclusion

The multimodal character of televised Christmas Messages – as demonstrated in this paper – often leads to a certain mismatch between what is shown and what is heard. In some cases, the clash of manner and meaning is undisguised. What you see is completely different from what you hear. The adaptation of the Message script to the medium television is predominantly restricted to the embodiment of the speaker as a person who is exposed to the viewers. Some speakers are more suitable for their role than others. Moreover, if representatives acknowledge the necessity of multimodal communicative practice and its relatedness to expectations that are, among other things, determined by media habits, then they are able to respect the visual layers that contribute decisively to the business of performing. Yet this is not only a question of personal inclination. It depends also on the willingness to pay more attention to the way public discourses are realised in general. This demonstrates that the cultural common ground, the anchoring and the adaptation to the medium features allow a considerable range of realisations. It is the domain of the semiotic resources that should be treated with more creativity and inventiveness, both from the perspective of analysis and from that of speech making. A lot of systematic work has to be done in order to discover how far one can go multimodally.

Although the speeches of our corpus may be regarded as tokens of a type, that is the genre of Christmas Messages, there are considerable differences concerning their use of multimodality. Because the semiotic resources of a culture, according to Kress and Van Leeuwen (2001:111), depend on the moment a "culture has made the decision to draw a particular material into its communicative processes" and therefore consider specific resources as part of this culture, the differences found in the corpus may also be seen as culture-related. However, how culture influences the multimodal discourses of Christmas Messages has not yet been worked out in full.

We distinguished two different groups of Messages: those by royal heads of state and those by elected ones. As far as multimodality is concerned, we made another distinction between a documentary and multimedia style transmission (GB and in Norway's closing sequence) and a sermon-like speech (by the majority of European representatives). We found that the sermon-like Messages used semiotic resources within a rather restricted framework. We also found that neither their royal nor their elected representativeness was able to explain the differences between them. The documentary or multimedia style of the British Queen, however, seemed to be affected by a strong inclination towards modernity, which is reflected in experimental, innovative TV performances. This turned out to be specific for the role of the monarchy in GB, which had been challenged by various attacks and problems (Wardle & West 2004). In the case of GB we thus detected a *cultural* element, an element specific of that culture of royal representation. It made the representation a media event. In the Norway Message, the closing sequence was culturally loaded too. It reflected the subtle ways of dealing with nature and the nation's landscape, which the verbal content of the Message just touched upon by shortly mentioning environmental problems. The association of Norwegian landscape and environment thus functioned as a cue of culture-related considerations and ideological claims.

The presidential Messages of our corpus in general hold a mirror to society. They either appeal to political activities in the immediate future, such as elections for the European Parliament or national elections (A, D, FIN), or they consider the state of the nation's mind, as was manifest in references to the country's need of moral support (D), in encouraging the people to behave decently and not nervously (A), or in encapsulating an atmosphere of hope and comfort (FIN). The three Messages have a presidential voice in common in which the sermon functions in a paternalistic culture (even if a woman fulfils the role of president). This entails that the nation from time to time needs a representative voice to be able to cope with identification problems and with confidence problems. However, without a closer investigation of the verbal content and the topics of the speeches, we cannot detect further cues. At least, the media features employed do not provide many other cultural cues. The sermon-like performances of the elected presidents rely heavily on the textual culture of rhetorical communication. It is this cultural pattern of Western civilisation and rhetoric that is predominant, although we may distinguish between a Southern European (Catholic) style (A, also E) and a Northern European (Protestant) style (FIN, also DK, N, NL). But there are also countries which have both (D, also B).

Clyne (1994: 3) opts for a pragmatic notion of culture and considers it "an *ensemble* of social experiences, thought structures, expectations and action practices, which has the quality of a *mental apparatus*". Clyne's publication centres upon *inter*cultural communication in spoken and written discourses as well as workplace encounters of members of different language backgrounds using English. Naturally, this focus is not applicable to our corpus, at least not in a direct way. However, it is likely that the concept of the mental apparatus that underlies the analysis of linguistic forms might also be useful in order to investigate multimodal communication phenomena, such as the televisuality of speeches. Even if these speeches do not include intercultural encounters between members of different cultures, in which cases one would exploit Clyne's approach directly, they make use of (socio)cultural practices.[15] I therefore intend to adopt the concept of mental apparatus also to the study of other semiotic resources than language and other practices than the ones of verbal actions. Here TV features play specific roles. They belong to the media practices considered. But at the same time they bear an *international* quality since the development of TV programmes is influenced by globalised formats and world-wide spread technologies. Television practices therefore have an inherent "intercultural" disposition (Fiske 1987) that may cause the impression that national forms seem to draw upon international formats. As far as Christmas Messages are concerned, their internationality is obviously restricted, although they may be induced by what other heads of state in Europe do, or what is seen as successful political communication in Europe.[16]

The mental apparatus is manifest in references to thought structures which are applied in the verbal content of Christmas Messages. Social experiences are related to both verbalisations and visualisations, while expectations and practices are examined separately. This is due to the fact that they concern not only the media features and the degree of multimodality in TV Messages, but also the ways heads of state act when being exposed to a mass public. They adjust the ways audiences respond to recipient-designed communicative practices transmitted on television. As regards the mental apparatus linked with Christmas Messages, two perspectives appear. On the one hand, the transmissions reflect a particular state of the mental apparatus in that they show how the public is assumed to be approached and entertained. Then the speakers' guarded conduct signals a cultivated air of representativeness in the European culture. The heads of state behave in a disciplined and discreet manner and carefully avoid eccentricity. Slight increases in the variations of realisations, according to the network of semiotic resources in Figure 5 (above), depend on individual solutions. The individuality

---

15. The British Message included spoken English texts by members of other cultures so that at least some intercultural elements were present. The Finnish Message comprised a speech in Finnish and in Swedish consecutively which opens a way for comparative intercultural examination. The Belgian King delivered two speeches too, one in Flemish and one in French, albeit in two different programmes. Even the fact that the Spanish King did not use Catalan, the second language of his country, might be worth mentioning as a political decision with intercultural implications.

16. Only with regard to international public televised commemorations we have found some indications that heads of state take the international context into consideration. But when it came to essential national problems that had to be referred to on the same occasion, the representatives normally chose a national perspective notwithstanding the other speeches (see the papers in Ensink & Sauer 2003).

of the representative bard as displayed in his or her Message style endorses the existing (present) political culture.

On the other hand, the mental apparatus of the members of a culture itself might be changing. Currently we experience an overwhelming production of visuals as contrasted with verbal products. The tension between the visual and the verbal culture and their respective domains has become a predominant pattern in the Western culture. Heads of state and other politicians cannot neglect this tension and have to respond to the tendency of visualised and visualisable representation. This is substantiated by the fact that a head of state appears on the television screen.[17] In such a way, the growing need of visual representations seems to determine the way political reality is depicted. The visual constituents of representation become more relevant and may outstrip the verbal constituents. Also the anchoring (the "discourse shadow") may shift and may be realised increasingly by visual features. The variations which characterise our corpus show that the transmissions of Christmas Messages tend to accentuate their visual or, more general, multimodal quality. It may be expected that the culture of political representation in the future will rely more and more on prolific forms of visual appearances. Consequently, we assume that the meaning of a Christmas Message depends rather on what viewers see than what they hear. They may hear only what their eyes can assess.

References

Atkinson, M. 1984. *Our Masters' Voices. The Language and Body Language of Politics*. London & New York: Methuen.

Barthes, R. 1977. *Image, Music, Text*. (transl. Stephen Heath). London: Fontana.

Bühler, K. 1990. *Theory of Language. The Representational Function of Language*. (transl. Donald Fraser Goodwin). Amsterdam/Philadelphia : John Benjamins (originally in German 1934).

Chandler, D. 1994. The 'Grammar' of Television and Film. http://www.aber.ac.uk/media/Documents/short/gramtv.html [accessed 9 November 2001]

Clark, H. 1996. *Using Language*. Cambridge: Cambridge University Press.

Clyne, M. 1994. *Inter-Cultural Communication at Work. Cultural Values in Discourse*. Cambridge: Cambridge University Press.

Ehlich, K. 1994a. "Funktion und Struktur schriftlicher Kommunikation". [functions and structures of written communication]. In *Handbuch Schrift und Schriftlichkeit [Handbook Writing and Its Use]*, H. Günther and O. Ludwig (eds.), Vol. 1, 18–41. Berlin & New York: De Gruyter.

17. The Dutch Queen delivered her Christmas Messages on radio alone until 2000. In 2000, she began delivering on TV too. The Swedish King still prefers radio.

Ehlich, K. 1994b. "Verweisungen und Kohärenz in Bedienungsanweisungen. Einige Aspekte der Verständlichkeit von Texten". [reference and coherence in manuals. Some aspects of usable texts]. In *Instruktion durch Text und Diskurs. [Instruction in Text and Discourse]*, K. Ehlich, C. Noack, and S. Scheiter (eds.), 116–149. Opladen: Westdeutscher Verlag.

Ensink, T. 1996. "The footing of a royal address". *Current Issues in Language and Society* 3 (3): 205–232.

Ensink, T. and Sauer, C. (eds.) 2003. *The Art of Commemoration. Fifty Years after the Warsaw Uprising.* Amsterdam/Philadephia: John Benjamins.

Ensink, T. and C. Sauer 2003. "The search for acceptable perspectives. German president Roman Herzog commemorates the Warsaw uprising". In *The Art of Commemoration. Fifty Years after the Warsaw Uprising,* T. Ensink and C. Sauer (eds.), 57–94. Amsterdam/Philadelphia: John Benjamins.

Fairclough, N. 1995. *Media Discourse.* London: Edward Arnold.

Fiske, J. 1987. *Television Culture.* London: Routledge.

Fiske, J. and Hartley, J. 1978. *Reading Television.* London & New York: Methuen.

Holly, W. 1995. "Secondary orality in the electronic media". In *Aspects of Oral Communication,* U. Quasthoff (ed.), 340–363. Berlin & New York: De Gruyter.

Jochum, M. 1999. "Der Bundespräsident als öffentlicher Redner. Zur Entstehung und Verbreitung der Reden Roman Herzogs". [The federal president as public orator. On the making and distribution of Roman Herzog's speeches]. In *Fest und Festrhetorik. Zur Theorie, Geschichte und Praxis der Epideiktik. [Festivals and Festive Rhetoric. Theory, History and Practice of Epideictic Speeches],* J. Kopperschmidt and H. Schanze (eds.), 141–147. München: Fink.

Kantorowicz, E. H. 1957. *The King's Two Bodies. A Study in Mediaeval Political Theology.* Princeton: Princeton University Press.

Kress, G. and Leeuwen, T. Van 1996. *Reading Images. The Grammar of Visual Design.* London: Routledge.

Kress, G. and Leeuwen, T. Van 2001. *Multimodal Discourse. The Modes and Media of Contemporary Communication.* London: Arnold.

Kress, G. and Leeuwen, T. Van 2002. "Colours as a semiotic mode: notes for a grammar of colour". *Visual Communication* 1(3): 343–368.

Lemke, J. L. 2002. "Travels in hypermodality". *Visual Communication* 1(3): 299–325.

Lim, F. V. 2004. "Problematising 'Semiotic Resource'". In *Perspectives on Multimodality,* E. Ventola, C. Charles and M. Kaltenbacher (eds.), 51–63. Amsterdam/Philadelphia: John Benjamins.

Lodge, D. 1997. "Novel, screenplay, stage play". In *The Practice of Writing,* D. Lodge, 201–217. Harmondsworth: Penguin.

MacArthur, B. 1999. "Introduction". In *The Penguin Book of Twentieth-Century Speeches,* B. MacArthur (ed.), xv–xxv. Harmondsworth: Penguin.

Neumann, I. B. 2004. "A speech that the entire Ministry may stand for, or: Why diplomats never produce anything new". Norwegian Institute of International Affairs, Oslo (unpublished paper).

Ong, W. J. 1982. *Orality and Literacy. The Technologizing of the Word.* London: Methuen.

Sauer, C. 1996. "Echoes from abroad – speeches for the domestic audience: Queen Beatrix's address to the Israeli parliament". *Current Issues in Language and Society* 3(3): 233–267.

Sauer, C. 1999. "Lobrede auf die befreiten Niederlande. Königin Beatrix am 5. Mai 1995 im 'Ridderzaal' in Den Haag". [Laudation of the liberated Netherlands. Queen Beatrix on 5 May

1995 in the "Ridderzaal" in The Hague]. In *Fest und Festrhetorik. Zur Theorie, Geschichte und Praxis der Epideiktik. [Festivals and Festive Rhetoric. Theory, History and Practice of Epideictic Speeches]*, J. Kopperschmidt and H. Schanze (eds.), 313–343. München: Fink.

Sauer, C. 2000. "Beatrix' kersttoespraak in 1994 en de politiek van de herinnering". [Beatrix's Christmas Message 1994 and the politics of memory]. In *Over de grenzen van de taalbeheersing. Onderzoek naar taal, tekst en communicatie. [On the Limits of Language Practices. Investigations of Language, Text and Communication]*, R. Neutelings, N. Ummelen and A. Maes (eds.), 393–404. Den Haag: Staatsdrukkerij Uitgevers.

Sauer, C. 2001. "Alle Jahre wieder. Weihnachtsansprachen und Massenmedien". [Year after year: Christmas messages and mass media]. In *Politische Kommunikation im historischen Wandel. [Historical Changes in Political Communication]*, H. Diekmanshenke and I. Meißner (eds.), 225–252. Tübingen: Stauffenburg.

Sauer, C. 2002. "Ceremonial text and talk. A functional-pragmatic approach". In *Politics as Talk and Text. Analytic Approaches to Political Discourse*, P. Chilton and C. Schäffner (eds.), 111–142. Amsterdam/Philadelphia: John Benjamins.

Sauer, C. 2005. "Christmas messages 1998 by heads of state on radio and TV: Pragmatic functions, semiotic forms, media adequacy". In *Dialoganalyse IX / Dialogue Analysis IX – Dialogue in Literature and the Media. Selected Papers from the 9th IADA Conference, Salzburg 2003*, A. Betten and M. Dannerer (eds.), Vol. 2, 95–106. Tübingen: Niemeyer.

Stöckl, H. 2004. "In between modes: Language and image in printed media". In *Perspectives on Multimodality*, E. Ventola, C. Charles and M. Kaltenbacher (eds.), 9–30. Amsterdam/Philadelphia: John Benjamins.

Tiemens, R. 2005. "A Content Analysis of Political Speeches on Television". In *Handbook of Visual Communication, Theory, Methods, and Media*, K. Smith, S. Moriarty, G. Barbatsis, K. Kenney (eds.), 385–404. Mahwah, New Jersey, London: Lawrence Erlbaum.

Van Leeuwen, T. 1999. *Speech, Music, Sound*. London: Macmillan

Van Leeuwen, T. 2000. "Some notes on visual semiotics". *Semiotica* 129 (1/4): 179–195.

Van Leeuwen, T. 2005. *Introducing Social Semiotics*. London: Routledge.

Wardle, C. and E. West 2004. "The press as agent of nationalism in the Queen's Golden Jubilee. How British newspapers celebrated a media event". *European Journal of Communication* 19 (2): 194–214.

Information meets entertainment

A visual analysis of election night TV programs across cultures*

Raimund Schieß
Goethe-University, Germany

The paper analyzes the semiotic work, techniques and conventions used by TV stations to articulate the transitions between studio and outside broadcasts and to produce a spatially fragmented yet coherent televisual text. The goal of TV stations and their news departments is not just to facilitate the information process, but to attract and involve viewers by projecting an identity that is serious and reliable yet at the same time high-tech, modern and dynamic. While none of the stations under investigation (BBC, BBC World, ITV, CNN International, NBC, ARD, RTL) is immune to the tension between the pressure to provide information and the pressure to increase audience appeal, the stations respond to it in different ways and to different degrees.

1. Introduction: Televised elections

"Computers, cameras and endless coffee – the stage is set at the BBC for the biggest show of the year. William Greaves watched the stars of Election 97 rehearse for the big night" – this is how the Radio Times (1997: 20), Britain's leading tv listings magazine, introduces an article on the BBC's preparations for the live broadcasting of the results of the British General Election on May 1, 1997. If it wasn't for the phrase "Election 97", this quotation, with terms like "stage", "show" or "stars", might as well be taken to refer to the final round of popular entertainment programs, such as "Idols" or "Big Brother", rather than to a news broadcast covering

*   This paper is part of the research project "Television Discourse", supported by the German Research Foundation (DFG) and directed by Gerda Lauerbach. The goal of the project is a comparative discourse analysis of election night television coverage in the United States, Great Britain and Germany (see also the papers by Becker and by Lauerbach, this vol.). I am grateful to the editors of this volume for valuable comments on previous versions of this paper.

an important political event. Is the Radio Times merely metaphorizing the BBC's election night coverage as a "show", in an effort to promote the program, or does the element of entertainment indeed manifest itself in the transmission of the election results?

On election day in many democratic countries, the media, and in particular television channels, have a field day. After weeks and months of covering the election campaign and the build-up to the campaign, the channels' work now culminates in the presentation of the election results: as the polls close, a media ritual is triggered, and the ensuing succession of exit polls, projections, analyses, commentaries, interviews etc. gives rise to the discourse type "election night program". For the broadcasters, this intense, high-profile moment of television culture, keenly expected and watched by millions of viewers across the country, is a chance to show themselves at their best and to parade their skills and competence. Election night programs differ from ordinary newscasts in a number of ways, some of which make the channels especially prone to assume the role of an entertainer in addition to – or at the expense of – their other functions, such as that of watchdog or moderator (cf. Blumler & Gurevitch 1995:14–23). On election night, audiences can choose between the results programs presented simultaneously by different channels (assuming a multi-channel media system). Hence, the broadcasters are in direct competition with each other, and this may lead producers to try to increase audience appeal (and thus ratings) by shifting towards the personal, the dramatic or the emotional (cf. Fairclough 1995:42–43). Another characteristic feature of election night programs is their length: depending on the electoral system and the counting procedure, it may take several hours for the results to come in, so that broadcasters may feel the need to keep viewers happy, and away from their remote control buttons, by making the program especially entertaining.

The present study explores the precarious boundary between information and entertainment within television news, and in particular within the election night coverage of three recent elections: the 1997 British General Election, the 1998 German Parliamentary Election, and the US Presidential Election of 2000. Unlike previous research on this particular issue, this paper investigates how broadcasts communicate *visually*, and the focus is therefore on visual components, such as the studio set and graphic displays. The paper is organized as follows: Section 2 outlines a framework for analyzing the visual dimension of election night broadcasts with an eye to the tension between information and entertainment. In Section 3, this framework will be applied to the opening phases of election night programs produced by public and private, national and international tv channels. Section 4 concludes by summarizing the results and by suggesting some directions for future research.

2. Theory: Visions of entertainment

The media's tendency to mix information and entertainment has received a fair amount of critical attention. Most analyses focus either on the topics covered by current affairs programs, or on linguistic features of the coverage. Newscasts that include human interest stories or other 'soft news' are criticized for becoming 'depoliticized'. Similarly, news discourse that uses a highly dramatic, sensational language faces accusations of 'going tabloid', and texts that exhibit features of what Fairclough (1995) calls "conversationalization" are viewed with suspicion: does the shift toward ordinary conversational practices serve ideological purposes, or is it indicative of a cultural democratization (cf. Fairclough 1995:13)?

One aspect that is often literally overlooked in this particular context is the programs' visual presentation: what happens visually in a news broadcast? What images do viewers actually get to see, and how do these relate to spoken language? How is a particular news topic visually represented? Some of the research on the information–entertainment tension has indeed attended to the visual aspects of news presentation (e.g. Muckenhaupt 1998; Ludes 1993; Klein 1998; Scollon 1998), yet on the whole, both media analysts and critical discourse analysts seem to have closed their eyes to visual analysis (cf. Kress 2004). As Graddol (1994: 137) notes: "The visual element of news is perhaps the most under-theorised element of an otherwise well researched genre" – and this despite early, groundbreaking work by the Glasgow University Media Group (1976, 1980) and numerous important reminders, such as Fiske and Hartley (1978: 15), who point out that the 'logic' of television is oral *and visual*. Only in recent years have there been signs that the reluctance to systematically explore the visual nature of tele-*vision*, or of 'texts' in general, is crumbling away: the approaches of social semiotics and multimodal discourse analysis (e.g. Kress & van Leeuwen 1996, 1998, 2001; Iedema 2001, 2003; Scollon 2004; see also Fairclough 1995), which take into account a variety of communicative modes and emphasize the interconnections between them, are making themselves felt in linguistics, discourse analysis and beyond.

Informed by this recent 'visual turn', the present paper analyzes to what extent TV news programs, and in particular special election night broadcasts, appropriate the visual style of entertainment programs. The analysis that follows in Section 3 is therefore an intertextual analysis that looks at traces of entertainment formats within the news genre. In the visual domain, a fairly well-researched example of generic heterogeneity is the mixing of current affairs programs with features of music videos, particularly a rapid editing rate (i.e. fast cuts). This has been observed for instance by Fairclough (1995: 8, 89) for the genre of scientific exposition in an education program, by Klein (1998) for arts and cultural affairs programs, by Schumacher (1991) for cultural affairs and political programs, and

Table 1. Categories of entertainment (from Klein 1998: 104)

basic category	subcategory
variety	speed, surprise, diversity, ...
light-heartedness	amusingness, fictionality, laid-backness, ...
interestingness	emotional and/or erotic stimulation, suspense, spectacularity, ...
catchiness	conventionality, simple structure, pleasant & trustworthy presentation, ...

by Muckenhaupt (1998) for daily news bulletins. While most of these studies concentrate on the programs' film component (news film with voice-over), the visual analysis presented below addresses four other selected elements of election night broadcasts: the title sequence, the studio setting, graphics, and the visual management of outside broadcasts. This choice of elements is in part motivated by Fairclough's (1995: 93) discussion of how narratives and 'stories' in the media achieve factuality:

> There is a range of devices within the rhetoric of factuality which are standardly drawn upon in the production of, for instance, news stories, involving *visual* and aural semiotics as well as language, including *the layout of the newsroom, the opening sequence* and theme music of the news programme, the appearance of the newsreader. One objective here has to be the creating of a sense of authority, *though even in news that may come into conflict with the pressure to entertain.* [emphasis added]

Yet what exactly does 'entertainment' mean? What makes a TV program entertaining? In order to approach this question, I draw on Klein (1997, 1998), who distinguishes four categories that are constitutive of entertainment-oriented communication: variety, light-heartedness, interestingness, catchiness.[1] These categories can be broken down into further subcategories, which often correspond to specific genres (Table 1).

Against the backdrop of these categories, Klein (1998) analyzes arts and cultural affairs programs broadcast on German television of the mid-1990s. Although his focus is on linguistic phenomena (e.g. on the use of formal vs. informal language), Klein also touches upon non-linguistic aspects, among them the content of visual images, and visual techniques. The category 'variety', for instance, can be visually realized by means of a high rate of image changes. Other visual phenomena observed by Klein for his data are for example the use of funny animated cartoons in combination with a voice-over commentary, and a preference for loud and flashy images. The election night programs to be analyzed here are

---

1.   Klein's original German terms for the four categories are *Abwechslung, Unbeschwertheit, Interessantheit, Eingängigkeit.* Klein derives the categories from audience reception research whose results he theoretically refines on the basis of the Gricean maxims.

more complex and heterogenous than Klein's data, and it is therefore necessary to expand and adapt his short list of micro-level visual features. Thus, I will also be looking at visual phenomena such as the following:

- images that have an emotional value, for instance by evoking a common cultural memory or national identity (thus realizing Klein's categories of interestingness and catchiness)
- visual practices that tie different segments of the programs together, creating a visual coherence and thus making it easier for viewers to follow the program (catchiness)
- the use of color as a source of affective meanings, dominated by the pleasure principle (interestingness, light-heartedness)
- practices that simulate a dialogue or interaction between viewers and on-screen participants, by means of direct visual address (interestingness)
- the contrast of moving and static elements, and of slow and fast movements (diversity)
- visual effects that positively stand out and arrest our attention, e.g special effects, computer animations, 3D-effects, oblique angles (interestingness)

In Section 3, these micro-level visual features, and their realization of Klein's categories, will serve as a template for the analysis of the four elements mentioned above – the title sequence, the studio setting, graphics, and the visual management of outside broadcasts. First, however, I briefly discuss the function that each of these elements has within television newscasts in general.

Title sequences (also called opening sequences) signal the beginning of a newscast and act as "boundary markers" vis-à-vis the previous TV program (Graddol 1994: 147). As Graddol (ibid.) points out, "[t]he integrity of the [news] genre is crucial to the perception of factuality [...]. Keeping news distinct requires clear boundaries to be created." Standard openings feature computer-animated graphics (e.g. a globe with an animated title over) and dramatic theme music (e.g. fanfares).[2] The sequences also play an important part in the overall opening frame of a news broadcast, which involves, as Scollon (1998: 73–74, 178–181) demonstrates, the establishment of the channel of communication, the (self-) identification of the presenter and the welcoming of the audience as well as the introduction of the first topic (see Lauerbach, this vol.). Allan (1998: 130) calls attention to the "larger performative task" of opening sequences and to "their dramatic role in attracting and maintaining the interest of the viewer". Given this

---

2. See Glasgow University Media Group (1980: 225–249) for an analysis of the opening and closing routines of British TV news bulletins from 1975.

particular function, openings seem to be predisposed to contain visual features that are perceived as entertaining.

The *television studio* is the physical setting in which newscasts are produced and through which the events of the broadcast are relayed. The central component of the news studio is the desk behind which the presenters sit (cf. Glasgow University Media Group 1980:250–258). The significance of the studio, and its relevance as an object of media analysis, are summed up by media researcher Paddy Scannell:

> Talk on radio and television comes from many locations but there is one that is primary and that is the broadcasting studio. [...] The studio is the institutional discursive space of radio and television. It is a public space in which and from which institutional authority is maintained and displayed. (Scannell 1991:2)

In the same context, he notes:

> Audiences are required to make sense of, to make inferences about, the design, content and manner of radio and television programmes on the basis that their design, manner and content is intended for listeners and viewers to make sense of. The design, layout and lighting of the studio; the age, appearance, sex and dress of participants; the manner and style of how they talk to each other – all these give rise to warrantable inferences about the nature of the event there taking place, the character and status of participants and the relationship of event and participants to viewers and listeners. (Scannell 1991:6; emphasis added)

Do the studios from which the election night broadcasts are presented also give rise to inferences about the programs' entertainment value?

Graphic displays on television have come a long way – from the chalk drawing held into the camera to the sleek, computer-generated 3D graphic called up at the touch of a button. With the recent developments in computer technology, graphics (such as charts, graphs, or maps) have become a mainstay of newscasts, displacing the talking heads more and more often. The media's tendency to graphically represent information – whether it's the weather forecast, currency reports or the trajectory of a cruise missile – is part of a larger development: as Mirzoeff (1998:4) observes, "human experience is now more visual and visualized than ever before." He goes on to argue that "visualizing does not replace linguistic discourse but makes it more comprehensible, quicker and more effective" (Mirzoeff 1998:7). Enhanced comprehension, speed und effectiveness are the primary reasons why producers of newscasts (say they) use graphics (cf. Schütte 1993), yet as

I will demonstrate, some state-of-the-art graphics also serve other, less information-oriented purposes.[3]

While the studio, as Graddol (1994: 148) puts it, "acts as a secure visual base from which forays into the hostile and troubled world may be made", that "hostile and troubled world" enters the studio, and thus the newscast and eventually the viewer's home, by means of *outside broadcasts* (OBs, also called remote broadcasts, or remotes). Live or on tape, a report filed from the very place of interest communicates authenticity and suggests that the information presented has been gathered first-hand. The geographical location of the outside broadcast is often signaled by well-known monuments or buildings visible in the background behind the speaker, such as the Eiffel Tower or Big Ben for reports from Paris or London, respectively. As Morse (1985: 8) points out, visual backings of this sort "may actually have no direct connection to an event, but they represent it symbolically." Another issue is the way in which the interaction between studio and outside location is mediated and how the transition from one location to another is visually managed.

Having thus briefly outlined and problematized the four basic elements of newscasts to be included in my visual analysis, I now turn to election night broadcasts in Britain, the United States and Germany. How were these elements realized by different channels in the specific context of an election night, and what does their realization tell us about the tension between information and entertainment?

3.   Visual analysis of election night coverage in Great Britain, Germany and the United States

3.1   Context and data

In this section, I analyze and compare data drawn from the election night television coverage of

– the British General Election of May 1, 1997,
– the German Parliamentary Election of September 27, 1998, and
– the US Presidential Election of November 7, 2000.

---

3.   I use the term "graphics" to refer to visualizations that are shown full-screen or appear on a studio monitor / video wall. For an analysis of graphic material that is superimposed on the primary television image, such as station logos and captions, see for instance Hofmann (2004), Schieß (2004 a, b).

All three elections resulted in historic changes of government: in Britain, the Conservative Party, under John Major, was defeated by the Labour Party, and Tony Blair became Prime Minister. After 16 years in power, German chancellor Helmut Kohl and his Christian Democratic Union lost to the Social Democrats, whose candidate, Gerhard Schröder, subsequently became the new chancellor. In the United States, the election night of November 7, 2000, turned into an 'election nightmare,' as the result of the presidential election remained disputed for some forty days; at the end of the 'Florida Recount', Democratic candidate Al Gore had to concede to his Republican opponent, Texas Governor George W. Bush.

For each of these elections, I explore the coverage by at least two major TV channels. For Britain, these are public service broadcaster BBC1, its commercial rival ITV as well as CNN International, the international branch of the US-based news channel CNN. Data for the German elections comes from public broadcaster ARD, commercial channel RTL, CNN International and from BBC World (the BBC's international commercial news channel). The corpus for the US elections has been constructed from the coverage by the commercial channels NBC and CNN. The analysis thus allows different comparisons: a cross-cultural comparison of the coverage in the three countries (each with its own culture, political system, media system etc.); a comparison between public service channels (funded mainly by license fees and bound by the obligations that the 'public service' approach implies) and commercial channels (dependent on advertising revenue); and a comparison between national and international (news) channels, the latter having to cater to diverse audiences around the world, with different interests and different levels of background knowledge.

Most of the channels started their coverage at or shortly before poll closing time, which is 10 pm in Britain and 6 pm in Germany. In the United States, the timing is more complex because of the country's numerous time zones and regulations that may differ from state to state. The first polls, for instance, close in the states of Indiana and Kentucky, at 6 pm Eastern Time. At that time, it is just 3 pm on the US West Coast, e.g. in California, where polls don't close until 8 pm Pacific Time (11 pm Eastern Time). These time differences do not only affect the ratings that a nationwide program is likely to achieve in different parts of the country, they may also influence the voting behavior: viewers in the West may base their decision to vote for a particular party or candidate (or whether to vote at all) on the results already coming in from the states further East.

In order to keep the analysis of nine different election night programs manageable, this paper concentrates on the programs' opening phases, i.e., on the first 15 to 20 minutes of the coverage. Such openings represent a condensation of the program's content and style, giving audiences a preview of the type of coverage they can expect to see over the following hours. The opening phase, as defined here, starts with the beginning of a program and ends once the main protagonists inside the television studio (anchors, experts, guests) and the major outside broadcasts have been introduced and the first results, exit polls or projections of the night have been announced. An exception is CNN's coverage of the US elections: since the special election night coverage started one hour before the first polls closed, the analysis includes both the very beginning of the program and the 're-opening' segment, broadcast one hour later, with the presentation of the first results. For the purposes of this paper, video recordings of the opening phases were transcribed, notating in detail both soundtrack and visual images, shot by shot.[4] The table below lists the data studied:[5]

UK 97: May 1, 1997
BBC: 9:55 pm – 10:13 pm local time
ITV: 10:00 pm – 10:20 pm local time
CNN-I: 9:57 pm – 10:21 pm local time

Germany 98: September 27, 1998
ARD: 5:45 pm – 6:08 pm local time
RTL: 5:55 pm – 6:11 pm local time
CNN-I: 5:57 pm – 6:18 pm local time
BBC World: 6:00 pm – 6:20 pm local time

USA 2000: November 7, 2000
CNN: 5:00 pm – 5:25 pm Eastern Time, 6:00 pm – 6:08 pm Eastern Time
NBC: 07:00 pm – 07:18 pm Eastern Time

To contextualize these primary data, I have also studied, albeit in less detail, the hours that follow the opening phases. In addition, the analysis draws on contextual information gleaned from research on the countries' media landscape and on the specific channels.

Section 3.2 explores country by country to what extent the nine news programs with their clearly prescribed political topic, contain visual traces of Klein's (1997, 1998) categories of entertainment. As the Glasgow University Media Group (1980: 194) points out, "[t]he work of visual analysis is extremely laborious ..."

---

4. See Thibault (2000) for an in-depth account of how to transcribe the different semiotic modes of television.

5. The times listed for CNN-I (UK 97) and CNN (USA 2000) include short commercial breaks, lasting two and three minutes, respectively. ITV's coverage contains an embedded news bulletin, with some five minutes of news unrelated to the UK election.

While this statement concerns first and foremost the analyst, those who read the results of visual analysis also face a number of difficulties. Visual analysis uses transcripts, i.e., verbalizations of visual resources, and presents its results in a written format. Thus, readers are twice removed from the original, audiovisual data. It takes quite a bit of imagination (and patience) to follow a written visual analysis of something one has never seen. Given the amount of data and the extent of features covered by the present paper, the inclusion of full transcripts or screenshots was not an option. As an alternative, the following sections are both descriptive, offering readers a chance to visualize the material studied, and analytical.

3.2 The British General Election of May 1, 1997

3.2.1 *BBC1: "Election 97"*
The BBC covered the May 1, 1997 British General Election live for some eight hours, starting at 9:55 pm, thus five minutes before polling stations in Britain closed. Following a short standard identification sequence which identifies the channel as BBC1, the program titled "Election 97" opens with a 50-second *title sequence* – a montage of moving images accompanied by a piece of instrumental theme music.[6] The short video clip, which does without any spoken language, starts with the program logo, a recurrent visual element throughout the night: the words "election 97" inside a large, pink/purple and orange, three-dimensional "e". Pieces of the logo then start rotating and fly out of the screen to make way for typical images of British geography, such as the White Cliffs of Dover. The clip goes on to show the leaders of Britain's three major political parties – John Major, Tony Blair, Paddy Ashdown – as well as generic scenes from the voting process (placing a cross mark on a ballot sheet, dropping the ballot in a ballot box). After giving us a glimpse of the Houses of Parliament and of the door to No. 10 Downing Street, the sequence ends with a sweeping crane shot of the studio, closing in on the "e" of the election logo, displayed in the center of a large, metallic round table, before it turns into the full "election 97" logo as seen at the very beginning.

This sequence of images is a visual shorthand for the theme of the program, elections in Great Britain. But the sequence does more than inform viewers about the topic in a conventional, catchy manner. The use of national institutions such as Parliament signals the importance of the program that is to follow. In addition, the stereotypical images of Britain invest the program with a 'Britishness', inviting

---

6. For an analysis of 'news music', see Glasgow University Media Group (1980: 230–233). The Group points out that the music of title sequences "often reflects the twin sources of television news practice – journalism and show business" (1980: 230). For a recent theoretical approach to the semiotics of music and sound, see van Leeuwen (1999).

a national identification on the part of the British audience. Thus, the sequence also has an emotional appeal, a quality that Klein subsumes under the category of "interestingness" (cf. Table 1 above).

Yet there is another important element to the BBC's opening sequence, beyond the use of national imagery. The sequence gains appeal through the way in which the various images are framed: most of them are not seen full-screen, in a direct, unmediated shot, but are shown as they appear on monitors and a video wall inside the television studio. Like the frame of a painting, the monitors act as a focusing device, giving viewers the impression that they are actively observing a scene through a window (cf. MacLachlan & Reid 1994: 20–21). At the same time, the title sequence is not only about seeing but also about showing: self-reflexively, the segment shows the BBC showing the election, thus anticipating the BBC's role during the night and in particular the large number of interactions between studio and outside locations, mediated via a video wall. The title sequence therefore combines and displays two themes: the election and the coverage of the election. By drawing the viewer into this self-reflexive media microcosm of seeing and showing, the opening sequence again scores high in terms of Klein's category of "interestingness". The fifty seconds that open the program thus contain several entertaining features: they offer easy to understand, catchy images that have an emotional appeal on account of their national connotations. The framing of the images and the element of visual reflexivity make the sequence even more interesting. Finally, the quick succession of images and diverse framings (full screen, monitor, video wall) square with Klein's category of "variety", though this element is by no means as pronounced as in music videos, for instance.

The huge *studio* where the BBC's election coverage originates from is Studio One of the BBC television center in London. The studio set, specially designed for the election, has a bright, modern, high-tech look and has in fact been compared with the bridge of Starship Enterprise (cf. Billen 1997), a comparison that suggests a visual link between the election broadcast and a popular entertainment series. The studio is large and complex, featuring different specialized areas that are grouped around the so-called "round table", from where the program is anchored. Each of these areas corresponds with an individual member of the studio team, who in turn has a specific task within the broadcast.

During the five minutes leading up to the 10 pm poll closings anchor David Dimbleby takes viewers on a guided tour of the studio and introduces the key members of his team, among them the BBC's star interviewer Jeremy Paxman and statistics expert Peter Snow. At the back of the studio, in front of pink/purple walls with the large "e" logo, we notice dozens of other people, who do not get a mention: they are busily working at computers, their backs turned to the camera. These faceless people, and in particular the numerous monitors in front of them,

signify immediacy and efficiency, the transmission of up-to-the-minute information gathered by means of the latest technology – a process made seemingly trans-
parent by placing the computer staff in front of the camera, rather than hiding
them out of view. All in all, the BBC's studio is no doubt an impressive, perhaps
even spectacular sight and promises variety through the sheer number of participants involved in the coverage.

The BBC uses a wide variety of *graphic displays* during the election night.
They range from simple pie charts and maps of Britain to more sophisticated and
imaginative computer animations, e.g. landslides that bury hapless candidates
(thus visualizing the literal meaning of the popular 'landslide' metaphor). These
animated graphics are presented by Peter Snow, a long-standing member of the
BBC's election night team. British television viewers are likely to associate Snow
with the 'swingometer', a gadget in the shape of a wheel with a large needle, which
serves to indicate the swing of the vote to or away from a particular party, illustrating the change, in percentage points, from the previous election. The swingometer is a fixture of the results coverage on British television and as such, adds
a certain nostalgic touch to the program. This nostalgia, however, is counter-bal-
anced by the swingometer's new, modernized look: once a mechanical device, the
BBC's swingometer of the 1997 election is computer-generated and displayed on
a video screen.[7] Beyond the swingometer, Snow promises to illustrate results "in
a more adventurous and inventive way" than ever before – an explicit reference
to the graphics' entertainment value. And he lives up to his promise: for instance,
in graphics sequences titled "battleground", building blocks representing target
seats are blown to pieces to the sound of explosions, a scenario reminiscent of
video war games (cf. Schieß 2000).[8] These particular graphics realize all of Klein's
categories of entertainment and blur the boundary between information and entertainment.

Another visual hallmark of the BBC's election coverage is the large number of
outside broadcasts that feed news and reactions from key areas into the program.

---

7. Four years later, for the coverage of the British elections of 2001, the BBC used a laser-beam
swingometer, projected in front of Snow.

8. Peter Snow's "battleground" even made its way into popular fiction. In Helen Fielding's
bestseller "Bridget Jones: The Edge of Reason" (1999), a book written in diary format, the entry
for May 2, 1997 in part reads as follows:

> When we went to bed Peter Snow was striding marvellously but incomprehensibly
> about and it seemed pretty clear the swingometer was to Labour but . . . Oh-oh. May-
> be we misunderstood. We were a bit squiffy and nothing made any particular sense
> other than all the blue Tory buildings on the map of Britain being blown up. (Fielding
> 1999:206)

Even before introducing the studio team, anchor David Dimbleby calls attention to the video wall behind him and points out some of the places the BBC will be reporting from. In Dimbleby's own words: "We are already at all the places that matter", "we'll be at the party headquarters, we'll be at the key marginal seats", "we'll be in hundreds and hundreds of places". The broadcast thus promises to become a complex, varied montage of inside and outside, of center and periphery (cf. Blumler & Gurevitch 1995: 125).[9]

Formally, the BBC handles the interaction between studio and outside broadcast in the following manner: correspondents and interviewees on location are first seen on the video wall inside the studio, as they are addressed by Dimbleby, who is visible in the foreground. This establishing shot is followed by a cut to a direct, unmediated shot of the outside broadcast that fills the entire screen. At the end of the segment, the speaker on location is once again framed on the studio screen, with Dimbleby in the foreground (cf. Marriott 2000: 134). During longer outside broadcasts, and especially during down-the-line interviews, the above convention is extended and produces a visual turn-taking that matches the dialogic structure of interviews, showing the establishing shot during Dimbleby's questions and the unmediated shot of the outside location during answers. This structure, with the establishing shot contextualizing the outside broadcast, gives coherence to the spatial transitions, a coherence that is all the more necessary given the large number and often rapid succession of outside broadcasts. The BBC's way of handling outside broadcasts, specifically the alignment of visual and verbal structures, makes it easier for viewers to follow the program and thus contains traces of Klein's category of catchiness.

Finally, there is one special type of outside broadcast that needs to be mentioned although it cannot be analyzed in any detail here: the reports presented by "roving reporter" Frank Skinner, a well-known stand-up comedian, who has been hired by the BBC to bring some comic relief to the results coverage. In the opening phase of the program, for instance, Skinner files a pseudo-live report from aboard a helicopter and tells the anchor that he will "supply sort of a low-brow, down-at-heel counterpoint to your intellectual analysis in the studio". Skinner is the clearest and most unequivocal element of entertainment to be found in the BBC coverage, and in fact in any of the election data.

3.2.2 ITV: "Election 97"

Commercial channel ITV (Independent Television) started its six-hour live election coverage at exactly 10 pm, i.e. at the time the polls closed. This timing

---

9. See Marriott (2000) for a detailed analysis of the interplay between different locations and of the "spatiotemporal dynamics" that obtained within the BBC's 1997 results coverage.

partly plays to ITV's advantage since 10 pm is usually the start of ITV's most famous news program, the "News at Ten" – it is thus a well-established timeslot for news bulletins, and viewers may be used to switching into ITV for news at that time.[10] The BBC's timing, with the program starting at 9:55 pm, gave the channel sufficient time for its elaborate opening sequence and studio tour before the anchor presented the first exit poll on the stroke of 10 pm. Given the importance of presenting the exit poll, ITV has no time to spare for introductions or even opening sequences. The program, titled "Election 97" just like its BBC counterpart, opens with a medium close shot of anchor Jonathan Dimbleby (brother of BBC anchor David Dimbleby), who after a quick "good evening" immediately announces the result of the exit poll: Labour is to win. Only then does the program's *title sequence* begin.[11]

The 30-second sequence is accompanied by instrumental theme music and has two parts. The first is a short video clip: the words "election 97" are slowly moving across a background of bluish, somewhat grainy and skewed images showing for instance a ballot with the names of the three party leaders, somebody marking a ballot with a cross, as well as extreme close-ups of Major, Blair and Ashdown. As the camera zooms slightly out, we see that these images are actually being displayed close-up on a battery of TV monitors, which explains their blue shine and grainy texture. Not unlike the BBC's opening, this portion of the title sequence shows a series of images that metonymically represent the night's topic, the election. And here as well, there is a self-reflexive element as ITV shows us the three party leaders appearing on a TV screen within the screen in front of us. By showing familiar images at such a close distance that viewers can make out their very texture, the images are defamiliarized, yet they become familiar again as soon as we realize that this effect is caused by a well-known technology. While this first part of the title sequence operates with images from the reality "out there", i.e. from the election itself, the second part focuses on the "inside", i.e. on the television studio. The camera quickly pans across the different sections of the studio, giving us a sense of its expanse, and finally closes in on

---

10. In fact, ITV tries to stick to its 10 o'clock news slot as much as possible: with some delay, at 10:05 pm, the anchor hands over to "News at Ten" newsreader Julia Somerville "for a brief round-up of today's news and weather". The special election coverage resumes some nine minutes later. (In 1999, ITV controversially moved the news bulletin from 10 to 11 pm. "News at Ten" was restored in 2000, only to be moved to a 10:30 slot in 2004.)

11. This format is a variant of the so-called "'hooker' opening" (Scollon 1998:179; see also Glasgow University Media Group 1980:322) in that the news topic is presented prior to the title sequence, thus reversing the prototypical structure of an opening sequence (cf. Lauerbach, this volume).

the anchor sitting at his desk. This fast-paced studio tour visually anticipates the more detailed introduction that the anchor will provide about one minute later. On balance, ITV's title sequence compares with the BBC's opening for variety, catchiness, and interestingness through visual reflexivity. A major difference is that ITV's sequence does not feature any British landmarks, and it therefore has a less national, less emotional appeal.

ITV's election *studio* is a huge, rectangular, multi-story space with lots of metal structures, a shiny floor, blue background lighting as well as numerous lights and cameras. Like the BBC's Studio One, it has a cool, modern, high-tech look – the New Statesman (Billen 1997) described it as "an underpopulated but space-age dungeon". The studio features four main areas:

- the anchor's desk, where anchor Jonathan Dimbleby is joined by Michael Brunson, ITV's political editor;
- the "results area", with computers, their operators as well as three election analysts, on whose expertise Dimbleby draws repeatedly throughout the night;
- a panel of voters, moderated by well-known ITV presenter Sue Lawley;
- a large video wall, on which Alistair Stewart, ITV's counterpart of the BBC's Peter Snow, illustrates results.

ITV's and the BBC's election studios thus share several features that are likely to engage the viewers' interest: the impressive size, the various special areas reserved for different members of the large studio team, and the overall modern, high-tech design. They differ for instance in their basic structure and in the formal arrangement of the special areas (circular vs. rectangular). Another important difference between the two studios is that ITV's anchor is placed in front of a semi-transparent blue partition, with broad yellow and pink vertical stripes. This salient, exuberant color scheme comes into view virtually every time we see a medium-close shot of the anchor, and it thus forms an important part of the program's overall look – a rather pleasant, colorful look, which, in Klein's terms, adds a 'lighthearted' touch to the program. Finally, while the BBC reserves a special area for star interviewer Jeremy Paxman, ITV features a panel of voters, which adds a certain democratic element to the program and is also reminiscent of the entertainment genre of the talk-show – thus both program orient to the high value currently placed on interactive talk (cf. Cameron 2000).

While anchor Jonathan Dimbleby presents the results coming in from individual constituencies, it is Alistair Stewart who *graphically* presents the larger picture, such as the possible distribution of seats in the new House of Commons. Stewart's job, as Dimbleby puts it, is to "bring clarity where confusion might otherwise reign" – compare this explicit reference to clarity (and thus catchiness) with Peter Snow's mission statement on the BBC, which promised an "inventive and adventurous" presentation. Stewart has two instruments at his disposal. One is a video wall large enough to list the names of dozens of constituencies all at once – it is reminiscent of the video walls often found in game shows. In addition, Stewart makes use of virtual reality graphics, projecting a "virtual House of Commons": as Stewart is standing in front of the video wall, facing the camera, we see benches appearing to his left and right, out of nowhere. As Stewart takes a few steps forward, he seems surrounded by the benches, which represent the government and the opposition benches of the House of Commons. Then, as if by magic, Members of Parliament suddenly appear on the benches, and they are colored according to their party affiliation. These graphics are likely to hold a great fascination for viewers as they see something that looks (almost) like a real, three-dimensional object, with Stewart right in the middle of it. The "'gee-whiz' value" (Robinson & Levy 1986: 140) of such graphics also derives from the fact that (at least still in 1997) they were not a very common sight on television. Apart from the virtual reality effect, however, Stewarts graphics are not particularly spectacular – the virtual House of Commons is, after all, just a static representation of something we have all seen many times before. In other words, it is the novel technology that makes these graphics so appealing. When it comes to creativity and new forms of representation, it is the BBC's Peter Snow who has the edge on Alistair Stewart. While Snow uses somewhat more conventional computer technology, his animated visualizations of metaphors such as "landslide" or "battlefield" are unparalleled.

Outside broadcasts play an important part in ITV's election night coverage.[12] Dimbleby tells viewers early on that "we'll be taking you out of the studio to every part of the nation, to the heart of the election story ...". Among the first outside broadcasts, for instance, are those that cover "the race to be first", i.e. the competition between three constituencies, each of which wants to be the first to declare the result. With a few exceptions, ITV handles the interaction between studio and outside location much like the BBC does: reports and interviews open with an establishing shot showing the reporter or interviewee on a video screen close to the anchor. Only then is there a cut to a full shot of the outside location. As on BBC, this technique provides viewers with a steady visual base, a fixed point of reference, from where they can venture out to the periphery of the broadcast and back.

---

12. While the BBC had 80 outside broadcast units in place, ITV had only 40 (Radio Times 1997).

3.3.3 CNN International: "Britain Decides"

How does the 24-hour international news channel CNN International (CNN-I) cover Britain's national elections and present this topic to an audience around the world? CNN-I changed its regular programming to bring special extended live coverage from its London studios. The main election special started some three minutes before poll closing time and lasted two hours.

Titled "Britain Decides", the program starts with a 13-second *title sequence*, accompanied by a lively instrumental theme tune. The clip features a sequence of images, asymmetrically superimposed on a fluttering Union Jack: a hand dropping a ballot in a ballot box, voters in front of a ballot box, and the leaders of the three major parties. The sequence ends as the large banners "Britain Decides" and "the vote" appear on the screen.

A striking feature of the title sequence is the use of Britain's national flag – an element that is noticeably absent from the coverage by the two national broadcasters, BBC and ITV. One way of explaining this difference is to point out CNN-I's status as an international channel with a global audience: by using national symbols (not only in the title sequence but also as part of its graphic displays, see below), CNN-I visually signals to its viewers around the world that it has temporarily and exceptionally focussed its coverage on one particular country (a focus that might otherwise be seen as running counter to the channel's international orientation). A sustained national focus by an international channel is a marked case, and as such, this focus also becomes visually marked. There is no need for such maneuvers on the BBC or ITV since it is obvious to a British audience which country these national channels are covering on election day in Britain.[13] An alternative explanation presents itself if one compares these data with the way in which CNN-USA (i.e. CNN's domestic network) covers the US election of 2000 (see 3.5.1 below). Here, the Stars and Stripes figures prominently throughout the program, something which can be attributed to the great role the US flag plays within the country's national culture in general. Seen against this backdrop, CNN-I's use of the Union Jack in its coverage of the British elections

---

13. The difference between national and international channels also affects the titles given to the election night programs: in Britain, viewers who tune into the BBC's or ITV's "Election 97" naturally interpret this title as referring to the British election. By contrast, the global audience of CNN International requires further information, and it is therefore necessary to use program titles such as "Britain Decides", which explicitly mention the country in question. These different naming practices are also found in the data on the German elections, see Section 3.4 below.

could be explained as a transferral of cultural practices from its own national (media) culture onto its international coverage.[14]

The *studio* from which CNN-I is covering the British elections does not compare with its BBC or ITV counterparts: it is small, unspectacular, plain if not modest, and its design bears no special relation to the election. Its centerpiece is an L-shaped desk with just enough room for anchor Richard Blystone and his two local experts. In the background, the studio wall shows what appears to be a collage of architectural elements taken from British historic monuments, as well as a large sign reading "CNN London", suggesting that the program is produced by a news team permanently based right in Britain.

CNN's *graphic displays* visualize exit polls and projections that have been provided by national British channels, such as the BBC. CNN-I borrows authenticity from the national broadcasters by crediting the data to them – after all, who, if not the venerable BBC, could be a more reliable source of information on the British elections? Visually, CNN's graphics are simple but sleek blockcharts that show photos of the party leaders next to the name of the respective party. The blocks are superimposed on a freeze-frame of a fluttering Union Jack, giving the graphic a three-dimensional, almost lively look.

CNN-I adds even more local flavor to its program by occasionally cutting to ITV, thus transmitting the British channel's election coverage live on CNN: at 10 pm, for instance, CNN viewers see ITV's Jonathan Dimbleby presenting the exit poll and introducing his studio team. ITV's coverage is integrated into the CNN program by means of a window which is overlaid on the Union Jack – yet another use of the national flag – and it is only the CNN logo at the bottom of the screen that tells viewers that they are actually tuned into CNN. Once CNN anchor Blystone takes over again, he summarizes ITV's coverage and repeats the result of the exit poll: "And the bottom-line behind all that flash and filigree was this, and it sounds very bad for the ruling Conservative Party ...". The first part of that sentence is revealing: Blystone's use of the phrase "flash and filigree" to characterize the ITV coverage captures the stylistic differences between the two channels – colorful, almost exuberant ITV meets plain, down-to-earth CNN International.

The Union Jack background also comes into play during *outside broadcasts*. CNN-I has just two remote locations: the headquarters of the Labour Party and of the Conservative Party. Unlike the BBC or ITV, CNN-I does not use establishing shots that show the anchor as he addresses the correspondent or interviewee on a studio screen. Instead, CNN-I has opted for another fairly common technique to

---

14. The US flag is less conspicuous in the election night coverage by US-channel NBC (see 3.5.2 below). Instead, NBC makes frequent use of the US Presidential seal, another national symbol.

contextualize the outside broadcast and to visually represent the interaction between studio and remote location: using a split-screen arrangement, CNN-I shows the anchor and the correspondent simultaneously in separate picture frames, superimposed on a still of a fluttering Union Jack. Once the anchor's turn is finished, the program cuts to a full-size shot of the correspondent. A characteristic feature of the use of the two simultaneous frames is that here, both anchor and correspondent are looking directly at the camera, and thus also at the viewers, but they are talking to each other (cf. Morse 1985:9). There is thus a certain disjunction between visual and verbal address: while anchor and correspondent verbally address each other, they visually address the viewers, who in turn have to reinterpret this direct visual address, this "visual 'you'" (Kress & van Leeuwen 1996:122), as being aimed at one of the participants on the screen. Whereas in the establishing shot of the type used by the BBC and ITV, viewers are onlookers watching the anchor address the correspondent on a large monitor, in a split-screen configuration, viewers can escape neither the anchor's nor the correspondent's gaze, and they may thus feel more actively involved in the on-screen interaction.

3.3.4 *Coverage of the British elections: A comparison*
It comes as no surprise that the most striking visual differences within the three election night broadcasts can be discerned between the national channels BBC and ITV on the one hand, and the international channel CNN International, on the other. CNN's small, modest studio and the simple, static graphics do not compare with the scale of the operation undertaken by the BBC and ITV, and this imbalance cannot be offset by fluttering flags or attention-grabbing split screens. CNN's coverage is visually solid and up to date, and it shows few signs of moving in the direction of entertainment. At least on the level of the visuals, the channel's election night special is a 'no frills' program, and this concentration on the essentials of news production corresponds with the "extreme cost-consciousness" and "commercial pragmatism" that Küng-Shankleman (2000:148) ascribes to CNN. Besides, CNN is a news channel operating in an international environment, and its viewers tune into the channel specifically for news, news that their national channels may not be able to offer them. As the world's self-declared "news leader", CNN has a strong position on the international news market and may thus feel less pressure to compete with other channels and to visually spice up its coverage.

Looking at the two national channels in more detail, it is worth recalling the significance of election night broadcasts as major national media events (cf. Lauerbach, this vol.). BBC political reporter Jonny Dymond (2000) describes the status that election results programs have attained in Britain as follows:

> It [election night] has become the behemoth of British television, a sprawling jungle of coverage in which the biggest beasts of broadcasting roam uttering strange war whoops and clashing with predators from all around the kingdom. Unrivalled as both news event and fantasy playground for computer whizzkids, Election night is now firmly fixed as a great television moment.

The BBC's and ITV's election night broadcast are scheduled directly against each other, and the competition is almost palpable. Each of the two programs has its own look, its distinct visual style, yet the similarities are also striking. Both broadcast from huge studios with a large on-screen staff, field well-known news personalities, and present computer-generated graphics displays. It is in the details that differences can be discerned. The BBC's title sequence, for instance, has a greater emotional appeal because of its visual references to national landmarks. One special highlight of the BBC's coverage are certainly the 'battleground' graphics presented by Peter Snow – they realize all of Klein's categories of entertainment and are unrivalled in any of the election data. Meanwhile, ITV's 'virtual House of Commons' is no doubt an interesting, if not spectacular sight, and is also a catchy visualization of election results, but it lacks the speed and the playful character of Snow's graphics.

Do the channels that covered the 1997 German Parliamentary Election divide along similar lines?

3.4 The German Parliamentary Election of September 27, 1998

3.4.1 *ARD: "Wahl '98"*
ARD[15] covered the German elections on September 27, 1998, with a special broadcast ("Wahl '98", 'Election '98') starting at 5:45 pm – 15 minutes before polls close in Germany – and lasting till 8 pm, with additional election specials following in the course of the evening. ARD opens the election special with a panoramic, bird's eye view of the city of Bonn and its government district, as seen from a helicopter. These images are accompanied by the anchor's live voice-over, declaring that the days of Bonn are numbered and that a touch of nostalgia has taken hold of the government district – references to the fact that at the time, the seat of the German government was about to move from Bonn to Berlin. The appeal of this title sequence, in which the images of Bonn function as a visual metonymy for the election, stems from the unusual perspective adopted, i.e. from the aerial view from which we look down at the city.

---

15. ARD (also called "Channel One") is a public service broadcasting system, and its position on the German media market is comparable to that of the BBC in Britain.

The program then cuts to the interior of the election *studio*, or rather to the place ARD is using as a studio especially for its election broadcast: the coverage is headquartered in Bonn, in a building called "Wasserwerk" ('waterworks'), which was the seat of the *Bundestag* (the lower house of the German parliament) from 1986 to 1992, while a new assembly hall was under construction. ARD thus covers the election out of a historic building and derives both prestige and authenticity from this locale and its aura. Accordingly, the producers did not have to (and probably were not allowed to) change the overall look of the Wasserwerk-cum-studio very much. Besides desks, chairs and monitors, they only added a few white and blue background panels with an election logo. The overall look of the 'studio' (always referred to as the 'Wasserwerk' by the participants) is bright, clear, sober, with no gimmicks or dramatic design elements. One special decorative object is the large metal eagle high up on one of the walls, behind what used to be the government benches: The 'federal eagle' ('Bundesadler') – Germany's official national symbol – is a visual reminder of the Wasserwerk's place in history as the prior seat of parliament. It might even lend ARD's election coverage a semi-official, authoritative touch.

The program is hosted by Marion von Haaren, at the time editor-in-chief of the regional ARD channel in charge of the Bonn election coverage. Von Haaren uses the opening phase of the program to introduce the studio team, whose members each have their own special area – as in the BBC's or ITV's case, the spatial division of the studio correlates with a functional differentiation among the participants. Striding through the studio, von Haaren first introduces her colleague Wolfgang Kenntemich, who in turn presents his panel of five "high calibre" studio guests whom he will interview during the course of the evening. In the back of the studio, members of a live audience can be seen at times, and they can be heard applauding while the team members and guests are introduced. The live studio audience, although never explicitly mentioned or introduced, gives ARD's coverage an air of democracy and transparency as the channel presumably allows average citizens to be present in the studio and to monitor its election coverage. A particularly important team member is journalist Uli Deppendorf, sitting below the eagle on a semicircular platform, thus occupying a central, priviledged position within the studio. Deppendorf is in charge of statistics and presents the results of exit polls, opinions polls and projections. The polls were commissioned by ARD and were conducted by the polling organization *infratest-dimap*, whose staff are also present in the studio yet remain anonymous. As with the BBC, these nameless experts visually represent part of the information process, suggesting that the information presented by Deppendorf does not come 'out of nowhere' but is the result of expert knowledge and computer technology. Even after this introductory round, anchor von Haaren, unlike her colleagues on the other channels, does not get to settle down behind a large, solid desk. Throughout the evening, she presents the program standing up, her only 'homebase' being a small high desk, resembling a lectern, with just enough room for some sheets of paper and a notebook computer. From here, she occasionally ventures to different parts of the studio, e.g. for a live studio interview with politicians.

The *graphics* that Deppendorf presents are computer-generated tables and blockcharts, overlaid on a light blue background that repeats the blue of the decorative panels put up in the Wasserwerk – blue being ARD's house colors. The design is sleek, modern and 3D but has little in common with the BBC's animated sequences or ITV's virtual-reality graphics. ARD does without any dazzling gimmicks or attention-getters and instead visualizes information in a sophisticated and modern yet simple, solid and well-established manner.

Throughout the program, ARD reports live from a number of remote locations, though the broadcast's "spatial fragmentation" (Marriott 2000: 140) does not match that of the BBC's *Election 97*. Visually, the *outside broadcasts* are presented in much the same way as on the two British channels: the correspondent is first shown on a large monitor inside the studio, conversing with the foregrounded von Haaren, who has turned around towards the monitor, leaning her right elbow on the high desk (a somewhat casual posture); the program then cuts to a full-size shot of the monitor image. The viewers are thus first onlookers, watching both anchor and interviewee from the sidelines, before they become more strongly involved in the interaction, as a result of the interviewee's direct visual address.

3.4.2   RTL: "Wahlen '98"

RTL is Germany's leading commercial channel and has a long history of competing with its public service rivals, such as ARD. When it comes to news programs, the public service broadcasters have always had a clear edge over RTL, both in terms of ratings and reputation. Since the mid-1990s, however, after changing the format of its newscasts (cf. Muckenhaupt 1998: 129–130), RTL has been able to improve its position and its image as a serious provider of news and information.

RTL covered the 1998 German election with a special broadcast that ran from 5:55 pm to 8:15 pm, and with another election special, starting at 10 pm. The special broadcast was preceded by a short segment that took a humorous look at the election, featuring funny vox pops and videoclips that mocked politicians.

"Wahlen '98" ('Elections '98') started with a short twelve-second *title sequence* which had been adapted from the regular news bulletin "RTL Aktuell". First, against a bright orange background we see a split screen showing Gerhard Schröder on the left and Helmut Kohl on the right – both are dropping a ballot in a ballot box, the stereotypical images from election day. The split screen visually polarizes the two candidates, much like the opponents of a boxing match. These images are captioned "Stunde der Wahrheit" ('The moment of truth'). On the very left of the screen, we see part of a rotating globe,[16] which soon expands to fill the entire screen and is then overlaid with the title "Wahlen '98. Die Entscheidung" ('Elections '98. The Decision'). As the globe and the titles shrink and move to the bottom-left of the screen, the studio, with the anchor's desk, comes into view. The sequence is accompanied by the theme music from 'RTL Aktuell' and by the anchor's voice-over: "Stunde der Wahrheit. Gerhard Schröder oder Helmut Kohl. Wer führt Deutschland ins nächste Jahrtausend?" ('The moment of truth. Gerhard Schröder or Helmut Kohl. Who will lead Germany into the new millennium?'). Both the voice-over and the visuals foreground the two main candidates, failing to mention parties or parliamentary seats – although it's a parliamentary election in a multi-party political system. The sequence – and in particular the images that visually oppose Kohl and Schröder – reduces the election to the competition between the two candidates. It simplifies and dramatizes a complex political process, scoring high in terms of Klein's categories of interestingness and catchiness.[17]

RTL's on-screen studio team consists of anchor Peter Kloeppel and political analyst Johannes Groß. The *studio* is divided into two areas: the anchor's desk and a special area for graphic displays. Kloeppel and Groß are sitting side by side at a large, wooden semicircular desk. Behind them, on the studio wall, is a large panel featuring a blue and yellow globe and the title "Wahlen '98". The panel is framed by a structure that echoes the warm colors of the anchor's desk and includes several small monitors on both the left and the right of the panel. This studio setting is solid, yet friendly and pleasant. For the presentation of *graphic displays* and for some of the outside broadcasts Kloeppel leaves the desk and walks a few steps over to the graphics area.

This area is a 'virtual studio', actually an empty area which only comes to life through computer technology. From here, Kloeppel presents for instance the first projection of the night, visualized by means of a bar chart. What's remarkable about this graphic is that it is not shown on a monitor or video wall but that it appears to be suspended in the air, to Kloeppel's left, in front of a background consisting of a stylized image of the German flag and the German eagle – the chart is a 3D-projection that uses a technology similar to ITV's "virtual House

16. As Maulko (1997: 163) notes, the globe is part of the corporate identity of many television channels and helps promote the myth of a medium that takes a god-like, all-embracing look at the world.

17. One might surmise that this poliarized form of representation has been influenced by US media practices, which reflect features of the US political system: the two-party system, and the presidential, rather than parliamentary, system of government.

of Commons". In fact Kloeppel later on shows a "virtual *Bundestag*" ("virtueller Bundestag"). Like ITV, RTL seems to bet on the astonishment that this type of graphics is likely to cause. The virtual graphics also have a practical advantage over graphics shown full-screen, as on ARD for instance: as Kloeppel explains a graphic, he can use his hands to point out certain sections or values displayed on it, thus making it easier for viewers to align his words with the visuals. This of course would also be possible by simply showing the graphics on a large monitor or video wall, yet these alternatives do not have the high-tech appeal and the effect of the technologically more advanced virtual reality graphics. Since the 1998 elections, the nimbus of such graphics has waned: at the time of writing this paper, RTL regularly used the virtual studio for presenting something as everyday as the weather report.

The area from where Kloeppel present the graphics is also used for some of the *outside broadcasts* from party headquarters. The technique employed by RTL resembles ARD's method: the program first shows the anchor addressing the reporter before it cuts to a direct shot of the outside location. On RTL, however, the reporter is not seen on an actual monitor or video wall, but on an artificially created screen that appears to be miraculously hovering above the ground, right next to the anchor. Just like the graphics discussed above, these outside broadcasts, presented via a virtual video wall, are thus loaded with a certain "gee-whiz value". A different type of outside broadcast originates at the anchor's desk. As Kloeppel hands over to his colleague on location, the screen image showing Kloeppel is reduced in size and moves down to the lower right corner of the screen, giving way to a large image of the outside location, which it slightly overlaps. The result is an asymmetrical screen layout which gives visual prominence to the outside location, thereby distorting the anchor's and the correspondent's proportions. Interestingly, Kloeppel's tiny head remains visible during the entire report – the two screen images do not alternate with a full-size shot of the outside location. Thus, as the correspondent is answering Kloeppel's question, we can see Kloeppel listening in silence to what the correspondent has to say, occasionally nodding his head. All the while, both anchor and correspondent are facing frontally, involving the viewer through their direct visual address.

3.4.3 *CNN International: "Germany Decides"*

CNN International's special broadcast on the German elections is formatted much like the channel's coverage of the British elections – from the small, plain studio, on to the graphics and outside broadcasts. Like "Britain Decides", "Germany Decides" started some three minutes before poll closing time and lasted two hours.

The 15-second *title sequence* that opens the program, accompanied by a piece of solemn, dramatic instrumental theme music, is visually more intricate than the one we saw for the British elections. Superimposed on a white background is a succession of lines and squares that scroll across the screen. In the upper and the lower sections of the screen, the squares are filled with black-and-white images of Germany and German politics: the Bundestag, the candidates Schröder and Kohl, people standing in line inside a polling station, factory chimneys, the Brandenburg Gate, etc. As thin lines – some of them black, red and yellow – move vertically down the screen, words such as "Germany", "elections" and "vote" float across the screen. At the end of the clip, appearing below an image of a hand putting a ballot in a ballot box, a large black, red and yellow banner reading "Germany Decides" appears and announces the title of the program. Like the sequence that opened "Britain Decides", this title sequence uses national colors as design elements – something the British or German national channels do not use in any prominent position. As above, this use of national colors may be explained either by CNN's status as an international channel, or by the possible influence of US cultural practices – or both. Another characteristic feature of the sequence is the fact that virtually all of its elements – lines, images, words – are in constant motion, vying for the viewers' attention.

The CNN *studio*, located in the buildings of CNN's German partner n-tv, in Düsseldorf, consists of a triangular desk where anchor Bettina Lüscher is joined by one local expert. In the background, we see several television monitors as well as a small office area with people working at computers, thus giving viewers a glimpse of some of the activity going on behind the scenes. The logo "CNN D" (short for "CNN Deutschland", 'CNN Germany'), visible on a column behind Lüscher, refers to CNN's small German-language window. At least for those viewers able to understand this reference, the logo suggests that CNN-I possesses local expertise drawn from a news staff permanently based right in Germany.

The *graphics* that CNN-I uses to illustrate the results of the German elections are mostly blockcharts overlaid on a white background with geometric shapes, i.e. the same background that was seen during the title sequence. And as with the British elections, CNN obtains its data from local, national channels. Another similarity is the technique used for *outside broadcasts*: superimposed on the same background as graphic displays, two windows show the anchor on the left and the outside location on the right, giving viewers simultaneous visual access to both locations.

3.4.4 *BBC World: BBC World News – "Germany Decides"*
Like its rival CNN International, BBC World is an English-language news channel and caters to viewers around the world. On the evening of the German elections, rather than to present one single election night program, BBC World broadcast several shorter news specials that covered events in Germany. In what follows, I

analyze a 20-minute segment that is formally part of the regular news bulletin "BBC World News" but exclusively focuses on the German election. This special coverage started at 6 pm, with the closing of the polls in Germany, and was hosted by BBC anchor Nik Gowing from Bonn.

The *opening* of the program has two parts: first, there is the station identification sequence that opens every BBC World newscast – a computer-animation of multi-colored (fictitious) flags, accompanied by dramatic theme music. Next, for some 15 seconds, the program cuts to a live shot of the outside of the German Bundestag in Bonn, with an unusually large "live" caption in white capitals on a red background in the lower left corner of the screen. The anchor's voice-over welcomes the viewers "live from Bonn, from outside the German Bundestag" and introduces the election topic. This verbal commentary explains to international viewers what they are currently seeing, a necessary explanation since the German Bundestag is a less common sight than for instance the British Parliament in London or the US Congress in Washington, DC. This opening sequence focuses on location, on the genius loci of the Bundestag, whose live image is employed to represent the election topic and to signal that BBC World is reporting right from the midst of ongoing events (although the main activity will be taking place in the party headquarters rather than the Bundestag).

From this opening sequence, BBC World cuts to the inside of the studio where we see anchor Nik Gowing and expert Heinz Schulte sharing a desk – a setting resembling that of the studio used by CNN-I for its coverage of the German and the British elections. The most conspicuous feature of this studio is the background: through a large pane of glass, we see part of the Bundestag, as introduced in the previous sequence. Again, this spatial proximity suggests that BBC World is literally close to the election and is thus in a position to inform viewers fast and first-hand. Given today's information technology, the same information would of course be available to Gowing if he were in the BBC's London studios. The decision to host the program from Bonn may thus at least in part be explained by the 'visual imperative'. The studio contains one other design element: during close-up shots of Heinz Schulte, and during some of the shots of Nick Gowing, we see panels with some of the flags shown at the very beginning of the program – these are elements from BBC World's corporate design, helping the channel project a unified image throughout the program.

BBC World uses *graphics* quite sparingly: just one during the entire 20-minute segment. This graphic, an exit poll, is a simple table consisting of two columns and five rows. It is overlaid on an image of the German eagle, in the colors of Germany's national flag. A small yet interesting detail is the fact that the German eagle has been placed at an oblique angle with the table, rendering the screen asymmetrical in a way that contravenes our viewing habits and is thus likely to engage our attention. On the whole, BBC World's rather plain, static graphics style resembles the graphics used by CNN International.

Outside broadcasts are handled in two different ways: for some of the reports, BBC World cuts directly from a medium close shot of the anchor to a medium close shot of the reporter on location. On another occasion, the channel uses a split screen, showing Gowing in a window to the left and the correspondent in a window on the right, over the same black, red and yellow background used for the graphics.

3.4.5 *Coverage of the German elections: A comparison*

Unlike the coverage of the British elections analyzed above, a comparison of channels ARD, RTL, CNN International and BBC World, and their coverage of the German elections, does not show a simple, clear-cut division between the national channels on the one hand and the international broadcasters on the other. While CNN and BBC World can be grouped together – both feature a small, static, unspectacular studio setting and make little use of graphics resources – the national channels ARD and RTL differ in a number of respects. ARD is broadcasting from the huge 'Wasserwerk', which compares to the studios used by the BBC and ITV in terms of size and variety, with the added appeal of the Wasserwerk's historic, national significance. By contrast, RTL's election coverage originates in a small, everyday news studio, which resembles the studios from which CNN and BBC World are broadcasting. A notable difference is the graphics area, from which RTL presents three-dimensional, attention-grabbing graphics, not unlike those seen on ITV. RTL' coverage – both the studio and the graphics – is generally more colorful than ARD's, which sticks to its serious, somewhat bland blue house color. A similar distinction applies to the title sequences: while ARD nostalgically shows an aerial view of Bonn, RTL focusses on candidates Kohl and Schröder, polarizing their images like the opponents of a boxing match. RTL's visual style thus exhibits a number of entertainment features, more so than ARD, and this difference between the two channels corresponds with their status as commercial and public service channels, respectively. Interestingly, the distinction between public and commercial channels was less pronounced in the data for the British elections, where the BBC's coverage was visually as appealing as ITV's, if not more.

Turning to election coverage in the United States, how does the line between information and entertainment fare in the country that is said to be the home of "infotainment"?

3.5 The US Presidential Election of November 7, 2000

3.5.1 *CNN: "Election 2000"*

CNN's[18] special coverage of election day 2000 started at 5 pm Eastern Time, one hour before the first polls closed. 5 pm is the time usually reserved for "Inside Politics", one of CNN's major political programs, and thus a well-established time slot for political coverage on CNN. The election special did not only take over the "Inside Politics" slot, it was also hosted by the program's two well-known anchors, Judy Woodruff and Bernard Shaw. Starting the coverage well before the first poll closings gave CNN ample time to present reports and background information on the election campaign, the candidates and the issues.

CNN's *title sequence* is the longest of all the election night broadcasts analyzed here. Lasting 2 minutes and 10 seconds, it is an elaborate, tripartite sequence that combines moving images, written and spoken language, and music. Part one identifies the station and announces that an "election 2000 special presentation" is about to begin. Part two, taking up the major portion of the sequence, fleshes out the topic "election day", before part three briefly introduces the on-screen studio team. In part two, CNN has opted to represent the election topic from a historical perspective and takes a look back at the twentieth century, from 1900 onward – it's a two-minute lesson (or crash course) in US and Presidential history. Each time the voice-over mentions a specific event or characterizes a specific era, we see an image of the President who was in office at that time. The visuals are in fact a complex, computer-animated collage consisting of the name and photo of the president in question, a large fluttering US flag, a moving time line on which specific years light up, and, at the bottom of the screen, small frames with news footage of events from the different eras. For instance, as the voice-over mentions the Great Depression, we see a photo of President Franklin D. Roosevelt, the year 1932 lights up on the time line and the three frames at the bottom of the screen show black and white images of soup kitchens. In a similar manner, the voice-over "the confusing contrast of tragedy and triumph" is combined with a photo of President Ronald Reagan and news footage showing Oliver North taking an oath, the Challenger explosion and the falling of the Berlin Wall. The historical review ends as a map of the United States blends into a ballot box, which in turn fades to images of candidates Al Gore and George W. Bush: "Today, America is again forging its future by choosing a man to lead it into the twenty-first century", the

---

18. CNN is actually a network of different channels, each catering to a different audience. The coverage of the British and the German elections was produced by CNN International, for an international audience. Coverage of the US elections, though broadcast around the world, was produced by CNN's domestic network, CNN-USA, which caters to the US market.

voice-over tells viewers. By historicizing the presidential election, CNN is able to show a wide variety of images that its (U.S.) audience can easily recognize and relate to and that in some cases have a strong emotional appeal. Thus, already on the level of visual content, i.e. the the people, places, objects, events depicted, the sequence is catchy, interesting and diverse. The latter two qualities are reinforced through visual effects, such as the fluttering of the US flag and the vertical movement of the time line.

The title sequence ends with a panoramic shot of CNN's vast broadcast *studio* and newsroom, closing in on the so-called "election desk", with anchors Judy Woodruff and Bernard Shaw as well as experts Jeff Greenfield (CNN's senior analyst) and Bill Schneider (CNN's senior political analyst). With this line-up of experienced and well-known anchors and experts, side-by-side at one desk, CNN has doubled its usual two-presenter format and signals the importance it attaches to the election coverage.

Behind the election desk, we see a large newsroom with numerous computers, monitors, clocks, and several people milling around. After commercial breaks, as the program re-opens and the camera zooms in on the election desk, further parts of the newsroom become visible in the foreground. The election desk is thus surrounded by the activities of electronic news-gathering, suggesting that rather than investing in fancy studio sets, CNN concentrates on the essentials of news production. In addition, by giving viewers some visual access to what is going on behind the scenes, CNN arouses and in part satisfies the viewers' curiosity about the mysteries of a TV news studio.

A fifth member of the on-screen studio team is Wolf Blitzer, CNN's senior political correspondent, who reports specifically on the night's Congressional and Gubernatorial elections. Blitzer is stationed in a separate area of the large CNN newsroom, in the midst of desks, monitors and busy staff – here again, the spatial contiguity of the processes of news gathering and news presentation are used to signal both immediacy and transparency.

The *graphic displays* presented by CNN have one conspicuous feature in common: their background is a digital, slightly blurred image of a fluttering US flag, as first seen in the title sequence. Whether it's a graphic that shows the winner of the Presidential race in a particular state, a list of important issues or winners of the Congressional elections, each and every graphic is backed by the Stars and Stripes. This background functions as an attention-getter on account of its fluttering movement and its value as a powerful cultural symbol. Overlaid on this motif, the results graphics for the Presidential race show a color photo of the winning candidate, next to his name, the number of electoral votes of the state in question, the word "winner" in capitals, and the remark "cnn estimate", in small print. At the top-left of the screen, next to the name of the state, there is a small frame with the Presidential seal, with stars rotating around it – another eye-catching moving element. An additional feature of CNN's graphics design is the three-dimensional look of some of the elements superimposed on the flag background, e.g. a map of the United States, or a pie chart. The 3D-look adds volume to these elements and enhances their visual presence (Maulko 1997: 166).

The US flag also functions as a backdrop to the picture frames in which the anchor and correspondents or interviewees appear during *outside broadcast*. CNN-USA uses the same split-screen technique as CNN International, visually involving the viewers by showing the participants as they face frontally at the camera.

3.5.2 *NBC: "Decision 2000: Election Night"*

On November 7, 2000, NBC's special election program started at 7 pm Eastern Time, i.e. one hour after the first poll closings. The program's anchor, Tom Brokaw, had already hosted NBC's 6:30 pm "Evening News", reporting on the first results of the night. The 7 pm special broadcast thus extends the previous program in terms of both topic and studio team, a scheduling strategy which is likely to provide for good audience flow. The coverage is periodically interrupted by commercial breaks and by election updates from a local NBC affiliate station.

As the 7 pm time slot coincides with several poll closings, NBC's "Decision 2000" begins with a variant of the "'hooker' opening", as did ITV's election night program (see above). Instead of an elaborate title sequence, we first see Tom Brokaw, one of the United States' best known news personalities, at his desk in the studio: he briefly welcomes the viewers, introduces himself and immediately goes on to announce the winners of the Presidential race in the six states where polls have just closed. After illustrating the results so far on a map of the United States, he promises to take viewers "on an exciting and bumpy ride". Only then, 90 seconds into the program, does the *title sequence* start.

The 30-second sequence is a computer animation accompanied by a piece of theme music that can faintly be heard during Brokaw's introduction. The main visual motif is the round Presidential seal. In the animation, the seal's round center and outer rings are detached from each other and start revolving on their own axes, as if suspended in the air. In the foreground, the words "NBC News", in large capitals, move across the screen, at an oblique angle, as if revolving around a globe. Similarly, a reel with images of former Presidents Carter, Reagan, Bush Sr. and Clinton turns around the seal and then fades into the NBC logo (a stylized, multi-colored peacock). Next, the dome of the US Capitol comes into view, rising from an area underneath the seal. Finally, "Decision 2000", in modern, shiny three-dimensional letters, appears on screen, forming the "Decision 2000, NBC News"-logo that will be a recurring graphic element throughout the night. As the logo is reduced in size and moves to the bottom of the screen, next to the words "Election Night", the computer animation gives way to a low-angle shot of Rockefeller Center (NBC's headquarters), with US flags in the foreground. Starting with the appearance of the words "Decision 2000", the sequence is accompanied by a male voice-over: "From NBC News, Decision Two Thousand, election night. Live from our election headquarters in New York, here is Tom Brokaw."

The sequence, short as it is, manages to realize all of Klein's categories of entertainment. It dazzles viewers with a rapid succession of well-known images and national symbols, some of which have been digitally enhanced, e.g. from flat and static, to three-dimensional and kinetic. While these features ensure that the sequence is varied, interesting and catchy, one can also detect aspects that even add a light-hearted touch: the bright orange background, and the portraits of former Presidents aligned in the shape of a film reel, which calls to mind actors and the entertainment industry, rather than politicians and national politics.

The expanse of NBC's election *studio* is visible only at the beginning of the program, during a long shot that shows the anchor's desk in front of several background panels, some of which feature the "Decision 2000" logo. Overwhelmingly, however, the camera focuses either on anchor Tom Brokaw or on Tim Russert, NBC's Washington bureau chief and moderator of the well-known interview program "Meet the Press", who is also sitting at the anchor's desk, to Brokaw's left. Shots that show both Brokaw and Russert reveal a central feature of the rather small studio set: on the wall behind the anchor's desk, appearing in between Brokaw and Russert, there is a large electronic outline map of the United States, on which states light up in different colors, depending on which of the candidates has won them. Not only does the map change in the course of the night, as more and more polls close, it is also surrounded by two thin rings on which the names of the 50 states circle the map – a moving element that catches the eye. Although the map is actually projected on a rectangular screen, we perceive the map as framed by the circles or rings. As a result, viewers see the United States as if through a porthole, from aboard a space ship – a futuristic variant of the "television as window to the world" metaphor. In an alternative reading, which is suggested by the circular shape and the shiny surface of the map, Brokaw and Russert are looking at a crystal ball inside of which the future of the United States is taking shape.[19]

The map functions both as a permanent decorative element of the studio setting and as a *graphic resource* that is repeatedly employed to illustrate results. During the sequences in which the map is actively used and referred to, Tim Russert uses a light pen to point out particular states. For example: "... right here in

---

19. See Glasgow University Media Group (1980: 274–275) on ITV's use of a 'crystall ball' icon as a backing image.

Pennsylvania and right here in Michigan. And, Tom, then we bounce over and have Wisconsin and Minnesota and Iowa and Missouri". The deictic adverb "here" is combined with Russert's pointing gesture, or rather with the appearance of a small point of light on a specific area of the map. By pointing out areas on the map, Russert acts as a facilitator and does not leave it up to the viewers, and to their knowledge of geography, to identify the states in question. This visual support increases the catchiness of the information presented.

Other graphics used by NBC do not appear on a studio screen but are shown in direct shots. The most common graphics are those indicating the winner of the Presidential election in a specific state: a close-up photo of the winning candidate is combined with written information such as "President", "Virginia", "Projected Winner", "13 electoral votes", and the name of the candidate.[20] The background on which the photo and the writing are superimposed is an artificial environment dominated by a tilted disk, possibly a variation on the "seal" motif introduced in the title sequence. There are several elements that add movement to the graphic: on the right and at the bottom of the screen, we see parts of two revolving circles made up of the words "Decision 2000". In the top left corner, stars are turning, like on the outer edges of the Presidential seal. The background is thus dominated by circles and curved forms, which contrast with the horizontal writing and provide coherence across different parts of the program: from the seal introduced during the title sequence, to the studio map surrounded by rings or circles, and on to graphic displays. The transition from one graphic to the next is achieved by a golden flash that quickly moves across the screen, from left to right, wiping out the information for one state and leaving new information in its trail. Another striking feature of NBC's graphics is the color scheme: the main colors used are bright orange and pink (also used to color in the names of Democratic candidates), in addition to blue (also used for the Republican candidates).

NBC's *outside broadcasts* from around the country are first shown in a separate picture frame next to an image of Brokaw, before the program cuts to a direct shot of the remote location. At the bottom of the screen, acting like a bridge between the two frames, is the NBC News "Decision 2000" logo. The images are backed by elements from the Presidential seal, as seen in the title sequence, and in particular a part of a large rotating ring with small stars, in the lower right portion of the screen, which repeats the effect used during graphics displays. Interestingly, the two frames are not aligned exactly at center screen – a slight asymmetry that adds salience to the frames and is likely to attract the viewer's attention.

---

20. Note that NBC's graphics carefully label the winning candidate as the "*projected* winner", while CNN uses the term "winner", adding the disclaimer "CNN estimate", in small letters, at the bottom of the screen.

A special type of outside broadcast are the reports by NBC's Katie Couric, who is stationed on Rockefeller Plaza, just a stone's throw from the studio. From here, Couric presents the results of various exit polls that have gauged voters' opinion on a number of issues. There is no immediate relation between Couric's location and the information she presents. Unlike correspondents reporting for instance from party headquarters, Couric does not present news that she has been able to gather first-hand, by virtue of being in a particular place. At least theoretically, anchor Tom Brokaw could have read out the very same exit polls right from his news desk inside the studio. Why then does NBC field Couric and place her on Rockefeller Plaza? Couric's outside broadcasts add several entertaining features to the program:

- variety, by shifting from Brokaw to Couric and back, increasing the number of front-stage personnel;
- interestingness, and even light-heartedness, by showing portions of Rockefeller Plaza in the background, including the famous skating rink (movement!), which is a New York landmark and likely to be recognized by most (U.S.) viewers;
- catchiness, by choosing Couric, who is a well-known and popular NBC moderator.

Finally, one might argue that there is after all a relation between Couric's location and the exit polls she presents: Rockefeller Plaza is a public square, frequented by people from all walks of life. Thus, Couric is physically close to "the people" (unlike for instance Brokaw, inside the studio), and it is also "the people" whose opinions have been captured by the exit polls. This link might add another popular touch to the program.

3.5.3 Coverage of the US elections: A comparison
Unlike the coverage by the BBC, ITV or ARD, the election night broadcasts presented by national channels CNN-USA and NBC do not originate in vast, compartmentalized studios in which the presenters are moving about, handing over to colleagues stationed in different sections of the studio. Rather, the two US programs feature relatively small on-screen studio teams, whose members are all sitting at the news desk from where the program is anchored. The remainder of the studio, as a three-dimensional space, has no or little active function and serves mainly as backdrop to the news desk. Neither of the channels uses particularly spectacular graphics, and this is somewhat of a surprise given the technological lead usually attributed to the U.S. media. A major difference between CNN and NBC is the color schemes they use for graphics and, in part, the studio. CNN has opted for a three-color design adopted from the US flag – red, white and blue,

with blue appearing as the background of most graphics. These three bold primary colors continuously call up the Stars and Stripes and thus give CNN's coverage a patriotic touch. At the same time, blue, as the dominant background color, lends the program an air of seriousness and soundness. By contrast, NBC's most dominant color is pink, together with bright orange and yellow. These exuberant or even garish colors are associated with popular culture, perhaps with a certain trendiness, thus giving the program a light-hearted, less serious look.

4.   Discussion and concluding remarks

Election night programs have, by definition, a mystery-element built into them: full of suspense, viewers and voters await the outcome of the election, which is still unknown – the results program becomes a "whowonit". Yet in a competitive media environment, channels need to do more than just broadcast the results. Just as during the campaign, the political parties had to face rival parties, swing voters or even voter apathy, TV channels, during election night, have to take into account factors such as competing channels, 'swing viewers' and viewer apathy. In situations like these, channels have been known to relax the boundary between information and entertainment, adding entertaining features to their news programs. The present paper has concentrated on the visual domain, analyzing how the pressure to entertain has affected the look and the visual practices of nine different election night broadcasts.

On balance, none of the programs offers full-fledged visual 'infotainment', whether it is a British, a German or a US channel, whether it is a public or commercial, a national or international broadcaster. We do not see, for instance, presenters sitting on sofas rather than behind desks, imitating the informal style of many morning news shows (cf. Coupland 2001:421). The importance of the political topic 'elections' seem to be a safeguard against moves that might be seen as undermining the channels' authority and reliability. Still, the notion of entertainment, as broken down into Klein's categories and realized by features such as the ones introduced in Section 2, is certainly present in the data, though it shows mostly in small details.

In Table 2, I have summarized my findings, assigning either a positive or a negative value for the realization of Klein's categories. These values are of course an abstraction and represent only a snapshot, as it were, of the detailed analysis presented above. From this table, several points emerge:

Table 2. Summary of visual analysis

	Title sequence v/l/i/c	Studio set v/l/i/c	Outside broadcasts v/l/i/c	Graphics v/l/i/c
UK97-BBC	☑☐☑☑	☑☑☑☑	☐☐☐☑	☑☑☑☑
UK97-ITV	☑☐☐☑	☑☑☑☑	☐☐☐☑	☑☑☑☑
UK97-CNN-I	☑☐☐☑	☐☐☐☑	☐☐☐☑	☐☐☐☑
FRG98-ARD	☐☐☑☑	☑☐☑☑	☐☐☐☑	☐☐☐☑
FRG98-RTL	☑☐☑☑	☐☐☐☑	☐☐☑☑	☑☐☑☑
FRG98-CNN-I	☑☐☐☑	☐☐☐☑	☐☐☐☑	☐☐☐☑
FRG98-BBC-W	☐☐☐☑	☐☐☐☑	☐☐☐☑	☐☐☐☑
USA2000-CNN	☑☐☐☑	☐☐☑☑	☐☐☑☑	☐☐☑☑
USA2000-NBC	☑☑☑☑	☐☐☑☑	☐☐☑☑	☐☐☑☑

v=variety, l=light-heartedness, i=interestingness, c=catchiness (cf. Section 2 above);
"☑" indicates that a category is distinctly realized or marked, "☐" indicates that a category is absent or almost absent.

1. Of the four visual features analyzed, outside broadcasts appear to be the least prone to become 'entertainized'. All nine OBs are catchy – creating visual coherence by means of split-screen arrangements, for instance – but only the outside broadcasts by RTL, NBC and CNN-USA have an added element of "interestingness", in Klein's terms. At the other end of the spectrum, title sequences seem to be the main playground for entertainment-oriented graphic designers.

2. The two British national channels, BBC and ITV, show the greatest number of entertaining features and are quite similar in this respect (see Section 3.3.4 for finer differences). By comparison, the differences between the German and the US national channels are less pronounced. Thus, the often voiced hypothesis that US news programs tend to move in the direction of entertainment much more so than their European (British, German) counterparts is not supported by my data.

3. A comparison between public channels (BBC, ARD) and private channels (ITV, RTL) shows that the differences between these two types of broadcasters are less marked in Britain than in Germany. While German broadcaster RTL offers its viewers more 'eye candy' than its public-service rival ARD, Britain's ITV and BBC are nearly equal in this respect.

4. The two international news channels, BBC World and CNN International, despite their different national origins, are remarkably similar in that they largely resist the pressure to entertain, doing without elaborate studio sets or glossy graphics.

My analysis raises a number of issues for future research. First, Klein's categories of entertainment were not developed for a cross-cultural, comparative analysis, and it may be necessary to review the values that attach to "variety", "light-heart-edness" etc. in different cultures. Similarly, the interpretation of micro-level visual features, such as the use of color or motion effects, is likely to differ across cultures. A color scheme that viewers in one country find pleasant and trendy may be considered brash and outdated by other audiences (this of course is a particularly important issue for the international channels and might explain their relatively reserved visual style). This aspect also makes high demands on the analyst, who would have to be able to "speak" and interpret different cultural visual styles – just as a linguistic analysis of British and US media discourse, for instance, would have to take into account differences between British and American English.

Another topic for future research is the relationship between entertainment in the visual and in the verbal domains. Does a high occurrence of visually entertaining features go hand in hand with, for example, a dramatization and conversationalization on the linguistic level (see Lauerbach, this vol.)? Do we find programs that are visually plain yet captivate viewers by means of powerful rhetoric strategies?

Finally, it has to be stressed that the research reported here has focused, somewhat one-sidedly, on entertainment, and has paid little attention to the notion of information. Although information and entertainment are often represented as binary opposites, they do not necessarily cancel each other out and may both be present in one and the same broadcast. Thus, from Table 2 it is not possible to deduce, for example, that the BBC's results program, with a high score in terms of Klein's categories of entertainment, is any less informative than the coverage presented by ARD or CNN International.

Comments made by the BBC's graphics expert Peter Snow serve to illustrate the still precarious boundary between information and entertainment. On a BBC website (Dymond 2000), Snow optimistically explain his role as follows:

> It's not an entertainment show, it's a show that explains how the vote is unravelling, how and why people are voting and what it's going to mean – it's a major national occasion. But ok, if we can have a bit of a laugh and entertain people a bit at the same time, all the better.

While this quotation suggests that Snow's graphics can easily accomodate both information and entertainment, comments he made elsewhere (Billen 1997:22) shed a somewhat different light on the 'battlefield' graphics he presented during the 1997 election night:

> "My own view is that we don't have enough time for factual background," he [Snow] says. "But the editor is so determined to have a quick-fire programme that no matter how complex the scene is in the South East, say, I know I've got precisely 30 seconds to get it across. That's the beauty of graphics. A table of fig-

ures is OK, but it is terribly difficult for people to read, so all the time you are looking for more and more colourful ways of bringing the battlefield to life on the screen."

Here, Snow draws attention to the time constraints that he is subject to. Complex information has to be presented in a way that complies with the editor's demand for a "quick-fire programme". Snow's graphics are catchy and spectacular, relieving viewers of the ever so 'terribly difficult' burden of reading tables. However, in the process, complexity is reduced and background information is minimized. At least in this example, entertainment has gained the upperhand over information.

References

Allan, S. 1998. "News from NowHere: Televisual news discourse and the construction of hegemony". In *Approaches to Media Discourse,* A. Bell and P. Garrett (eds.), 105–141. Blackwell: Oxford.

Billen, A. 1997. "Beamed up, beamed down". *New Statesman,* May 1997 special ed., 28–29.

Blumler, J. G. and Gurevitch, M. 1995. *The Crisis of Public Communication.* Routledge: London.

Cameron, D. 2000. *Good to Talk? Living and Working in a Communication Culture.* Sage: London.

Coupland, N. 2001. "Stylization, authenticity and tv news review." *Discourse Studies* 3(4): 413–443.

Dymond, J. 2000. "The oldest swingometer in town." http://news.bbc.co.uk/1/hi/uk_politics/655207.stm [date last visited: March 20, 2007]

Fairclough, N.1995. *Media Discourse.* Arnold: London.

Fielding, H. 1999. *Bridget Jones: The Edge of Reason.* Picador: London.

Fiske, J. and Hartley, J. 1978. *Reading Television.* Methuen: London.

Glasgow University Media Group. 1976. *Bad News.* Routledge & Kegan Paul: London.

Glasgow University Media Group. 1980. *More Bad News.* Routledge & Kegan Paul: London.

Graddol, D. 1994. "The visual accomplishment of factuality". In *Media Texts: Authors and Readers,* D. Graddol and O. Boyd-Barrett (eds.), 136–160. Multilingual Matters and The Open University: Clevedon.

Hofmann, S. 2004. "Mediale Umbrüche? Schrift im Massenmedium Fernsehen". In *Lateinamerika. Orte und Ordnungen des Wissens. Festschrift für Birgit Scharlau,* S. Hofmann and M. Wehrheim (eds.), 225–242. Narr: Tübingen.

Iedema, R. 2001. "Analyzing film and television: a social-semiotic account of *Hospital: An Unhealthy Business*". In *Handbook of Visual Analysis,* T. van Leeuwen and C. Jewitt (eds.), 183–204. Sage: London.

Iedema, R. 2003. "Multimodality, resemiotization: Extending the analysis of discourse as multi-semiotic practice". *Visual Communication* 2(1): 29–57.

Klein, J. 1997. "Kategorien der Unterhaltsamkeit. Grundlagen einer Theorie der Unterhaltung mit kritischem Rückgriff auf Grice". In *Pragmatik. Implikaturen und Sprechakte.* (= Lin-

guistische Berichte, special issue 8/1997), E. Rolf (ed.), 176–188.Westdeutscher Verlag: Opladen.

Klein, J. 1998. "Boulevardisierung in TV-Kulturmagazinen?". In *Medien im Wandel*, W. Holly and B. U. Biere (eds.), 103–111. Westdeutscher Verlag: Opladen.

Kress, G. 2004. "Commentary. Media discourse – extensions, mixes and hybrids: Some comments on pressing issues". *Text* 24 (3): 443–446.

Kress, G. and van Leeuwen, T. 1996. *Reading Images. The Grammar of Visual Design*. Routledge: London.

Kress, G. and van Leeuwen, T. 1998. "Front pages: (The critical) analysis of newspaper layout". In *Approaches to Media Discourse*, A. Bell and P. Garrett (eds.), 186–219. Blackwell: Oxford.

Kress, G. and van Leeuwen, T. 2001. *Multimodal Discourse*. Arnold: London.

Küng-Shankleman, L. 2000. *Inside the BBC and CNN. Managing Media Organisations*. Routledge: London.

Ludes, P. 1993. *Von der Nachricht zur News Show*. Fink: München.

MacLachlan, G. and Reid, I. 1994. *Framing and Interpretation*. Melbourne UP: Melbourne.

Marriott, S. 2000. "Election night". *Media, Culture & Society* 22: 131–150.

Maulko, R. 1997. "Vom einfachen Kürzel zum stilisierten Gütesiegel – Wie Senderkennspots auf PRO SIEBEN 'Marke machen'." In *Trailer, Teaser, Appetizer. Zu Ästhetik und Design der Programmverbindungen im Fernsehen*, K. Hickethier and J. Bleicher (eds.), 155–186. LIT: Hamburg.

Mirzoeff, N. 1998. "What is visual culture?". In *The Visual Culture Reader*, N. Mirzoeff (ed.), 4–13. Routledge: London.

Morse, M. 1985. "Talk, talk, talk". *Screen* 26(2): 2–15.

Muckenhaupt, M. 1998. "Boulevardisierung in der TV-Nachrichtenberichterstattung". In *Medien im Wandel*, W. Holly and B. U. Biere (eds.), 113–134. Westdeutscher Verlag: Opladen.

Radio Times, 1997. "Election 97: The night watchmen". 26 April – 2 May, 20–22.

Robinson, J. P. and Levy, M. L. 1986. *The Main Source. Learning from Television*. Sage: Beverly Hills.

Scannell, P. 1991. "Introduction: The Relevance of Talk". In *Broadcast Talk*, P. Scannell (ed.), 1–13. Sage: London.

Schieß, R. 2000. "Of ballots and battlegrounds: Metaphorizing elections as war". Paper presented at the Annual Meeting of the British Association for Applied Linguistics (BAAL). Cambridge.

Schieß, R. 2004a. "Reading the television screen: text, texture, screen design". In *Text and Texture. Systemic Functional Viewpoints on the Nature and Structure of Text*, D. Banks (ed.), 411–428. L'Harmattan: Paris.

Schieß, R. 2004b. "'Too close to call': CNN's politics of captions in the coverage of the Florida Recount". In *Communicating Ideologies*, M. Pütz et al. (eds.), 637–665. Lang: Frankfurt am Main.

Schütte, G. 1993. "Aktualisierung und Visualisierung aus der Perspektive der Macher". In *Von der Nachricht zur News Show*, P. Ludes (ed.), 119–145. Fink: München.

Scollon, R. 1998. *Mediated Discourse as Social Interaction. An Ethnographic Study of News Discourse*. London: Longman.

Scollon, R. (ed.). 2004. *Discourse and Technology. Multimodal Discourse Analysis*. Georgetown UP: Washington, DC.

Schumacher, H. 1991. "Infotainment-Ästhetik im berichterstattenden Magazin". In *Bausteine II. Neue Beiträge zur Ästhetik, Pragmatik und Geschichte der Bildschirmedien. Arbeitshefte Bildschirmmedien 30*, H. Kreuzer and H. Schanze (eds.), 67–70. Universität-GH-Siegen.

Thibault, P. 2000. "The multimodal transcription of a television advertisement: theory and practice". In *Multimodality and Multimediality in the Distance Learning Age*, A. Baldry (ed.), 311–365. Palladino Editore: Campobasso.

van Leeuwen, T. 1999. *Speech, Music, Sound*. Macmillan: London.

Presenting television election nights in Britain, the United States and Germany

Cross-cultural analyses

Gerda Eva Lauerbach
Goethe University Frankfurt, Germany

The paper presents a comparative analysis of the practices of presenting television election nights in Britain, Germany and the USA. The data are from two national channels per country, one public, one private where applicable, as well as from two international channels covering the same elections. The method applied is sequential frame and micro-level analysis. The results show different national profiles on the level of sequential generic patterning, with the international channels CNN International and BBC World grouping with their national counterparts. By contrast, micro-level analysis yielded strong differences between the national and the international channels. As regards the national channels, the differences on the micro-level were not across cultures but between the public and private national channels, as well as between the two national ones from the US. Due to within-culture variation, no culture-specific profile could be constructed for the national channels. Rather, the findings point to channel-specific subcultures.

1. Introduction

In contrast to interviewing or news-reading, the practice of presenting news and current affairs television does not seem to have received much attention in discourse-analytic media research. It is a challenging activity that requires the coordination of the many voices that make up today's news and current affairs programmes and to present this polyphonic discourse to the audience in a coherent and comprehensible manner. The object of this paper is precisely such a study, which is moreover designed as a comparative analysis of presenting practices in the US, Great Britain, and Germany, as well as on international television.[1] The basic premise from which the study departs is that the mass media are carriers of culture not merely through the specific content they transmit, but also, significantly, through the very practices with which this content is constructed discursively.

The data for the analysis to be presented in this paper are the opening sections of the television coverage of three national election nights – of the British parliamentary elections of 1997, the German parliamentary elections of 1998, and the American presidential elections of 2000, both in two national channels each and in the international channels CNN International and BBC World, where applicable. For the European data, the national channels chosen for analysis were a public and a private one each.

Election night broadcasts are well suited for comparative analysis. Like royal weddings or funerals, they are important national media events, but unlike such very culture-specific happenings, and in spite of national differences in political systems and mass media regulations, they are highly ritualised cross-culturally. Like all television spectacles, and in times of increasing audience fragmentation, they generate a unified mass audience (Gurevitch & Kavoori 1992:415). For national and international channels alike, they are sites of competition for that audience. Election night broadcasts have similar goals, deal with similar topics, use similar types of discourse strategies and a similar variety of media formats and genres to realize them. Due to the fact that they are broadcast live, they provide good data for a comparative analysis not only of scripted but also unscripted yet routinised discourse practices. Through these practices, the privileged reading positions for the event and the culturally specific identities and relations for the media, for politics, and for the public are constructed. Since there is so much similarity in the social and discursive frameworks of such broadcasts, it will be interesting to find out where the differences in terms of culturally specific realizations lie and where homogenisation processes of a global television culture may be at work.

In addition, these election night broadcasts are special in another way. They are probably the only news format in which the viewers are not merely unseen witnesses or overhearing audience (cf. Heritage, Clayman & Zimmerman 1988; Heritage & Greatbatch 1991; Allen 1998). On election night, the national television audience at least, is to a considerable extent identical with one of the major

---

1. The research reported in this paper is part of the project "Television Discourse", funded by the German Research Council (DFG) and directed by the author. The goal of the project is the cross-cultural and transcultural analysis of discourse practices in covering election nights in the US, Great Britain and Germany on national and international television.

newsmakers of the day – how they have voted is after all what the programme is about. Also, unlike tomorrow's newspaper or next week's news magazine, television is on the spot, broadcasting live on the results of the election as and when they are announced. But this is only the basis for realizing a cluster of further important functions that television fulfils on election night.

Election night programmes provide the arena in which politicians, experts, and representatives of the powerful social institutions can engage, under the direction of the presenters, in the conflictual negotiation over what the results of the election mean (cf. Stiehler 2000). They provide a stage on which (and stage directions according to which) the participants involved can transform the numerical election results into social facts. By offering its forum to a multitude of voices, television offers a multitude of explanations of the election results from which viewers can construct their own.

These explanations concern prospectively what follows from the numerical results in terms of who are the winners and losers, in terms of who will be the next President, Prime Minister or Chancellor, in terms of which party or parties will form the next Government, what policies to expect in the next legislature and what they will mean for different parts of the electorate and the individual viewer. Similarly, television analyses retrospectively voter turnout and voters' movements, and provides an arena for the exchange of different opinions on the strengths and weaknesses of the election campaigns and party platforms, on the allocation of credit and blame.

In sum, by staging the multi-voiced discourse of election night, television offers the spectacle of a battle of interpretation over what the elections results mean for the voters, for the country at large, and for international relations. Stiehler (2000: 109), writing from a political communication perspective, argues that research on what happens in the media after an election is over has been neglected in favour of studying what happens before, i.e. during election campaigns. He claims that it is, however, only this final review of the outcome of the election that concludes an important act of political participation, and that this review is well worth our analytical attention.

From a more specifically discourse-analytic perspective, TV election nights are different from other media events like for instance cup finals, in that they are not broadcast live from one location. During the broadcasts, politicians are in their constituencies all over the country, awaiting the declaration of their results (in Britain), or in their national party headquarters or local party offices (in Germany), or in their home states (in the US). The national channels, and to a lesser extent also the international 24-hour news channels, have correspondents and camera teams in the important places to bring the news from these outside locations into the studio (see Schieß, this volume).

It is the task of the presenters of such programmes to construct, for the television audience, a comprehensible and coherent whole from these many simultaneous events in different locations. They do this by commenting on live events like declarations of results, by introducing live reports by correspondents, or by interviewing newsmakers on outside locations. But the complexity does not stop there. The anchor, as the central person in the studio, interacts with participants in the studio as well. Presenters talk to experts and interviewers, may themselves interview politicians in the studio, may talk to studio guests, possibly a studio audience and, mainly in the case of things going wrong, to members of the production team, all of this for the benefit of an overhearing audience. But they also, particularly in the opening stages of the night and in announcing media genres like reports and interviews, talk to the television audience directly. Presenters have to be able to change their footing constantly (Goffman 1981), not only from one interlocutor to another, but also between talk *to* an audience to talk *for* an audience.

It is the discursive practices of presenters that are the object of this paper: the practices with which the presenters construct and organize the broadcasts and orchestrate the multitude of voices that make up the discourse of election night. In the following section, the discourse model guiding the analysis will be briefly presented, while the analysis itself will follow in Section 3. In order to keep the analysis within manageable limits, the data for this paper have been restricted to the opening sequences of our election night data, each about three minutes in length. The criteria for setting a boundary at around that time were that all the stages of opening sequences that lead up to the main topic should have occurred.

The reason for focussing on openings is that we regard them as particularly significant types of sequences that display and foreshadow not only the character of what is to follow but also the discourse practices with which it is going to be talked about. At the same time, they are discursively salient sites for presenters to position themselves in relation to their audiences, to their journalistic colleagues and expert guests, and to their topic of politics and the politicians as its representatives. The analytical results of the opening sequences should therefore provide a fairly good indication of the culture-specific discourse practices that we can expect to find in the rest of the data.

2.   A discourse analytical approach to presenting practices

2.1 Openings – the power of projection

Openings are frames in the Goffmanian sense in that they put a particular perspective and focus on the perception of an event. Frames provide the basic organization for our understanding of natural and social events and steer our definitions and interpretations of situations. In Goffman's words, frames enable us to structure our experience and to answer the question: "What is it that is going on here?" (1974: 8). For social events that are speech events, conversation analysis provides us with a relevant method for the analysis of their opening and closing frames. The projective character of openings was pointed out early on by Schegloff (1979) in his paper about telephone conversation openings, when he noted that openings and closings are the places where the characteristic features of different types of discourse can be most easily discerned:

> It is in the overall structural organization of a conversation – in its opening and closing – that the distinctive "types" of conversation may most prominently appear. The opening is a place where the type of conversation being opened may be proffered, displayed, accepted, rejected, modified – in short, incipiently constructed by the participants to it. With all the similarity between talk on the telephone and other talk settings (...) openings are a likely place in which to find differences (Schegloff 1979: 25).

In the openings of telephone conversations, the prime concerns are the opening of the channel, the identification, recognition and mutual greeting of the participants, and the introduction of the (first) topic (Schegloff 1972, 1979; Scollon 1998). There are similarities and differences to openings in mass media communication genres. One crucial difference is that mass media communication is one-way in that one of the participants, the audience, is in the invisible onlooker position and unable to reciprocate (other than switching off). Another is that it is public communication addressed to a mass audience which as a rule however is received by individual members of that audience in their private home environment.

The differences between natural conversation and mass media communication give rise to particular features of the openings of television broadcasts which affect the construction of participant relations (see below), as well as the introduction of topics. In conversation, capturing the interlocutor's attention and obtaining the go-ahead for prolonged talk on a topic like telling a story is done interactively. The broadcast media, however, have to generate the audience's attention and interest unilaterally. This is regularly done by formulating the topic in a manner that on the one hand appeals to audience interest and on the other foreshadows the way in which it is going to be dealt with. In doing this, the media construct the particular frame (focus, perspective) under which the topic is to be perceived. In his analysis of interview openings, Clayman (1991: 70) notes:

> Indeed, it is misleading to conceive of occurrences as having a singular, determinate character prior to the occasion of talk, for those occurrences may be characterized in divergent and contrasting ways, each of them in some sense 'correct'.

> But as they are formulated within the opening, occurrences take on a particular shape and form because of the manner in which they are going to be talked about; they are selected and assembled in order to lead up to the kind of interview that is about to take place.

For 'interview' we can easily substitute 'broadcast' without having to modify any of Clayman's claims. Consequently, we depart not only from the assumption that by analysing openings we will be able to capture the significant features of the broadcasts that they introduce, but also that these openings will display in a significant manner the ways in which national election night broadcasts are done in Great Britain, Germany and the USA, as well as the way in which the international channels CNN International and BBC World orient to their transnational audiences. To say that openings possess this power of projection is of course a simplification – the power rests not so much in their structural properties as in the privileged reading positions they invite and ultimately with those who have the prerogative of constructing such positions in the public sphere.

2.2   The discourse practices of presenting

In a study comparing the generic structure of public and private prime-time newscasts in Germany, Püschel (1992) observed that in the broadcasts of the public channels (ARD and ZDF), the hierarchical inverted-pyramid structure of news stories described by Bell (1998) was still the dominant format. As in the print media, newsreaders unfolded the story from the lead sentence, proceeding from the central events of the story on to background or expected follow-ups, constructing connections to other happenings, etc., and then going on to the next story. By this linear ordering, coherence was constructed implicitly. Things were different with the commercial channels (RTL and SAT 1), where often after the presenters' framing of the story, the provision of further detail, background, etc. was delegated to a number of different participants in different locations.

The story was thus not developed in a linear and hierarchical fashion from the lead sentence, but through a variety of texts clustering around the lead as a core, which presented the story from different perspectives. In such a *cluster* structure, involving different genres and participants, the organization of the discourse has to be done explicitly, the orientation of the audience at each new turn becomes vital and the framing role of the presenter a pivotal one. This format of presenting the news story from different perspectives, using different genres and participants, has become more or less the rule nowadays, although cultural differences are still to be expected. For our election night data, the cluster metaphor is certainly an apt one.

In election night broadcasts, as in other news and current affairs programmes, the presenter is the central person who instigates and coordinates all communication, just as the studio is the central place where all lines of communication converge (Marriott 2000). The manifold functions of presenters that have been discussed in communication studies (e.g. Straßner 2000; Muckenhaupt 2000; Allen 1998; Coupland 2001) can be subsumed in discourse-analytic terms under the three types of meaning distinguished in Systemic Functional Linguistics: on the textual level, presenters have to organize the discourse and construct textual coherence; on the interpersonal level, they have to construct and maintain identities and relations; and on the topical level, they have to construe information in a manner that is comprehensible to a mass audience (cf. Halliday 2003; Fairclough 1995: 58).

Drawing on this model as well as on Goffman's frames and the conversation analytic work on openings, Scollon (1998) has subjected these functions to what he calls *"maxims of stance"*. These maxims apply generally to all types of verbal interaction, but have to be specifically modified to regulate particular genres of discourse. For opening an interaction they are (my comments added in brackets): (1) attend to the channel frame (differs according to various modes – from face-to-face dialogue to electronically mediated asymmetric mass communication), (2) attend to the relationship frame (this frame concerns participant identities and relationships and differs according to participant role, social power and distance), and (3) attend to the topic frame (differs according to (1) and (2) above).

The maxims of stance regulate a set of "implicationally nested social practices" (Scollon 1998: 70) in that they are hierarchically ordered and in the unmarked case are worked through in that order, which is reversed in closings. As with Gricean maxims (Grice 1975), if they are intentionally violated, this triggers special effects like enhancing audience attention through highlighting and dramatization in "hooker frames" (Scollon 1998: 179), when e.g. presenters appear speaking on topic before the channel, they themselves or the topic have been introduced. The maxims of stance work on various levels of discourse: In mono-topical talk they organize the opening, the topic-oriented talk and the closing of the speech event on the global level of textual organization. In complex dialogic interactions, they have to be applied again and again for the framing of new participants, genres, and topics in the organization of internal structure on the middle level. On the local level at last we find the semiotic means with which the maxims can be realized.

The practice of presenters goes of course beyond organizing the programme by framing participants and their talk – for example they also give reports and conduct interviews themselves. Yet their organizing and managing function stands out as the most important and salient part of their discourse. It is this function which is typical for presenting practice and which makes it different from reporting or interviewing. At the same time, the practice of framing goes significantly beyond mere organisational functions in that it sets the focus and the perspective under which that which is framed is to be perceived (see Section 2.1).

The analysis to be presented in Section 3 of this paper will focus on framings, as well as on micro-level realisations. It is our expectation that the focus on framing will aid the discovery of culture-specific discourse practices of presenting. The reason for this is that the occurrence of many discourse practices is constrained by discourse position, and that frames are the significant discourse positions for the practice of presenting. The categories developed for the analysis will be briefly presented and discussed in the next sections.

2.3   Types of frames and framing in presenting news discourse

2.3.1 Pre-opening frame
Pre-opening frames open programmes by opening the channel, relationship and topic frames. In television news and current affairs programmes, the pre-opening frames are the title sequences which provide channel and sometimes programme identification and appeal to audience attention. The audience is mainly in the invisible onlooker position, rarely do we find direct audience address (like, *You are watching BBC-World*). Pre-opening sequences are carefully constructed from a combination of images, language and sound and serve as a channel's and programme's fingerprint with high recognition value (see Schieß, this volume). The language part appears typically as voice-over announcement and/or as text-inserts on the screen. Sometimes the voice-over is done by the presenters themselves.

2.3.2 Hooker frame
Hooker frames are realized by violating the unmarked, expected order of Scollon's maxims of stance, e.g. by presenters' topic-oriented talk before the relationship frame has been opened. Hooker frames are designed to capture audience attention and lead up to the "real" opening frames.

2.3.3 Opening frame
These are the frames in which presenters orient to constructing the relationship with their audience and project their channel's identity – in Scollon's (1998) terms the channel and relationship frames. In the fully elaborated version, presenters greet and welcome the audience, identify themselves and the channel, and announce or repeat the programme title. The mode is presenter live to camera in direct audience address.

This stage has received attention in communication studies on two counts: First, the presenters through their appearance (formal) and style of speaking (authoritative) are expected to project seriousness and reliability (Allen 1998; Coupland 2001). Also, the same journalists tend to present the same programmes over long periods of time, so that they are familiar to the audience, and through this familiarity can promote audience attachment to channel and programme (Straßner 2000: 78). The second point concerns the attempt to construct co-presence – shared time and space – in a simulated dialogic relationship with the audience. This becomes most pronounced in presenters' self-identification, audience greeting and address (Allen 1998: 124f.). In symmetric mediated communication, e.g. in telephone conversation, this would require signals of recognition as well as reciprocal identification and greeting by the interlocutor. Yet television is asymmetric communication. Consequently, the audience's recognition, etc. cannot be communicated, while the presenters' recognition of, as well as their orientation to, their audience is reduced to an abstract concept of their channel's and programme's viewers. This concept is presumably less problematic for national than for international channels.

2.3.4 *Agenda projection frame*
In this frame, realized in direct audience address and/or pre-recorded footage, presenters give an overview over the broadcast's topics as well as the manner in which and by whom they are going to be dealt with. In national election night broadcasts, this can be very elaborate, involving an introduction of journalists and experts in the studio and of reporters on outside locations, with short sample performances by some of those thus introduced. In that case, the floor and the mode of direct audience address is delegated briefly to these performers. International channels, with their reduced local studio space and resources, handle this phase in a much more restrained manner.

2.3.5 *Pre-headline frame*
Pre-headlines frame topics. They are designed to provoke the audience's attention and interest, e.g. by asking a question or posing a puzzle (Clayman & Heritage 2002). The mode is direct audience address, but can also be pre-recorded footage.

2.3.6 *Headline frame or lead*
The headline frame likewise is a topical frame. It corresponds to what in printed news stories is done in the lead sentence, covering the central event of the story by giving the actors, action, circumstances (place, time), causes and perhaps manner in which things were done or happened (the well-known five Ws – who, what, where, when, why – and one how, cf. Bell 1998; Muckenhaupt 2000). This frame

is usually realized in the mode of direct audience address but, as Clayman (1991) notes, it may also present pre-recorded material with voice-over narration. As mentioned above, this frame covers not only what, but also the way in which it is going to be talked about (Clayman 1991). After the presenter's framing of the story through the headline, the complex process of presenting the story from different perspectives, in different genres, by different participants in different locations may begin.

What happens, though, if there is no story, because that which is to be reported on has not happened yet, or is in the process of happening? This is the situation at the opening of election nights, or of sports and other live media events. Do such genres have no headline frames or leads? How do journalists deal with the problem of capturing the audience's attention in the absence of news? In our data, they refer to what sort of outcome can be expected on the basis of exit poll projections or, if these are not yet available, of the opinion polls of the election campaign. Likely headlines, then, are phrases like *an era may be ending; a landslide is expected; it is going to be an historic evening; it's a neck-to-neck race; the race is too close to call; we can expect a cliffhanger/a nailbiter; we won't know the result for hours*, etc.

2.3.7 Background frame

In the background frame, the presenter can contextualise the topic, constructing the perspective under which it is to be perceived, for instance before delegating the floor to another journalist for supplying further detail.

2.3.8 Analysis frame

This is the frame in which presenters can initiate interpretation-oriented talk, either by themselves or by another participant. In the latter case, this can be done by sketching possible dimensions of analysis before delegating the floor.

2.3.9 Delegation frame

In this frame, presenters handle the delegation of the floor to some other participant, be it an expert, interviewer or co-presenter in the studio, or a reporter or correspondent on outside location. There will usually be a pre-introduction, giving advance information about the topic (Clayman 1991:56), before the interlocutor is introduced with name, location, and possibly function within the broadcasting organization. This is followed by the first question. Scollon (1998:159–178) has shown how introduction and first question are a site for constructing interlocutor status and presenter-interlocutor relations, e.g. by using titles, full names, functions (also in captions), or first names. The first question can impose strong topical control, or leave more freedom. Also the choice between using recorded footage or trusting the reporter live is a distinction that constructs status. Delegation frames start in direct audience address mode, then move to interlocutor address, with the audience assuming the invisible onlooker position. After this, the new floorholders address their contribution either to the audience or to the presenter, and then give the floor back to the presenter.

2.3.10   Formulation frames

The practice of formulating has been described as an interviewer resource for summing up the gist of an interviewee's response or for requesting confirmation or disconfirmation for a clarification or interpretation of the answer (Heritage & Watson 1979). In presenting, this is sometimes done after the floor had been delegated to another participant, e.g. to a reporter on outside location or an expert in the studio. In contrast to interviews, the presenter's formulation generally closes delegation or story sequences and does not expect a response – the formulation thus establishes the final perspective under which the preceding contribution is to be seen. The practice is also used by journalists at the end of their turns, for example by reporters or experts at the end of their contributions. In that case, their formulation can support a position or argument that is being built jointly between presenter and one or more journalists.

2.3.11   Teaser frames

These occur at the end of a sequence, they are boundary markers, in private channels often before a commercial break. They are realized in direct audience address, often with imperatives (*stay with us, stay tuned*), and usually contain short agenda projections for the segment after the commercial break to induce the audience to stay with the channel.

2.4   The micro-level of semiotic realization

In this section, I will briefly look at local structure, focussing on the linguistic means with which the above frames can be realized. One of the hypotheses of our election night project is that cross-cultural variation in the discourse practices of political reporting is to be expected especially along the dimension of constructing identities and interpersonal relations (see Section 1). The identities involved in our data are, on the part of the broadcasters, those of the presenter and other channel personnel like experts, interviewers, and reporters. However, studio design and other production factors (see Schieß, this volume) are part of a channel's and programme's style, image, or identity as well.

In addition, an important part of a channel's and programme's identity is also the manner in which the broadcasters relate to each other as well as to their audience and, for the purposes of this study, to their object of reporting on a political topic like a national election. This is a complex matter. Concerning the audience, the relation is expressed in the ways in which broadcasters address their audience and design their message for a mass of projected recipients. Through the nature of these practices, a channel's or programme's conception of its audience is discursively exhibited, constructed and maintained. At the same time, these practices and this audience construction become part of the channel's identity. The same holds for the relations between the broadcasters themselves, as it does for those between them and their topics of politics and its agents, the politicians.

Thus channel identity, as exhibited in a broadcast, feeds on two sources: on the one hand, there is a fairly stable and channel-specific "potential" – of studio, technology, journalistic personnel and discourse strategies – and on the other a set of typical technical and discursive realization practices with which the night's broadcast is constructed. Both – the potential as well as the realization practices – are exhibited to the analyst in the multimodal text of the broadcast itself.

The analysis in the next section will focus on frames and framing practices, and on the micro-level semiotic features with which these are realized. These features can be used to express interpersonal distance or closeness, to construct power or equality, and to invite a particular perspective and/or evaluative stance. They are briefly described below.

2.4.1 Speech acts/communicative acts

Speech acts that are particularly significant for interpersonal positioning are those involved in opening the discourse – greetings; identification of self, programme, and channel, acts of discourse organization like introductions, delegating the floor, etc. However, all other types of speech acts are relevant as well, like representatives, directives, commissives and declaratives, with the possible exception of expressives. Some of the frames listed above make certain speech acts more expectable than others. Since all communicative functions listed above can be, and are, performed through the visual modality as well, it is more appropriate to speak of "communicative acts" in our context.

2.4.2 Address terms

Address terms are first and second names, honorifics, titles, function, or descriptions of participant role (e.g. *viewers*). The choice of address terms constructs individual and group identities and relations in the domains of social distance/closeness and power/solidarity (cf. Levinson 1983: Ch. 2).

2.4.3 *Personal pronouns*

Personal pronouns are a core domain of grammar that can be used for the construction of power and solidarity (cf. Brown and Gilman 1972). For our data, it is above all the use of *I, we, you* and *them* that requires particular attention in the negotiation of interpersonal positioning regarding responsibility, bias, status, solidarity, or the construction of groups and institutions (cf. Fowler & Kress 1979; Wilson 1990).

2.4.4 *Descriptive expressions of persons, objects, places, times and actions*

This is the classical domain of *recipient design* as formulated within conversation analysis (Schegloff 1972, 1979; Sacks 1972; Sacks & Schegloff 1979; Clayman 1991): descriptors are formulated to be optimally relevant to the recipient (cf. also Sperber and Wilson 1995) and therefore indicate speakers' concept of the identity, background knowledge and value systems of their audience. Due to the fact that in the asymmetric communication of the mass media, there is no possibility for the interactive resolution of comprehension problems of the recipients, journalists have to take particular care with their descriptive expressions. The problem can be expected to be aggravated for channels addressing an international audience.

2.4.5 *Evaluative expressions, modality, and emphasis*

The most concise approach to evaluative language as a tool of interpersonal positioning can be found in *Appraisal Theory* (cf. Eggins & Slade 1997; Martin 2000; White 2003). In this approach, the resources of evaluative meaning are brought together in a unified framework comprising three semantic domains or systems: *Attitude, Engagement* and *Graduation*. Through their choices from these resources, journalists will exhibit, construct and maintain their conception of their readerships' or audiences' value systems, thereby of the identity of their readership or audience, of the image they have of their own paper or broadcasting station, and of the relations between their readership/audience and their paper/broadcasting station. A high ratio of appraisal or evaluative stance in hard news discourse is generally associated with lower factuality and stronger orientation towards entertainment. It will thus presumably be found more in the rainbow press than in the broadsheets, and more in the newscasts of commercial channels than in those of public service television. However, this is an empirical question, as is the question of how the degree of evaluation in the genre of hard news varies cross-culturally.

3.   Presenting election nights: Analysis

3.1 Overview

The analysis below will proceed chronologically from the British Parliamentary Election 1997, through the German Federal Elections 1998 to the American Presidential Elections 2000. Within each set of election night broadcasts, the discourse practices of the presenters of all the channels in the data will be documented and analysed, focussing on their practices of opening the programmes during the first few minutes. The presentation of the data that follows is based on transcripts of video recordings which account not only for the verbal text, with pauses, break-offs, emphatic stress and overlapping talk, but also for the visual and verbal information that can be seen on the screen, recording camera movements, types of shots and cuts, as well as illustrations and graphics. All of this has been used for the analyses presented below, but the full-blown transcripts had to be omitted for reasons of space and clarity of presentation.

The analysis will be presented as follows: First, the situational context of the data will be briefly characterised. Secondly, an analysis of about the first three minutes of the opening section of each of the channels under review will be presented, employing the categories of frames and micro-level realisation features introduced in 2.3 and 2.4 above. The analysis will be based on tables, which provide frames and communicative acts in the left column, and the corresponding text of the sequence on the right. Lastly, the micro-level of semiotic realization will be analysed. The following questions will be addressed: Firstly, what frames are employed, and what is the sequence's structure? Secondly, how does this structure interact with micro-level realisation features in the positioning of the presenters and other journalists relative to their audience, their journalistic colleagues and expert guests, and relative to the topic of politics and the politicians mentioned or addressed? An evaluation of the findings will follow in Section 4.

3.2 The British Parliamentary Election of 1997

The election of 1997 was the one in which New Labour under Tony Blair ousted the Tory Party after eighteen years of Conservative rule, first under Margaret Thatcher and then under John Major. Labour's victory was not unexpected, but its landslide proportions were a surprise, as was the fact that many leading Conservatives, or Tories, lost their seats in parliament, and that the smaller third party, the Liberal Democrats, gained more seats than ever before. It was assumed that John Major would resign shortly, and a struggle over the leadership of the Tory

Party was expected. All of this made the election of 1997 a memorable one, and an exciting election night for television broadcasters and audiences alike.

The data are from the openings of the election night broadcasts of the two leading national channels BBC1 (public service television) and ITV (commercial), as well as from CNN International (CNN I), the US-based 24-hour international commercial news-channel. The three stations did not all start their broadcasts at the same time, which affected the way their opening stages were done: The BBC began five minutes before polls closing time at 9.55 p.m., which gave it five minutes to introduce the night's programme, including the journalists and experts in the studio, two reporters on outside location in the Tory and Labour headquarters, and the BBC's "roving reporter" in a helicopter, while all the time leading up to the climax of announcing the exit polls at 10 p.m. CNN I started about 5 minutes before polls closed and used that time for an introduction and two brief outside broadcasts from Labour and Tory Party headquarters, taking over the announcement of the exit poll results through live footage from ITN, ITV's news channel. ITV, on the other hand, started at exactly 10 o'clock, its regular slot for the evening news, opening with a "hooker" frame and announcing the exit poll results before the proper opening.

Table 1 shows the excerpt of the first three and a half minutes of the BBC's opening section, analysed as to frames and communicative acts, both verbal and visual. The analysis is in the left column, the excerpt on the right. Frames are printed in upper case, except when they are embedded in a higher frame and appear in subordinate position. Framing can be done either through verbal or through visual acts, or by both simultaneously. Visual acts and descriptions of visual representations are printed in italics, in both columns.

First, to textual structure: The first part of the text constructed by the BBC presenter exhibits the elements and sequence typical for the opening sections of television news programmes (cf. 2.3 above): The PRE-OPENING frame or title sequence, followed by the OPENING frame, the PRE-HEADLINE and the HEADLINE.[2] Apart from the music, the communicative acts of the pre-opening are totally visual: the channel is identified through the BBC logo, the programme is identified through the election broadcast logo, and the topic is implicitly introduced through images symbolizing country/nation/state and parliamentary elections. In the opening frame the presenter greets the audience, in the pre-headline, he builds suspense by linking the past election campaign with the results of the election that will presently become known, and in the headline, he announces the likely outcome. This sequence concludes with a TEASER announcing "a very,

---

2. Cf. Schieß, this volume, for a detailed analysis of the visual elements in the pre-opening sequences of these data.

Table 1. UK97.BBC: Frame analysis of opening section

PRE-OPENING	Title sequence:
id channel	*BBC logo throughout the broadcast; drums and instrumental music;*
id programme	*text insert: programme logo "election 97";*
id topic	*images of "Britishness" (landscapes), of election symbols:*
	parliament, Downing Street, ballot box); of the Conservative, Labour and Liberal
	party leaders; all shown on monitors making up a large video wall in the studio
OPENING	*(presenter standing in front of video wall showing images of Britain, live to camera)*
greet audience	good evening
PRE-HEADLINE	for weeks we've watched the politicians slugging it out together, tonight at last we hear the voters' verdict as they tell us who has won.
HEADLINE	If the opinion polls through this campaign are borne out tonight, we're likely to see one of the biggest political upsets since the Tories were swept out of office in 1945.
TEASER	It is at any rate going to be a very, very exciting political night.
AGENDA-PROJECTION	We are already at all the places that matter, the count in Sedgefield for Tony Blair, his Labour Club *(pointing to monitor in video wall)*, with the Tories in Huntingdon *(pointing)*, with the Liberal Democrats in Yeovil *(pointing)*, and we'll be following the party leaders *(starts walking around the studio)*, we'll be at the party headquarters, we'll be at the **key** marginal seats where the battles are being fought and people are discovering whether they've lost or won. Er, in a moment, when the polls close, I'll bring you what I really promise is the last poll of this election, our exit poll based on **talking** to people today as they come out of the voting booths and said how they'd cast their vote. The last poll that is before we add up the real votes.
delegation to interviewer	All through the night, politicians will be coming here and be called to account by Jeremy Paxman (JP)
JP	Yes, *(to cam)* over the next 18 hours we shall have a succession of victors, vanquished and walking wounded up here to explain what went right, what went wrong, and what happens now in their respective parties. We'll be joined in a moment by (...)
delegation to statistics expert	*(pres points to computer section)* And here all the results are phoned in to us from across the country (...) and when the facts are marshalled they are given to Peter Snow (PS) who will illustrate what's happened on the battlefield.
PS	Yes David, *(to cam)* and we'll be illustrating this battle in a more adventurous and inventive way than we've ever done before (...)
introduction of pol. experts	*(pres points to tables with analysts)* it's not just the way we voted that we'll be looking at, it's why we voted the way we did in different parts of the country, our experts up there are looking at all of that, and Peter Kellner will tell all, and over here at the round table with me, Robin Oakley, the BBC's political editor will be looking at the battles that lie ahead, and Professor Anthony King of Essex University will place this, which could well be the last general election of this century, into context.

very exciting political night". We note that the presenter is neither identified in this section, nor does he identify himself. Obviously this is not deemed necessary since he is known to the audience. We can take this then as a marker of familiarity between presenter and audience.

Were this a normal news broadcast, the story would now have to be developed with respect to its protagonists, significant events, background and expected consequences, either by the presenter himself, or by a number of other participants doing report, interview, analysis, or commentary. However, since this is a media event projected to last through the night, what is done next is an AGENDA PROJECTION, displaying how the public service broadcaster BBC is going to fulfil its remit of informing its audience on this significant national day. The presenter first introduces the outside locations, supported by images on the monitor wall, then the studio staff, and briefly delegates the floor to two of them. So what the audience will expect is a varied broadcast of the cluster-structure type, with the presenter introducing core topics and organizing their development and discussion from a number of perspectives, from different locations and through other participants and genres (cf. 2.3).

For reasons of space, the full length of the agenda projection cannot be shown here. After the end of the excerpt, the presenter goes on to introduce the BBC's "roving reporter" in a helicopter, designed to land in different places and get "the word on the street", does two brief down-the-line interviews with correspondents at the headquarters of the Conservative and Labour parties, and finally, as Big Ben strikes ten, announces the results of the exit polls.

Turning to the micro-level of linguistic realizations, what kinds of interpersonal identities and relations does the BBC presenter construct, regarding his audience, his journalistic colleagues, and the politicians he will be reporting on? Looking at personal pronouns, we note a high density of *we/us/our*. Four of these are audience-inclusive and occur in the pre-headline and headline, where the presenter constructs two groups: the BBC and its audience on the one hand, and the politicians and the voters on the other. The divide is deepened as the presenter invites the audience's complicity with the BBC against the politicians: the viewers are nudged to share the presenter's negative evaluation of the politicians' way of conducting the election campaign (*slugging it out*). Another indication of how the BBC positions itself vis-à-vis the politicians comes in the agenda projection when the interviewer is thus introduced: *politicians will come here and be called to account by Jeremy Paxman*. The BBC thus assumes what has been called the "watchdog" position towards the politicians (cf. Blumler & Gurevitch 1995:15).

What is strange is the positioning of the voters in the pre-headline: many members of the audience must be assumed to be also voters, yet the voters are constructed in the *they*-position. Gone their brief moment of agency in making their cross on a ballot – they are now unambiguously back in the passive audience position. This is aggravated by the fact that the overall majority of the tokens of *we/us/our* are audience-exclusive. All of these occur in the agenda projection, where *we here at the BBC* tell the audience what *we* have in store for *them*. Thus, a strong contrast between channel and audience is constructed, which is also supported by the only tokens of *I* and *you: I'll bring you what I really promise is the last poll of this election.*

As to evaluative and emphatic elements, there is a fair share: not surprisingly, we see gradation and intensification regarding the political outcome (e.g. *one of the biggest political upsets since the Tories were swept out of office in 1945*, in the headline). However, by far the larger share of such elements goes into stressing how well the BBC is equipped and prepared for election night, in the agenda projection. The sheer introduction of all the participants involved, or of the locations covered (*we are already at all the places that matter*), which are enumerated in a rhetorically effective three-part list (cf. Atkinson 1984), or the preview of the manner in which the graphics are going to be handled (*we'll be illustrating this battle in a more adventurous and inventive way than we've ever done before*) – all of this constructs the BBC as richly provided with communicational resources, and as efficient and creative in using them.

By contrast, what the experts and other participants will be doing is phrased in very understated terms: they will *look at, tell all, place in context.* This may suggest that the self-reflexive hype of infotainment extends to the on-stage side of the broadcast only, while background research, reporting and analysis are intended to remain serious and objective. The question arises if the two things can be kept apart, and the metaphors used in reports and analysis suggest that it cannot (cf. Scheithauer, this volume).

All in all, the presenter positions himself as the leader of a strong team and the representative of a powerful and authoritative broadcasting company – a company which works hard to fulfil its public remit towards the audience, which acts as watchdog over the politicians by "calling them to account", and whose institutional voice can, minutes later, dramatically, declare victory for Tony Blair: *Ten o'clock, and we say: "Tony Blair is to be Prime Minister".*

The frame analysis for BBC's commercial rival ITV is given in Table 2 below. In terms of structure, ITV differs markedly from the BBC. As mentioned above, this is due to the fact that its programme starts at exactly the time the polls close. The programme opens with a normal title sequence in which the channel is identified both verbally and visually, but between this and the real opening, a HOOK-ER frame is inserted with its own internal structure of opening, pre-headline and headline. This sequence serves to announce the victory of Labour, and its boundary is marked with a teaser frame. In the "real" PRE-OPENING, channel, topic

Table 2. UK 97.ITV: Frame analysis of opening section

PRE-OPENING 1	Title sequence: *Carlton logo changes to ITV logo, which*
id channel	*remains visible throughout the broadcast; male voice over music:*
id channel	This is Carlton, it's exactly ten o'clock.
HOOKER	*(presenter sitting at desk, to camera, pre- recorded)*
greet aud	good evening
pre-headline	the votes are cast, the polling stations are closed
headline	our prediction based on the Mori exit poll for ITV is that Labour have clearly won this election with what appears to be a massive majority
agenda projection	in the crucial hours ahead we'll see just how accurate that forecast is, we'll report on the results flooding in from around the country and we'll find out who are the winners and the losers
	(zoom away from desk with presenter and expert to bird's eye
id topic	*view of studio, pictures of three candidates on monitors, election*
id progr	*logo "Election 97")*
teaser 1	here in the hub of ITV's election studio we're poised to share
id channel	with you the drama ahead, for tonight is decision night for the
id programme	nation in election ninety-seven.
PRE-OPENING 2	Title sequence: *Theme music;*
id channel	*ITV logo throughout;*
id topic	*footage of campaign and election symbols, photos of three party leaders on monitors;*
id programme	*animated text insert: "election 97"; bird's eye view of studio.*
OPENING	*(presenter sitting at desk, live to camera)*
greet audience	Welcome
id programme	to election 97, the results programme
id channel	on ITV
teaser 2	we'll be here live throughout the night and we'll be back again tomorrow to bring you all the election news as it happens.
PRE-HEADLINE	And now to our exit poll with the reminder that these can at best prove a rough estimate how the country has voted, and they have been wrong in the past.
HEADLINE	But our prediction based on the Mori exit poll is that Labour will win this election with a huge majority of one hundred and fifty-nine seats.
STORY	That figure is in line with the campaign polls, it's based on the Mori poll carried out for us today with fifteen thousand voters outside polling stations in a hundred marginal constituencies. Part of the drama of election night is to see how close our forecast is to the actual results. But unless there's quite a remarkable upset what does now seem certain is that Labour will form the next government, and the scale of this victory would mean that the people who tonight are holding the great offices of state, many of them will not only be out of power but some of them without a seat,
TEASER 3	so stay with us to witness what is undoubtedly one of the great moments in British post-war politics. For unless the exit poll is wildly out, tonight represents a truly seismic shift in the public opinion of the nation. Our aim is to bring you the fastest, the clearest and the friendliest election night service.

and programme are introduced visually. Then comes the OPENING with the welcoming of the audience and the verbal identification of channel and programme. This sequence, too, concludes with a teaser frame.

There follows a second sequence of PRE-HEADLINE and HEADLINE, both dealing with the exit poll results and Labour's victory. This is elaborated in the STORY sequence, which once again concludes with a teaser. This second structure of pre-headline, headline and story, is the unmarked one of the inverted pyramid, where the story is developed from the lead or headline by the presenter alone. What is marked, however, is that pre-opening and opening occur twice in the excerpt. In such a structure, the positions for self-identification occur repeatedly, and such positions can be and are used here for self-promotion, e.g. by mentioning the name of the channel (five times, verbally and visually). Additional and quite blatant features of advertising are introduced through the use of TEASER frames as regular sequential boundary markers, rather than merely as frames around commercial breaks.

On the micro-level, ITV positions itself as quite distinct from its audience – there is no audience-inclusive *we* at all, against 13 tokens of exclusive *we*. Interestingly, the 3 explicit *we-you*-contrasts that occur are one in each of the three teasers (*we are poised to share with you; we'll …bring you; our aim is to bring you*), and in the last one we also find the only audience-addressed imperative (*stay with us*).

The positioning in relation to the politicians casts the losing Conservatives as plain *people*, while the winners are referred to as plain *Labour*, and the greatest winner of all, Tony Blair, is not mentioned at all. Against the BBC and, as we shall see, the international broadcaster CNN as well, this is a strongly marked omission. It raises the question about how ITV will position Labour under Tony Blair, while not yet allowing any specific hypothesis (but see Lauerbach 2006).

Evaluative and emphatic elements abound, but seem to be more evenly distributed over the topic of the election results and ITV's coverage of them than was the case with the BBC. This is probably due to the fact that the excerpt contains only a very brief agenda projection sequence (an extended one comes later). On the other hand, the night's broadcast is conceptualised as *drama*, and this, for ITV, arises not only from waiting how the results turn out, but also from the suspense of finding out how close their own forecast is to the actual results. This adds something of a sporting and betting spirit to the political character of the night.

The British elections of 1997 were also covered by CNN International, and Table 3 shows the frame analysis of its opening section.

In terms of structure, the first part of the CNN International opening is very similar to the BBC: PRE-OPENING, OPENING, PRE-HEADLINE, HEADLINE. In the pre-opening frame, channel, topic and programme are first introduced visually, as with the BBC. The opening frame, however, is filled differently. Where

Table 3. UK 97.CNN International: Frame analysis of opening section

PRE-OPENING	Title sequence: *theme music;*
id channel	*CNN-INTERNATIONAL Live;*
id topic	*election images of polling stations and voting, of the three party leaders, against background of British national flag;*
id programme	*animated inserts: "Britain Decides. The Vote"; insert: LIVE.*
OPENING	*presenter sitting at desk in studio; live to camera;*
id presenter/loc	*inserts: Richard Blystone, London,*
id channel	*CNN INTERNATIONAL Live*
greet aud	Hello
welcome aud	and welcome
id programme	to our live coverage of Britain's election
self-id presenter	I'm Richard Blystone
PRE-HEADLINE	the last votes are being cast right now
HEADLINE	and if the polls are right, an era is ending
DELEGATION	for the polls for weeks have said 18 years of conservative rule by Margaret Thatcher, carried on by John Major is about to end in a Labour Party landslide. In those 18 years, Britain has changed profoundly. What Labour offers is less than chrystal clear, but we'll get
to reporter 1	insights live from Christiane Amanpour (CA) at Labour headquarters. Christiane.
CA	Richard, as you say, it is a new era, a new generation. The old
background	ideological divides have gone, the divides that split the two parties, and nobody symbolizes that more than Tony Blair (…)
formulation	He is poised, if the polls are to be believed, to become the first Labour prime minister elected in twenty-three years.
id reporter/loc.	*caption Christiane Amanpour, Labour Headquarters*
DELEGATION	Now at Conservative Central Office, we'll hear from Siobhan
to reporter 2	Darrow (SD).
greet rep	Hello, Siobhan.
SD	Hello, Richard. Things are pretty quiet down here, most of the
report	MPs are in their constituencies waiting for word on the vote count (…)
formulation	Now if the polls are anywhere near correct, we're expecting a very gloomy atmosphere down here all evening (…)
id reporter/loc	*caption: Siobhan Darrow, Conservative Heaquarters*
DELEGATION	The British Broadcaster ITN is just about to give us its first exit
TO ITN	poll results. Here they are.
	(follow 4 minutes live coverage of ITN opening/ exit polls results, cf. Table 2)
FORMULATION	*presenter at desk, inserts:*
id progr	*"Britain Decides",*
id channel	*CNN INTERNATIONAL Live*
	All right, that was ITN, and the bottom line behind all that flash and filigree was this, it sounds very bad for the ruling Conservative Party. A 159 seat majority for the Labour Party in the next British parliament, that's based on 15.000 people polled on exiting the polls by the Mori organisation. Jonathan Dimbleby there, the preven/the presenter, promised friendly coverage. Their political expert was saying this is a decisive turn.

the BBC presenter (and that of ITV) just greets the audience, the CNN International presenter welcomes the audience, identifies the programme once more, stressing that it is live, and identifies himself, while being identified visually by caption at the same time.

Where the BBC then continues with a lengthy agenda projection frame in order to display its studio and outside resources, the CNN I presenter starts a DELEGATION sequence in which two reporters are given the floor, one after the other. We have a cluster structure here (cf. Püschel 1992 and Section 2.2), in which the reporters elaborate from different perspectives on the presenter's headline *if the polls are right, an era is ending*. The first reporter, located at the headquarters of the winning Labour Party, supplies BACKGROUND regarding the *new era* and finishes with a FORMULATION that supports the presenter's headline through stressing the historic quality of the imminent change of power: *He (Tony Blair) is poised, if the polls are to be believed, to become the first Labour Prime Minister in twenty-three years.* The second reporter provides BACKGROUND atmosphere from the headquarters of the Conservative Party, and concludes with a FORMULATION that supports the presenter's headline from the perspective of the prospective losers of the election: *Now if the polls are anywhere near correct, we're expecting a very gloomy atmosphere down here all evening.* After this, CNN I takes over the announcement of the exit polls results from the British commercial channel ITN, ITV's news channel associate, so that CNN I viewers will see the segment shown in Table 2 above.

What may be strange to viewers unfamiliar with CNN I practices is the summary or formulation immediately after the ITV footage. However, to summarize something that has just been said is a routine practice with CNN International. In contrast to the reporters' formulations described above, such presenters' formulations may be motivated by two reasons: firstly, the informative imperative of a 24-hour news channel, according to which continuous orientation cues have to be provided for viewers who may just have tuned in. Secondly, they may be motivated by CNN I's recipient design for an audience that is international or, in the case of CNN I's American home audience (which is selectively tuned in), non-British. An international or "foreign" audience needs more aid in understanding reports on regional topics – it may not have sufficient background information on the one hand, and on the other, comprehension may be impaired for linguistic reasons, for instance the audience's English may not be perfect nor tuned to, in this case, a British accent. This means for the broadcasters that they have to provide frequent orientations regarding channel and programme as well as repetitive recyclings and summaries of the news items. The multiple identifications in opening frames are a part of this practice, too.

What is striking is the critical stance in which the summary of the ITV footage is realized: There is a clear reaction to what is evaluated as an exaggerated and non-factual style of reporting against which the CNN presenter positions his channel as factual and matter-of-fact: *the bottom line behind all that flash and filigree was this.* Also, the quote from ITV's final teaser frame – *Jonathan Dimbleby there, the preven/presenter, promised friendly coverage* – is remarkable in several respects: (1) it focuses on the style in which ITV positions itself towards its audience, over and above on the contents reported on; (2) it selects from what the ITV presenter actually said (*Our aim is to bring you the fastest, the clearest and the friendliest election night service*) only the adverb *friendly* (presumably as particularly newsworthy); and (3) it invites the inference of further negative evaluation through the aborted slip of the tongue which could well be heard as *preventer.* Clearly, the presenter of CNN International feels a need to indicate to his international and American audiences that he wishes to distance himself from the ITV style of reporting.

However, the style of CNN International is not entirely free of appraisal items itself (*an era is ending, has changed profoundly, the first Labour Prime Minister elected in 23 years*). Yet it is important to note that all of these expressions refer to the topic of the broadcast and not to the channel's way of reporting on it. Under the circumstances, they can almost be considered justified.

The informative imperative of an international news channel also holds for what kind of information is given at all – for instance in naming the programme in the pre-opening and opening frames, CNN I needs to mention that it is the British election that is being reported on, something a national channel can of course omit. Complex descriptive expressions are another sign of orientating to a non-national audience, e.g. *18 years of conservative rule by Thatcher and carried on by Major* – this is information that national channels can presuppose as known by their audiences.

Regarding CNN I's positioning to their audience through the use of personal pronouns, there are only 5 tokens of *we/us/our* in the segment. Three of these are audience-inclusive and establish a grouping of presenter and audience who together are going to hear what outside reporters and ITN have to tell them. The only occurrence of *you* is addressed to the presenter by the reporter Christiane Amanpour, which may be an indication of a certain directness and familiarity in interpersonal relations between the journalists of CNN I. This would also be indicated by reciprocal first name address in delegation frames. CNN I's position towards the politicians projects a sober, but not uncritical approach, as evidenced in evaluative vocabulary (*what Labour offers is less than crystal clear*).

Let us review, at the end of this section, some of the dimensions of variation in audience design and in constructing channel identity that will play a role in the following analyses as well. Structurally, both the BBC and CNN I presenters use clusters in their opening sequences, projecting a style of reporting in the rest of the broadcast which is characterised by teamwork and the presentation of topics from different perspectives and by different participants. ITV, on the other hand, opens with the classical inverted pyramid structure, projecting more such linear structures under the control of the presenter. This expectation receives some confirmation from the fact that all political interviews of the night's broadcast were done by the ITV presenter himself and not by an interviewer in the studio or by outside reporters (Lauerbach 2006). Also, ITV, with its hooker frame and multiple teaser frames, massively introduces features of advertising into the opening segment, to a much greater extent than does the other commercial channel in the data, CNN International.

Regarding the opening frames, the BBC's presenter opens with a sparse *good evening*. This contrasts with CNN I's more elaborate frame: the greeting and welcoming of the audience, the identification of the programme (and pointing out that it is live) plus the self-identification of the presenter. The difference between the national and the international opening frames attests to the different audiences they are orienting to: The presenters of the two national channels can take for granted a high degree of familiarity with their audiences, no self-identification being necessary beyond voice and image. Addressing an international audience, however, the presenter of CNN International has to explicitly identify himself as the anchor of the programme and must also specify which election is being covered.

We can see recipient design at work here: the national broadcasters can follow the conversational preference for minimal forms over elaborate ones (Sacks & Schegloff 1979), which the international one cannot. The omission of self-identification is the most preferred minimal form. It carries the inference of familiarity that such in-group markers do, and thereby constructs and reaffirms a relation of closeness between presenter/channel and audience. This relation is also strengthened by the employment of audience-inclusive *we*. The presentation of information is subject to recipient design as well – this is the reason why descriptive expressions have to be far more elaborated when addressing an international audience which is unfamiliar with local persons, locations, election systems, etc. But the two national channels, as well, exhibit differences between their opening frames: The BBC's *good evening* contrasts with ITV's advertising style in the opening frame – the naming of the product ITV, again, and the pointing out of its outstanding service, which continues the chain of commissives from the hooker frame.

3.3 The German parliamentary elections of 1998

Similar to the 1997 elections in Great Britain, the German parliamentary elections of 1998 brought about a change of power from a conservative to a social-democratic government. The long-ruling Christian Democrats under Chancellor Helmut Kohl lost to the Party of the Social Democrats under his challenger Gerhard Schröder, who eventually formed a coalition with the Green Party. Unlike Britain, Germany has a multi-party system, and the 1998 election was the first time that a transition of power came about through general elections, and not through changes in the ruling coalitions. It was also the last election before the German Government moved from Bonn to Berlin after German re-unification. The data for the analysis are from the opening sections of two German national television channels, the public channel ARD, and the commercial channel RTL, as well as from two international channels, the British-based BBC-World and the US-based CCN-International. The ARD started their election special 15 minutes before the polls closed at 6 p.m.; RTL began 10 minutes and CNN International 5 minutes before, while BBC-World started at 6 p.m. sharp. Table 4 shows the frame analysis of the opening section of the ARD.

Table 4. FRG 98.ARD: Frame analysis of opening section

PRE-OPENING	Title sequence: *footage of arial view of the*
id topic	*government district of Bonn, pre-recorded,*
id channel	*insert: ARD logo throughout the broadcast; female presenter's voice-over:*
id topic	So the days of Bonn are numbered. A touch of nostalgia lies over the government district.
	(Die Tage Bonns sind also gezählt. Ein Hauch von Nostalgie liegt über dem Regierungsviertel.)
PRE-HEADLINE	*presenter standing at small high table, live to camera*
id topic	Well, the days of Bonn are numbered but today the city holds centre stage one more time, one last time for a general election. For a super election day is ending. Now comes the hour of the pollsters, the vote counters, the statisticians.
	(Tja, die Tage von Bonn sind gezählt, aber heute steht die Stadt noch einmal voll im Zentrum des Geschehens, ein letztes Mal zu einer (.) Bundestagswahl. Denn ein Superwahltag geht zuende. Jetzt beginnt die Stunde der Demoskopen, der Stimmenzähler, der Hochrechner.)
AGENDA PROJ	How you, dear viewers, have voted today,
id statistics expert	Uli Deppendorf *(medium shot Uli Deppendorf at desk)* and the team from Infratest dimap will tell you presently, in a few moments,
	(Wie Sie, liebe Zuschauer, heute gewählt haben, das sagt Ihnen gleich Uli Deppendorf und das Team von infratest dimap)
DELEGATION to	and how the results are to be interpreted will be discussed by Wolfgang Kenntemich (WK) with our guests
interviewer	(und wie das Wahlergebnis zu bewerten ist, das wird Wolfgang Kenntemich in Erfahrung bringen mit unseren Gästen)

Table 4. (*continued*)

id programme	*(insert) Wahl 98*
id interviewer	*(insert) Wolfgang Kenntemich*
	(co-presenter standing in front of table with expert guests)
headline WK	Yes, dear viewers, whether the election will be the cliffhanger we all expect – we'll find out in a moment.
report	to help you find your way in the maze of prognoses, speculations, projections, coalitions, concepts, we have invited some high-calibre guests and experts for you here into the Waterworks who will be with us all evening, and we have also asked these experts and guests beforehand as to their prognosis.
	(Ja, liebe Zuschauer, ob die Wahl die Zitterpartie wird, die wir alle erwarten – wir werden's gleich sehen. Damit Sie sich etwas besser im Wust von Prognosen,Spekulationen, Hochrechnungen, Koalitionen, Konzepten zurechtfinden können, haben wir hochkarätige Gäste und Experten hier ins Wasserwerk für Sie eingeladen, und wir haben sie auch vorher, diese Experten und Gäste, kurz befragt, was sie denn für eine Prognose abgeben.)
id guest	Here is Dieter Schulte *(medium shot DS)* the chairman of the German Trade Union Council.
	(Hier ist einmal Dieter Schulte, der Vorsitzende des Deutschen Gewerkschaftsbundes.)
quote guest	He says that he expects a Red-Green, but narrow majority.
	(Er sagt, dass er mit einer Rot-Grünen, aber knappen Mehrheit rechnet.)
id guest	*(insert) Dieter Schulte, DGB*
quote guest	*(insert) "rechne mit einem knappen Sieg für Rot-Grün";*
id programme	*(insert) Wahl 98*
	Next to him ...(neben ihm ...)
	(This procedure is followed in identical manner with four more invited experts: the chairman of the Federal Union of German Industry; the chief economist of Deutsche Bank; Germany's only female bishop; and a professor of politology, who is quoted like the others but is also given the opportunity to endorse his quoted statement live.)

Structurally, the ARD sequence differs from the British and International channels covering the British election night in several respects. Like them, it has a PRE-OPENING sequence in which the topic of politics and elections is introduced both visually and verbally through footage of the government district, with the female presenter's voice-over narration to the effect that soon, Bonn will no longer be the seat of the German Government. Unlike them, however, the channel is identified through the channel logo only, and the programme is not identified at all.[3]

---

3. It was at first assumed that this might be due to the fact that maybe our recording started a few seconds late. A comparison with the ARD's pre-opening frame for the election night of 2002 shows however that it was just as abrupt and likewise had no explicit channel, programme or presenter identification.

Another difference is that there is no OPENING frame in which the audience is greeted, the programme named, the presenter identified, either by self-identification or by on-screen characters. Instead, there is a PRE-HEADLINE frame in which the presenter, live to camera and thus in direct audience address, creates suspense regarding the outcome of the election (*a super election day is ending, now comes the hour of the pollsters, the ballot counters, the statisticians*). As with the British BBC and ITV, we could conclude that, since the presenter is not identified, she is a journalist of high recognition value and maybe regularly hosts the evening news or another high-profile programme, so that she is familiar to the audience. But this is not so. Up to the election of 1998, election nights on ARD were regularly hosted by the editor-in-chief of the broadcasting corporation of North-Rhine Westphalia, the federal state in which Bonn, up to then the German capital, is located. Marion van Haaren, the presenter, happened to be editor-in-chief at the time, and she had little screen presence outside of her federal state. Yet we do not learn her identity until three minutes into the broadcast, at which point she is addressed by name by a journalist in the studio, when he gives the floor back to her. The programme title, too, is not supplied until well into the following agenda projection frame, when the floor has been taken over by the interviewer – and then only by on-screen characters.

The data show no HEADLINE frame. Instead, the PRE-HEADLINE frame is followed by an AGENDA PROJECTION frame. It is in this frame that the audience appears for the first time, not through being greeted, but in a direct address (*dear viewers*) that precedes a projection of what the polls and statistics expert will be telling them. The expert is identified both verbally and visually by caption. After this, the floor is passed to the broadcast's interviewer in a DELEGATION frame. The interviewer is likewise doubly identified by verbal and visual means and he takes over the floor by directly addressing the audience and finally supplying a HEADLINE: *Yes, dear viewers, whether the election will be the cliffhanger we all expect – we'll find out in a moment.* This makes his role somewhat ambiguous between interviewer and co-presenter. He holds the floor to the end of the excerpt, in a special kind of interaction with five *high-calibre guests and experts* who were asked about their prediction on the outcome of the election before the programme (see below). He is the one who returns the floor to the presenter and, in saying "weiter mit Marion van Haaren" (*we continue with MH*), finally names her.

We now turn to interpersonal positioning and begin with the channel's construction of its own identity. The missing identification of a relatively unknown presenter discussed above implies that it does not really matter who animates what the ARD has to say. This foregrounds the institution rather than the person of the presenter. The fact that the programme is identified so late points in a similar direction: what else could the ARD be doing just before 6 o'clock on Election

Day? There is an inference of authoritativeness that may still go back to the time when the ARD was Germany's sole television station. As regards interpersonal relations between the channel's journalists, first and last name address is used throughout, and greetings, e.g. in delegation frames, are formal.

Regarding channel-audience relations, the ARD constructs a certain immediacy towards its viewers: there are, in the excerpt, 7 direct addresses (*dear viewers 2, you 5*). Also, the audience's role as voters and thereby newsgivers is acknowledged (*how you, dear viewers, have voted today*). If we take the interviewer's introductory text into account as well, the channel-audience relation is further specified: the ARD sees it self as a mediator between the complex issues of the election process and its audience, its role is *to help you find your way* .... This implies a clear grouping of channel as expert on the one hand and an audience in need of guidance on the other (this is supported by there being only 2 inclusive *we*'s).

The channel-guest relation is very interesting: The guests have been invited *for you*, the audience, and they are *high-calibre* personages, representatives of the key institutions of German society: the unions, industry, finance, religion, education. This enhances the channel's standing as a social institution equal to the others and widens the gap between channel and the everyday world of the audience.

The way in which the guests' prognoses on the outcome of the election are presented is quite remarkable. One guest after another is shown full screen listening to the interviewer's live voice-over giving an indirect report of what he or she has said in an interview with him before the programme. The interviews themselves are not shown. Representing in indirect speech previous utterances of co-present participants must be a fairly unique practice on live television – unless, of course, the quotes serve as a preface to something else, for instance an upcoming interviewer question. But this is only done once, with the last guest, who is asked if he sticks with his opinion. Presumably this procedure is owed to a need to strictly control time until 6 p.m., when the polls close and the results of the exit polls can be announced. But it adds another facet to the emerging image of the ARD: one of non-spontaneity and controlled interaction.

Channel-politics relations are very much backgrounded. Issues of politics enter the programme for the first time through the quoted prognoses of the celebrity guests referred to above. Their utterances focus on issues of political parties, coalitions, and a possible change of government, dealing with the topic of politics in a quite de-personalised manner. A personalisation of politics occurs much later, when the presenter introduces a sequence of delegation frames to reporters by saying: *It is going to be a neck-to-neck race, that is what the polls had predicted for today. The incumbent Chancellor Helmut Kohl against challenger Gerhard Schroeder* (not included in the table).

As regards expressions of appraisal in terms of attitude, gradation and evaluation on the micro-level of linguistic expression, we find several in the presenter's pre-headline and in the interviewer's introduction of the guests (*centre stage, one last time, super election day, now comes the hour of …; cliffhanger, maze, high calibre*). They serve to enhance equally the importance of the election and the quality of the ARD's presentation of it, and to create some suspense as to the outcome. But in comparison with the British channels, this must be called restrained.

The election special by the commercial channel RTL was entitled *Stunde der Wahrheit: Wahl 98. Die Entscheidung* (Hour of Truth: Election 98. The Decision). It started at 5.50 p.m., 10 minutes before the polls closed. Table 5 presents the frame analysis of its opening section.

Structurally, the sequence of frames in the RTL excerpt up to the pre-headline frame is very much like the ones of the British and International channels. In the

Table 5. FRG 98.RTL: Frame analysis of opening section

PRE-OPENING	Title sequence: *split screen showing Helmut Kohl, and Gerhard Schröder with his wife, casting their ballots, music*
id programme	*(animated inserts) HOUR OF TRUTH, followed by ELECTION 98, THE DECISION*
	(STUNDE DER WAHRHEIT: WAHL 98. DIE ENTSCHEIDUNG)
id channel	*RTL logo throughout*
	(Presenter's voice-over)
id programme	Hour of truth *(Stunde der Wahrheit)*
HOOKER	
PRE-HEADLINE 1	Gerhard Schroeder or Helmut Kohl – who will lead Germany into the next millennium?
	(Gerhard Schröder oder Helmut Kohl – wer führt Deutschland ins nächste Jahrtausend?)
OPENING	*(Presenter, sitting at desk with expert, live to camera)*
greet audience	Good evening and a really hearty welcome
	(Guten Abend und ganz herzlich willkommen)
id programme	to our special election broadcast on the parliamentary elections 1998.
	(bei unserer Wahlsondersendung zur Bundestagswahl 1998.)
introduce expert	As always on such days I welcome my dear colleague Johannes Groß here with me in the studio.
	(Wie immer an solchen Tagen begrüße ich meinen lieben Kollegen Johannes Groß hier bei mir im Studio.)
PRE-HEADLINE 2	What is at stake? (Worum geht es?)
BACKGROUND	What is at stake first of all is – who is going to be the next chancellor? Will Helmut Kohl remain chancellor or will the next chancellor be SPD challenger Gerhard Schröder, who of course was ahead in so many polls in the last weeks.
	(Es geht in erster Linie darum – wer wird neuer Bundeskanzler? Bleibt es Helmut Kohl oder wird es der SPD-Kanzlerkandidat Gerhard Schröder, der in so vielen Umfragen in den letzten Wochen ja vorne gelegen hat.)

Table 5. (*continued*)

DELEGATE/clip	We'll briefly present to you the two gentlemen once more.
	(Wir stellen Ihnen die beiden Heren noch mal ganz kurz vor.)
video clip	(follows footage characterising Kohl and Schroeder in personal and political
BACKGROUND	terms, and on how they spent the day, with presenter voice-over narration)
DELEGATE/exp	*medium shot presenter and expert sitting at desk*
	Johannes Groß, it is the battle of battles, as it were, the last parliamentary elections in this millennium; what are the salient elements, would you say, in this parliamentary election campaign?
	(Johannes Groß, es ist die Schlacht der Schlachten, könnte man fast sagen, die letzte Bundestagswahl in diesem Jahrtausend; was sind so die herausragenden Momente, würden Sie sagen, in diesem Bundestagswahlkampf?)
id exp/genre	*caption: JOHANNES GROSS, RTL-Analyse*
JG	Well, the parliamentary election campaign was of course strangely
analysis	devoid of content, though not of tension. It was staged as a pure personality contest between the two top candidates who kept accusing each other of not speaking sufficiently about factual issues – which did not prompt them however to talk on issues themselves…
	(Also der Bundestagswahlkampf war ja auf eigentümliche Weise inhaltsleer, wenn auch nicht spannungsleer. Er war aufgezogen als reiner Personalwettbewerb zwischen den beiden Spitzenkandidaten, die sich immer gegenseitig vorgeworfen haben, es würde nicht über Sachfragen genügend gesprochen, was sie aber nicht veranlasst hat, selber über Sachfragen zu sprechen.)

PRE-OPENING frame, there is footage symbolising the topic of elections, showing the two main candidates as they cast their ballots, on a split screen. The programme is identified both with on-screen characters and by presenter's voice-over saying *Hour of Truth*. The channel is identified through the RTL logo. As with the ARD, we have no presenter identification in the pre-opening or opening frames. But as with the BBC and ITV, in the case of RTL, this is unmarked since the presenter Peter Kloeppel also presents the channel's main evening news and is thus a well-known figure to the RTL audience. In the HOOKER frame, the theme of the split-screen footage is taken up verbally: *Gerhard Schroeder or Helmut Kohl – who will lead Germany into the next millennium?*

In the OPENING frame, the audience is greeted and bid a hearty welcome, the programme is once more identified and the studio expert is introduced. There is no need for an agenda projection frame for introducing additional channel personnel, since the presenter and the expert do the election special between them. The comparative sparseness is in part compensated by the advanced electronic equipment of the RTL studio (see Schieß, this volume).

The second PRE-HEADLINE frame continues the theme of who is going to be the next chancellor – Kohl or Schröder? In not following this up with a HEADLINE frame, RTL is like the ARD. Yet where the ARD follows its pre-headline frame with an agenda projection, RTL goes on to provide BACKGROUND footage on the two candidates Kohl and Schroeder. After this, the presenter DELEGATES to the studio expert and enters into a sustained sequence of talk with him.

Turning to the construction of identities and relations on the micro-level, we find appraisal language leading to dramatisation in both the channel's construction of its own identity and of the topic in the pre-opening frame: The name of the programme itself, *HOUR OF TRUTH. ELECTION 98. THE DECISION*, is very dramatic in its high-noon character. The fact that it is supplied both by on-screen characters and through presenter's voice-over lends this further emphasis.

RTL's relation to its audience is personalised and familiar (*good evening and a really hearty welcome*). This does not lead to the construction of an in-group of channel and audience, however. On the contrary, the only occurrence of personal pronouns (in the background frame: *We'll briefly present to you*) clearly positions channel and audience as two separate entities, with the audience as recipients of entertaining footage (see below). Closeness and familiarity also characterise the presenter's relation to his journalistic studio guest (*I welcome my dear colleague J.G.*).

What are the identities constructed for the political process and the politicians, and for the channel-politics relations? Again we find personalisation and dramatisation in the reduction of the election and its issues to the confrontation of the two top candidates. The dramatisation starts with the split-screen footage in the pre-opening frame, continues in pre-headline 1 in the hooker frame (*Gerhard Schroeder or Helmut Kohl – who will lead Germany into the next millennium?*), which casts the election as a historic contest between two protagonists, and is taken up again in the question of pre-headline 2 (*who is going to be the next chancellor?*). The presentation of *"the two gentlemen"* in the footage supplied in the background frame, with the presenter's live voice-over supplying details as to marital history and personal predilections, constructs two men who are different not merely in their political orientation but also in character and biography. The effect is very sensationalist and personalised, the contrast to ARD very pronounced.

The hype continues in the delegation of the floor to the studio expert (*it is the battle of battles, the last parliamentary elections in this millennium*). There lies a certain irony in the expert's subsequent reply, in that he criticises the election campaign as *strangely devoid of content* and *staged as a pure personality contest between the two top candidates*, because this is of course exactly what RTL has been doing up to now, as well. The expert goes on to supply a succinct analysis of the campaign (not shown in the excerpt), only to be asked by the presenter *But of course above all it is about this duel between these two opponents*. It seems almost like a "good cop – bad cop" – division of labour: the presenter does the dramatisation, the expert the sober analysis.

As is to be expected, this role distribution is clearly reflected in the two journalists' differential use of expressions of appraisal: of affective and evaluative
terms, of weak and strong modality, and of up-graded or downgraded language.
For lack of space, this cannot be demonstrated here beyond the examples already
given. Comparing ARD and RTL, the use of appraisal terms does differ as predicted in Section 2.4 the presenter of the commercial channel uses more and stronger
appraisal terms than the journalists of the public service one.

Table 6. FRG 98.CNN International: Frame analysis of opening section

PRE-OPENING	Title sequence:
id channel	*CNN-INTERNATIONAL logo throughout the broadcast*
id topic	images of the German Parliament, the candidates Kohl and Schröder, polling stations, ballot boxes
id programme	inserts: Germany DECIDES, over German national colours; dramatic theme music
OPENING	presenter sitting at desk, live to camera
id programme	*insert: Germany DECIDES, followed by*
id presenter	*insert: Bettina Lüscher, Düsseldorf, Germany, followed by insert: Bettina Lüscher, German Election Center*
greet audience	Hello and welcome
id.channel/progr.	to CNN special coverage of the German vote,
self-id.presenter	I'm Bettina Lüscher.
PRE-HEADLINE	In just a few moments polling stations here will close and the first exit polls will be announced.
BACKGROUND	Four-term Christian Democrat Chancellor Helmut Kohl has been locked in a tough campaign with Social Democratic challenger Gerhard Schröder.
DELEGATION	
del. preface	
id reporters/loc	*split screen Jonathan Mann, caption SPD / Jim Bitterman, caption CDU*
id programme	*Germany Decides*
id reporter 1/loc	CNN's Jonathan Mann joins us tonight from the SPD headquarters in Bonn
id reporter 2/loc	CNN's Jim Bitterman is nearby at the CDU headquarters
delegation to rep 1	and we begin with Jonathan Mann (JM) at the SPD, John?
id reporter/loc	*Jonathan Mann, caption Jonathan Mann, SPD Headquarters, Bonn, Germany*
JM	Bettina, Gerhard Schroeder is trying to achieve something that
analysis	others before him have found impossible – unseat an icon and jump German politics forward a generation while guaranteeing stability and delivering change. It is a very tall order.
background	Schroeder began his campaign with a very commanding lead, one that one poll-ster called "solid and historic", but somehow, over the last few weeks, that has been whittled away and now the race is too close to call.
formulation	So, over the next few minutes, perhaps even the next few hours, we'll have to wait and see whether Gerhard Schroeder has held on to that early support, enough of it at least to finally put a Social Democrat in the Chancellor's office in Germany.

Table 6. (*continued*)

delegation to rep 2	
JM	Let's go now to the other side of the contest, the Christian Democrat headquarters, and Jim Bitterman (JB), Jim?
id rep1/rep2	*split screen Jonathan Mann, caption SPD/Jim Bitterman, caption CDU*
id programme	*Germany Decides*
id rep 2/loc	*Jim Bitterman, captions Jim Bitterman, CDU Headquarters, Bonn, Germany*
JB	Jonathan, one way or another, it's going to be an historic evening.
headline	We're either going to see a four-term chancellor get elected to his fifth term, and that'll be surprising, or we're going to see a chancellor turned out of office after so many turns/so many years in office, after being one of the longest-serving democratic leaders in history.
delegation to pres	
JB	Those results are about to come in now, Bettina, so let's take a look at them together
STORY	*screens in studio showing ARD and ZDF live reporting of exit polls results*
preface	Basically, what we're doing to inform our viewers is that we are taking the polls that the ARD and ZDF networks are providing.
story	And we're getting the first numbers (gives results).

The German election night of 1998 was also covered by CNN INTERNA-
TIONAL, and the frame analysis of its opening section is shown in Table 6.

The frame structure of CNN I's opening sequence is very much like that
of CNN I's coverage of the British elections (cf. Table 3). The PRE-OPENING
frames with the visual identification of channel, topic and programme are more
or less identical, as are their OPENING frames with the greeting and welcoming
of the audience, the self-identification of the presenters, and the naming of the
programme with reference to the country covered. Both have PRE-HEADLINE
frames referring to the imminent closing of the polls. The presenters are different: while the anchor for the British elections was a male American foreign correspondent, the one for the German elections is a female German journalist, head
of CNN's Berlin office.

Against the background of such sequential similarity, if not standardisation, it
is striking that in the German data, the presenter does not provide a HEADLINE.
In the British data, BBC, ITV and CNN I alike use the predictions of the opinion
polls of the campaign to produce some sort of a headline oriented to future news
to the effect that Labour will win this election. The presenter of CNN's coverage
of the German election, on the other hand, refers to the past campaign solely
as BACKGROUND: *Four-term Christian Democrat Chancellor Helmut Kohl has
been locked in a tough campaign with Social Democratic challenger Gerhard Schroeder*. Yet the opinion polls of the campaign would have supported a prediction

about the outcome of the election in Germany as well, if only to the effect that it was hard to say.

As in the CNN I British data, there is no AGENDA PROJECTION frame. Instead, there follow two DELEGATIONS to reporters at the headquarters of the two major parties. These are preceded by their introduction in a DELEGATION PREFACE. Such prefaces are very common in serial delegation sequences. What is unique in this sequence, though, is the manner in which the floor is delegated here: from the presenter to reporter 1 to reporter 2 and back to the presenter. The effect of this practice is to reduce the hierarchy between presenter and reporters.

In the delegation sequence, reporter 1 supplies ANALYSIS and BACK-GROUND, concluding with a FORMULATION which would support a present-er's headline (had there been one) to the effect that it will take time until the outcome of the election will be known, thus creating audience suspense. He then delegates the floor to reporter 2 who produces what serves as a PRE-HEADLINE and HEADLINE, before passing the floor back to the presenter for the presentation of the results.

As with the British elections, CNN I bases its announcement of the German exit polls results on information from national television channels of that country. But unlike in Britain, where CNN I delegated the floor to ITV to carry that station's announcement live, in the German data the results are read by the CNN I presenter from a piece of paper while we see the graphics of the ARD results and those of ZDF, another German national channel, on two screens in the studio background.

Turning to the construction of interpersonal identities and relations on the micro-level, we start again with the construction of the channel's own identity. As with CNN I's coverage of the British elections, again we have the attention to clear presentation of information: this pertains to establishing the channel's own identity as well as to its recipient design for an international audience in providing more information than the national channels and using complex descriptive expressions to do it. The relations between the channel's journalists are constructed as informal – through first-name basis – and more team-oriented than in the British data – through the egalitarian delegation practices. First names, as used in the excerpt, serve simultaneously as terms of address and as signals of delegating, respectively accepting, the floor. As with the British CNN I data, the overall impression is one of high professionality.

Channel-audience relations are polite and matter-of-fact. There is direct audience address up to the delegation sequence, when presenter and reporters start addressing each other but sometimes also the audience, in the delegation frames. A case in point is the second reporter's *Those results are about to come in now, Bettina, so let's take a look at them together.* Although the reporter directly addresses the presenter in passing the floor back to her, *let's look at them together* addresses both her, the audience, and the overhearing first reporter. Thus *let's* is simultaneously an audience-and addressee-inclusive *we*. The excerpt also has 7 tokens of audience-inclusive and 4 tokens of audience-exclusive *we*. All of the latter occur in the presenter's story-preface frame, in which she sources the exit polls data to ARD and ZDF.[4] Thus it is only at the very end of the opening sequence that a construction of channel and audience as clearly separate groups occurs.

As regards the construction of politics and the politicians involved, we find again, as with ARD and RTL, the characterisation of the election as one between two protagonists. At the same time, personalisation is weak, since the politicians are expressly linked to their parties, to the extent that the second reporter manages not to use names at all. Helmut Kohl is referred to merely as *chancellor*.

Turning to the use of appraisal language, we do find, in the reporters' contribution, the construction of suspense by the skilful juxtaposition of the two possible outcomes of the election. The means to achieve this are metaphors (*unseat an icon*), up-grading terms like *very*, upgraded superlatives (*one of the longest-serving democratic leaders in history*), and generally the stressing of the "historic-ness" of the event (*a solid and historic* lead in the polls, *an historic evening*). Yet what is absent is any talk of opponents, adversaries, battles or duels. Also, this type of dramatisation only applies to the topic and not to CNN I's coverage of it.

The German elections of 1998 were covered not only by one but by two international channels. Table 7 shows the frame analysis of the opening sequence of BBC-WORLD.

BBC World started its broadcast at 6 p.m. sharp, that is, at the time the polls closed and the exit polls were announced. In its frame structure, the PRE-OPENING frame exhibits the usual features, alluding to the topic visually, and identifying the channel both visually and verbally. There follows a HOOKER frame in which, in presenter's voice-over, the audience is welcomed to the channel and to a live transmission from outside the German parliament, and, in a PRE-HEADLINE frame, told that the polls just closed. Note the reference to Germany and its general election, and to the number of people living there – pieces of information recipient-designed for a non-German audience.

---

4.   One wonders who the addressees of this preface might be since the audience is referred to in third person (*what we're doing to inform our viewers*). We take this as a sort of oblique audience address, parallel to cases like *my little boy needs to go to bed now,* said by an adult to a small child. Possibly, by addressing their audience with *our viewers,* CNN I assumes a likewise adult or higher status position towards them. If so, this would implicate a similar channel-audience relation to the one that the German channel ARD constructs.

Table 7. FRG 98.BBC WORLD: Frame analysis of opening section

PRE-OPENING	Title sequence: *images of animated multi-coloured BBC-WORLD flag, music*
id topic	*images of German Bundestag*
id channel	*BBC-WORLD logo throughout the broadcast, insert: LIVE*
id channel	*Male voice-over:* You're watching BBC-WOLRD, the BBC's international news channel
HOOKER	*Presenter's voice-over*
id channel	Welcome to BBC World News,
id location	live from Bonn, from outside the German Bundestag.
pre-headline	In Germany, across this nation of eighty million people, the polls closed just a few seconds ago in the general election.
OPENING	*presenter sitting at desk in studio, live to camera:*
id channel	*Insert BBC WORLD LIVE*
id programme	*GERMANY DECIDES*
greet audience	Hello and welcome
id. ch/progr/loc	to BBC World News from Bonn,
self-id. pres	I'm Nik Gowing.
id programme	*caption GERMANY DECIDES*
id presenter/loc	*caption Nik Gowing in Bonn*
HEADLINE	And already the polls are suggesting a significant lead for the Social Democrats
STORY	The polls suggest that the Social Democrats of Gerhard Schröder have won forty-one per cent of the vote, and the CDU/CSU alliance have won just thirty-five per cent, that's Chancellor Helmut Kohl. So that's a significantly larger gap between the Christian Democrats and the Social Democrats than was predicted by the opinion polls.
DELEGATE	Well, joining me now to look immediately at that first result from
to expert	the exit polls, conditional of course on the final results, is Heinz Schulte (HS).
expert interview	Heinz, what do these figures now tell us?
id expert	*Heinz Schulte, caption HEINZ SCHULTE, German affairs analyst from Bonn*
HS	Nik, they tell us that Helmut Kohl's Christian Democrat Party is out, that Helmut Kohl will not be chancellor, we're gonna get a coalition led by Gerhard Schröder of the SPD and likely to be a grand coalition because of the PDS, the East German party coming in with more than five per cent. And that means it's not enough for Red-Green.
PRES	So let's just be clear. On the basis of these exit polls, we have what for the Greens and also the Free Democrats, the Liberals?
HS	Both the Greens and the Liberal Party will be in parliament with 6.5%.
PRES	Each?
HS	Each. But that means that Red-Green, which would have a majority over the existing coalition, will not/that will not be enough if the PDS comes in with more than 5%. That will water down the coalition Red-Green, and that means a grand coalition with the SPD in the driving seat.
PRES	Let's just be clear, the terms we are using here. Red-Green is Social Democrats with Gerhard Schröder?
HS	That's right.
PRES	and the Green Party?

Table 7. (*continued*)

HS	Exactly
PRES	Now who else might they therefore have to do a deal with?
id expert	*Heinz Schulte, caption HEINZ SCHULTE German affairs analyst from Bonn*
HS	He has to do a deal with Helmut Kohl's Christian Democratic Party, but bear in mind without Helmut Kohl. Helmut Kohl has said consistently that he will not be a partner in a grand coalition, and particularly not if it is the junior partner.
PRES	And particularly eventually if the result is as bad as this?
HS	Exactly. I think Helmut Kohl is out, that seems to be clear on the basis of these exit polls.

In the OPENING frame, the channel is identified again through on-screen characters, as is the programme *GERMANY DECIDES*, while the presenter greets and welcomes the audience live to camera, identifying the channel BBC World News and the location of the transmission, Bonn, and introducing himself. This is accompanied by two captions, one naming the programme *GERMANY DECIDES*, and the other identifying the presenter and his location. There are, in the pre-opening, hooker and opening frames, quite a number of verbal and visual references to the location of Bonn. To be in Bonn may be a mark of distinction, since the only other channel broadcasting from the German capital is the German public service channel ARD, while BBC World's global rival, CNN International, airs from its studio in Düsseldorf. The opening sequence of BBC World is very similar to that of CNN International, both in the German and the British data.

As with CNN International, there is no agenda projection frame. After the opening frame comes a HEADLINE based on the results of the exit polls *And already the polls are suggesting a significant lead for the Social Democrats*. Its pre-headline was in the hooker frame, and the headline continues this even syntactically. The result is a conjunctive structure that joins pre-headline and headline over the interruption by the interspersed opening frame (*In Germany ... the polls closed ..., and already the polls are suggesting ...*). The STORY then opens with the lead sentence, which gives the gist of the news, and evaluates the result against that of the opinion polls, in the classical inverted pyramid structure.

The DELEGATION frame to the studio expert and the subsequent interview with the expert guest is then devoted to the interpretation of what these results mean in terms of political consequences (cf. Stiehler 2000). In his first reply to the presenter's question *what do these figures now tell us?*, the expert supplies a complex answer as to the likely constitution of the new government against the background of Germany's multi-party system and its consequent tradition of forming coalitions. He is immediately checked by the presenter, who first wants to establish the results for the smaller parties, which the audience does not know yet. His *so let's just be clear* is the first of a series of clarification questions initating a repair sequence in which the presenter attempts to get the expert to present his information about the results step by step, clearly and in detail, to refrain from using insider terms like *Red-Green* without explanation, and to supply missing pieces of information.

The way in which this repair is done is mainly through polarity questions inviting a positive answer, to which the expert can only reply by confirmation (*that's right, exactly*). But wh-questions are used as well, and when the presenter asks his last one of those (*now who else might they therefore have to do a deal with?*), he sounds like a teacher nudging his pupil to knowledge in a sort of didactic dialogue. But of course the expert knows all these things, knows them too well, in fact. It is the international audience that needs such help. In order to be able to assemble the puzzle of a complex state of affairs in a different culture, the audience needs "foreign" knowledge broken down into in small pieces on the one hand, and on the other also to be presented with such pieces of information that a native of the culture would take for granted.

The stretch of talk with the political expert very clearly shows the problems an international channel can be confronted with in trying to mediate regional information to a global audience with the help of a local expert. This is not the only such example in our data – it seems that local experts are not yet used to the modifications required in addressing international audiences. As we have seen, this requires quite specific and additional repair work on the part of the presenters.

Turning to the construction of identities and relations, what is the identity that BBC World projects for itself? The construction of the opening sequence exhibits professionalism, and in the dialogue with the political expert, a didactic endeavour to mediate complex issues to an international audience manifests itself. Presenter/expert guest relations are informal, first name terms and direct communication strategies are used (cf. Becker, this volume). At the instigation of the presenter, both are collaborating in the construction of local knowledge that is comprehensible to a global audience.

Channel-audience relations are neutral. There is a fair share of inclusive *we* which casts presenter and audience as recipients of the expert's contribution. However, there is also a clear differentiation between channel and audience when identities are established in the opening section (*you are watching BBC World ..., I'm Nik Gowing*), and when things start getting didactic about the terms *we* are using. The construction of politics and the politicians is matter-of-fact, without personalisation or evaluation. Names are linked with parties and possible coalitions in a new government.

As regards uses of appraisal language, we find a number of features of gradation that emphasize the channel's coverage of the German election: the repetition of the channel's name, of the fact that the programme is transmitted live, and from

Bonn, as well the emphasis on *immediately* discussing the results with the expert. This can be read as an attempt to position BBC World as a serious competitor vis-à-vis its rival CNN International. There is no notable appraisal language regarding politics, or the audience.

3.4 The American Presidential Election of 2000

This was the election that George W. Bush narrowly won against Vice President Al Gore after a 5-week long post-election contest between the Republicans and the Democrats over who had won Florida's 25 electoral votes. The election night was dramatic. The networks declared Florida first for Bush, retracted, then for Gore, retracted again, then ultimately declared for Bush. Since the margin between the two candidates was so narrow, Gore refused to concede defeat, and machine recounts were automatically done in some counties. In a dispute over subsequent manual recounts and overseas votes, both sides filed lawsuits in county, state and federal courts. This series of legal battles only came to an end when, on December 12th, 2000 and on a vote of 5 to 4, the United States Supreme Court ruled to end all counts of Florida's disputed votes and effectively decided the election in favour of George W. Bush.

Our data are from the American national channels CNN USA and NBC, both commercial networks, again from the opening sections, when the dramatic development of the night was still in the future. Yet with the benefit of hindsight, some of the things said at the beginning of that night, and recorded in the following excerpts, sound prophetic. The mixed-programming channel NBC started its special at 7 p.m. Eastern Standard Time, one hour after polls closing time in the East, and coinciding with polls closing in a number of other states. The presenter of NBC's election special also hosts the regular evening news of that channel. The 24-hour news network CNN USA started its election special at 5 p.m. EST, one hour before the polling stations closed in a number of states in the East. The time was the regular slot for the daily political news show *Inside Politics*, and the presenters were the same as those that host that show. Table 8 shows the frame analysis of its opening sequence.

The frame structure of the CNN USA opening sequence is similar to those of the British and German data for CNN International, but at the same time it is more elaborate in a number of respects. In the PRE-OPENING sequence, we have multiple identifications of channel and programme in the verbal and visual modalities. The footage identifying the programme is very long (for a description, see Schieß, this volume) and very much focused on American history. There is a

Table 8. USA 2000.CNN: Frame analysis of opening section

PRE-OPENING	Title sequence
id. channel	*animated inserts CNN, CNN logo throughout*
id. programme	*"election 2000, special presentation" against background of animated US flag; male voice over theme music:*
id. channel/progr.	This is a CNN election two thousand special presentation
id. topic	*two-minute footage on American presidential history of the 20th century, voice-over narration, stately background music*
id. programme	*insert "Election 2000" over animated US flag, pan across studio and presenters' desk*
id. channel/progr.	*presenter Bernard Shaw (BS) voice-over*
	This is CNN's coverage of election two thousand.
OPENING	Now from the election desk,
id. presenters	here are Judy Woodruff (JW), Jeff Greenfield (JG) and Bill Schneider (WS).
id presenters	*medium shot of election desk with BS, JW, JG, WS.*
id channel/prog	*insert CNN live/ Election 2000*
welcome aud.	and welcome to viewers around the world watching
id. channel	CNN International
thank audience	thank you for joining us
teaser	as we begin what promises to be a remarkable and a suspenseful evening
PRE-HEADLINE	*Judy Woodruff to camera*
JW	As voting continues literally at this hour and will continue across the nation,
HEADLINE	there is every indication that George W. Bush and Al Gore are indeed locked in a presidential race that may be too close to call for hours.
DELEGATION	
to expert 1	*election desk with BS, JW, JG, WS*
JW	Jeff Greenfield, our senior analyst, this is the kind of election those of us who love politics have been living for.
id expert 1	*Jef Greenfield, caption Jef Greenfield, CNN Senior Analyst*
JG	If you've ever wanted, Judy, and folks out there, if you've ever longed for those nights when/that you've heard about when people waited late to find out who their their leader was, pull up a chair, this may be it. If you want to know how tight this presidential race is,
background	you only have to know this: This afternoon the Al Gore campaign dispatched Reverend Jesse Jackson to Pennsylvania. At this hour, they asked Senator Kennedy to dispatch a hundred of his advisers and supporters, union people, labor activists, environmentalists up across the border to New Hampshire where that race is apparently so tight, the Presidential race, we're hearing, Senate race after Senate race –
formulation	we simply don't know. It's an election like we haven't seen in decades.
DELEGATION	
to expert 2	*election desk with BS, JW, JG, WS*
BS	And Bill Schneider, people are leaving the polling booths, how can we characterize some of the things they are saying?

Table 8. (*continued*)

id expert 2 WS analysis	*William Schneider, caption: William Schneider, CNN SR. POLITICAL ANALYST* Well, I think we can say that voters in this election – it's very unusual – they're very two-minded, they are of two minds. You know, in any election in this country, usually one of two themes dominates. Either people say they've never had it so good or they say it's time for a change. What's really rare is for people to believe both, and they do. They believe they've never had it so good – their financial situation is good, they've never seen an economy this good. On the other hand, they want a change of leadership, a change of leadership but not a change of direction.
formulation	And I think it all stems from their views of Bill Clinton, the President. He gets a very high job rating, which ought to elect Al Gore, but a very low personal approval rating, so people want a change of leadership.
FORMULATION BS	Feels like a long night.

team of two presenters, one male, one female, and they are assisted by two well-known CNN Senior political analysts.

The OPENING frame is done by the male presenter (presenter 1) who introduces the female co-presenter (presenter 2) and the two experts by name, although the latter will be introduced and captioned with their full status within CNN USA later on in the delegation frames. Presenter 1 then goes on to welcome the viewers of CNN International. He does not self-identify himself, nor does he greet or welcome his American audience. By this omission, a special relation between this presenter and his American audience is implicated, on the basis that they meet each day at the same time for the news show *Inside Politics*. The other journalists of the team do not have quite the same status. The international audience is welcomed as a sort of special guest who is thanked for coming. Thus no special accommodation to a global audience can be expected, such as that provided by CNN International. The opening frame concludes with a teaser foreshadowing *a remarkable and suspenseful evening*.

There is no agenda projection frame. The following sequence of PRE-HEADLINE, HEADLINE, DELEGATION 1 and DELEGATION 2 is identical with the cluster structure of CNN I's coverage of the British elections, and similar to that of the German ones. The female presenter 2 takes over and begins a topic-oriented frame with pre-headline and headline, continuing the theme of suspense, and stressing *that the presidential race may be too close to call for hours*.

She then delegates to the co-present analysts for BACKGROUND and ANALYSIS. The political analyst comments on how close the race is going to be, provides information about mobilising the vote and, like his colleagues reporting on the British and German elections for CNN International, concludes with a formulation supporting the presenter's headline *that it is a very close race*. The second expert to whom the floor is delegated is CNN USA's polls and statistics expert. In his contribution, he provides analysis based on opinion polls and, like expert 1, concludes with a formulation which supports the presenter's headline by explaining *why the presidential race is so close*. Presenter 1 then closes the sequence with a FORMULATION frame that mirrors the headline of presenter 2: *Feels like a long night*.

It seems that we are looking at a prototypical CCN cluster structure, involving one or two presenters, about two reporters on outside locations and about two experts in the studio, and a sequence of pre-headline, headline, a number of delegations, and a concluding formulation by a presenter. Each of the frames contributes something to the headline, and the nature of this contribution is made explicit in the journalists' formulations which conclude their turns.

The delegation sequences are worth looking at in more detail, as well. In the first delegation, presenter 2 personalises the election topic in strongly affective terms (*the kind of election those of us who love politics have been living for*), and this stance is taken up by the analyst in his contribution. While it remained open in the delegation whether *those of us who love politics* referred only to journalists, the analyst's response makes it clear that the audience is definitely included in this group. In acknowledging the floor, expert 1 addresses not only the presenter who delegated it to him, but also the audience: *Judy, and folks out there*. This is quite unique in our data. In his following discourse he addresses the audience explicitly in the first half, evidenced by a high density of *you* and one audience-addressed imperative which approaches teaser status (*pull up a chair*). In our data so far this, too, is rare in analysis frames.

The second delegation, to the polls expert, foreshadows discourse **about** and not directly **to** the audience. Yet discourse about opinion polls of election campaigns is also discourse about those members of the audience who are also voters, and about all the other members of the audience who, by definition of what opinion polls show, share the attitudes reported on. Nevertheless, this section is all third-person discourse about *people* and what *they* believe and want, with the audience in the overhearer's position. (As in other election night broadcasts, later on in the night, the discourse will be about how *they* have voted, but *they* will have totally disappeared behind figures and percentages.) This discourse practice of the media of reporting to the public about the public through third person reference in report and analysis frames is nowhere more striking in our opening sequences than in the juxtaposition of the contribution of CNN USA's expert 2 with the audience-oriented contribution of expert 1.

While the structural and functional pattern of the opening sequences is very similar between CNN International and CNN USA, the identity that CNN USA constructs for itself in our data is far more personalised than that of CNN International. In both, a high degree of professionalism shows itself in the design of the pre-opening sequences. But in the opening frame, where the relationship to the audience is established, we find a much closer channel-audience relation being constructed by CNN USA than by CNN International, viz. the implicated familiarity between the first presenter and the American home audience, in which the international audience has no part.

Familiarity towards the audience is also evidenced through the use of personal pronouns and direct audience address terms (*you, folks out there*). However, as the use of audience-inclusive and audience-exclusive *we* shows (2 to 6 in the excerpt), familiarity does not necessarily mean the construction of an in-group with the audience. Another sign of familiarity and informality is casual language. This latter pertains to the relation to the home audience (*pull up a chair*), to people and their beliefs according to opinion polls (*people say they've never had it so good*), and to the relation between the presenters and experts themselves, through usage of first name address. It is also reflected in the delegation routines with which the two presenters distribute the right to the floor to the analysts. Turn-taking becomes successively relaxed in evaluation and interpretation sequences about an hour later, approaching at times those of everyday conversation. The familiarity does not extend to the construction of politics and the politicians however.

To conclude again with appraisal language, this is heavily used, not merely in gradation terms, but also in affect-laden and evaluative language. It can refer to the topic of the election (*it's an election like we haven't seen in decades, a tight race*), or to CNN's coverage of it (*promises to be remarkable and suspenseful evening*), sometimes to both in combination (*the kind of election those of us who love politics have been living for*).

What kind of politics is it though that people love when they love *a tight race*, and what is it they love about it? It sounds very much like a spectacle, something that entertains and titillates through suspense, and like events that provide the media with an opportunity to stage a contest of heroes, which lets the audience witness, and by proxy share, the big emotions of the winners and losers. Is there any difference then between the lover of politics and the soccer fan that wants his team to win? Well, the fan is partisan – the polit-junkie, not necessarily. But he loves a good show. The opening segment of CNN's election night shows how the channel positions itself to provide just that, a good show for an audience constructed as sharing the team's love of politics.

The other national channel in our data was NBC, the mixed-programme television station of a network that grew out of America's oldest broadcasting company. Table 9 shows the frame analysis of its opening section.

When NBC started its election special *Decision 2000. Election Night* at 7 p.m. EST, polls had already closed in some Eastern states at 6 p.m., and in six more

Table 9. USA2000.NBC: Frame analysis of opening section

HOOKER	*Presenter Tom Brokaw (TB) sitting at desk, on wall behind him, map of US, showing states; TB live to camera*
opening	
greet aud. TB	good evening
self-id/id loc	I'm Tom Brokaw in New York
pre-headline	It's been a long campaign, it appears it will be a long and exciting evening before we know who is the next President of the United States.
headline	Polls have just closed in six additional states, representing sixty electoral votes; let's take you through them now.
story	*graphics and inserts throughout the sequence, voice over TB*
	First of all, in South Carolina, NBC projects that Texas Governor George W. Bush is the winner of those eight electoral votes. In Virginia, solid Republican territory, again Governor Bush the projected winner there. In New England, in Vermont, three electoral votes, Vice President Al Gore the projected winner there. But look at these states that are too close to call, even though the polls have closed now. Here we are in Georgia with thirteen electoral votes, New Hampshire with four, and the big prize, the brass ring for this evening to start everything off, the state of Florida, twenty-five electoral votes.It's been the most hotly contested race in this election so far.
formulation	We'll know before this night is out whether Jeb Bush in Florida is his brother's keeper or not.
illustration	*TB voice over graphics of US map:* So, we'll light up the states in our map, red for Governor Bush, blue for the Vice President. Governor Bush has already won Indiany and Kentucky.
agenda projection	We'll add it all up for you throughout the evening, we'll take you through what it all means, first man to 270 electoral votes wins.
teaser	Stay with us, we`re about to take you on an exciting and bumpy ride
PRE-OPENING	Title sequence:
id topic	*animated Presidential Seal, images of former presidents Carter, Reagan, Bush and Clinton, of the Capitol and of*
id.channel	*Rockefeller Center (NBC headquarters); NBC logo throughout;*
id progr	*animated inserts "NBC News", "Decision 2000", "Election Night"; music. TB voice-over:*
id. channel	From NBC News,
id. programme	Decision two thousand election night live
id. location	from our election headquarters in new York
id pres	here is Tom Brokaw
OPENING	*Presenter Tom Brokaw (TB) sitting at desk, on wall behind him, map of US, showing states; TB live to camera*
greet aud TB	good evening,
address aud	everyone
PRE-HEADLINE	It was not a false promise when we told you yesterday and the day before and all last week this promises to be one of the closest races in American presidential history,
HEADLINE	it is shaping up as just that tonight.

Table 9. (*continued*)

DELEGATION	Let's begin with
id co-pres	NBC's Washington Bureau chief, moderator of *Meet the Press,* Tim Russert (TR). All eyes on Florida at this hour, Tim, both campaigns made an enourmous investment there. The governor is another Bush, Jeb Bush. But at 4 o'clock this morning, Al Gore was still in Florida.
id. co-pres.	*Tim Russert, caption Tim Russert, NBC News*
TR	because George W. Bush knew, Tom, that he had to win Texas and Florida, his
background	linchpins, because all along Gore had been suggesting he could win New York and Califoria. With Florida, a battleground, Gore believes he can beat Bush there, he can change the whole dynamic of the race.
analysis	We've been talking to voters all day in Florida and quite striking, Tom, everyone assumed it was going to be social security, the big issue. In fact, those 65 and older split evenly amongst the candidates. What we're looking at are the younger voters. The younger voters appear to have been much more favorably disposed towards Al Gore – why, because of the economy.
formulation	The race too close to call, we don't know yet about the African-American turnout in Florida (…)
TB	All right, Tim, let's take a look at the map …

states at 7 p.m. The 6 p.m. projections had been reported in NBC's evening news at 6.30 p.m., by the same journalist who presents the election special.

Just like the British channel ITV, which started its broadcast after the polling stations had closed, NBC begins with a HOOKER frame to report the projected results for the states in question right at the start. The hooker frame has its own opening, in which the audience is greeted and the presenter, Tom Brokaw, introduces himself. Since Tom Brokaw had been the sole anchor of "NBC Nightly News" since 1983, this is surprising. By contrast, there is no identification of the channel, over and above the NBC Logo, or of the programme. In the pre-headline frame embedded in the hooker, the presenter does the usual looking back at the campaign and preview of the evening to come, and in the headline frame he announces that polls just closed in six more states. In the story frame, he reports on the projected results, following this up with a look at the states that are still too close to call, ending with Florida's 25 electoral votes.

The story concludes with the formulation *We'll know before this night is out whether Jeb Bush in Florida is his brother's keeper or not.* This requires context for comprehension: Jeb Bush is the brother of presidential candidate George W. Bush, and Governor of Florida. We assume that this context was provided in the preceding news and/or that after the campaign this could be presupposed as known by an American audience. The critical inference invited by this remark is that if Bush wins Florida, it will be due to his brother's help, and if he does not, then his brother will have let him down. A more general, and no less critical, inference is that the Governor of a state can influence the outcome of the presidential election.

There follows a sequence in which the results are graphically represented on the map of the US visible behind the presenter on the wall, by marking the states that have been decided in the colours red and blue for the respective winner. The hooker frame ends with a brief agenda projection and a teaser frame: *Stay with us, we're about to take you on an exciting and bumpy ride*.

It is only after this that the body of the opening sequence of the broadcast begins, with pre-opening, opening, pre-headline and headline frames, and a delegation frame in which the floor is passed to the political analyst and polls expert in the studio. In the PRE-OPENING frame, topic, channel, programme and, again, the presenter, are introduced both visually and verbally in presenter's voice-over, and special emphasis is laid on the fact that NBC broadcasts from its prestigiously located headquarters in Rockefeller Center, New York City. In the OPENING frame, we finally see the presenter on the screen, greeting the audience, again, and familiarly addressing them with everyone. PRE-HEADLINE and HEADLINE frame focus on the closeness of the election. Without projecting the agenda for the evening, the presenter then DELEGATES to the studio expert, introducing him with his high status functions within NBC, and topically focusing on Florida, with another reference to its Governor Jeb Bush. The expert provides some background and a brief analysis of the importance of the state of Florida in deciding the election, reports on opinion polls conducted with voters there by NBC, and, like the CNN journalists, closes with a formulation that supports the presenters pre-headline and headline.

What is the channel identity that NBC constructs for itself in this opening segment? Compared to the other channels opening with a hooker frame – ITV for the British elections and BBC World for the German ones – it is remarkable that NBC does not use this frame for additional advertising of channel or programme. On the other hand, the presenter is identified in both the hooker and the pre-opening frame. This differs markedly from the European national channels BBC, ITV, ARD and RTL, and also from CNN USA. In all these channels, the presenters who opened the broadcast remained unidentified. It was claimed above that non-identification presupposes and constructs familiarity and in-group membership between presenter and audience, because presenters can rely on audience recognition of the sort "if it is the BBC, it is David Dimbleby". With NBC, this seems to be the other way round: "If it's Tom Brokaw, it is NBC". So the presenter Tom Brokaw is constructed as standing for NBC, and NBC's full identification ritual unfolds only later in the pre-opening frame.

The assumption that journalists' high status may be an important facet of NBC's projected identity is supported by the attention paid to status in the presenter's introduction of the expert in the delegation frame: *let's begin with NBC's Washington Bureau chief, moderator of Meet the Press, Tim Russert*. On the other hand, relations **between** the two journalists are constructed as informal by using first name terms in delegating and accepting the floor. This corresponds to the practices we have found in all the other Anglo-Saxon channels. Yet the expert addresses the presenter by name not only in accepting the floor, but also in the middle of his contribution. What the audience sees at the time is the two journalists sitting at their desk looking at each other, with the expert addressing the presenter. Instances like these, which we also find in the CNN USA data, seem to confirm Scollon's (1998) finding that media discourse on the news is primarily social interaction between journalists, and not between journalists and the audience. Our impression is, however, that such cases of explicit address in the body of longer contributions occur rarely in the European data, so that for the European media different channel identities and audience relations may be implicated. More research is needed here.

If we look at audience-inclusive and exclusive *we*, the relation of 2 to 7 confirms that the channel is not constructing an in-group with its viewers. Also, let's have a look at *let's*. This is normally always addressee-inclusive, which is why *Let's go to see you tomorrow* is not acceptable (Levinson 1983:69). There are three occurrences of *let's* in the excerpt, but only the one quoted in the previous paragraph is audience-inclusive. The last utterance of the excerpt, *All right, Tim, let's take a look at the map*, excludes the audience. The first token of *let's*, which prefaces the story in the hooker frame, *let's take you through them now* looks like the kind that according to Levinson's criteria would have to be judged unacceptable. But it can of course be seen as an authoritative, addressee-exclusive *we* as in teacher to students: *Let's give you your essays back*. This would add another note of authoritativeness to NBC's identity vis-à-vis its audience.

Other indications point in the same direction: *we'll add it all up for you* offers help in doing difficult sums, while *stay with us, we're about to take you on an exciting and bumpy ride* has something of an adult-to-child ring to it. NBC is not the only channel doing this – the German ARD and CNN International reporting on the German elections exhibit traces of this attitude as well (see above).

Turning to channel-politics relations, we have already noted the presenter's critical and suspicious attitude towards Jeb Bush, the Governor of Florida. This points to a watchdog role definition towards politics, but may also exhibit a partisan, non-neutral stance, depending on whether or not this kind of remark is evenly distributed over the political camps in the rest of the broadcast. Then there is the inevitable casting of the election as a race, and a very close one at that. Brokaw's laconic *first man to 270 electoral votes wins* might just as well state the rules for a high school athletic contest, judged by how little respect it conveys.

Regarding appraisal language, we find high degrees of gradation, also in metaphors (*most hotly contested race, the big prize, the brass ring, linchpin, battle-*

ground), and attitudinal colouring (*an exciting and bumpy ride*). As with CNN USA, the appraisal terms refer both to the topic of the election and to NBC's coverage of it. Bearing in mind that the American networks had advance information on the projected results of the election – which they could not broadcast as long as voting was still going on across several time zones (cf. Greenfield 2001) – and knowing in retrospect how the night turned out, the tangible excitement of the journalists may be understandable.

4.   Comparison and discussion

The comparisons in this section are between the election night openings of the channels shown in Table 10. Such data offer various possibilities of doing comparative analysis. If we can find culture-specific discourse styles in the national channels, we can compare presenting practices in Great Britain, Germany and United States. Should this prove difficult because the differences between public service (ps) and commercial channels (com) turn out to be too pronounced, we can carry out a comparison nationally and cross-culturally between those two types of channels. We can look at the international channels and see what specific discourse practices are employed in mediating political news to international audiences and ask how they differ from those used to address national ones. And lastly, we can study the way in which national and international channels differ even if they operate under the roof of the same broadcasting corporation, as is the case with CNN USA/CNN INTERNATIONAL and BBC1/BBC-World. With these questions in mind, I will first look at sequential structure across the various channels, and then at micro-level realisations and the construction of channel identity, of the relations between channels and their audiences, and between channels and the domain of politics.

Based on the frame analysis of Tables 1–10, the channels analysed exhibit the sequential patterns shown in Figure 1. In this figure, the frames realised by all the channels listed at the end of a path are printed in bold. Those that are not in bold are only realised by the channels listed for them. The exception is in the box, where the internal frame structure of hooker frames is shown and where this

Table 10. Television Channels

	GB	FRG	USA
national	BBC1 (ps)	ARD (ps)	NBC (com)
	ITV (com)	RTL (com)	CNN USA (com)
international	CNN I	CNN I	
		BBC World	

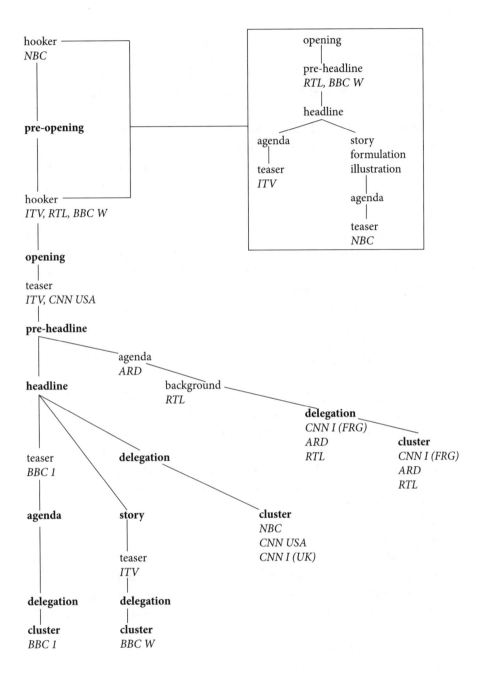

Figure 1. Sequential patterns

distinction is not made. The figure shows that, with the exception of hooker and teaser frames, there is homogeneity in sequential structure from pre-opening to pre-headline, at which point different sequential types begin to branch out.

Turning first to hooker frames, they are optional and only used by some of the channels. They violate Scollon's (1998) unmarked order of opening frames by providing on-topic talk before the channel has been opened and/or the relationship to the audience has been established. Figure 1 shows that hooker frames occurred in two variants. In one, they were used by the channels that began their broadcast at a time when there were already results to report (ITV/UK; NBC/USA), and presenters delivered the results live to camera before the pre-opening frame. This variant is structurally more complex than the other one, which is not motivated by breaking news but houses a pre-headline in which suspense is built up at the end of the pre-opening frame and before the audience is greeted in the opening frame (RTL/FRG; BBC World/FRG). Both types offer opportunities for the channels' self-presentation and promotion, as well as for capturing audience attention. We have seen that the British commercial channel ITV made the most extensive use of this, and the commercial US channel NBC the least. NBC, however, employed the longest, most informative and most complex hooker frame of all, taking up almost half of its opening segment. The other channels did not use hookers at all.

Another optional and "promotional" type of frame is the TEASER frame. Interestingly, such frames are employed by the presenters of the Anglo-Saxon national channels only, that is neither by the German channels, nor by any of the international ones reporting on the British or German elections. While the American channels CNN USA and NBC, and the British channel BBC1, have one each of these frames, the BBC's commercial rival ITV employs three (one each at the end of the hooker, the opening and the story frame).

All channels, save the German ARD, which has no opening frame, share the sequential pattern of pre-opening, opening, and pre-headline frames. After this, there is a bifurcation into those channels that have a headline, and those who do not. The "headline-channels" branch into three sequential patterns: one for the British public service channel BBC 1, one for its commercial rival ITV and the Britain-based BBC World, and a third one for the north-American channels NBC, CNN USA and CNN International (on the British elections).

The difference, however, between the two British patterns, BBC1 on the one hand, and ITV and BBC World on the other, is a superficial one: It is due to the fact that BBC 1 started broadcasting before, and the other two after the exit polls were announced. That is why BBC 1 has time for its elaborate agenda projection, and ITV and BBC World already have a story to report. But for this, we have one sequential pattern for the two British national channels and the British international one. All three share not only the headline frame, but also some intervening material before they come to the delegation frame and start a cluster structure, in which the headline and story can be elaborated upon by studio interviewers and various experts.

It is interesting that BBC World should be in this British group. There is a sequential difference, though, between the international channel and the two national ones, and it lies in the agenda projection frames. The British national channel BBC exhibits a very elaborate sequence, displaying with a flourish the spatial, technical and human resources of the BBC, as well as the rhetorical skills of its personnel. The BBC's rival ITV provides a short agenda projection in its hooker frame and another sequence later on, (not included in Table 2), which is as impressive as the BBC one. The only other national channel offering something approaching an agenda projection is the German channel ARD (ps), but it is a minimal version, foreshadowing the contribution of only one journalist, the statistics expert. The two British national channels are thus unique in our data in positioning themselves in this manner. BBC World, by contrast, has no agenda projection frame.

The pattern is different for the third, the North-American branch, including CNN International reporting on the British elections. Presenters go straight from headline frame to delegation and, together with studio experts or reporters on location, collaboratively construct different perspectives on the topic in a cluster structure. As we have seen, this happens in a very regular manner, according to which experts or reporters supply analysis and background and conclude with a formulation that supports the presenter's headline frame. There is hardly any difference in sequential patterning between CNN USA and CNN International.

The channels that use no headline frame are the German public service ARD, the German commercial channel RTL, and CNN International reporting on the German elections. Although all three started their broadcast before the exit poll results were in, this is no explanation for not using a headline frame. Since the presenter of BBC World, the other international channel involved in reporting on those elections, did use a headline, this omission cannot be ascribed to the fact that the situation might not have yielded one at the time of reporting (see Section 3). Different generic conventions seem to be in play here, possibly a longer introductory phase being favoured by German text construction principles.

Even though CNN International is being anchored by the German head of CNN's Berlin office, it is remarkable that the presenter should still follow German generic conventions. It could be assumed that she would have had a thorough secondary discourse socialisation, as it were, into the CNN channel culture. But the RTL presenter, too, spent several years working for American television in the USA, so an adaptation to the US pattern might be expected from him, as well.

Instead, our findings suggest that such textual construction principles are very deep-seated and hard to replace or use at will (cf. e.g. Clyne 1987).

But there is also a difference between CNN International/FRG and the German national channels. ARD and RTL go from the pre-headline frame to a brief agenda projection (ARD), or supply background (RTL), before they come to the delegations to studio interviewer or expert. CNN International, by contrast, goes straight from pre-headline to delegation. In this, it is more like the American patterns. What we are looking at, then, in CNN International's broadcast on the German elections by a German presenter, is a hybrid. In not having a headline frame, it has features of the generic conventions of the local host culture. In going straight from superordinate headline-type frame to delegation and cluster structure, it has features of the generic conventions of North-American/international channel culture. The two German national channels, for their part, in having material intervening between a superordinate headline-type frame and the delegation/cluster structure, are similar to the British national channels. In this respect, and in contrast to the North-American sequential pattern, the British and German channels seem to share a "European" text construction principle.

Turning to the comparison of micro-level realisations, let us begin with the construction of channel identity. The primary discourse positions for doing this explicitly are pre-opening and opening frames. We have seen that most national channels make the most of this, investing much effort in well-crafted and visually and emotionally appealing pre-opening frames (see also Schieß, this volume), above all the British BBC and ITV, CNN USA and NBC. Some also had dramatic high-noon programme titles, like the German commercial channel RTL (*Hour of Truth. The Decision*). The biggest difference between public service and commercial channels in this and the subsequent opening frame is that between the German ARD (ps) and all other national public service and commercial channels alike, since the ARD does not introduce the name of its programme at all.

Apart from channel and programme identification, what can be done in pre-opening and opening frames is the introduction of the presenters. This was omitted however in most of the national channels (BBC1, ITV; ARD, RTL; CNN USA). The inference from this was that the presenter was so well known to the audience that there was no need for an introduction and that this was a sign of in-group membership and familiarity between presenter and audience. There were two exceptions to this. One was the German national channel ARD, whose presenter was not introduced although she was not a well-known screen personality. The other was NBC, where the presenter was identified although he was one of America's best-known newscasters. We took the first to be a case of strengthening the authoritativeness of the institution ARD (inviting the inference that it did not matter who spoke for it), and the second as a case of strengthening the status of the NBC presenter (inviting the inference that the presenter stood for NBC).

The big contrast in the pre-opening and opening frames is between the national and the international channels, since the presenters of the latter cannot rely on being familiar to an international audience and take great care to introduce themselves. Also, their programme names typically refer to the country whose election is being covered, which would be redundant for a national channel.

Implicit constructions of channel identity and of the relations between their journalists can be observed in presenters' delegation frames to other journalists by studying the address terms and forms of greeting used. In this, we observe a difference between the German channels and all Anglo-Saxon ones – national and international, public service and commercial alike. The typical form of address in the British, American and international channels is first names, in the German channels it is first and last name. Greetings, too, are much more formal in the German channels.

Channel-audience relations can likewise be inferred from forms of address and greetings. National channels like the British BBC or ITV just either greet the audience or welcome it (*good evening,* or *welcome*), the German commercial channel RTL does both emphatically (*good evening and a really hearty welcome*). CNN USA does neither to its domestic audience but welcomes the international audience to their election special. The only national channel that both greets and addresses the audience in the opening frame is the American NBC (*good evening, everyone*). The exception is again the German ARD, whose presenter neither greets nor welcomes the audience, but addresses it as *dear viewers* in the agenda projection. The international channels exhibit both greeting and welcome (*hello and welcome*),all three in an identical manner.

Further manifestations of channel-audience relations can be found in the commissive and directive speech acts as well as the appraisal language the channels addressed to their audience in teaser frames. While the international as well as the German channels did not have such frames at all, their realizations differed across the Anglo-Saxon national frames from neutrally projecting a really exciting night (BBC 1/UK, CNN USA), to stressing the channel's readiness to provide excellent election night service (ITV/UK), to promising to take the audience, like children eager for a rollercoaster ride, on an *exciting and bumpy ride* (NBC/USA). Commissives also occurred at the boundaries of other frames, such as in the German ARD's introduction of its guests: *to help you find your way ...,* or in NBC's *we'll add it all up for you,* in which the channels position themselves as helpful experts towards an audience in need of such help.

There is a cline here in the audience roles (and the reciprocal channel identities) that are being constructed by such utterances: from fairly equal recipients of an exciting news show (BBC1), to the customers of a service provided with a dramatic stance (ITV), to charges in need of help to understand the complexities of politics (ARD), to curious viewers eager to be served tidbits of politicians' personal lives (RTL), to excited children being promised a special treat (NBC), or, as in the case of CNN USA's *pull up a chair*, to onlookers invited to watch a spectacle. Needless to say, the international channels do not do this sort of thing at all.

Turning to the construction of the channel-politics relationship by the national channels, and again paying attention to the use of appraisal language, both the British BBC and the American NBC manifest disrespect and even distrust of the politicians (BBC: *watched the politicians slugging it out together; politicians will ... be called to account;* NBC: *first man to 270 electoral votes wins; we'll know ... whether Jeb Bush in Florida is his brothers keeper or not*). The British ITV, while talking neutrally about the projected winners of the election, emotionalises about the losers (*the people who tonight are holding the great offices of state, many of them will not only be out of power but some of them without a seat*). The German commercial channel RTL constructs the election as a duel between the two top candidates, neglecting the complexities of the German multi-party system. It is the channel in our data whose presenter personalises politics the most – but he is checked by his political expert, who provides more differential analysis. For CNN USA the politicians are like performers in a spectacle, which the audience is invited to watch. In spite of all its journalistic professionalism, CNN USA thus casts itself implicitly as the channel that presents political struggle as entertainment, and in addition presents this in casual everyday language. Its four-strong election night team, of all channels, also approaches most closely a conversational style in talking about politics and the public sphere.

The German public service channel ARD again stands out from this array. Politics only enters its opening section through the comments of its celebrity guests (who however are not permitted to speak for themselves). These high-ranking guests comment in a quite depersonalised manner, refer to the elements of Germany's political landscape – a number of parties and possible coalitions between them – and do not name the top candidates. In this, the ARD is very close to the way in which politics is constructed by the international channels CNN International and BBC World.

The international channels differ from the national ones in several respects. We have seen that in the pre-opening and opening frames, they use multiple identifications of channel, programme and presenter, both in the verbal and the visual mode, state their location and name the country whose election they are covering. They do no agenda projection like e.g. the British channels BBC1 and ITV, broadcast from a small studio and approach the topic of politics in a very matter-of-fact manner. This contrasts with the style of the national channels (cf.

the CNN International presenter's critical summary of the British ITV's *flash and filigree* footage). The same difference between a dramatising and a matter-of-fact approach can, however, also be observed between the internationals and their national sister channels, so that the American presenter could have reacted in the same manner to CNN USA's opening sequence.

The construction of local information for a global audience that the international channels have to do is not without its problems. For authenticity and immediacy, and to provide the dialogical element no television channel nowadays can do without (except perhaps the German ARD), they recruit local experts, even local presenters, to explain the local political system and interpret the election results. We have seen how this can go wrong in the data from BBC World covering the German elections, and how presenters must be able to do extensive repair work in order to recipient-design, in collaboration with the local expert, the type of knowledge a global audience can understand. A similar example occurs in the data of CNN International on the German elections, but it comes later in the night.

To sum up, our study has shown clear differences in the domain of sequential patterns, between the Anglo-Saxon channels on the one side and the German ones on the other. Within the Anglo-Saxon group, there was also a clear distinction between the British and the North-American channels. For the international channels, there is a tendency to group with their base cultures, that is for CNN International to follow the sequential pattern of CNN USA, and for BBC World to follow that of BBC 1.

The exception was the broadcast of CNN International on the German election. This was presented by a German journalist and shared the sequential structure of the German national channels in not having a headline frame, but also that of the American ones, including CNN International, by going straight from a superordinate frame into delegation and cluster structure. It is thus an example of a hybrid between the American pattern of CNN International and the German generic patterns. The German national channels, on the other hand, shared sequential features with the British ones by having intervening material between some sort of head frame and the start of delegation frames and cluster structure. This points to a difference between European and North American generic conventions for the discourse type studied.

Compared to the findings for the level of sequential patterns, in the domain of micro-level realisations it is the differences between national and international channels that are much more clearly pronounced. Differences to the national channels exist in the way the international broadcasters project their own identity, construct their relation with their audiences and with the political world, as well as in the discourse practices of recipient design and repair with which they work at mediating the topic of elections for international, non-local audiences. The level of personalisation, between journalistic colleagues, in relation to the audience and to the political topic, is considerably lower in the international channels than in the national ones – again with the exception of the German public service channel ARD.

As regards the differences between the British, American and German national channels, however, they are not as clearly pronounced on the micro-level as they were sequentially. True that the British channels are unique in the corpus in broadcasting from mega-studios and having an extensive agenda projection frame devoted to introducing these and their studio and outside personnel, and that this exercise involved high-densitiy use of appraisal language. Granted also that the German public service channel ARD differs from the British and American ones in the way in which it relates to its audiences in a more authoritative manner, and that both German channels interact more formally with their journalistic colleagues.

But the picture becomes blurred because there are differences between the national channels as well. They are most pronounced in Germany between the public service broadcaster ARD and the commercial channel RTL, but they can also be observed between the British BBC1 and ITV, in terms of higher degrees of commercialisation of the latter in constructing it own identity, and in terms of the personalisation of the audience-channel relation and of politics. BBC1, for its part, casts itself in the critical role of watchdog vis-á-vis the political sphere, but also embraces entertainment features for presenting this. Thus it is not possible to discern a national style of presenting for either Germany or Britain (as it proved impossible for interviewing styles in Britain, as well, cf. Lauerbach 2004, 2005b).

As to the two American Channels CNN USA and NBC, both commercial networks, the NBC presenter is more critical of the political process and at the same time positions itself in the role both of an editorial guide for its audience and a parent promising to provide fun. His style is one of critical commitment on the one hand and a chummy familiarity on the other, and while there is certainly a sense of drama in the air, neither he not his expert strive for entertainment. The CNN team, by contrast, addresses its audience on equal terms and projects a high degree of professionalism. At the same time, its two presenters and two analysts, who also regularly present the daily news show *Inside Politics*, not only make up a well-functioning, rhetorically sparkling studio team whose members at times interact in an almost conversation style. They also know how to be entertaining, without belittling the importance of the political process.

This may be as far as we can get on the micro-level with qualitative methods in comparative analysis. In ongoing work on these data, we are employing quantitative methods in an effort to capture the dimensions of variation more precisely. The case studies in this paper are more than a necessary prerequisite for this, however. They are presented here to document the data, to introduce and test the method of frame and microanalysis, to provide insights of what discourse practices are involved in anchoring a complex news programme, and to trace dimensions of variation between national and international, public service and commercial practices.

5. Conclusion

The complex findings of this study are not easy to interpret. On the level of generic patterning, we found clear sequential differences between the Anglo-Saxon channels on the one hand, and the German ones on the other. But within the Anglo-Saxon channels, too, there was a difference between the British ones, including the Britain-based international BBC World, and the US channels, including the US-based CNN-International. Some generic features were also shared between the German channels and the British ones, suggesting a European tradition of text construction principles which is distinct from the US one. It looks as though European practices have not been adapted to American standardised genre patterns. However, the use of hooker and teaser frames by European and American commercial channels alike does indicate transcultural influence on discourse practice in that particular sector of media production.

In spite of discernable national profiles on the level of sequential structure, there were pronounced differences on the level of micro-level realisations **between** national channels. It was therefore impossible to distinguish homogeneous cultural styles of broadcasting for the genre studied on that level. This was the more surprising because elections are national events, and the television event of *Election Night Special* is a well-established traditional genre across cultures. Therefore, culturally delimited and differentiated styles of presenting might have been expected.

However, the differences between the national channels should not really have come as a surprise. In reporting on the same event, broadcasting channels compete for a national audience on the same national media market. In such a situation, it would be quite counter-productive to deliver identical or similar products. Instead, it makes eminent sense to design different products that appeal to different sections of the audience in an effort to try and secure the best share of the audience ratings. Of course, this pressure to be different from the competitor applies not only to reporting on big media events, but to all the products of a media channel. In fact, it is desirable for channels to develop their own recognisable culture or brand. It could be objected to this (cf. Hofmann 2006) that public service television is not subject to the pressures of the market to the same extent as privately owned channels because it is mainly funded by public licencing fees and not by advertising venue. However, this does not consider the way in which viewing habits have changed since the arrival of the commercial channels, nor the resultant pressure on public broadcasting to respond to this, at least in Europe. The situation is different in the United States, where public service television exists on a small scale, but television culture has been dominated by private broadcasting companies from the start.

It follows that the complex of discursive (as well as social and economical) practices of a television channel can be considered to make up its specific channel culture. The media culture of a nation, then, turns out to be a collection of different broadcasting subcultures. Cross-culturally comparative media discourse research has to take this into account when selecting its objects of analysis so as not to obscure culturally internal differences.

Just as the specific profile of national channels is the result of competitive product design for a national market, the profile of international channels is the outcome of competition for audiences on the international market. As this study has shown, both CNN International and BBC World were close to their related national channels CNN USA and BBC 1 in their generic structure. In designing their products for an international, English-speaking information elite however, BBC World and CNN International rely on serious, matter-of-fact reporting in a non-dramatic, neutral style. This makes their products different from those of their national counterparts. Both international channels studied are experimenting with different formats of presenting, and with local experts, even presenters, to provide for local authenticity, as well as analytical and political expertise, in their broadcasts. The study has shown how specific discourse practices on the part of the presenters are used to repair the hitches that arise when those local experts are unfamiliar with orienting to transnational audiences.

At present, the world of global television is very much in flux. BBC World and CNN International are no longer the only transnational players, nor is English the only language for transnational television. Deutsche Welle broadcasts worldwide in German, English, Arabic and Spanish on German and European topics, CNN en espanol in Spanish to audiences in the US and Latin America, Al Jazeera in Arabic to the Arab world, and 2006 has seen the arrival of Al Jazeera English and the first transnational French channel, France 24. This situation calls for new dimensions in doing cross-cultural discursive media analysis. The study of discursive practice in the domain where transnational media culture interacts with local ways of doing things promises to add new insights to our understanding of media discourse.

References

Allen, S. 1998. "News from NowHere: Televisual News Discourse and the Construction of Hegemony." In *Approaches to Media Discourse*, A. Bell and P. Garrett (eds), 105–141. Oxford: Blackwell.

Atkinson, M. 1984. *Our Masters Voices – The Language and Body Language of Politics*. London/ New York: Methuen.

Becker, A. 2003. "Interviews in Election Night Broadcasts: A Framework for Cross-Cultural Analysis." This volume.

Bell, A. 1998. "The discourse structure of news stories." In *An Approach to Media Discourse*, A. Bell and P. Garrett (eds), 64–104. Oxford: Blackwell.

Bell, A. and Garrett, P. (eds). 1998. *Approaches to Media Discourse*. Oxford: Blackwell.

Brown, R. and Gilman, A. 1972. "The pronouns of power and solidarity." In *Language and Social Context*, P. P. Giglioli (ed.), 252–282. Harmondsworth: Penguin.

Blumler, J. G. and Gurevitch, M. 1995. *The Crisis of Public Communication*. London: Routledge.

Clayman, S. 1991. "News Interviews Openings – Aspects of Sequential Organization." In *Broadcast Talk*, P. Scannel (ed.), 48–75. London: Sage.

Clayman, S. and Heritage, J. 2002. *The News Interview. Journalists and Public Figures on the Air*. Cambridge: Cambridge University Press.

Clyne, M. 1987. "Cultural differences in the organization of academic texts." *Journal of Pragmatics* 11: 211–247.

Coupland, N. 2001. "Stylization, authenticity and TV news review." *Discourse Studies* 3 (4): 413–442.

Eggins, S. and Slade, D. 1997. *Analysing Casual Conversation*. London: Cassell.

Fairclough, N. 1989. *Language and Power*. London/New York: Longman.

Fairclough, N. 1992. *Discourse and Social Change*. Cambridge: Polity Press.

Fairclough, N. 1995. *Media Discourse*. London: Arnold.

Fowler, R. and Kress, G. 1979. "Critical Linguistics." In *Language and Control*, R. Fowler, B. Hodge, G. Kress and T. Trew (eds), 185–213. London/Boston/Henley: Routledge and Kegan Paul.

Fowler, R. 1987. "Notes on Critical Linguistics." In *Language Topics: Essays in Honour of Michael Halliday*, T. Threadgold and R. Steele (eds), 481–492. Amsterdam: John Benjamins.

Fowler, R. 1991. *Language in the News: Discourse and Ideology in the Press*. London: Routledge.

Goffman, E. 1974. *Frame Analysis – An Essay on the Organization of Experience*. Boston: Northeastern University Press.

Goffman, E. 1981. "Footing." In *Forms of Talk*, E. Goffman (ed.), 124–157. Oxford: Blackwell.

Greenfield, J. 2001. *"Oh Waiter! One Order of Crow!" Inside the Strangest Presidential Election Finish in American History*. New York: Putnam.

Grice, H. P. 1975. "Logic and Conversation." In *Syntax and Semantics 3: Speech Acts*, P. Cole and J. Morgan (eds), 41–58. New York: Academic Press.

Gurevitch, M. and Blumler, J. G. 1990. "Comparative Research: The Extending Frontier." In *New Directions in Political Communication. A Resource Book*, D. L. Swanson and D. Nimmo (eds), 305–325. Newbury Park/London/New Delhi: Sage Publications.

Gurevitch, M. and Kavoori, P. 1992. "Television Spectacles as Politics." *Communication Monographs* 59 (4): 415–420.

Hall, S. 1973. "A World at One with Itself." In *The Manufacture of News*, S. Cohen. and J. Young (eds), 85–94. London: Constable.

Halliday, M.A.K. 2004. *An Introduction to Functional Grammar.* London: Arnold.

Heritage, J. and Watson, R. 1979. "Formulations as Conversational Objects." In *Everyday Language*, G. Psathas (ed.), 123–162. New York, Irvington.

Heritage, J., Clayman, St. and Zimmerman, D. 1988. "Discourse and Message Analysis – The Micro-structure of Mass Media Messages." In *Advancing Communication Science: Merging Mass and Interpersonal Processes*, R. P. Hawkins, J. Wiemann and S. Pingree (eds), 77–109. Newbury Park: Sage.

Heritage, J. and Greatbatch, D. 1991. "On the Institutional Character of Institutional Talk: The Case of News Interviews." In *Talk and Social Structure*, D. Boden and D. Zimmerman (eds), 93–137. Cambridge: Polity Press.

Heritage, J. and Roth, A. L. 1995. "Grammar and Institution: Questions and Questioning in the Broadcast News Interview." *Research on Language and Social Interaction* 28 (1): 1–60.

Hofmann, S. 2006. "Spanisch im Massenmedium Fernsehen: Sprachliches Design, sprachliche Variation und mediale Räume in Lateinamerika". Habilitationsschrift. Frankfurt am Main.

Lauerbach, G. 2004. "Political interviews as a hybrid genre." *TEXT* 24 (3): 353–397.

Lauerbach, G. 2005. "Election nights: A cross-cultural analysis of presenting practices." In *Dialogue Analysis IX. Dialogue in Literature and the Media. Selected Papers from the 9th IADA Conference, Salzburg 2003, Part II: Media*, A. Betten and M. Dannerer (eds), 31–43. Tübingen: Niemeyer:

Lauerbach, G. 2006. "Discourse representation in political interviews: The construction of identities and relations through voicing and ventriloquizing." *Journal of Pragmatics* 38: 196–215. (Special Issue *Political Discourse in the Media*, Fetzer, A. and Weizman, E. (eds)).

Levinson, S. 1983. *Pragmatics.* Cambridge: Cambridge University Press.

Marriott, S. 2000. "Election Night." *Media, Culture & Society* 22: 131–150.

Martin, J. R. 2000. "Beyond Exchange: Appraisal Systems in English." In *Evaluation in Text – Authorial Stance and the Construction of Discourse*, S. Hunston and G. Thompson (eds), 142–175. Oxford: Oxford University Press.

Muckenhaupt, M. 2000. *Film- und Fernsehanalyse.* Stuttgart: Metzler.

Püschel, U. 1992. "Von der Pyramide zum Cluster. Textsorten und Textsortenmischung in Fernsehnachrichten." In *Medienkultur – Kulturkonflikt. Massenmedien in der interkulturellen und in der internationalen Kommunikation*, E. Hess-Lüttich (ed.), 233–258. Opladen: Westdeutscher Verlag.

Sacks, H. 1972. "On the Analyzability of Stories by Children." In *Directions in Sociolinguistics*, J. Gumperz and D. Hymes (eds), 325–345. New York: Holt, Rinehart & Winston.

Sacks, H. and Schegloff, E. 1979. "Two preferences in the organization of reference to persons in conversation and their interaction." In *Everyday Language. Studies in Ethnomethodology*, G. Psathas (ed.), 15–21. New York: Irvington.

Sarcinelli, U. 1994. "Fernsehdemokratie." In *Öffentlichkeit und Kommunikationskultur*, W. Wunden (ed.), 21–41. Hamburg: Steinkopf.

Schegloff, E. 1972. "Notes on a conversational practice: Formulating place." In *Studies in Social Interaction*, D. Sudnow (ed.), 75–119. New York: Free Press.

Schegloff, E. 1979. "Identification and recognition in telephone conversation openings." In *Everyday Language. Studies in Ethnomethodology*, G. Psathas (ed.), 23–78. New York: Irvington.

Scheithauer, R. "Metaphors in election night television coverage in Britain, the United States and Germany." This volume.

Schieß, R. "Lights, Camera, Action: Visualizing Election Nights Across Cultures." This volume.

Scollon, R. 1998. *Mediated Discourse as Social Interaction – A Study of News Discourse*. Harlow, Essex: Addison Wesley Longman.

Sperber, D. and Wilson, D. 1995. *Relevance – Communication and Cognition*. Oxford: Blackwell.

Stiehler, H.-J. 2000. "'Nach der Wahl ist vor der Wahl': Interpretationen als Gegenstand der Medienforschung." In *Wahlen und Politikvermittlung durch Massenmedien*, H. Bohrmann, O. Jarren, G. Melischek and J. Seethaler (eds), 105–120. Wiesbaden: Westdeutscher Verlag.

Straßner, E. 2000. *Journalistische Texte*. Tübingen: Niemeyer.

White, P. 2003. "Beyond modality and hedging: A dialogic view of the language of intersubjective stance." *TEXT* 23 (2): 259–284.

Wilson, J. 1990. *Politically Speaking – The Pragmatic Analysis of Political Language*. Oxford: Blackwell

Wodak, R. and Meyer, M. (eds). 2001. *Methods of Critical Discourse Analysis*. London: Sage.

Index

Pragmatics & Beyond New Series

A complete list of titles in this series can be found on the publishers' website, *www.benjamins.com*

135 **ARCHER, Dawn:** Questions and Answers in the English Courtroom (1640–1760). A sociopragmatic analysis. 2005. xiv, 374 pp.

134 **SKAFFARI, Janne, Matti PEIKOLA, Ruth CARROLL, Risto HILTUNEN and Brita WÅRVIK (eds.):** Opening Windows on Texts and Discourses of the Past. 2005. x, 418 pp.

133 **MARNETTE, Sophie:** Speech and Thought Presentation in French. Concepts and strategies. 2005. xiv, 379 pp.

132 **ONODERA, Noriko O.:** Japanese Discourse Markers. Synchronic and diachronic discourse analysis. 2004. xiv, 253 pp.

131 **JANOSCHKA, Anja:** Web Advertising. New forms of communication on the Internet. 2004. xiv, 230 pp.

130 **HALMARI, Helena and Tuija VIRTANEN (eds.):** Persuasion Across Genres. A linguistic approach. 2005. x, 257 pp.

129 **TABOADA, María Teresa:** Building Coherence and Cohesion. Task-oriented dialogue in English and Spanish. 2004. xvii, 264 pp.

128 **CORDELLA, Marisa:** The Dynamic Consultation. A discourse analytical study of doctor–patient communication. 2004. xvi, 254 pp.

127 **BRISARD, Frank, Michael MEEUWIS and Bart VANDENABEELE (eds.):** Seduction, Community, Speech. A Festschrift for Herman Parret. 2004. vi, 202 pp.

126 **WU, Yi'an:** Spatial Demonstratives in English and Chinese. Text and Cognition. 2004. xviii, 236 pp.

125 **LERNER, Gene H. (ed.):** Conversation Analysis. Studies from the first generation. 2004. x, 302 pp.

124 **VINE, Bernadette:** Getting Things Done at Work. The discourse of power in workplace interaction. 2004. x, 278 pp.

123 **MÁRQUEZ REITER, Rosina and María Elena PLACENCIA (eds.):** Current Trends in the Pragmatics of Spanish. 2004. xvi, 383 pp.

122 **GONZÁLEZ, Montserrat:** Pragmatic Markers in Oral Narrative. The case of English and Catalan. 2004. xvi, 410 pp.

121 **FETZER, Anita:** Recontextualizing Context. Grammaticality meets appropriateness. 2004. x, 272 pp.

120 **AIJMER, Karin and Anna-Brita STENSTRÖM (eds.):** Discourse Patterns in Spoken and Written Corpora. 2004. viii, 279 pp.

119 **HILTUNEN, Risto and Janne SKAFFARI (eds.):** Discourse Perspectives on English. Medieval to modern. 2003. viii, 243 pp.

118 **CHENG, Winnie:** Intercultural Conversation. 2003. xii, 279 pp.

117 **WU, Ruey-Jiuan Regina:** Stance in Talk. A conversation analysis of Mandarin final particles. 2004. xvi, 260 pp.

116 **GRANT, Colin B. (ed.):** Rethinking Communicative Interaction. New interdisciplinary horizons. 2003. viii, 330 pp.

115 **KÄRKKÄINEN, Elise:** Epistemic Stance in English Conversation. A description of its interactional functions, with a focus on *I think*. 2003. xii, 213 pp.

114 **KÜHNLEIN, Peter, Hannes RIESER and Henk ZEEVAT (eds.):** Perspectives on Dialogue in the New Millennium. 2003. xii, 400 pp.

113 **PANTHER, Klaus-Uwe and Linda L. THORNBURG (eds.):** Metonymy and Pragmatic Inferencing. 2003. xii, 285 pp.

112 **LENZ, Friedrich (ed.):** Deictic Conceptualisation of Space, Time and Person. 2003. xiv, 279 pp.

111 **ENSINK, Titus and Christoph SAUER (eds.):** Framing and Perspectivising in Discourse. 2003. viii, 227 pp.

110 **ANDROUTSOPOULOS, Jannis K. and Alexandra GEORGAKOPOULOU (eds.):** Discourse Constructions of Youth Identities. 2003. viii, 343 pp.

109 **MAYES, Patricia:** Language, Social Structure, and Culture. A genre analysis of cooking classes in Japan and America. 2003. xiv, 228 pp.

108 **BARRON, Anne:** Acquisition in Interlanguage Pragmatics. Learning how to do things with words in a study abroad context. 2003. xviii, 403 pp.

107 **TAAVITSAINEN, Irma and Andreas H. JUCKER (eds.):** Diachronic Perspectives on Address Term Systems. 2003. viii, 446 pp.

106 **BUSSE, Ulrich:** Linguistic Variation in the Shakespeare Corpus. Morpho-syntactic variability of second person pronouns. 2002. xiv, 344 pp.

105 **BLACKWELL, Sarah E.:** Implicatures in Discourse. The case of Spanish NP anaphora. 2003. xvi, 303 pp.

104 **BEECHING, Kate:** Gender, Politeness and Pragmatic Particles in French. 2002. x, 251 pp.

70   **SORJONEN, Marja-Leena:** Responding in Conversation. A study of response particles in Finnish. 2001. x, 330 pp.

69   **NOH, Eun-Ju:** Metarepresentation. A relevance-theory approach. 2000. xii, 242 pp.

68   **ARNOVICK, Leslie K.:** Diachronic Pragmatics. Seven case studies in English illocutionary development. 2000. xii, 196 pp.

67   **TAAVITSAINEN, Irma, Gunnel MELCHERS and Päivi PAHTA (eds.):** Writing in Nonstandard English. 2000. viii, 404 pp.

66   **JUCKER, Andreas H., Gerd FRITZ and Franz LEBSANFT (eds.):** Historical Dialogue Analysis. 1999. viii, 478 pp.

65   **COOREN, François:** The Organizing Property of Communication. 2000. xvi, 272 pp.

64   **SVENNEVIG, Jan:** Getting Acquainted in Conversation. A study of initial interactions. 2000. x, 384 pp.

63   **BUBLITZ, Wolfram, Uta LENK and Eija VENTOLA (eds.):** Coherence in Spoken and Written Discourse. How to create it and how to describe it. Selected papers from the International Workshop on Coherence, Augsburg, 24-27 April 1997. 1999. xiv, 300 pp.

62   **TZANNE, Angeliki:** Talking at Cross-Purposes. The dynamics of miscommunication. 2000. xiv, 263 pp.

61   **MILLS, Margaret H. (ed.):** Slavic Gender Linguistics. 1999. xviii, 251 pp.

60   **JACOBS, Geert:** Preformulating the News. An analysis of the metapragmatics of press releases. 1999. xviii, 428 pp.

59   **KAMIO, Akio and Ken-ichi TAKAMI (eds.):** Function and Structure. In honor of Susumu Kuno. 1999. x, 398 pp.

58   **ROUCHOTA, Villy and Andreas H. JUCKER (eds.):** Current Issues in Relevance Theory. 1998. xii, 368 pp.

57   **JUCKER, Andreas H. and Yael ZIV (eds.):** Discourse Markers. Descriptions and theory. 1998. x, 363 pp.

56   **TANAKA, Hiroko:** Turn-Taking in Japanese Conversation. A Study in Grammar and Interaction. 2000. xiv, 242 pp.

55   **ALLWOOD, Jens and Peter GÄRDENFORS (eds.):** Cognitive Semantics. Meaning and cognition. 1999. x, 201 pp.

54   **HYLAND, Ken:** Hedging in Scientific Research Articles. 1998. x, 308 pp.

53   **MOSEGAARD HANSEN, Maj-Britt:** The Function of Discourse Particles. A study with special reference to spoken standard French. 1998. xii, 418 pp.

52   **GILLIS, Steven and Annick DE HOUWER (eds.):** The Acquisition of Dutch. With a Preface by Catherine E. Snow. 1998. xvi, 444 pp.

51   **BOULIMA, Jamila:** Negotiated Interaction in Target Language Classroom Discourse. 1999. xiv, 338 pp.

50   **GRENOBLE, Lenore A.:** Deixis and Information Packaging in Russian Discourse. 1998. xviii, 338 pp.

49   **KURZON, Dennis:** Discourse of Silence. 1998. vi, 162 pp.

48   **KAMIO, Akio:** Territory of Information. 1997. xiv, 227 pp.

47   **CHESTERMAN, Andrew:** Contrastive Functional Analysis. 1998. viii, 230 pp.

46   **GEORGAKOPOULOU, Alexandra:** Narrative Performances. A study of Modern Greek storytelling. 1997. xvii, 282 pp.

45   **PALTRIDGE, Brian:** Genre, Frames and Writing in Research Settings. 1997. x, 192 pp.

44   **BARGIELA-CHIAPPINI, Francesca and Sandra J. HARRIS:** Managing Language. The discourse of corporate meetings. 1997. ix, 295 pp.

43   **JANSSEN, Theo and Wim van der WURFF (eds.):** Reported Speech. Forms and functions of the verb. 1996. x, 312 pp.

42   **KOTTHOFF, Helga and Ruth WODAK (eds.):** Communicating Gender in Context. 1997. xxvi, 424 pp.

41   **VENTOLA, Eija and Anna MAURANEN (eds.):** Academic Writing. Intercultural and textual issues. 1996. xiv, 258 pp.

40   **DIAMOND, Julie:** Status and Power in Verbal Interaction. A study of discourse in a close-knit social network. 1996. viii, 184 pp.

39   **HERRING, Susan C. (ed.):** Computer-Mediated Communication. Linguistic, social, and cross-cultural perspectives. 1996. viii, 326 pp.

38   **FRETHEIM, Thorstein and Jeanette K. GUNDEL (eds.):** Reference and Referent Accessibility. 1996. xii, 312 pp.

37   **CARSTON, Robyn and Seiji UCHIDA (eds.):** Relevance Theory. Applications and implications. 1998. x, 300 pp.

36 CHILTON, Paul, Mikhail V. ILYIN and Jacob L. MEY (eds.): Political Discourse in Transition in Europe 1989–1991. 1998. xi, 272 pp.

35 JUCKER, Andreas H. (ed.): Historical Pragmatics. Pragmatic developments in the history of English. 1995. xvi, 624 pp.

34 BARBE, Katharina: Irony in Context. 1995. x, 208 pp.

33 GOOSSENS, Louis, Paul PAUWELS, Brygida RUDZKA-OSTYN, Anne-Marie SIMON-VANDENBERGEN and Johan VANPARYS: By Word of Mouth. Metaphor, metonymy and linguistic action in a cognitive perspective. 1995. xii, 254 pp.

32 SHIBATANI, Masayoshi and Sandra A. THOMPSON (eds.): Essays in Semantics and Pragmatics. In honor of Charles J. Fillmore. 1996. x, 322 pp.

31 WILDGEN, Wolfgang: Process, Image, and Meaning. A realistic model of the meaning of sentences and narrative texts. 1994. xii, 281 pp.

30 WORTHAM, Stanton E.F.: Acting Out Participant Examples in the Classroom. 1994. xiv, 178 pp.

29 BARSKY, Robert F.: Constructing a Productive Other. Discourse theory and the Convention refugee hearing. 1994. x, 272 pp.

28 VAN DE WALLE, Lieve: Pragmatics and Classical Sanskrit. A pilot study in linguistic politeness. 1993. xii, 454 pp.

27 SUTER, Hans-Jürg: The Wedding Report. A prototypical approach to the study of traditional text types. 1993. xii, 314 pp.

26 STYGALL, Gail: Trial Language. Differential discourse processing and discursive formation. 1994. xii, 226 pp.

25 COUPER-KUHLEN, Elizabeth: English Speech Rhythm. Form and function in everyday verbal interaction. 1993. x, 346 pp.

24 MAYNARD, Senko K.: Discourse Modality. Subjectivity, Emotion and Voice in the Japanese Language. 1993. x, 315 pp.

23 FORTESCUE, Michael, Peter HARDER and Lars KRISTOFFERSEN (eds.): Layered Structure and Reference in a Functional Perspective. Papers from the Functional Grammar Conference, Copenhagen, 1990. 1992. xiii, 444 pp.

22 AUER, Peter and Aldo DI LUZIO (eds.): The Contextualization of Language. 1992. xvi, 402 pp.

21 SEARLE, John R., Herman PARRET and Jef VERSCHUEREN: (On) Searle on Conversation. Compiled and introduced by Herman Parret and Jef Verschueren. 1992. vi, 154 pp.

20 NUYTS, Jan: Aspects of a Cognitive-Pragmatic Theory of Language. On cognition, functionalism, and grammar. 1991. xii, 399 pp.

19 BAKER, Carolyn and Allan LUKE (eds.): Towards a Critical Sociology of Reading Pedagogy. Papers of the XII World Congress on Reading. 1991. xxi, 287 pp.

18 JOHNSTONE, Barbara: Repetition in Arabic Discourse. Paradigms, syntagms and the ecology of language. 1991. viii, 130 pp.

17 PIÉRAUT-LE BONNIEC, Gilberte and Marlene DOLITSKY (eds.): Language Bases ... Discourse Bases. Some aspects of contemporary French-language psycholinguistics research. 1991. vi, 342 pp.

16 MANN, William C. and Sandra A. THOMPSON (eds.): Discourse Description. Diverse linguistic analyses of a fund-raising text. 1992. xiii, 409 pp.

15 KOMTER, Martha L.: Conflict and Cooperation in Job Interviews. A study of talks, tasks and ideas. 1991. viii, 252 pp.

14 SCHWARTZ, Ursula V.: Young Children's Dyadic Pretend Play. A communication analysis of plot structure and plot generative strategies. 1991. vi, 151 pp.

13 NUYTS, Jan, A. Machtelt BOLKESTEIN and Co VET (eds.): Layers and Levels of Representation in Language Theory. A functional view. 1990. xii, 348 pp.

12 ABRAHAM, Werner (ed.): Discourse Particles. Descriptive and theoretical investigations on the logical, syntactic and pragmatic properties of discourse particles in German. 1991. viii, 338 pp.

11 LUONG, Hy V.: Discursive Practices and Linguistic Meanings. The Vietnamese system of person reference. 1990. x, 213 pp.

10 MURRAY, Denise E.: Conversation for Action. The computer terminal as medium of communication. 1991. xii, 176 pp.

9   LUKE, K. K.: Utterance Particles in Cantonese Conversation. 1990. xvi, 329 pp.

8   YOUNG, Lynne: Language as Behaviour, Language as Code. A study of academic English. 1991. ix, 304 pp.